Reconsidering (Post-)Yugoslav Time

Studies in Slavic Literature and Poetics

Editors

O.F. Boele (*Leiden University*)
S. Brouwer (*University of Groningen*)
J. Niżyńska (*Indiana University Bloomington*)
A. Rogatchevski (*Arctic University of Norway*)
M. Rubins (*University College London*)
G. Tihanov (*Queen Mary University of London*)
S. Vervaet (*University of Oslo*)

Founding Editors

J.J. van Baak
R. Grübel
A.G.F. van Holk
W.G. Weststeijn

VOLUME 65

The titles published in this series are listed at *brill.com/sslp*

Reconsidering (Post-)Yugoslav Time

Towards the Temporal Turn in the Critical Study of (Post-)Yugoslav Literatures

Edited by

Aleksandar Mijatović
Brian Willems

BRILL

LEIDEN | BOSTON

The Library of Congress Cataloging-in-Publication Data is available online at https://catalog.loc.gov
LC record available at https://lccn.loc.gov/2021046066

Typeface for the Latin, Greek, and Cyrillic scripts: "Brill". See and download: brill.com/brill-typeface.

ISSN 0169-0175
ISBN 978-90-04-50313-7 (hardback)
ISBN 978-90-04-50314-4 (e-book)

Copyright 2022 by Koninklijke Brill NV, Leiden, The Netherlands.
Koninklijke Brill NV incorporates the imprints Brill, Brill Nijhoff, Brill Hotei, Brill Schöningh, Brill Fink, Brill mentis, Vandenhoeck & Ruprecht, Böhlau Verlag and V&R Unipress.
All rights reserved. No part of this publication may be reproduced, translated, stored in a retrieval system, or transmitted in any form or by any means, electronic, mechanical, photocopying, recording or otherwise, without prior written permission from the publisher. Requests for re-use and/or translations must be addressed to Koninklijke Brill NV via brill.com or copyright.com.

This book is printed on acid-free paper and produced in a sustainable manner.

Contents

Acknowledgements IX
Notes on Contributors X

Introduction 1
    Aleksandar Mijatović and Brian Willems

PART 1
The Concept of (Post-)Yugoslav Time

SECTION 1
Time Unbound: De-synchronized Temporalities of Modernity, the (Neo-)Avant-Garde, Post-modernity, and the Concept of (Post-)Yugoslav Literature

1   Past Fragments, Future Change: Dubravka Ugrešić, Vladan Desnica, Sanja Iveković, and Dalibor Martinis   25
      Brian Willems

2   The "Historical Moment before Our Eyes": On Producing Post-Yugoslav Literature   39
      Tijana Matijević

3   Whose (Neo-)Avant-Garde? The Poetry of Josip Sever, Yugoslav Modernity, and the Problem of Mononational Literary History   57
      Lujo Parežanin

SECTION 2
From the Time That Belongs to No-One to Temporalities of Non-belonging

4   The End of the World as We Know It? Anti-utopia in Post-Yugoslav Literature   81
      Boris Postnikov

5   Post-Yugoslav Dystopian Dilemmas and Writing the History of the Future: Alternative Version or Parodic Subversion?   93
    Miranda Levanat-Peričić

6   Kant Has Some Relevance Here: On a Fictional Theory of Quentin Meillassoux and the Theoretical Fiction of Luka Bekavac   107
    Ante Jerić

7   The Narrative Out of Time: The Nonhuman World of Luka Bekavac's Fiction   127
    Matija Jelača and Anera Ryznar

PART 2
Application(s) of/to (Post-)Yugoslav Time

SECTION 1
Unhinging Memory and Space: Remembering (Post-)Yugoslav Time

8   Re-reading/Writing Yugoslav Pasts and Presents in Post-Yugoslav Literature: Between (Yugo-)Nostalgia and "Lateral Networks"   149
    Mirko Milivojević

9   Spaces of Memory in Dragan Velikić's Novel *Investigator*   172
    Danijela Marot Kiš

10 In Search of Home Time   191
    Kujtim Rrahmani

SECTION 2
De-composing Broken Bonds: The Culture of Non-relational Relation

11 Transition, Trauma, and Culture in Croatia (Notes on Post-war Literature and Film)   205
    Saša Stanić and Marina Biti

12   Writing against the Code and Fitting in with the Code: Reading
     Dubravka Ugrešić in the Context of the International Literary
     Field   239
        Iva Kosmos

13   Narrations of Lost and Found: The Twists and Turns of the Friendship
     Discourse in the (Post-)Yugoslav Environment   261
        Zala Pavšič

     Index   273

Acknowledgements

The research and writing of this book were supported by two research projects, Politics of Time in post-Yugoslav Prose: Imagining Temporalities of Literary Cultures of Transnationality (IP-2016-06-9548) and Literary Revolution (IP-2018-01-7020), funded by the Croatian Science Foundation. We express our gratitude to the Croatian Science Foundation for its continuing support.

We owe a personal and intellectual debt to many colleagues and friends. The idea for this volume germinated from the conference Lost Discontinuity, Lost Fragmentarity: Conflict, Composition and Temporalities of Post-Yugoslav Literature(s) and Culture(s), held at the Faculty of Humanities and Social Sciences, University of Rijeka, October 12–13, 2018. Many thanks to all participants of Rijeka's conference for their intellectual engagement and courage to reconsider the field of (post-)Yugoslav studies.

We appreciate all the efforts by Masja Horn and Christa Stevens, acquisition editors of the BRILL series Studies in Slavic Literature and Poetics. We owe much to the anonymous reviewers for their rigorous and lucid reading of the book. We are grateful to the editorial board of SSLP for their invaluable recommendations and for guiding us in every step of the publishing project.

Aleksandar Mijatović, Brian Willems
Rijeka, Split, September 14, 2021.

Notes on Contributors

Marina Biti
is professor at the Department of Croatian Studies (University of Rijeka) and at the Department of Media, Communication and Journalism (University North). She was the founder of the Department of Cultural Studies in Rijeka and the initiator/coordinator of two interdisciplinary doctoral programmes. Her research interests predominantly lie in the field of cognitive poetics, as best documented by the book *The Poetics of Mind* which she co-authored with Danijela Marot Kiš in 2008. In more recent articles she specifically focused on examining literary trauma from a cognitive perspective, as in The *Silenced Narrator and the Notion of "Proto-Narrative"* (with Iva Rosanda Žigo, 2021). In her other books and scientific articles, she explored topics in cultural and digital cultural studies, discourse theory, critical discourse analysis, stylistics, etc.

Matija Jelača
is Assistant Professor at the Faculty of Humanities and Social Sciences of the Juraj Dobrila University of Pula (Croatia) where he teaches courses in literary theory, history of literature, comparative literature and semiotics. He has given talks and published papers (in English and Croatian) at the intersection of contemporary continental (G. Deleuze, speculative realism) and analytic philosophy (W. Sellars, R. Brandom) (most notably "Sellars Contra Deleuze on Intuitive Knowledge," 2014), on H.P. Lovecraft's weird fiction ("On the Horror of Knowledge: Speculative Realism and H.P. Lovecraft," 2019), and on the TV series The Wire ("From Rationalism to Realism in The Wire," 2016).

Ante Jerić
is lecturer at the Department of Croatian Language and Literature, Faculty of Humanities and Social Sciences, University of Rijeka. His research moves between philosophy, narratology and film studies. He is the author of the book *Uz Malabou: profili suvremenog mišljenja* (Zagreb, Multimedijalni institut, 2016).

Danijela Marot Kiš
is Associate Professor of Literary Theory at the Department of Croatian Language and Literature of the Faculty of Humanities and Social Sciences, University of Rijeka. She is an executive editor of Fluminensia, a journal for philological research published by the Department of Croatian Language and Literature; the co-author of monographs Poetics of Mind – Winning, Question-

ing and Saving Meaning and Exile and Trauma: Examples from Post-Yugoslav Prose (with Marina Biti) and Personifications – Literary Subject and Politics of Impersonality (with Aleksandar Mijatović).

Iva Kosmos

is a researcher at ZRC SAZU, Institute of Culture and Memory Studies. Kosmos graduated from the University of Zagreb (2015), was a Fullbright fellow at UW-Madison (2014) and a guest researcher at the Center for Southeast European Studies at University of Graz (2016–2017). She graduated with a thesis on contemporary post-Yugoslav writers on the international literary market. Recently she is focused on memory politics of remembering Yugoslavia in art and everyday practices. She has published in Slovenian, Croatian and international journals and editions, including *East European Politics and Societies* and *The Slavonic and East European Review*. She co-edited the monograph *Stories from Tin Cans: History of the Fish Canning Industry in the Northeast Adriatic* (in Slovenian, translated to Croatian, 2020).

Miranda Levanat-Peričić

is an associate professor at the Department of Croatian Studies, University of Zadar, where she teaches courses in comparative literature, contemporary literature and literary theory. Her research interests include literary posthumanism, speculative fiction and dystopian novels, monster theory / monster studies, post-Yugoslav literature and Balkan studies. Recently she published two books in Croatian: *Introduction to the Monster Theory: from Humbaba to Caliban* (2014) and *Comparative Binoculars: on Croatian Literature and Culture* (2017) and co-edited two books, also in Croatian: *Liber Monstrorum Balcanorum* (2019) and *The First May of Brešan* (2020).

Tijana Matijević

is an independent researcher and a teaching associate at the Universities Martin Luther in Halle and Friedrich Schiller in Jena. She is interested in feminist and counter-hegemonic explorations of post-Yugoslav literature and culture, and writes texts that utilize feminist knowledge and expand on continuities between Yugoslav and post-Yugoslav literatures. In 2014 she published the book *Post-Yugoslav Film and Literature Production: An Alternative to Mainstream Political and Cultural Discourse*, and in 2018, co-edited the volume *Schwimmen gegen den Strom? Diskurse weiblicher Autorschaft im postjugoslawischen Kontext*. Her book *From Post-Yugoslavia to the Female Continent: A Feminist Reading of Post-Yugoslav Literature* came out in 2020 in transcript Verlag.

Aleksandar Mijatović

is an Associate Professor of Literary Theory and History at the Department of Croatian Language and Literature, Faculty of Humanities and Social Sciences, University of Rijeka. He has recently authored the book *Temporalities of Post-Yugoslav Literature: The Politics of Time* (2020) with Lexington Books, an imprint of Rowman & Littlefield.

Mirko Milivojević

is an independent researcher and PhD candidate in Literary and Cultural Studies at Justus-Liebig University Giessen, Germany. He is a former research assistant and lecturer in the Slavic Department at Justus-Liebig University Giessen and holds M.A. in Comparative Literature (Erfurt University, Germany). His main research interests include contemporary (Post-)Yugoslav literature and popular culture, memory studies (primarily Southeast European and post-socialist contexts, transmedial and transnational practices), and cultural theory. He is an author of several essays and articles/reviews on contemporary post-Yugoslav cinema and literary production, published in edited volumes (*Introducing Wounds: Challenging the 'Crap Theory of Pain' in Nikola Lezaić's Tilva Roš*, 2015), and in scientific journals (*Rat i pitanje postmoderne e(ste)tike*, 2019).

Lujo Parežanin

is a doctoral candidate at the Postgraduate Programme in Literature, Performing Arts, Film and Culture at the University of Zagreb, where he is writing his thesis on the poet Josip Sever. His research primarily focuses on Yugoslav culture and neo-avant-garde art and literature in the Cold War context. He is a researcher at the *Modernism and the Avant-garde in the Yugoslav Context and Drežnica: Traces and Memories 1941–1945* projects and the co-editor of the books *Criticism in Transition: A Glossary of Visual Arts Criticism* (Kulturtreger, Kurziv, Zagreb, 2019) and *Unrepressed Subjectivity: A Glossary of Performing Arts Criticism* (Kulturtreger, Kurziv, Zagreb, 2019).

Zala Pavšič

is Assistant Professor at the Faculty of Media, Ljubljana, and has responsibility for the course Contemporary History. Her main research areas include friendship studies, memory studies, the disintegration of Yugoslavia and gender studies. She is the 2021/2022 Max Weber Postdoctoral Fellow (EUI, Florence), where she will work on a project further investigating gender aspects of the discourse of friendship. Active as a translator, her translations of Mikhail Lermontov's poems were included in the 2014 book of new translations published to honour the 200th anniversary of the poet's death. She is the recipient of various Slovenian and international fellowships and grants.

Boris Postnikov
is a PhD candidate at the Faculty of Philosophy and Social Sciences in Zagreb, working on a thesis on Post-Yugoslav Literature: The Construction of a Field. The cultural editor of a Novosti weekly (Zagreb) and author of weekly radio broadcast The Glossary of Post-Yugoslav Literature (Croatian National Radio, 2012–2015), he is also a contributor of many cultural and literary media in Croatia and post-Yugoslav region, writing predominantly essays, comments and literary reviews; further, he is an author of books of collected essays *Post-Yugoslav Literature?* (Sandorf, Zagreb, 2012) and *And Now a Word from Our Sponsor* (V.B.Z., Zagreb, 2013), co-author of policy paper *National Report on the State of Media* (Croatian Ministry of Culture, 2015) and co-editor of a post-Yugoslav war literature anthology *Once there was a Country* (Paralela 45, Bucharest, 2018).

Kujtim Rrahmani
is a senior researcher/professor of literature at the Institute of Albanology in Prishtina, Kosovo. Rrahmani's research focuses on the intersections between poetics and emotions, intertextuality and orality, myth, epics, and fairy tale, and polis and poiesis. He is e widely published author, author of five monographs – including *Anthropoetics* (Prishtina, aikd 2008) and *Warrior Naturalis* (Prishtina, iap 2020) – and winner of national prizes for novel/short stories (1994, 2017) and literary studies (2020). He has been a visiting research fellow at many universities abroad (George Washington University, University of Michigan, LSE in London, *Maison des Sciences de l'Homme* in Paris, Heidelberg University, Free University of Berlin, University of Freiburg etc.).

Anera Ryznar
is an assistant professor at the Chair for Stylistics, Department of Croatian language and literature, Faculty of Humanities and Social Sciences, University of Zagreb. She teaches courses in stylistics and literary criticism and specializes in the study of contemporary Croatian fiction. She is the editor of the academic portal Stilistika.org and of the Journal of the Faculty of Humanities and Social Sciences, University of Tuzla. She is the author of the monograph *Contemporary Novel in the Jaws of Life: A study in Interdiscursivity* (Disput, Zagreb, 2017), a translator of several monographs in linguistics and literary theory (G. Lakoff and M. Johnson, M. Dolar, R. Felski) and the editor of many collective works.

Saša Stanić
is an assistant lecturer at the Department of Croatian Language and Literature of the Faculty of Humanities and Social Sciences in Rijeka. He teaches courses on literary theory and stylistics. His primary interests are contemporary Croatian literature, popular culture, media and cinema in theoretical and practical terms. He is a co-author of a book *Fragmented Images of the World: Critical Analysis of Contemporary Film and Media Production* along with Boris Ružić (Facultas, Rijeka, 2012) in which he tackles the theoretical principles of a film making process with the emphasis on the phenomena of the spectacle.

Brian Willems
is associate professor of literature and film at the Faculty of Humanities and Social Sciences, University of Split. His most recent books are *Zugov učinak* (Multimedia Institute Zagreb, 2022) and *Sham Ruins: A User's Guide* (Routledge, 2021).

Introduction

Aleksandar Mijatović and Brian Willems

1 An Outline of the Temporal Turn in the (Post-)Yugoslav Studies

Almost three decades after the dissolution of Yugoslavia and the Yugoslav wars from 1991 to 1995, the concept of Yugoslavia still haunts present generations. The transition the former Yugoslav republics went through seems like a failure and it is viewed as incomplete. However, the case of Yugoslavia is not only indicative of the nations of its former republics. Throughout these past 30 years, it turns out that the Yugoslav scenario hovers over the oldest and seemingly the most stable, western liberal democracies. A belief, sprouted from the ruins of World War II, in a multinational, multiethnic, and multiracial coexistence in the globalized world is now faced with the rise of populism, nationalism, chauvinism, xenophobia, and the adoration of the authoritarian model of governing.

The corrosion of the firm ground of liberal democracies, through the processes of illiberalization, is to a certain extent pre-figured in the dissolution of Yugoslavia. The Yugoslav scenario incorporates two constituents. The first relates to the disruption of the multinational and multiethnic state, and the second involves the dismantling of socialism. As we shall discuss shortly, these two constituents form an ideological ethno-nationalist and neoliberal compound that imposes sequential temporality. This sequential temporality assumes two types of teleological and nostalgic remapping. While in the teleological type, the future determines the past, in the nostalgic counterpart, the future is conditioned by the past. Thus, the socialist and communist past simultaneously performs two functions. On the one hand, the transition into oxymoronic national-liberal and capitalist democracies is brought into discontinuity with the renounced past. On the other, continuity with the renounced past is revoked as an explanation for the shortcomings of the new political and economic order.

The rise of nationalism in the second Yugoslavia during the 1980s was disguised as the intellectual and democratic reclaiming of civic and political rights.[1] Notwithstanding attempts to (re)build the political culture of the sec-

---

[1] For how that could be avoided, see a recent study by Wachtel and Štiks (2019) which presents a kind of synthesis of their previous arguments independently delivered in Wachtel (1998) and Štiks (2015).

ond Yugoslavia on egalitarian grounds, at the end of the 1980s this rapidly backslides into a hidebound chauvinism and nationalism. Political and civic values and rights were abused in order to unfetter the foreclosed nationalist drive. At the outbreak of 1989, nationalist hatred was ignited by the misuse of a political reformation in the direction of liberal democracy and an economic transformation from socialism to the capitalist free market and self-regulated economy. During the 1990s, political and economic reformatting was coupled with the painful and traumatic experience of war. Bearing in mind that in the 1990s the neo-liberal transmogrification of the nation-state was indivisible from the war, one may bitterly pun with paronomasia that the socialist welfare state declined into the warfare state.

Yet, the first millennial decade showed that the war conditions, as a state of exception that temporarily cancels and constrains human, political, and civic rights, in effect sustains and supports the neoliberal position.[2] The neoliberal infringement of political domain with economic techniques of deregulation is accompanied by the ethno-nationalist state of war. In the post-crisis decade after 2008, this neoliberal and ethno-nationalist correlation resurfaces in the form of a populist backlash and revival of authoritarian forms of governing. While all former Yugoslav republics attempt to detract from their erstwhile common historical episodes, some other aspects of this bygone life shed more light on the contemporary decline of democracy and freedom in the world shaken by enduring global economic insecurity. The political and economic order of the second Yugoslavia is usually considered as the epitome of the ideas of equality, unity, parity, and solidarity. In order to debunk this bucolic image, neoliberal derogators, boosted by ethno-nationalist concomitants, repeatedly disparage the second Yugoslavia as a totalitarian regime.

While it may come true that this halcyon *locus amoenus* of equality and unity was more advertised and professed than genuinely embodied during the second Yugoslavia, many elements of governmentality pertaining to those values, as well as the political engagement inherent to them, were engendered in the political, social, economic, and civic life of Yugoslavia. A critical revision of the political, social, civic, and economic experience of the second Yugoslavia cannot directly counter and contest the neoliberal and

---

2   The term 'neoliberalism,' which has almost too many meanings to be useful, is being used here in Wendy Brown's sense: "[N]eoliberal rationality disseminates the *model of the market* to all domains and activities – even where money is not an issue – and configures human beings exhaustively as market actors, always, only, and everywhere as homo oeconomicus" (Brown 31), while at the same time, it should be remembered that neoliberalism is something that, as Maurizio Lazzarato says, "is always *in the process of being made*" (Lazzarato 107).

ethno-nationalist unmasking of the Yugoslav socialist Arcadia. Such a revision would be intrigued by the idyllic stereotype. Any forced forgetting cannot be countered by compulsory remembering, just as foreclosure and reclaiming are not opposed to disease and recovery. The primary object of reevaluation and retracing should be precisely this socialist *locus amoenus*, and not only attempts to demystify it. The Yugoslav past is simultaneously shaped as the *locus amoenus* and *locus horridus*, a socialist utopia and a totalitarian dystopia. The point is not to prove that there was any kind of real socialism, or a genuine social life, feigned behind its distorted appearance in order to be debased from the neoliberal and ethno-nationalist points of view. On the contrary, this revision should demonstrate that dissimulation is forged precisely within the same movement of its purported uncovering. The constitution of the object to be unveiled is coeval with the very act of its unveiling.

Daily political feuds are inundated not only with rehearsals of the socialist past as being directly responsible for the ensuing drawbacks but also with the shortcomings of the new political and economic order, which are vindicated by appealing to their communist and socialist antecedent. The consecutiveness of the political and economic order is manipulated so to create the deceptive effect of *post hoc ergo propter hoc*, that is to deceitfully conflate the logical and temporal arrangement of events. From this confusion of causality and succession, sustained by a linear chronology, the preceding time is reframed and re-enacted within the margins of the succeeding time. It is not only that *après coup* and *déjà vu* blend with each other to the point of their indiscernibility. Their interpenetration is still invested with a linear chronology. Due to that, the teleological confusion or conflation of outcomes and causes turns every attempt of the replenishment of the Yugoslav experiment into a nostalgic inability to distinguish between the already-have-been and the never-have-been, the always-already, and the never-to-come. And (post-)Yugoslav literature is a privileged place to witness this time which, as Zoran Roško describes it in his novel *Minus sapiens* (2017), is "a time that lasts but does not pass" (Roško 113). Nothing new can arise from this teleological remapping and nostalgic reliving of the past and the future. Teleological remapping undermines endeavors to seize the past in hindsight and to envisage the future and recover withheld possibilities and curbed insurgencies.

Coevality and sequentiality are not two separate temporalities. Instead, they form a two-tiered structure. Therefore, every critical study of literature, culture, and society seeks to establish non-coinciding fault-lines within this coexistence, as well as to find ways to re-enter them into the consecutive order of events. As we shall shortly discuss, one sets out to transform sequences into the coeval multitude of enduring processes with many loops and twists which are capable of disarraying time-lines and disrupting time-layers in order to question and restitute both discontinuities and continuities.

The topic of time is clearly important in exploring (post-)Yugoslav literatures and cultures. The prefix and punctuation of (post-)Yugoslav refer to the literatures and cultures that were emerging after the collapse of the second Yugoslavia. These literatures and cultures are frequently regarded as responding to the nationalist onslaught in the second Yugoslavia and its final collapse. Therefore, the prefix and hyphen involved in the word formation of the (post-)Yugoslav refer to wavering inbetween the interstitial realm of the before and after of the demise of the second Yugoslavia. Due to this wavering, both the before and the after could be extended and stretched in time to encompass various historical events. By departing from the 'post-' as wavering it could be possible to escape from both a teleological explanation of the slow and dramatic destruction of the second Yugoslavia and its nostalgic restoration. Nostalgic reinvigoration is a backlash to the teleological ingraining of the fallout into the origin. Refraining from teleological explanations means curbing retroactive deductions of causes from the outcomes. Holding back from nostalgic restoration blocks hooking the future onto the past.

(Post-)Yugoslav literary, artistic, and cultural practices do not only attempt to portray the demise of the state and the succeeding war between its former republics; they also critically reflect on and engage with the processes taking place before and after the dissolution in order to capture the collapse itself. Nevertheless, the (post-)Yugoslav character of this literary, artistic, and cultural production does not arise from its *thematic* framework. The collapse, the emergence of new states, and the subsequent interactions of individuals and collectives outside the boundaries of these states cannot be captured by turning them into the topic of an artistic world, the object of performance, or the product of a culture.

(Post-)Yugoslav literature(s) and cultures are preoccupied and enthralled with the temporality of the before and the after as well as with the middle that evanescently lingers between them. Research into the growing field of (post-)Yugoslav studies has so far been focused on the topics of memory, trauma, exile, nostalgia, melancholy, community, identity, and popular culture.[3] From both theoretical and historical points of view, it would be fruitful

---

3   In *The Cultural Life of Capitalism in Yugoslavia*, Jelača, Kolanović, and Lugarić cover a variety of topics related to the socialist Yugoslavia and former Yugoslav states in the post-socialist era. The volume examines transformations of class, labor, the market, consumerism, feminism, the body, education, and sexuality in the ongoing transition from socialism to a neo-liberal market economy.

INTRODUCTION 5

and promising to reconceptualize and redescribe the current state of debate by connecting the thematic research program with the framework of temporality.

(Post-)Yugoslav literature(s) and culture(s) do not only depict what happens after the dissolution and how the past is extended into the future. Indeed, the structure of the 'post-' is not determined by a succession of moments; the temporal structure of the 'post-' is not derived from the movements between objects, events, and persons. This means that the temporal structure of the 'post-' is not delimited by the existence of Yugoslavia and its dissolution.

In this panoply of essays, the authors were asked to search for the possibility of explicating the temporal structure underlying the theoretical and analytical concepts employed in understanding (post-)Yugoslav literature(s) and culture(s). This turn from the *thematic* to the *temporal* in critical (post-)Yugoslav studies follows the shift from state-centered research presumptions and corresponding frameworks methodologies to non-institutionalist, even anti-institutionalist, fields and objects of study (Gordy). The authors were asked to look into the potentials of the temporal turn to unravel the interdependencies of the social background, cultural context, and political and historical events.

Concepts related to time have been used to study (post-)Yugoslav literature(s) and culture(s), however, the concept of time itself has not been directly engaged. The literature(s) and culture(s) that emerged after the dissolution of the second Yugoslavia could be written in both the singular and the plural. This ambiguity indicates a proliferation of temporal frames, time-scapes, layers, and lines, including the processes of their constant divergence and convergence and ever shifting time scopes. Scholars of (post-)Yugoslav literature(s) and culture(s) are aware of these multiplying and heterogeneous chronologies. This theoretical, analytical and interpretive awareness is both implicit and explicit.

Various studies highlight the importance of time in apprehending these theoretical, interpretative, and analytical concepts, such as Rakočević (2011), Williams (2013), Matijević (2016), Beronja and Vervaet (2016), and Brebanović (2017).[4] Beronja and Vervaet (5–6) introduce the notion of a (post-)Yugoslav constellation in order to explicate the shift from historical sequences to their mutual influence. Drawing on Hirsch's (2012) seminal study, Beronja

---

4 This is not an exhaustive list. One may add a recent collection by Marčetić et al. (2019) or the more historically and culturally oriented papers such that of Velikonja (2017) and collections such as the previously mentioned Jelača et al. (2017).

and Vervaet underline how sequences coming into this constellation have an "ongoing influence" (6) upon each other. This alteration of theoretical focus could bring forth important interpretive and analytical results. First, the study of the 'post-,' as Beronja and Vervaet compellingly show, would no longer be limited to the research of the period that comes after, while the preceding period is considered an unalterable cause. Second, the passing between periods has both destructive and transformative effects and outcomes. Third, this transformation is effective in both directions of the past and future. Hence, the post is the "ongoing influence" itself, possessing its own temporality. It is not temporality that is derived from the break between the before and after; rather, it is the temporality of an enduring influence that divides. Departing from this temporality of division, the 'post-' becomes a mobile quality that switches between temporal frames, flows, lines, and layers independently from and across their sequential order.[5]

However, despite being acknowledged across the field of (post-)Yugoslav studies, these multiplying and heterogeneous chronologies are not susceptible to being easily taken as an autonomous object of study. With this volume we suggest a possible outlook on how these multilayered temporality/ies could be accessed in the study of (post-)Yugoslav literature(s) and culture(s).

To disclose one of the temporal structures underlying the other theoretical, analytical, and interpretative concepts employed in the field of (post-)Yugoslav studies, we set forth the concept of (post-)Yugoslav time as the object of research. (Post-)Yugoslav time is defined and revealed by using terms and concepts such as exile, melancholy, memory, and trauma. It is a thought experiment in which understanding the collapse of Yugoslavia would depend on shifting the theoretical focus from Yugoslavia itself to the question of time. Concomitant to this transposition is a shift from the (post-)Yugoslav to literature alone. [6]

By abstracting both (post-)Yugoslav time and literature from the history of both Yugoslavia and its dissolution, one shifts from the history to the process as well as the processual characters of historical events themselves. Following

---

5 For developing such an in-between temporality in the field of (post-)Yugoslav art, see Čvoro (2018).

6 Koczanowicz (2008) examines the post-communist condition by reconsidering post-communist time. He describes the transformations of post-communist Poland from a liberal democracy to an illiberal republicanism in terms of a temporal dynamics divided between social and political time. Without going further into his extremely important and intricate argument, we will in passing conclude that he tries to elaborate a political capacity of time to empower the multitude of social agents lacking political power.

Braudel (1969), Elias (2007), and Abbott (2001; 2016), emphasis on the process and processual character of society and culture does not mean overlooking their historical character. On the contrary, in leaving enduring processes behind, one reassesses the history of societies and cultures from the standpoint of time. In subsuming time under history, culture, and society, research would be confined to their products, neglecting a variety of interwoven trajectories from which social and cultural objects and events upsurge. By adopting the conceptual primacy of time, an entirely different object of study arises in the field.

As Abbott (*Processual Sociology* 4) put it: "The social process doesn't have outcomes. It just keeps on going." Earlier, Abbott (*Time Matters*) attempted to grasp that ongoing processuality of the social world through Bergson's concept of time as duration, and Whitehead's notions of process and relationism. The social and historical world is caught in the continuous "process of making, remaking, and unmaking" (ix). These recent achievements in the fields of sociology and historiography are concomitant with the simultaneous historical (re)turn in literary studies. Echoing Jameson's famous theoretical slogan to "always historicize" stated in *The Political Unconscious* (1981), Bru and his collaborators announce a "turn to history in literary studies" (Bru et al. 1). They attempt to resuscitate long-outmoded theoretical terms such as 'Generation' and 'Period' (178–205) and to link them with concepts such as 'Time' and 'Event' (137–152; 164–178).

These processes do not take place in history and society; instead, they create history and society. The processual character of history, society, or politics is attained by extricating the time that governs other concepts, describing how individuals and collectives interact, counter and mourn their losses and traumas, as well as how they recall and commemorate their past. Critical (post-)Yugoslav studies need to disentangle the concept of time from history, society, and politics in order to show how individuals and collectives transform the temporal character of their interactions just as they are simultaneously transformed by them. Returning to Bru and his collaborators' restoration of literary history within the field of literary theory, one does not only seek to pinpoint the historical framework of theoretical concepts, for: "Even scholars of literature now, apparently, cannot avoid thinking in *historical* terms" (1, emphasis added). Concepts and time, literary theory and history are not, however, divided. The temporal structure of concepts knots together their quality of being historical and theoretical, which pushes them beyond both oppositions of receptivity and spontaneity, passivity and activity, and beyond the spiritual movement of a concept that needs to be embodied into history. Instead of thinking in historical terms propelled by a manic pursuit of overcoming an alleged theoretical sterility, one could attempt to temporalize both history and theory coevally – *always temporalize* – in order to expound how are both concrete events and the standpoints of their apprehension is concurrently transformed and transmogrified, mutated and mutilated.[7] Following on the recent work of the Invisible Committee (190), Nick Srnicek and Alex Williams (61), as well as Thomas Piketty (7), this strategy of delineating the material properties of ideological positions is essential in reducing specters that seem too large and pervasive to change, such as neoliberalism, to their parts which can then be challenged, reformulated, or discarded.

As argued above, Beronja's and Vervaet's (2016) edited collection, with its overtly stated research agenda, presents an instance of using the temporal turn to the study of (post-)Yugoslav literature(s) and culture(s). Beronja and Vervaet, in the Introduction, reassess to (post-)Yugoslav time in linking the most recent (post-)memory studies with Walter Benjamin's notions of the constellation and dialectics at a standstill.

Beronja's and Vervaet's volume engages the compelling legacy of critical theory (Benjamin) and more recent postmemory studies (M. Hrisch, M. Rothberg) in order to counter both ethno-nationalist and neo-liberal excoriations and condemnations of the quondam country and to envision looming forms of community and identity as emerging outside the limits of institutionalized legitimation. Through the shift from the static to the dynamic model of cultural memory, this enduring influence reframes the coeval temporalities of the before and the after, putting them into interaction.

Reconsidering (Post)-Yugoslav Time endeavors to recover the multiplicity and heterogeneity of (post-)Yugoslav chronologies in a variety of concepts deployed in studies of (post-)Yugoslav literature(s) and culture(s). It is not possible to adequately understand the dissolution of Yugoslavia, its subsequent events, and their intricacies without re-considering and re-conceptualizing the multiple and conflicting timelines along which they are arranged, rearranged, and disarranged. An adequate theoretical account should display how (post-)Yugoslav literature(s) and culture(s) capture the processual character of the (post-)Yugoslav condition. With temporal complexity placed at the center of the theoretical reflections and interpretative

---

7 Williams (2013) develops the notion of literature of ruin (*Trümmerliteratur*) in order to explain topics of nostalgia, melancholia, and memory that pervades (post-)Yugoslav literature in the era after the collapse of Yugoslavia. Although Williams addresses "the time in between" (Williams 175) transformation and destruction, restoration and annihilation, he conceptualizes the notion of time indirectly, in terms of the processes of fragmentation and their dialectics with regaining totality.

procedures of reckoning with (post-)Yugoslav literature(s) and culture(s), the (post-)Yugoslav condition could be grasped as an ongoing process. The processual character of the (post-)Yugoslav condition requires an investigation into the co-existence of multiple temporal layers. The chronology of discrete timelines reduces processes and the processual quality of society and politics to sterilized outcomes (Abbot 2016). The multidimensionality of timelines and time-scapes disrupts the sequential view of history.

The essays in *Reconsidering (Post)-Yugoslav Time* indicate that *the before* and *the after* of Yugoslavia is involved in an incessant shifting backwards and forwards. The 'post-' designates that toing and froing, veering between *the before* and *the after*, thereby putting the temporal dividing line into continuous movement. The errant movement of this dividing line, its ever-shifting character of toing and froing, outlines a swirling of ephemeral (Manning) zones of traversals in-between identities.[8] The swaying of time-line(s) backwards and forwards introduces time-lags (Bhabha) in their simultaneity.

Viewing the (post-)Yugoslav condition as a sum or assembly of discrete parts causally connected in the stereotyped solidity of historical lineages entails the risk of limiting analyses and theoretical elaborations to what Althusser termed a Hegelian conception of time, or an "ideological conception of historical time" (Althusser et. al. 279). By shifting from the simultaneity of heterogeneous temporal levels and flows to their homogenous contemporaneity, there is a danger of overlooking how they change between themselves and within themselves as they cross and traverse each other.

Notwithstanding their simultaneity, the temporalities of active metamorphosis and passive transformation do not synchronize with each other. This non-coinciding simultaneity opens a gap or a scission that coordinates temporal layers without subordinating them to a unifying timeline. This non-coalescent simultaneity of multilayered temporality was previously described as "the contemporaneity of the noncontemporaneous" (Koselleck) and by Bloch (1977; 1985; 1991) as a non-synchronous heterogeneous contradiction. Both Kosselleck's and Bloch's notions appear in Rethmann's (2016) attempt to accommodate Yugoslavism within Bloch's politics of hope. Rethmann's maneuver is provocative since she extends it to the (post-)Yugoslav condition. She displaces "an historical imagination of linear progress, of ending and failure" with "a temporally uneven and densely layered present" (169) If Rethmann is right in describing Yugoslavism as "an invitation to think 'otherwise' to produce 'otherwhiles'" (170), then it merges a divergent diversity of

---

[8] For a possibility of developing a (post-)Yugoslav community along similar lines see Kovačević (2018).

temporal lines, strata and layers, withdrawing from their synchronization. Following Rethmann, the task of critical (post-)Yugoslav studies is then to avoid and thwart synchronization through a commitment to the multiplicity of co-existing temporalities.

2   A Note on the Corpus and Division of the Volume

Readers will note that the corpus covered in the collection does not encompass all the (post-)Yugoslav literatures and authors. The volume's topic is the concept of (post-)Yugoslav time and examining alternative routes in critical (post-)Yugoslav studies. Therefore, with the volume in its readers' hands, we intend to expound on different methodologies and outline possibilities of the temporal turn in the field of (post-)Yugoslav studies instead of presenting all post-Yugoslav literatures and languages.

Before presenting single chapters, we explicate a blueprint of the division and subdivision of the volume. The array of essays is divided into two parts titled 'The Concept of (Post-)Yugoslav Time' and 'Application(s) of/to the (Post-)Yugoslav Time,' each then branching into two sections. The first part is devoted to elaborating the concept of temporality. The second part outlines the scopes and limits of the concept of temporality in memory studies and cultural analysis. The chapters are ordered according to the following schema:

Part 1. The Concept of (Post-)Yugoslav Time
   1. Time Unbound: De-synchronized Temporalities of Modernity, the (Neo-)Avant-Garde, Post-modernity, and the Concept of (Post-)Yugoslav Literature
   2. From the Time that Belongs to No-One to Temporalities of Non-belonging

Part 2. Application(s) of/to (Post-)Yugoslav Time
   1. Unhinging Memory and Space: Remembering (Post-)Yugoslav Time
   2. De-composing Broken Bonds: The Culture of Non-relational Relation

3   Presentation of Chapters

The first part of the book, The Concept of (Post-)Yugoslav Time, begins with the section "Time Unbound: De-synchronized Temporalities of Modernity, the (Neo-)Avant-Garde, Post-modernity and the Concept of (Post-)Yugoslav

Literature," contains four contributions. Brian Willems, in "Past Fragments, Future Change: Dubravka Ugrešić, Vladan Desnica, Sanja Iveković, and Dalibor Martinis," outlines a transversal trajectory from Yugoslav to (post-)Yugoslav time. Willems juxtaposes the seemingly diverse literary works of Vladan Desnica's *Proljeća Ivana Galeba: Igre Proljeća i Smrti* (1957) and *Pronalazak Athanatika* (1957), as well as Dubravka Ugrešić's *Europe in Sepia* and (2014) *Baba Yaga Laid an Egg* (2009), with artistic performances by Dalibor Martinis (1978, 2010) and Sanja Iveković (1979). By outlining how these writers and artists establish links between immortality, communism, and fragmentation, Willems demonstrates how these political and economic regimes preempt the transformative character of the future through the appropriation of death. He reads these works and performances as hallmarks of "(...) the death of a hegemonic view of time." He convincingly shows that finitude and contingency need to be transferred from the individual to the collective domain of communities, states, and regimes. By reclaiming the experience of death, the future is re-appropriated by re-inventing the past as that which has "never been experienced by anyone."

Tijana Matijević's contribution "'The Historical Moment Before Our Eyes': On Producing Post-Yugoslav Literature" offers a comparative reading of Slobodan Tišma's novel *Bernardijeva soba* (2011) and Judita Šalgo's novel *Put u Birobidžan* (1997). Matijević explores the paradoxical temporality of non-objects (car wrecks, furniture, and armor), non-spaces (rooms), and non-bodies that are metamorphosed into memory machines. By drawing on a feminist critique of Deleuze and Guattari's concept of becoming-woman, Matijević underscores gender as a site of interplay between various temporal layers, both individual and collective. She demonstrates how characters could unleash femininity from the universalizing constraints of Deleuze's and Guattari's notion of becoming-woman. As the argument unfolds, Matijević showcases how subjectivation enters a realm of potential multi-layered temporality/ies that removes the now from being contemporary with itself. This temporalization of the subject of femininity engenders a diffusion of non-coinciding correspondences among various social, political, and historical strata.

This section concludes with Lujo Parežanin's article "Whose (Neo-)Avant-garde? The Poetry of Josip Sever, Yugoslav Modernity, and the Problem of Mononational Literary History" opens with a challenging thesis, according to which: "The conceptual triangle, comprising Yugoslavia, Yugoslav literature, and post-Yugoslav literature, entices ambiguity in what sense post-Yugoslav literature is post-Yugoslav, and what defines it as post-Yugoslav literature." He intriguingly engages with this thesis by coupling the modernist literary scholar

Svetozar Petrović and neo-avant-garde poet Josip Sever. Parežanin employs this juxtaposition to dismantle the Yugoslav national(ist) project and its academic underpinnings in literary history. He retrieves the revolutionary background of the project of Yugoslavia, actualizing the temporal framework in which Petrović attempts to conceptualize Yugoslav literature. Parežanin shifts from the modernist temporalization to the (neo)-avant-garde attempt to free time from an already determined point of reference. The (neo)-avant-garde impulse to be ahead of its time disrupts both the modernist's contemporaneity with one's own time and the progressist's obsession to surpass the past. Petrović tries to surmount the perplexities of the notion of Yugoslav literature by relocating it to the modernist temporality. However, as Parežanin shows, this modernist temporality is disrupted by the unsettling anticipatory movement of the (neo)-avant-garde.

The section "From the Time that Belongs to No-One to Temporalities of Non-belonging" moves from dystopian to speculative time. It comprises four articles. In "The End of the World as We Know It? Anti-Utopia in Post-Yugoslav Literature," Boris Postnikov compares the following novels: *Promijeni me (Change Me)* (2008), written by Slovenian author Andrej Blatnik, *Planet Friedman*, written in 2012 by Bosnian-Herzegovinian author Josip Mlakić, and *Lomljenje vjetra (Breaking the Wind)* written by Croatian writer Edo Popović in 2011. While Mlakić's and Popović's novels appeared in the culmination of the economic crisis, Blatnik's novel was published in the wake of the recession. Countering Frederic Jameson's thesis, or rather H. Bruce Franklin's, that it is easier to imagine the end of the world than to imagine the end of capitalism, Postnikov puts forth the thesis that these novels do not raise "fictional critiques of capitalism." Instead, they excoriate neoliberalism as an "exaggerated 'malformation'" of capitalism. Postnikov sees the decay of capitalism, its downturn into neoliberalism as an inseparable part of the breakdown of socialism. However, the temporalities of capitalism and socialism are simultaneous because the destruction of collective life is followed by disempowering the individuals and their lack of capability for change. The simultaneous destruction of collective and individual life divests the community of its political character. Postnikov seeks to de-synchronize this destruction of community, which disables the production of collective and individual resistance.

Miranda Levanat-Peričić's "Post-Yugoslav Dystopian Dilemmas and Writing the History of the Future: Alternative Version or Parodic Subversion?" proceeds with an exploration of the temporality of (post-)Yugoslav literature. Her goal is to redefine the genre of dystopia regarding its relationship with the past and the future. She distinguishes between an anti-modernist dystopia and, relying on Bakhtin's theory of genre, Menippean dystopia. While the first dystopia opposes the past to the drawbacks of the future, the second kind of dystopia subordinates the past to a sweeping appraisal. In this Levanat-Peričić underscores the de-synchronizing impact of Menippean dystopia.

The two concluding chapters of this section of the volume are dedicated to the Croatian writer Luka Bekavac and his recent literary work. Ante Jerić's contribution "Kant Has Some Relevance Here: On a Fictional Theory of Quentin Meillassoux and the Theoretical Fiction of Luka Bekavac" focuses on philosophical aspects of Bekavac's prose. Matija Jelača's and Anera Ryznar's contribution "The Narrative Out of Time: The Nonhuman World of Luka Bekavac's Fiction" amounts to a narratological account of Bekavac's prose.

Luka Bekavac was one of the 2015 European Union Prize winners for his novel *Viljevo* (2013). He has also received national awards for his literary work. He blends fictional characters and settings with historical (Croatian Homeland War/*Domovinski rat* and the siege of Osijek during the early 1990s) and the topographical (Osijek and near villages) references. However, this is far from the metahistoriographic devices familiar from postmodernist fiction, which have been employed in (post-)Yugoslav literature. Bekavac's prose, following the threads of speculative fiction, installs an alien zone that co-exists with its historically and topographically discernible fictional settings. These zones are incompatible and yet they interpenetrate each other, transpiring therewith to a temporality that expunges history from an uncontestable familiarity. Through the interplay of zones, time is extirpated from history. By becoming thereby unknown, history is rendered into present experience and reframes the horizon of expectations.

Due to its untranslatability into habitual experience, history, as a site of contestation, demands a coeval reading of the past and the present. Jerić, Jelača, and Ryznar focus on this new stance toward time and history, relying on different methodologies. Whereas Jerić is oriented to recovering a philosophical backdrop of this history of the non-human, Jelača and Ryznar examine Bekavac's prose using post-classical narratological tools. To some extent, Bekavac's prose has a notable predecessor in David Albahari's Canadian Trilogy (*Snežni čovek/Snow Man*, (1995), *Mamac/Bait*, (1996), and *Mrak/Dark*, (1997)). Nevertheless, Bekavac's implementation of speculative fiction to forge a transhistorical world embedded in history, in effect to excavate history from history, could open new paths in the study of (post-)Yugoslav literature(s) and culture(s). This is why we conclude this subsection with two pieces devoted to Luka Bekavac's prose.

Jerić navigates Bekavac's novels *Drenje* (2011), *Viljevo* (2013), and *Policijski sat* (2016), as well as the collection *Galerija likovnih umjetnosti u Osijeku* (2017). As a departing point, Jerić engages with a recent philosophical and theoretical discussion on speculative realism. He connects Quentin Meillassoux's divinology with Bekavac's re-conceptualization of diegetic temporality. In Bekavac's prose, the reader is confronted with the temporality of something that does not exist but might come about. The experience of return is displaced by the experience of the radically contingent event of arrival. Its radicality lies not only in its modality, but also in its temporality. The fortuitous arrival, a simultaneous possibility both of its advent and a withdrawal from it, supersedes a longing to resuscitate something that once was. It is a yearning for something unknown, exceeding cognitive boundaries, and whose foreignness stems from a perpetual delay in an unprecedented future; it is something that certainly could have arrived, but its arrival is interminably delayed. Jelača and Ryznar combine a narratological analysis and philosophical meditation. They argue that Bekavac's fiction disrupts the mimetic illusion of temporality by laying bare the textual mechanisms of its production. Bekavac's fiction instills a "temporal entropy," foregrounding a sense of "eerie" time that exists outside the human reach and yet determines our approach to the world. In the unfolding of a narrative world, the temporality of the eerie alternates between anticipation (flashforward, prolepsis) and retrospection (flashback, analepsis).

The second part of the collection, Application(s) of/to (Post-)Yugoslav Time, begins with the section "Unhinging Memory and Space: Remembering (Post-)Yugoslav Time," which consists of three contributions. In "Re-Reading/Writing Yugoslav Pasts and Presents in Post-Yugoslav Literature: Between (Yugo-)Nostalgia and 'Lateral Networks,'" Mirko Milivojević studies the vicissitudes of the notion of nostalgia in the work of Dubravka Ugrešić, Miljenko Jergović, and Aleksandar Hemon. Milivojević aims to debunk the notion of Yugonostalgia and replace it with the notions of lateral networks and minor transnationality. In employing these concepts, Milivojević rethinks a turn to a future-oriented nostalgia within the field of (post-)Yugoslav studies. This nostalgia is a lateral operation that cuts across given boundaries and identities. Its de-synchronizing effects cannot be reduced to envisaging the future from the point of view of restoring broken links between the present and the past. Instead, in Milivojević's chapter, the future is unraveled as a zone of traversals between heterogeneous layers of time.

Danijela Marot Kiš, in "Spaces of Memory in Dragan Velikić's Novel *Investigator*," describes how the subject of memory patches together various places and objects that metonymically displace each other. She examines how memories revolve around familiar places, restoring their initial strangeness. The adjacent strangeness of familiar objects, surroundings, and persons reveals their evanescent and ephemeral belonging. Marot Kiš pinpoints the temporality of simultaneity and co-existence, which transforms memory from a site of loss into a site of rebirth and renewal. The temporalized structure of memory turns remnants into empty places, obliterated from previous content. Instead of being reminders of the previous order, empty places commemorate the alien identities, uncharted possibilities, and unforeseeable outcomes of historical processes. They are not only empty places in the present, evacuated from any content coming from the past. In addition, temporalized memory recovers the vacant sites in the past. For something to become past it needs to be gone and to disappear. That passing in time is reinscribed in memory as searching for traces (lat. pl. *vestigia*) of a time that is yet to come. Hence, to consider memory as incomplete, as hindered by a lack, is to conceive it as a storage of feeble representations of the past. Following Marot Kiš, explicating the temporal structure of memory means transforming the resistance of memory to be fulfilled into a condition of the resuscitating the futurity of the past alone.

Kujtim Rrahmani's "In Search of Home Time" offers an astounding blend of theoretical and poetical meditations combined with an autoethnographical approach to the topic of home time. In reassessing home time as the temporality of elsewhere, Rrahmani draws striking parallels between Dubravka Ugrešić and Zejnullah Rrahmani. Kujtim Rrahmani's theoretical framework is Gaston Bachelard's phenomenology of time employed in relation to the poetics of home. Yet, as he shows, home is not only an abode of intimacy or a spotlight of recovery of the lost past. Taking a clue from Bachelard that home surmounts its physical limits, Rrahmani traces homelessness, epitomized in the fractal temporality of elsewhere and nowhere, as a new form of dwelling. By this, Bachelard's poetics of home is merged with the contrapuntal condition of being expropriated from home, elaborated by Georg Lukács as transcendental homelessness. In weaving intimacy and distance, proximity and remoteness, Rrahmani moves to the poetics of homelessness, wherein home is divested from its origins and roots. Such a temporalization of home is foremost deployed in relation to the homeland, which needs to be estranged from within.

The section, "De-composing Broken Bonds: The Culture of Non-relational Relation," consists of three articles. Saša Stanić and Marina Biti, in their chapter "Cultural Values and the Circularity of 'Transition' in Croatia: Postwar Literature and Film," explore the period of transition of Croatia from a (post-)communist country to a neoliberal state. Along with this political and economic transition, nationalism slides from the ideological to the cultural realm. Considering the historical context and yet focusing more narrowly on processes in the cultural field, which are most clearly reflected in narrative genres – literature and film, Stanić and Biti view the transition as a recurring process simultaneously addressing both the past and the future. This swirling transition involves a continuous and still ongoing back and forth movement under the lid of prevailing ideological and market values, with a suffocating effect on artistic expression and literary and cultural critique. Stanić and Biti provide a meticulous cultural analysis of the relationship between commodification and conservative politics. Accordingly, to disrupt this link they reconsider the concept of transition as a political and economic process that conceals both its beginning and ending. The transition is ideologically distorted by employing linear temporality. In this consecutive order, what comes after is contrived as unrelated to what was before. Instead, the authors revise the notion of transition as a recursive process entangling discontinuity and continuity, regression and progression, retrospection and anticipation. Both past and future are uncharted realms toward which transition steers.

In the contribution "Writing Against the Code and Fitting in with the Code: Reading Dubravka Ugrešić in the Context of the International Literary Field," Iva Kosmos reconsiders the notion of exile and its contemporary (re)production, in which the structural conditions that enable the position of exile writers from Eastern Europe have changed. Kosmos questions the function of (post-)Yugoslav exile writers as native informants on their region as well as the reception of their representations of Yugoslav socialism in countries abroad. She argues that the criticism of (post-)Yugoslav writers, leveled against their home region(s), could be in the service of the reaffirmation of Western values and the confirmation of its feeling of supremacy over the Orientalist "other." She engages with the notion of temporality to avoid the understanding of a "context" as a homogenous set of cultural codes, practices, and discourses. Thereby, each context is showcased as being composed of multidimensional timelines and timescapes, along with their attendant discourses, codes, associations, and implications.

In "Narrations of Lost and Found: The Twists and Turns of the Friendship Discourse in the (Post)Yugoslav Environment," Zala Pavšič explores the complicity of politics and spectacle. Pavšič turns to Boris Dvornik's (1939–2008) and Bata Živojinović's (1933–2016) mutual renouncement of their renowned friendship in the 1990s and their reconciliation in the 2000s. Croat Dvornik and Serb Živojinović were the most popular Yugoslav actors and great friends in real life until the 1990s, when they ended their friendship. Hence, the vicissitudes of their friendship, its recurring integration, and disintegration, are rendered into a symbol of Yugoslav unity and its subsequent dissolution. In the early 2000s, Dvornik and Živojinović attempted to regain their friendship publicly. Taking the symbolic and affective charge of the ending of a seemingly enduring friendship, as well as its restoration, Pavšič examines friendship as a temporal experience. Drawing on Derrida's analyses of the relationship between friends, Pavšič shows that friendship is never given. Rather it is ceaselessly exposed to the risk of separation and partition. This finitude is ingrained in friendship as a temporal interval that simultaneously conjoins and disjoins. The finitude of friendship, its mortality, overruns any claim on the eternity of its bonds. Pavšič studies friendship as a possible pattern for superseding the nationalist governmentalities of newly constructed states. Pavšić traces the discourse of the lost and recovered friendship in the newly established and conflicting (post-)Yugoslav states. Through the narrative of reconciliation, the (post-)Yugoslav states are de-synchronized both between and within themselves. The friendship regained discloses equality as a category that enables the disruption of policies that blur and redraw the lines between friends and enemies, neighbors and strangers.

What ties these chapters together is the way they all foreground the incongruous mutuality of toing and froing that confronts the reader with the fortuitous discovery of something where nothing was expected, as well as the obverse, an unforeseen encounter with nothing where something once was. (Post-)Yugoslav time places the subject within the haphazard asymmetrical interplay and dissonant interchangeability between something and nothing. The subject of experience structured by (post-)Yugoslav time wanders through the temporality of what lies in-between both presence and absence.

References

Abbott, Andrew. *Time Matters: On Theory and Method*. University of Chicago Press, 2001.
Abbott, Andrew. *Processual Sociology*. University of Chicago Press, 2016.
Althusser, Louis, et. al. *Lire le Capital*. PUF, 1965.
Beronja, Vlad and Vervaet Stijn (Eds.). *Post-Yugoslav Constellations: Archive, Memory and Trauma in Contemporary Bosnian, Croatian, and Serbian Literature and Culture*. De Gruyter, 2016.
Bhabha, Homi. *The Location of Culture*. Routledge, 1994.
Bloch, Ernst. "Nonsynchronism and the Obligation to its Dialectics," *New German Critique*, vol. 11, 1977, pp. 22–38.
Bloch, Ernst. *Erbschaft dieser Zeit*. Suhrkamp, 1985.
Bloch, Ernst. *Heritage of Our Times*. Neville and Stephen Plaice (Trans.). Polity Press, 1991.
Braudel, Fernand. *Écrits sur l'Histoire*. Flammarion, 1969.

Brebanović, Predrag "Jugoslavenska književnost: stanovište sadašnjosti," *Tranzicija i kulturno pamćenje*, Virna Karlić, Sanja Šakić and Dušan Marinković (Eds.), Srednja Europa, 2017, pp. 57–65.

Brown, Wendy. *Undoing the Demos: Neoliberalism's Stealth Revolution*. Zone Books, 2015.

Bru, Sascha, Ben De Bruyn, and Michel Delville (Eds.). *Literature Now: Key Terms and Methods for Literary History*. Edinburgh University Press, 2016.

Čvoro, Uroš. *Transitional Aesthetics: Contemporary Art at the Edge of Europe*. Bloomsbury Academic, 2018.

Elias, Norbert. *An Essay on Time. Collected Works, Vol. 9*. University College Dublin Press, 2007.

Gordy, Eric. "On the Current and Future Research Agenda for Southeast Europe." *Debating the End of Yugoslavia*. Florian Bieber, Armina Galijaš and Rory Archer (Eds.). Ashgate, 2014, pp. 11–23.

Hirsch, Marianne. *The Generation of Memory: Writing and Visual Culture After the Holocaust*. Columbia University Press, 2012.

Invisible Committee, The. *To Our Friends*. Robert Hurley (Trans.). Semiotext(e), 2015.

Jelača, Dijana, Maša Kolanović, and Danijela Lugarić (Eds.). *The Cultural Life of Capitalism in Yugoslavia: (Post)Socialism and Its Other*. Palgrave Macmillan, 2017.

Koczanowicz, Leszek. *Politics of Time: The Dynamics of Identity in Post-Communist Poland*. Berghahn, 2008.

Koselleck, Reinhart. *Futures Past: On the Semantics of Historical Time*. Keith Tribe (Trans.). Columbia University Press, 2004.

Kovačević, Nataša. *Uncommon Alliances: Cultural Narratives of Migration in the New Europe*. Edinburgh University Press, 2018.

Lazzarato, Maruizio. *The Making of the Indebted Man: An Essay on the Neoliberal Condition*. Semiotext(e), 2012.

Manning, Erin. *Ephemeral Territories: Representing Nation, Home, and Identity in Canada*. University of Minnesota Press, 2003.

Marčetić, Adrijana, Bojana Stojanović-Pantović, Vladimir Zorić, and Dunja Dušanić (Eds.). *Jugoslovenska književnost: prošlost, sadašnjost i budućnost jednog spornog pojma/ Yugoslav Literature: The Past, Present and Future of a Contested Notion*. Čigoja Štampa, 2019.

Matijević, Tijana. "National, Post-national, Transnational: Is Post-Yugoslav Literature an Arguable or Promising Field of Study?" *Grenzräume – Grenzbewegungen*. Nina Frieß, Gunnar Lenz, Erik Martin (Eds.). Universitätsverlag Potsdam, 2016, pp. 101–113.

Piketty, Thomas. *Capital and Ideology*. Arthur Goldhammer (Trans.). Harvard University Press, 2020.

Rakočević, Robert. "Post-jugoslovenska književnost? Ogledala i fantomi." *Sarajevske sveske*, vols. 35–36, 2011, pp. 202–210.

Rethmann, Petra. "Yugoslavism: History, Temporality, and the Search for Alternative Modes of Political Critique." *Time, Globalization, and the Human Experience*. Paul Huebener et al. (Eds.). Routledge, 2016, pp. 160–174.

Roksandić, Drago. "Yugoslavism before the Creation of Yugoslavia." *Yugoslavia from a Historical Perspective*. Latinka Perović, Drago Roksandić, Mitja Velikonja, Wolfgang Hoepken, and Florian Bieber (Eds.). Helsinki Committee for Human Rights in Serbia, 2017, pp. 29–65.

Roško, Zoran. *Minus sapiens*. OceanMore, 2017.

Štiks, Igor. *Nations and Citizens in Yugoslavia and the Post-Yugoslav States: One Hundred Years of Citizenship*. Bloomsbury, 2015.

Velikonja, Mitja. "Ways of Remembering Yugoslavia. The Yugoslav Rear-View Mirror." *Yugoslavia from a Historical Perspective*. Latinka Perović, Drago Roksandić, Mitja Velikonja, Wolfgang Hoepken, and Florian Bieber (Eds.). Helsinki Committee for Human Rights in Serbia, 2017, pp. 515–551.

Wachtel, Andrew. *Making a Nation, Breaking a Nation: Literature and Cultural Politics in Yugoslavia*. Stanford University Press, 1998.

Wachtel, Andrew and Igor Štiks. "Squaring the South Slavic Circle: Ethnicity, Nationhood, and Citizenship in Yugoslavia." *Civic Nationalisms in Global Perspective*. Jasper Trautsch (Ed.). Routledge, 2019, pp. 54–69.

Williams, David. *Writing Postcommunism: Towards a Literature of the East European Ruins*. Palgrave Macmillan, 2013.

PART 1

The Concept of (Post-)Yugoslav Time

SECTION 1

*Time Unbound: De-synchronized Temporalities of
Modernity, the (Neo-)Avant-Garde, Post-modernity,
and the Concept of (Post-)Yugoslav Literature*

CHAPTER 1

Past Fragments, Future Change: Dubravka Ugrešić, Vladan Desnica, Sanja Iveković, and Dalibor Martinis

Brian Willems

1   A Future Decided

Dubravka Ugrešić, Vladan Desnica, Sanja Iveković, and Dalibor Martinis. Two authors and two artists. Despite their many differences, they all have at least three themes in common: immortality, communism and fragmentation. What unites these themes is a reading of the meaning of *time*. This reading is used to argue that in order to open the future to change, the past must be fragmented. Doing so is key for us now, since it seems like the future has already been decided for us. The rest of our lives are already trapped in decades of debt payments, austerity programs decided by other countries, and retirement plans we know will go bankrupt. The present is claustrophobic, and without any room to breathe there is not even a chance to image a different future for ourselves. Foregrounding the fragmented nature of time offers one possibility for opening up the future to change.

Why does the future seem already decided? Elena Eposito argues that we live in the time of financial logic and credit, in which the future is already used-up by the present (137–9). The future is already being created in the present by our current financial models. As Eposito says, ours is "a present facing the openness of a future that is unknowable and indeterminate not because it is independent from us, from our actions and our expectations, but precisely because it is constructed by the (contemporary) present and would not come about without our intervention" (143). This is an expression of what Mark Fisher has developed under his expanded definition of *capitalist realism*, in which everything is subsumed under capitalism, even anti-capitalism, since anti-capitalism is just another product for capitalism, creating even more products (marches, films, posters, video hits) which enrich capitalism's gains (Fisher 12–14; cf. Shaviro 39). This is also what Stipe Grgas describes as the "structure of the American present," meaning "facing a future that is constantly perpetuated. It is constantly being emptied of content, so it is often used as a picture of something porous in it that affects and expires time" (Grgas 30). However, the Americanness of the present is now global in nature.

Yet a fetish should not be made of the impregnability of the future, nor of any abstraction of 'capitalism' which does not take its specific functions, institutions, and history into account. The capitalist realism that Fisher describes is the product of material forces that can be changed, tied to actual institutions, processes, abstract ideas, and people.

A similar approach on the financial market is taken by The Invisible Committee in *To Our Friends* (2014). Its anonymous author(s), which most probably include Julien Coupat, an anarchist convicted of sabotaging the French high-speed train network in 2008, argue(s) that

> Rather than seeing Wall Street as a celestial raptor dominating the world as God used to, we would have much to gain by determining its material, relational networks, tracking the connections from a trading floor out to their last fiber. One would find, no doubt, that the traders are just idiots, that they don't even deserve their diabolical reputation, but that stupidity is a power in this world. (190)

Seeing the future as changeable means locating the people, institutions, and networks that have given rise to global phenomena, thus putting individuals face-to-face with the hegemonic through concrete lines of labor and production. The future is not monolithic, but rather full of material cracks and chinks which can be pried apart. Nick Srnicek and Alex Williams follow a similar path in their development of the global intervention (Srnicek and Williams 75–78; cf. Willems, "Things" 54–5). In order to show how contemporary global capitalism is not just a given, they follow the particularities of its rise, arguing that in the 1970s those who became neoliberals "had both a diagnosis of the problem" of the combination of high employment and high inflation "and a solution" (Srnicek and Williams 61). This solution was not inevitable, just available, offering a "plausible solution" to government officials who were lost in the crises. The solution was always meant to be global, meaning it was long-term, including post-Bretton Woods committees committed to de-regulation, the use of right-leaning university textbooks for Economics Departments, and ready-made policies for politicians who had no other solution at hand (ibid.). Srnicek and Williams use this history to argue that neoliberalism "was not a necessary outcome, but a political construction" (ibid.). The solution to such seemingly universalism is not a set of local disruptions, but rather an alternative which is also universal, long-term and concrete. One example is a recommendation for a more progressive Economics textbook at universities, such as William Mitchell and Randall Wray's *Modern Monetary Theory and Practice* (230n67). Setting out such concrete strategies for change is what is meant by treating the future as fragmentary: new pieces can be added or taken away.

In other words, time is not monolithic, as seen in capitalist realism, but fragmentary, as argued by Srnicek and Williams. This fragmentation is actually a more accurate description of what time is, rather than what it feels like. Time is a "complex collection of structures, of layers" (Rovelli, *The Order* 4). There is no time, but times. Einstein's special theory of relativity, published in 1905, uncovers the way that there are many *local* times, rather than one Newtonian universal time. Time passes faster on top of a mountain than at its base, and faster on a planet 100 light years away and on Earth. This is because time and space are not separate, but are rather spacetime, which is a field which is bent and warped by the mass of objects (76). Imagine a vinyl record with its hole in the middle. The circumference of the hole is less than the circumference of the outer edge. There is 'less circumference' at the inside of the record than at the outside. Since time is not just time but also space, there is actually less 'time' at the record hole than at its edge, just like there is less space. If we replace the record with the earth, then the base of the mountain is closer to the center of the earth, closer to the hole, and hence there is less spacetime there than the top of the mountain, which is located closer to the edge of the 'record,' where there is more spacetime. Where there is more time, time moves faster; where there is less, it moves slower. This phenomenon was first measured in the 1970s when very accurate clocks were put on international flights (38). The clocks on the planes went faster, or experience 'more time,' than the clocks on the ground, because they covered more space. Both times are valid, they are just different. Thus there is not one time but many times. Time is fragmented, not continuous.

Yet time is fragmented in an even more fundamental way, and this 'way' will be used as an interpretive strategy for the novels and art under discussion here. Going back to Einstein's 1905 paper on special relativity, a fundamental formulation of quantum mechanics appears: that at its smallest (what came to be known as the Planck scale), time and space are granular, meaning composed of discrete, unconnected units, or fragments: "'the energy of a light ray spreading out form a point source is not continuously distributed over an increasing space but consists of a finite number of "energy quanta" which are localized at points in space, which move without dividing, and which can only be produced and absorbed as complete units'" (qtd. in Rovelli, *Seven Brief Lessons* 15). While we now call these "energy quanta" photons, an important take for a discussion of time and fragmentation is that at this level, the smallest level there is, "The world is subtly discrete, not continuous" (Rovelli, *The Order* 84). The experience of time as continuity is fake because it is not how the world works, but rather how we experience it at the local level. Yet even our 'fake' experience of continuous time is not real, because there is no single time-telling part of the brain. Rather, our experience of time is also fragmented, since our brain has different areas for understanding different intervals: "Evolution has endowed the brain with a multitude of different-clocks-for-different-timescales strategy," which Dean Buonomano calls the *"multiple clock principle"* in differentiation from mechanical clocks (33). Thus we have a fragment experience of a fragmented world. Below it is argued that the novels of Desnica and Ugrešić represent the fragmented world, while the art of Iveković and Martinis represent our fragmented experience of it. The addition to the discussion offered by the artists is the answer to how to move from the stasis of fragmentation to the movement of change. The answer is heat.

2 Communist Immortality

In *Europe in Sepia* (2013), Ugrešić argues that in order to find a different future than the one already decided for us by long-term debt obligations and irreversible ecological damage we have to look for a different 'local clock' in the past. She argues that one thing Yugoslavia shared with other, less liberalized communist dictatorships, was a strong sense of the future. Capitalist clocks ran at a different speed than the "socialist clock," she says, ran at a different speed than the capitalist one, since the latter was "always rushing on ahead into the *brighter future*, toward *progress*, a tomorrow envisaged as a majestic fireworks display of a thousand shapes and colors" (*Europe* 20). In other words, "In the time of communism watches sped ahead" because it was "an epoch that believed it was creating a new world" (76). This is in part because, as Anya Bernstein argues, "from the mid- nineteenth century onward, in Russia, the Soviet Union, and the Russian Federation that succeeded them, the theme of technologically enabled human immortality has been consistent across diverse intellectual circles in a way...that we do not find elsewhere in the world at least until the 1960s" (Bernstein 4).

In *Baba Yaga Laid an Egg* (2007), a re-telling of the Slavic myth of Baby Yaga in three parts, Ugrešić locates this specific clock in the connection between communism and immortality. The three sections of the novel focus on female ageing. The second section features Pupa, Beba and Kukla looking for the secret of youth at a Czech health spa. They are treated by Dr Topolanek, who gives a speech on the history of longevity, starting with Noah, Abraham and Moses before describing the long lives of ancient Greeks and Africans. Later,

Topolanek prepares another speech he would like to give on the communist idea of longevity. However, no one comes to listen, so he just goes through the speech in his head.

The point here is not to find a new correct sense of time, but rather to look into the past to find a different one, thus showing how all senses of time are local, and can thus be changed. Dr Topolanek rejects the Darwinian theory of evolution, accusing it of being a version of capitalist inheritance; a communist clock of immortality is suggested instead: "The new communist man had to live long, collectively and industriously, by the strength of his own will.... For inheritance, even genetic, was not acknowledged" (*Baby Yaga* 145). This temporal perspective actually falls into the Lamarckian idea that genetic characteristics are not inherited but are acquired during one's lifetime and dependent on the way that life is lived. Such a view, in the words of Steven Jay Gould, "appeals to common sense not only for its simplicity but perhaps even more for its happy implication that evolution travels an inherently progressive path, propelled by the hard work of the organisms themselves" (76).

While Lamarck's ideas are pertinent for changes in human *cultural* evolution, their adoption as the official *genetic* science of the Soviet Union, through the work of botanist Ivan Michurin and his protégé T.D. Lysenko, has found no scientific validation (Weiner 133). However, this belief in acquired characteristics does support a special clock for a future-oriented society geared toward five-year plans full of hard work and communal support. It also finds resonance in the taking matters into one's own hands of some versions of Yugoslavian self-management (*samoupravljanje*) (Jakovljević 57–61).

This alternative view of genetics also encourages making extreme interventions into the ageing process, as Ugrešić mentions in her novel. These are the material lines of change as outlined by Srnicek and Williams. For example, Alexander Bogomolets and his assistants developed the Antireticular cytotoxic serum in 1936 and saw it as a cure for ageing. Bogomolets connected the aging process to the deterioration of the macrophage system, which is related to the capacity of the body to ingest foreign materials and bacterial organisms. As Ugrešić mentions, the serum was meant to regenerate this system (*Baba Yaga* 146).

However, the preparation of the serum indicates more than just regeneration. It attempts to directly inject the genes of the recently dead into the still living. As Frederic Ilfeld describes it in a 1948 review of the process:

> The serum is prepared by removing spleen and bone marrow from cadavers less than twelve hours postmortem. The cleanly removed tissues are weighed in sterile dishes; four parts of spleen to one part bone marrow

> are minced with scissors and ground in a mortar with five volumes of normal saline solution. This mixture is centrifuged and the cloudy supernatant fluid used as antigen. The antigen is injected into rabbits and goats at intervals of three days for six doses. On the third to fifth day following the last injection the rabbits are bled by cardiac puncture and the goats from the jugular vein. The resultant serum contains the anti-reticular cytotoxic antibodies. (117)

The injection of the dead in order to prolong the living is a rather too-literal reversal of Karl Marx's famous quote on the vampire-like qualities of capital. Ugrešić, through the thoughts of Dr Topolanek, sees the serum as "part of the megalomaniac communist delusion," although current clinics offer a modernized version of the treatment through expensive "complete blood transfusions" (Ugrešić, *Baby Yaga* 146) which are also aimed at capturing the fountain of youth. And unfortunately this is not just a scene in a novel. In 2012 a woman died in Hong Kong after being injected with the blood of teenagers at a beauty center.

Although real danger is involved with the direct manipulation of the understanding of time, and the body, there is also a potential for liberation. Along with a number of precursors for connecting feminism to technological intervention, including Shulamith Firestone's *The Dialectic of Sex* (1970) and Donna Haraway's *A Cyborg Manifesto* (1985), the Laboria Cuboniks collective's *Xenofeminist Manifesto* (2015), and especially collective member Helen Hester's personal take on the subject, *Xenofeminism* (2018), provide a clear contemporary view on the subject.

Focusing on Hester's work, xenofeminism connects feminism to technology in three ways: technomaterialism (using technology to free the body from its gendered roles), anti-naturalism (against any assumptions as to the nature of gender) and gender abolitionism (not the end of gender, but rather its multiplication to the point of no longer being of interest) (Hester 3–4). Ugrešić's figure of Topolanek advocates a position closest to that of technomaterialism.

Technomaterialism "thinks about technology as an activist tool" (7), but in the most mundane sense, looking at how technology is an almost invisible part of our everyday, domestic lives, rather than a feature of far-flung science fiction futures.[1] For Hester, technologies "need to be conceptualized as social phenomena, and therefore available for transformation through collective struggle" (11). The most developed example in her book, the DIY Del-Em

---

[1] This is similar to how "The everyday, the trivial are just as important in Ugrešić's early writing as is the magical and the problematisation of matters from literary theory" (Lóránd 110).

menstrual extraction kit created in the US in the 1970s, is a key example of "collective struggle" and feminism coming together. Because the kit had to be assembled and home, and it could not be self-administered, using the Del-Em "typically involved people narrating their experiences of the procedure and inserting their own specula, for example, and encouraged the framing of menstrual extraction as a group experience – a technique learned and performed among solidarity networks taking ownership of their collective health by experimenting on one another" (111), which was supported by the illegality of the act at the time.

Hester's work on technomaterialism and Ugrešić thought aimed at changing some of the fragments of the future. Technology is key for this orientation because it intervenes into the direct material lines of oppression, whether cultural or natural, thus freeing a woman from either reproductive constraints or ageing. However, there is an important connection between the two in the way technology is used. Although the Del-Em was a valid scientific instrument, it was illegal. This is one factor which led to its being an object of collective struggle. The technology that Ugrešić describes is not so much illegal as illicit.[2] Both examples exist outside of the legal framework of the time. Both examples are sub-cultural. Both examples are 'local.'

Another instance of this in *Baby Yaga Laid an Egg* is the Romanian Ana Aslan's anti-ageing cream Gerovital H3, developed in 1952. Ugrešić says that the cream is "made from the placenta," which "could only have been invented under communism, when abortion was the most common means of contraception…" (*Baby Yaga* 146). Although this ingredient is disputed, the cream is said to have been used by many famous people, including Pablo Picasso and John F. Kennedy. In Ugrešić's novel, both these examples illustrate the relentless march toward the future that was part of the war communism waged on "the task of living as long as possible and looking as good as possible" (147). For the story went that "In communist dictatorships people lived longer and healthier lives. Promised a brighter future, many were convinced they'd live to see its dawn" (Ugrešić, *Europe* 126).

On the one hand these examples criticize how the Lamarckian march toward progress steamrolls over the health and stability of real individuals. Yet there is also a feeling that this view of the future, as damaging as it might be, was at least *a* view of the future, and as such shows how the future is

---

2 Illicit technology is a central theme in Paul Preciado's *Testo Junkie*, which combines fiction and non-fiction to describe the journey Beatrice Preciado had in using testosterone to become Paul. One of the key factors of the text is that the testosterone is neither obtained nor administered in a legal fashion.

not monolithic, but granular, thus functioning as a counter-example to what Ugrešić calls the "absence of future projections" (22) caused by what Esposito's time of finance and Fisher's capitalist realism. The key to this view is that it is located in a fragmented past. Dr Topolanek even imagines that after his treatments become famous, there will be a museum devoted to the process in the past: "the Museum of the History of Longevity" (Ugrešić, *Baby Yaga* 185). The possibility for an immortal future is located in a re-imagining of what came before. This is the logic of foregrounding the fragmented nature of time: it can lead to a more varied version of the future than we can presently imagine.

3 Limitless Lasting

The connection of a piecemeal view of the future to the past can already be found in two works by an earlier writer, Vladan Desnica, in *Proljeća Ivana Galeba* (1957) and the related, but unfinished, dystopian novella *Pronalazak Athanatika* (1957).[3] The first edition of *Proljeća Ivana Galeba* contained 71 chapters. In later editions two more were added, one of which was the initial material for *Pronalazak Athanatika*. However, I will not attempt to engage with the long critical tradition surrounding Desnica's work. Instead, I will use a few key passages from the novels to help develop a way of looking at the future.

The subtitle of *Proljeća Ivana Galeba* is *Igre proljeća i smrti*.[4] The novel is full of the memories of Ivan Galeb, who is recovering from an operation in a hospital. As indicated in the subtitle, one of Ivan's main occupations is death. More specifically, although the traditional role of death as the cornerstone of self-reflection is acknowledged, death is mainly seen as something to be resisted, whatever the cost: "You must hate death/Treba mrziti smrt," Ivan thinks, "You must negate death, without a pause, by any means, every step of the way/Treba pobijati smrt, bez predaha, svim sredstvima, na svakom koraku" (Desnica, *Proljeća* 70).[5] Although this is a "fight for the impossible/borba za nemoguće" (72), the newly inserted chapter mentions one of the "means/sredstvima" that could be used in this fight for immortality.

---

[3] I keep the titles of these novels in the original since they have not been translated into English. Approximations of the titles would be *The Spring of Ivan Galeb* and *The Discovery of Athanatik*, respectively.
[4] *Games of Spring and Death*, approximately.
[5] Translations from both of Desnica's novels are mine.

The novella *Pronalazak Athanatika*, an unfinished expansion of the inserted chapter, features the character Krezubi, who tells Ivan about the fantastic dystopian novel he is writing. The novel features a drug, *Athanatik*, which guarantees immortality for all who take it. The drug is discovered in the midst of what is already a utopia: "It took place in one fantastic land in which all the previous social, economic and similar problems have already been solved, all inequalities have been abolished, and misery has been put away / Stvar se dešavala u jednoj fantastičnoj zemlji u kojoj su već prethodno svi socijalni, ekonomski i slični problemi riješeni, sve nejednakosti ukinute, i bijeda obješena o klin" (Desnica, *Pronalazak* 10). All cares were taken care of. It was a place "where the nation was already satisfied *per definitionem* / gdje je narod bio zadovoljan već *per definitionem*" (37).

However, this utopia is a sham. The drug is under the complete control of the dictator Maman-Mamon, who distributes it according to a strict hierarchy, starting with heads of state and ministers and moving down the line to deans, vice-deans and other academics. This uneven distribution of immortality creates a dystopia among the masses, who engage in a 'cannibalistic' fight amongst themselves, even bringing back the gas chamber from the Second World War (15).

There is a possibility here for imagining a different future. Desnica's connection between utopianism and oppression is in line with the recent work of Gregory Claeys, who has traced the connections between utopia and both Nazism and Stalinism. Claeys argues that the violence of totalitarianism finds a parallel in the conformity demanded by utopias, even of the most innocent variety: "when utopia demands the extreme sacrifice of individual well-being to the group and coincides with hysteria and hatred of and extreme violence toward outsiders, we verge on dystopia, understood as a regime of maximized coercion, violence, and fear" (Claeys 44). In Desnica's novella, eventually the people reject their utopia by demanding "GIVE US BACK OUR CANCER! GIVE US BACK OUR DEATH! / VRATITE NAM NAŠ RAK! VRATITE NAM NAŠU SMRT!" (*Pronalazak* 78), thereby cancelling out the future by showing how death is preferable to the totalitarian immortality of utopia.

In other words, as Ante Jerić says in his chapter on immortality from *Uz Malabou*, "To be immortal – that means to be less than human / Biti besmrtan – to znači biti manje od čovjeka" (Jerić 42).[6] However, there is something else going on in the novel. The way the immortality drug is described points toward a better way to look at the future, through the lens of fragmentation.

---

6 Translation mine.

When looked at closely, Desnica's drug does not actually guarantee immortality. Instead it combines a "limitless lasting" (*beskonačno trajanje*) and "eternal regeneration" (*vječita regeneracija*) (*Pronalazak* 9). This description is crucial because it combines a monolithic view of the future as everlasting ("limitless lasting") with the material processes needed for such everlasting to take place ("eternal regeneration"). The process of regeneration is, like the perception of time in the brain, not a single process but many. Physiological regeneration, which Desnica is presumably referring to here, includes the shedding cycles of skin, the renewal of the endometrium after menstruation, and the regeneration of antlers which is based on cycles of light (Carlson 4). Eternal life is fragmented into a number of material processes that can make it happen, with a technomaterialist intervention. It is this fragmentation which allows for a potentially different view of the future to take place, one different from that of the current age, in which our "futures have no future" (Ugrešić, *Europe* 124). The next step is to develop the connection between fragmented, granular spacetime and the forward momentum for change.

4   Heating Up the Past

Iveković and Martinis bridge the granularity of time and a new vision of the future by applying some heat. But this 'heat' is not figurative, it is thermodynamic. Time and heat are connected. This is because "There is a detectable difference between the past and the future only when there is flow of heat" (Rovelli, *Seven Brief Lessons* 69). All movement involves friction, which creates heat. Taking a step on the ground creates heat, as does the movement of muscles in the body. When you are cold you rub your hands together, creating heat, and you are no longer as cold now as you were in the past. In fact, any time the past and future are distinguished, heat is involved: "Friction produces heat. And immediately we are able to distinguish the future… from the past." (53). Although there is much more involved in this topic,[7] the artwork discussed below mirrors the fragmentation of the past in order to see what kind of 'heat' was applied to understand it. This is done to try and change the kind of heat

---

7   The main line of reasoning that is being cut here is that the transfer of heat from a hot object to a cold one is due to chance: atoms move faster when heated than when cooled, and thus the faster atoms have a higher chance of 'hitting' colder ones and transferring heat to them. For an accessible explanation of this process, see Johnson.

that was used. In other words, they attempt to change the material forces that were used to create the future in order to create a different one.[8]

One powerful example of fragmentation is found in the documentation of Sanja Iveković's 1979 artistic performance *Triangle*. The photographs of her performance show different perspectives of a parade held by Tito in Zagreb on the 10th of May of that year. There are separate photographs of Tito in his car, of the crowd watching with a Jugoslav flag hanging above, one of a building with someone standing on the roof, and one of Iveković on a balcony masturbating. The photographs are accompanied by a text in which the artist narrates the scene:

> Due to the cement construction of the balcony, only the person on the roof can actually see me and follow the action. My assumption is that this person has binoculars and a walkie-talkie apparatus. I notice that the policeman in the street also has a walkie-talkie.
>
> The action begins when I walk out onto the balcony and sit on a chair. I sip whiskey, read a book, and make gestures as if I perform masturbation. After a period of time the policeman rings my doorbell and orders that "the persons and objects be removed from the balcony." (qtd. in Bryzgel 104)

What is most important for us at the moment is the form of the documentation of the performance. It functions as a refiguration of a past event. The parade is too large to be contained in one picture. As curator Ruth Noack has argued, chopping the event into different frames and perspectives foregrounds the constructed rather than hegemonic nature of totalitarianism (Noack 8–9). The way this construction happens is the 'heat' referred to above. Rather than being seen as a conforming, oppressive whole, the state is broken up into its constituent parts: a flag, a crowd, a leader, the police, an individual woman in her semi-private space. The presentation of this piece, at least in this final form it eventually stabilized into, shows the application of hegemony to the actual fragmentation of a past event.

Dalibor Martinis, who took the photos in Iveković's piece, has made a number of artistic works which combine three of the elements under discussion

---

8 In *Déjà Vu and the End of History* (2015) Paolo Virno makes a similar argument about history, meaning that there is an equivalence to be drawn between the past and potential (Virno 61; cf. Willems, "The Potential" 167–8). Rather than seeing the future as the privileged location for change, the potentiality for something different and new is actually something which comes before rather than something which lies ahead.

here: immortality, communism and fragmentation. One major project of his is a series of work called *Data Recovery 1969–2077*. The location of the end of this work, presumably after Martinis' death (the artist was born in 1941, which would make him 136 years old in 2077), gives the whole project a futuristic bent. And the fragmentation of time and perception are found in of a number of the works found within.[9]

The two examples used here were broadcast on the Croatian National Television program *Drugi format*. The first is *Proba TV Dnevnika 4. svibnja 1980.*, from 2017. In this piece, Martinis re-enacts a recorded test from the past for the televised announcement of the death of Josip Broz Tito, breaking up the solemn broadcast into numerous fragments. The video shows Martinis dressed as a newscaster. He goes through all the procedures before the newscast, walking the halls of the TV studio, having make-up put on, getting his text ready. Then when he reads the actual official announcement of Tito's death, the words are interrupted continually by a multitude of cuts, so that they can never come out fully. This most solemn event in Yugoslav history is, just as the parade of 1979, broken up into its constituent elements. Doing so traces the people, institutions and networks that are the 'heat' which gives rise to totalitarian phenomena.

In *Martinis 1978 talks to Martinis 2010*, a similar fragmentation takes place, although on a more personal scale. While in Vancouver in 1978, Martinis recorded a series of questions addressed to himself in 2010. Then, in 2010, Martinis answered the questions from his own interview.

The first question that 1978 Martinis asks himself is whether he is still alive. In his answer, 2010 Martinis raises the material concerns regarding longevity. 2010 Martinis' answer is that the difficulty was not so much in staying alive himself, but rather in preserving the archival material containing 1978 Martinis' interview.

Other parts of the interview stress the differences between the two speakers rather than their obvious similarity. 1978 Martinis' questions are said to come from a time that no longer exists, and when 1978 Martinis asks if he and 2010 Martinis are the same person, or whether they no longer have anything in common, 2010 Martinis answers with a quote from Jacques Lacan about the separation of the real and the symbolic. For Martinis, just as everyone is

---

9   A connection can be made between Martinis and Ugrešić also, for he designed the original movie poster for the film based on her novel *Štefica Cvek u raljama života* (1981). A connection can also be made between Einstein and Yugoslavia, since, with Heinrich Mann, he wrote a letter to the International League of Human Rights protesting the death of Croatian scientist Dr Milan Sufflay (Brian 220–1).

separated from the real by their entry into symbolic language, "I am neither here nor there, just as you are not. If we are all the same person, that person is neither you nor I." In other words, neither of them really exist, although they are both obviously in the same room together.

Perhaps the most relevant part of the interview for this essay is the end, when 1978 Martinis asks if the artistic questions of the 1970s are still relevant in 2010. The answer is that the question of the death of art from the 60s and 70s is still relevant, although the issue has been transformed. Rather than being about the end of art, 2010 Martinis says that the death of art is necessary for the creation of a new life.

This is the death of time, and of space, but it is also the new life being born out of death in Bogomolets's process for creating Antireticular cytotoxic serum, as well as Desnica's description of his drug as "eternal regeneration." As such, the death Martinis refers to is not the literal death of animals and humans, but rather the death of a hegemonic view of time. Yet this death is not located in the future but in the past, in a new past never experienced by anyone and which is aimed at changing the future.

References

Bernstein, Anya. *The Future of Immortality: Remaking Life and Death in Contemporary Russia*. Princeton University Press, 2019.

Brian, Denis. *Einstein: A Life*. J. Wiley, 1996.

Bryzgel, Amy. *Performance Art in Eastern Europe Since 1960*. Manchester University Press, 2017.

Buonomano, Dean. *Your Brain is a Time Machine: The Neuroscience and Physics of Time*. W.W. Norton and Co., 2017.

Carlson, Bruce. *Principles of Regenerative Biology*. Elsevier, 2007.

Clayes, Gregory. "When Does Utopianism Produce Dystopia?" *Utopian Horizons: Ideology, Politics, Literature*, edited by Zsolt Cziganyik, CEU Press, 2017, pp. 41–61.

Desnica, Vladan. *Proljeća Ivana Galeba: Igre Proljeća i Smrti*. Matica Hrvatska, 1977.

Desnica, Vladan. *Pronalazak Athanatika*. VBZ, 2006.

Esposito, Elena. "The Construction of Unpredictability." *The Time Complex: Post-Contemporary*, edited by Armen Avanessian and Suhail Malik, [NAME] Publications, 2016, pp. 135–143.

Fisher, Mark. *Capitalist Realism: Is There No Alternative?* Zero Books, 2009-.

Gould, Steven Jay. *The Panda's Thumb: More Reflections on Natural History*. Norton and Co., 1980.

Grgas, Stipe. "Reading Richard Powers at the Turn of the Century." *Mapping the World of Anglo-American Studies at the Turn of the Century*, edited by Marija Krivokapić and Aleksandra Nikčević-Batrićević, Cambridge Scholars Publishing, 2015, pp. 3–20.

Hester, Helen. *Xenofeminsim*. Polity Books, 2018.

Ilfeld, Frederic. "Antireticular Cytotoxic Serum: A Review." *Journal of the National Medical Association*, vol. 40, no. 3, 1948, pp. 116–119.

Invisible Committee, The. *To Our Friends*. Semiotext(e), 2015.

Jakovljević, Branislav. *Alienation Effects: Performance and Self-Management in Yugoslavia, 1945–91*. University of Michigan Press, 2016.

Jerić, Ante. *Uz Malabou: Profili Suvremenog Mišljenja*. Multimediljanli institut, 2016.

Johnson, Eric. *Anxiety and the Equation: Understanding Boltzmann's Entropy*. MIT Press, 2018.

Lóránd, Zsófia. *The Feminist Challenge to the Socialist State in Yugoslavia*. Palgrave Macmillan, 2018.

Noack, Ruth. *Sanja Iveković:* Triangle. Afterall, 2013.

Preciado, Beatriz (Paul). *Testo Junkie: Sex, Drugs and Biopolitics in the Parmacopornographic Era*. Feminist Press, 2013.

Rovelli, Carlo. *The Order of Time*. Riverhead Books, 2018.

Rovelli, Carlo. *Seven Brief Lessons on Physics*. Riverhead Books, 2015.

Shaviro, Steven. *No Speed Limit: Three Essays on Accelerationism*. University of Minnesota Press, 2015.

Srnicek, Nick and Alex Williams. *Inventing the Future: Postcapitalism and a World Without Work*. Verso, 2015.

Ugrešić, Dubravka. *Baby Yaga Laid an Egg*. Canongate, 2010.

Ugrešić, Dubravka. *Europe in Sepia*. Open Letter, 2014.

Virno, Paolo. *Déjà vu and the End of History*. Verso, 2015.

Weiner, Douglas. *A Little Corner of Freedom: Russian Nature Protection from Stalin to Gorbachev*. University of California Press, 1999.

Willems, Brian. "The Potential of the Past: *First on the Moon*." *Science Fiction Film and Television*, vol. 9, no. 2, 2016, pp. 159–179.

Willems, Brian. "Things that Go Nowhere: Scale, City and the List in Richard Price's *Lush Life*." *Umjetnost riječi*, vol. 42, no. 1, 2018, pp. 51–70.

CHAPTER 2

The "Historical Moment before Our Eyes": On Producing Post-Yugoslav Literature

Tijana Matijević

> the modern work of art is a machine and functions as such. ...Why a machine? Because the work of art, so understood, is essentially productive ...; the work of art is a form of production that it does not raise a special problem of meaning, but rather of use.
> GILLES DELEUZE, *Proust and Signs*

∴

In Slobodan Tišma's 2011 novel *Bernardijeva soba* (*Bernardi's Room*), two critical narrative objects – the eponymic furniture set 'Bernardi's room,' a remnant from the family's past, and the Mercedes car wreck in which the protagonist Pišta Petrović finds his new home – are to an extent two paradoxical objects: they are non-objects. The car is a non-car, a former car which is now only the shell of a car, while the furniture is non-furniture, a set which notwithstanding its present obsoleteness (it stands in the room covered with white sheets) has never been functional: "though it was a pleasure watching it, it was pretty uncomfortable" (Tišma, *Bernardijeva soba* 17).[1] Though their *meaning* relates to the past – they point to absent time, space, and people – the two objects have seemingly no *use*, and this precisely qualifies their capacity to get across something about that past.

The past narrativized in the novel is clearly defined as the Yugoslav past. This past is also – predictably – a necessary backdrop for any attempt to theorize a post-Yugoslav literary discourse, or to conceive the post-Yugoslav literary field.[2] The past that is present in two objects is either "antiquated" (Benjamin, "The Interior" 217) or materialised through "presencing" (Osborne) which is

---

[1] In Serbo-Croatian: "bio je prilično neudoban, ali zato beše užitak za oko," (all translations from this novel are mine).

[2] The application of the Bourdieusian theoretical materialist paradigm in interpreting (post-Yugoslav) literature could be found in the works of several authors from Croatia (Duda,

why the analysis of the two possibilities can be transposed onto a debate about the post-Yugoslav literary discourse. This discourse relates to its Yugoslav forerunner in one of the modes (antiquated/presenced), and while the choice of the mode affects the very definition of post-Yugoslav literature, this receptiveness to the questions of temporality facilitates a literary historization as an ultimate act of legitimization of this problematic body of literature.[3] Simply put, this paper represents an attempt of establishing a historical link among late Yugoslav and post-Yugoslav literatures.

If – as stated in the epigraph – the work of art is a *machine*, we readily enter into a discussion on the work of art as a mechanically reproduced object, activating and recovering the materialist interest in its production, and the conditions accompanying it. That is, we are trying to answer "what is the literary work's position *within* the relations of production of its time?" (T. Eagleton 28). The machine is also a concept that could be used when discussing matters of history and historization, for it is precisely the machine that, according to Deleuze, opposes the structure. The machine indicates instead "repetition [...] that is, repetition as difference" (Dosse 127). Post-Yugoslav literature – comparable to Deuleze's machine – happens "[a]gainst structure" (ibid.). For, it relates to its (Yugoslav?) past in a not necessarily linear, or analogous way, but through a repetition. Indeed, theorizing the continuity between the Yugoslav and post-Yugoslav literatures would appear as a result of recognizing precisely a "repetition as difference" in the novel *Bernardi's Room*.

Examining the two 'non-objects' also in their conceptual, artistic capacity (and lack thereof) supports the argument about post-Yugoslav literature as a specific aesthetic (the *meaning*), yet one which is *used* in the situation of "the deterritorialization of language, the connection of the individual to a political immediacy, and the collective assemblage of enunciation" (Deleuze and Guattari, *Kafka* 18). Taking these three Deleuze and Guattari's characteristics of minor literature as a reference point, this paper offers a reading of post-Yugoslav literature which integrates Benjamin's theorization on the work of art and the past, together with a take on alienation, and a Deleuzian *machinic*

Postnikov, Kosmos, Kreho), resulting in the recent circulation of the concept of literary and cultural fields: Dean Duda, "Prema genezi i strukturi postjugoslovenskog književnog polja"; Dinko Kreho, "O čemu govorimo kada govorimo o postjugoslavenskoj književnosti?". See References.

[3] A number of recent studies define already Yugoslav literature as a contested or even a phantom notion: *Jugoslovenska književnost: sadašnjost, prošlost i budućnost jednog spornog pojma/Yugoslav Literature: The Past, Present and Future of a Contested Notion*, edited by Marčetić, Adrijana et al.; Svjetlan Lacko Vidulić, "Jugoslawische Literatur. Kurzer Abriss zur langen Geschichte eines produktiven Phantoms." See References.

imagery which offers language to discuss phenomena beyond structures, but as processes, as *production*. Some of the novel's central motifs will be analysed using this language to describe peculiar bodily, creative, and desiring narrative 'machines' that are also seen as affecting the properties of post-Yugoslav literature itself, particularly when they are put under feminist scrutiny.

The protagonist's concerns and fantasies are imbedded in the past, but in a way which involves the matters of (his) body and sexuality and their transformation. This fusion of contemplation and enactment (of both corporeal and temporal matters) conjure Deleuze and Guattari's concept of *becoming* as generating a new way of being, that is, creating something new (Deleuze, "Contrôle et devenir") which "incarnates, actualises and expresses immanence, yet without having any priority" (Thiele 127). Yet, though placing analytical trust in Deleuze and Guattari's *becoming* as "the affirmation of the positivity of difference, meant as a multiple and constant process of transformation" (Braidotti 111), it is critical seeing the *becoming* as a "sex-specific, sexually differentiated, and consequently [taking] different forms according to different gendered positions" (121).

Hence, occupying the space in-between the above-quoted three characteristics of minor literature by Deleuze and Guattari and their feminist expansion, this paper has been written by "discursive positioning," a concept Elisabeth Grosz uses to theorize a feminist literary approach which integrates "complex relations between the corporeality of the author, that is, the author's textual residues or traces, the text's materiality, and its effects in marking the bodies of the author and readers, and the corporeality and productivity of readers" (Grosz 18).[4] The materiality of the text, which has its effects on its author(s) and readers, is here also read temporally, as a historically traceable literary fact needed for the 'production' of post-Yugoslav literature.

1 Bernardi's Room: "The Localized Essence of Time" as/and the Fetish

Slobodan Tišma is a conceptual Neo-avant-gardist author from Vojvodina, the "most influential representative" (Kopicl 103) of the group KôD who established "one of the most challenging poetic concepts which, with its public

---

[4] Quite in the fashion of theoretician Jasmina Lukić, who in her texts, by theorizing (post-)Yugoslav women's writing, integrates a feminist *positioning* and transnationalism studies: "Tijelo i tekst u feminističkoj vizuri"; "Žensko pisanje i žensko pismo u devedesetim godinama"; "Rod i migracija u postjugoslovenskoj književnosti kao transnacionalnoj književnosti." See References.

and 'underground' impact, has lasted until today" (104). Besides his prevalent 'underground impact,' his recent admission into the contemporary literary centre after receiving the NIN award[5] for *Bernardi's Room* stirred and expanded the discourse of contemporary mainstream literature, at the same time actually enabling the reassessment of some (post-)Yugoslav literary and artistic traditions.

Bernardi's room is a prestigious Yugoslav modernist design set that Pišta's parents purchased in 1966; it is an emblematic project of a middle-class Yugoslav family in the period of the commodification of everyday family life. It is a type of a Yugoslav souvenir – made in Yugoslavia by Yugoslav designer Bernardo Bernardi, a member of the avant-gardist group Exat 51, whose envisioning of the design integrated both conceptual and applied approaches. Indeed, the narrator states that besides music, design "is probably the only modern art in which the famous idea about the original work of art in the era of mechanical reproduction has been fully materialised" (Tišma, *Bernardijeva soba* 44).[6] Hence, the symbolism of the furniture set feeds on Yugoslav avant-gardists traditions, but also on the character of the product, in a Benjaminian fashion, as an "original work of art, made in the era of the mechanical reproduction of art, a paradox worth its weight in gold" (17). It is indeed seen as "pure art" (ibid.).[7] The conceptual character of the set, at once also a signal of its obsoleteness (hence: pointing out the *meaning*, but leaving the question of *use* open) is narrativized over the protagonist Pišta's act of wrapping it in plastic, so he could "imagine it" (42):

> In the very centre of the room I put all the pieces in a heap and covered them with white cloths to preserve them from the dust ... Also, I wrapped the whole pile with thin rope, I packed it all nicely into a single whole, so that it resembled a modernist piece of art. (19)[8]

The proof of the furniture set being a true work of art is precisely its ghostly presence, ridiculed by the use of plastic wrapping, but still suggesting inaccessibility, distance: the "strange tissue of space and time: the unique apparition

---

5   The highest award given for a novel in Serbia (and previously in Yugoslavia).
6   "Dizajn je, pored muzike, možda jedina moderna umetnost gde se sasvim ovaplotila čuvena ideja o originalnom umetničkom delu u eri tehničke reprodukcije."
7   "originalno umetničko delo, nastalo u eri tehničke reprodukcije umetnosti, što je bio paradoks zlata vredan. ... Čista umetnost!"
8   "U samo središte sobe, poslagao sam sve komade i prekrio ih belim plahtama, da ne pada prašina po njima ... Takođe, čitavu gomilu sam uvezao tankim konopcem, upakovao sam sve to lepo u jednu celinu, tako da je ličilo na neko modernističko umetničko delo."

of a distance, however near it may be" (Benjamin, "The Work of Art, Second Version" 23). What Benjamin comprehends as the *aura* is here put into relation to Bernardi's room conceptualized as a capacity to evoke nostalgic memories, those that devise a chronotopic figuration of the times past. The furniture set preserves a distance, symbolically referred to as the 'absence in furniture.' The assumed physical, sensory resemblance of the back of the Bernardi's office chair and shutters trigger the memory of the protagonist looking through the shutters somewhere on the Adriatic coast:

> That office chair was somehow always connected to summer, to the sun: You could see the sea through a hollow backrest of the office chair. That hollow backrest actually resembled the shutters of some coastal house. A return to the house by the sea? ... I saw a lot with these eyes: wide and green agave leaves and a blue lizard which suddenly moves while the purple waves foam in the cove. Nothing was more valuable than that. The shutters close down like eyelids and the white room turns dark. But outside there was an incredibly gleaming light. Eternity is sometimes so close. It is present. The world spreads, it is real. Immutable! If you don't have a house, you can always have that chair, those shutters, actually. That is enough. (Tišma, *Bernardijeva soba* 68)[9]

A bright summer day on the Adriatic coast is the measure of reality: there was nothing "more valuable," the "Eternity" was in and of itself. The "intrinsic connectedness of temporal and spatial relationships" (Bakhtin 84) forge Yugoslavia as a chronotopic literary figuration, a "carefully thought-out, concrete whole" (ibid.): an epiphanic moment in which – unlike present-day alienation and loneliness – Pišta felt he was one with the outside world. The perfect past is unalterable, and besides serving as a critical attribute of the Yugoslav past's chronotopic capacity, it suggests the solidity, the totality of an imagery which offers consolation. The narrator repeatedly mentions the year 1966 in relation to the furniture, which also lends a chronotopic quality to the furniture as an object.

---

[9] "Taj kancelarijski stolac bio je nekako uvek povezan sa letom, sa suncem: U nekoj kancelariji leti kroz rebrasti naslon stolice videlo se more. Zapravo, taj rebrasti naslon podsećao je na šalukatre neke kuće na moru. Povratak u kuću na moru? ... Video sam tim očima svašta: široke zelene listove agave i plavog guštera koji se iznenada pomeri dok u uvalama pene tamnoljubičasti talasi. Ništa nije bilo vrednije od toga. Šalukatre se spuste kao očni kapci i u beloj sobi zavlada tama. Međutim, napolju sve blešti u neverovatnoj svetlosti. Večnost je nekada tako blizu. Ona je tu. Svet se prostire, stvaran je. Nepromenjiv! Ako nemaš kuću, ipak, uvek možeš imati taj stolac, zapravo, te šalukatre. I to je sasvim dovoljno."

Describing the perception of aura in the work of art, Walter Benjamin compares it to the awareness of distance in/from nature, and the enthusiasm it prompts: "To follow with the eye – while resting on a summer afternoon – a mountain range on the horizon or a branch that casts its shadow on the beholder is to breathe the aura of those mountains, of that branch" (Benjamin, "The Work of Art, Second Version" 23) Variating Benjamin's motifs throughout the narration, Tišma applies almost the same rhetoric of nostalgia: "But the freshness of youth, youth itself... The first green willow leaves in the early spring, is there anything so tender? *Tenderness* as freshness. Ah, that is everything! Eternal youth on the couch on a December Sunday afternoon. We were born for that moment only." (Tišma, *Bernardijeva soba* 76)[10] Narrativized as the object of admiration and veneration, a flawless piece of sublime formal characteristics (in the shape of a cube), the furniture set *embodies* the idealistic (or also: perfectionist) relationship to the past. It is the perfect medium of 'traditionalization' (it is 'antiquated'), suggesting that the past is always lost anyways: "He created that wonderful furniture, eternal, indestructible. The hours of our lives which passed by it, where are they? The furniture stands still, the heart beats in Agram, Đurvidek, on the Adriatic highway." (63)[11] The search for lost time is directed by the certainty that the "[r]oom is just a space of purely aesthetic phenomena, that is, a configuration" (Tišma, *Velike misli* 180).[12] It restores an 'essence,' what Deleuze quoting Proust explains as what is "[r]eal without being present, ideal without being abstract" (Deleuze *Proust* 58). The way Proust's "madeleine enfolds an essence of Combray, a pure past that has never been actually present" (Bogue 290), Bernardi's room arouses "what Proust calls 'a morsel of time, in the pure state,' or in Deleuze's words, 'the localized essence of time'" (ibid.). "The hours of our lives which passed by" materialized as fictionalized 'toponyms of nostalgia' (Zagreb as Agram, Novi Sad as Đurvidek), turn up "here and now" (Benjamin, "The Work of Art, Second Version" 21). The "here and now" of the work of art and its "unique existence in a particular place [...] bears the mark of the history to which the work has been subject" (ibid.). Bernardi's room preserves and perpetuates the Golden (Yugoslav) past, that chrontopical past which could be also described as an aestheticized and fictionalized past.

---

10   "Ali svežina mladosti, zapravo, sama mladost... Prvo zelenilo vrba u rano proleće, ima li ičeg nežnijeg? *Nežnost* kao svežina. Ah, to je sve! Neprolazna mladost na kauču u decembarsko nedeljno poslepodne. Rodili smo se samo zbog tog časa."
11   "Stvorio je taj predivni nameštaj, koji je večan, neuništiv. Sati naših života koji su proticali pored njega, gde su? Nameštaj miruje, damari biju u Agramu, u Đurvideku, na Jadranskoj magistrali."
12   "Soba je samo prostor estetskog fenomena, tj. konfiguracija."

Likewise, the 'presence of distance' in the work of art 'Bernardi's room' is what informs its proneness to enclosing absent time and space together with those who occupied it. Based, again, on its physical, aesthetic characteristics, one of the suggestive and repetitive ways of describing the furniture set is its capacity to enclose someone's absence:

> Furniture is the very idea of an art work, the most precious thing, as it were, a negative of sculpture, adjusted to a human body which is absent, as I saw it. Bernardi's design precisely highlighted that spatial absence, an empty place. Simply, nobody should sit in that armchair or that chair which is a pure being. Or somebody sits but is invisible. That is even more interesting. (Tišma, *Bernardijeva soba* 44)[13]

Furniture which represents the family gathered together (like they were back in the past) is defined by its lack, its absence. Pišta and his parents, who are now absent, used to occupy the dents in the modernist chairs. Also, more specifically, the long, almost ever-absent protagonist's mother indicates an invisible presence (together with the absence of home that she represents). Yet, the narrator's contemplation of 'authenticity,' of 'aesthetics,' of one in fact mechanically reproduced object (an industrial furniture set), provokes a discourse of alienation beyond the protagonist's psychological trauma of a mother's unavailability, the detachment from home, and homelessness.

The protagonist's melancholic obsession with 'what is missing' (time, people, objects) is permeated by the Marxist theorizing on the humans' relationship to objects, importantly, the objects of their labour: the alluded 'product' character of the furniture and car facilitates their description as an "alien object" (Marx in Elster 37). Though they are venerated as the commodities of the Yugoslav past, the narrator's attachment to the products (of the factory workers' labour) is narrativized as alienation – a further stage in the process of objectification.[14] Pišta Petrović's affection for non-objects could be,

---

13 "Nameštaj je pojam umetničkog dela, nešto najdragocenije, kao negativ kiparstva, prilagođen je ljudskom telu koje je odsutno, tako sam razmišljao. Bernardijev dizajn je upravo podvlačio tu prostornu odsutnost, upražnjeno mesto. Jednostavno, ne treba niko da sedi u tom naslonjaču ili na tom stolcu koji je samo čisto biće. Ili neko ipak sedi, ali se ne vidi. To je još zanimljivije."

14 "The product of labour is labour which has been embodied in an object, which has become material: it is the *objectification* of labour. Labour's realisation is its objectification. Under these economic conditions this realisation of labour appears as *loss of*

hence, read as a Marxist critique of capitalist production, which pauperizes the working class; not by chance is the protagonist one of those "humiliated and insulted" (Tišma, *Bernardijeva soba* 27), "the miserable" (72). The absence integrated into the narrativized objects appears to be the absence of people in the process of their alienation from the products they have made. The objects are the melancholic reminders of people's absence, understood both nostalgically and politically. Therefore, as 'products of labour' become fetish, appearing "as independent beings endowed with life" (Marx in Elster 65), it is possible to employ a Marxist rhetoric to convey the possibility of possessing, that is, commodifying the past that exists in 'industrial artefacts,' consequently also constructing that same past as a fetish.

However, while the room is a fetishist 'configuration,' the "[w]reck is closer to the body, similar to a shell, to armour. It represents a time machine, a place of memory, imagination. It symbolizes both motion and stasis" (Tišma, *Velike misli* 180).[15] In the room absence is definitive, making it appear as an ideal object of chronotopic 'fixation.' To that end, instead of the melancholic image of the ideal past, a Mercedes car wreck, that would become a *desiring machine* will enable the process of *becoming* of the protagonist.

2   A Car Wreck: A Desiring Machine

Pišta spends time in a Mercedes car wreck, daydreaming about the past, haunted by an accident which caused the death of a young woman he had raced against. This episode, a memory, is an *event*, as that which opposes essence, and "cannot be explained by the situations that gave rise to [it]" (Deleuze, *Negotiations* 176). It appears "for a moment, and it is that moment that matters, it's the chance we must *seize*" (ibid.).[16] The episode gets complicated as Pišta cannot tell with certainty if a young woman died or not, since he suspects that there were *two* women in *two* different cars, but *simultaneously* racing against him: the "truth is that in reality everything happens simultaneously" (Tišma, *Bernardijeva soba* 94).[17] In other words, the past cannot be represented since "[w]riting is a question of becoming, always incomplete,

---

      realisation for the workers; objectification *as loss of the object and bondage to it*; appropriation as *estrangement, as alienation*" (Marx in Elster 37).
15   "Olupina je bliža telu, kao ljuštura, oklop. Ona predstavlja i vremensku mašinu, mesto za sećanja, za maštanje. Ona simbolizuje i kretanje i stanovanje."
16   Italics mine.
17   "Istina je da se u stvarnosti sve događa istovremeno."

always in the midst of being formed, and goes beyond the matter of any livable or lived experience. It is a process, that is, a passage of life that traverses both the livable and the lived" (Deleuze, *Essays* 1). In this sense it is possible to relate the main activity of the protagonist and the very process of writing, that is, of the production of the novel's text: as I would show next, his doing is a figure of this production.

"Body" is the first word of the novel, immediately followed by "Armour," hence constituting an analogy among the car body shell and the protagonist's human body: "Body. Armour. Armour around what? Emptiness, an echo? A car left on the parking lot, forgotten. Maybe the owner died, or just can't remember where he had parked his car." (7)[18] The aptitude of the car and the body to enclose something, or someone that is *missing* has been underscored: "Armour around what?" The measure of this missing is the past, configured as the dead, and the unavailability, the absence of the past (literature, writing "consists in inventing a people who are missing" (Deleuze, *Essays* 4)).

The metaphor of a shell ("školjka" as the *body* of the car) also effortlessly leads to Pišta's inhabiting this shell, giving it a new body: "I would creep into the shell, crouch inside the sleeping bag as a fetus on the back seat" (Tišma, *Bernardijeva soba* 8).[19] Nevertheless, the protagonist feels his own body to be also incomplete:

> I often imagined myself as somebody else. I wanted to change my sex, preconditions were there. My testicles never dropped. At erection my penis was 3 centimetres long, better to say short (Tišma, *Bernardijeva soba* 30);[20]
>
> I didn't have to serve in the army, for reasons well-known, the thing between my legs was untrustworthy. (69)[21]

In this sense, both the Mercedes car wreck and the protagonist's body are 'bodies without organs.' The BwO – body without organs – is a puzzling and

---

[18] "Telo. Oklop. Oklop čega? Praznina, jeka? Automobil ostavljen na parkingu, zaboravljen. Možda je vlasnik umro, ili samo ne može da se seti gde je parkirao svoj auto."
[19] "Uvukao bih se u olupinu, skupio se u vreći kao fetus, na zadnjem sedištu."
[20] "Često sam zamišljao sebe kao nekog drugog. Želeo sam da promenim pol, imao sam uslova za to. Testisi mi se nikada nisu spustili. Moj penis u erekciji bio je dugačak, bolje reći kratak, tri santimetra."
[21] "Oslobođen sam vojske iz već poznatih razloga, ona stvar među mojim nogama nije im ulivala poverenje."

contradicting concept from Deleuze and Guattari which takes up a peculiar image of the body to theorize materiality beyond structure, beyond 'organised organism': "insofar as the organism is a stratum (a centralized, hierarchical, and strongly patterned body), a BwO is a destratified (decentralized, dehabituated) body" (Protevi 257). Body of the protagonist and the analogous body of the car wreck are dehabituated, decentralized, but they also – quite literally – miss organs. The author clearly described his protagonist as a body without organs by pointing out his egg form, which is one of the BwO manifestations: "he lost shape, resembles an egg, has no limbs" (Tišma, *Velike misli* 167). The self-mocking ambiguity of the protagonist himself also suggests the BwO. Furthermore, the expositional image of the relic car wreck left on the parking lot indicates a body without organs:

> First the air in tires leaked. Then someone stole the wheels. ... One by one, smaller, lighter parts, the rear-view mirrors, the headlights, the gear stick, the windshield, then the leather seats and in the end the engine was out, actually, first the carburettor and then the engine. The heart. It went fast. The body rots fast in the jungle, it starts dissolving and smelling. (Tišma, *Bernardijeva soba* 7)[22]

The image of the car as a body without organs to which the protagonist lends his own body, his own organs, shows again that "the BwO is the organism moved from equilibrium, out of a stable state or comfort zone" (Protevi 258). Seen as leaving his parents' home, and subsequently deserting the convention of residing inside a house, to be 'moved from equilibrium' in truth refers to the protagonist's bodily and sexual disposition. Pišta started dwelling inside a car wreck after an attempt to live in a male commune with his friends and acquaintances had failed. This informal group occupied the flat after Pišta's parents had successively left their family home, and what at first seemed to be Pišta's 'life-style' choice (to live in a car wreck) becomes a compulsory residence after they were all together evicted from the flat. Hence, the homeless protagonist Pišta in his immobile wreck is reminiscent of a "desert traveler and nomad of the steppes" (Deleuze and Guattari, *Plateaus* 150), which is how those in search of the body without organs are described by Deleuze and Guattari. Also, his quest is framed ironically: Pišta is in the process of separation

---

22   "Prvo su se spuvale gume. Zatim je neko skinuo točkove. ... Redom, sitniji, lakši delovi, retrovizori, farovi, ručica menjača, šoferšajbna, zatim sedišta presvučena kožom i na kraju je izvađen i sam motor, zapravo, prvo karburator, pa onda motor. Srce. Brzo je to išlo. U džungli telo se brzo pokvari, počne da se raspada, da zaudara."

from his parents; he is in his late thirties and desires to change his sex due to existing "preconditions" (Tišma, *Bernardijeva soba* 7). His hopes for that reason manifest as a body without organs, as "nondesire as well as desire" (Deleuze and Guattari, *Plateaus* 149).

Spending time in a Mercedes car wreck daydreaming about the past, 'putting the wreck on' as his own shell suggests the impossibility of reaching the body without organs, because "you can't reach it, you are forever attaining it, it is a limit ...; it is already underway the moment the body has had enough of organs and wants to slough them off, or loses them" (150). Though this clearly correlates to Pišta's "preconditions," but also to the Mercedes car 'loss of organs,' the body without organs remains a mere description of their static state, for the BwO is the "uninterrupted continuum [...], immanence, immanent limit" (Deleuze and Guattari, *Plateaus* 154). Though the BwO has been theorized as "the field of immanence of desire, the plane of consistency specific to desire" (Deleuze and Guattari, *Plateaus* 154), it, as already written, stays ambivalent, and in many respects contradicts the concept of a desiring-machine. A relatively steady distinction between the two is that the body without organs indicates the final decision to renounce the desire, while the desiring-machine, quite the reverse, constructs, produces a desire.

Hence, once the 'uninterrupted continuum' of the body without organs is interrupted by Pišta's entering the wreck – which also marks 'cutting through' his own corporeality and sexuality – the fusion of the two 'bodies' could be seen as a desiring-machine. That is how the central image of the novel – the protagonist's entering and inhabiting a deserted and dilapidated car shell – becomes in reality an activity, a narrative entity beyond a (represented, representable) structure. It occurs as a process, and is a movement "[a]gainst structure, which is defined by its ability to exchange its particular elements" (Dosse 127). Pišta's and the wreck's 'organs' fuse, organizing instead (of a structure) "the machine [which] would stress repetition ... repetition as difference, 'as a conduct and as a point of view [that] concerns nonexchangeable and nonsubstitutable singularities'" (ibid.). His body temporarily restores the car parts that are missing, while the speculation that the Mercedes previously belonged to a young woman who died in a car crash enables the identification of the two 'owners,' that is, the protagonist's *becoming*. Precisely his writing/thinking about the past produces his transformation: "Writing is inseparable from becoming" (Deleuze, *Essays* 1). That there is a young woman (or: someone) who died, is formative for the protagonist, and though ambivalent, the answer to the question in which way he is responsible for someone's death – even if he is not, strictly speaking, guilty – remains open, and disturbing.[23] The writing of this novel revolves around this loss.

Moreover, while Pišta's communication in, or 'through' the car wreck enables the 'presencing' of the past, unlike the aestheticized configuration of the Bernardi's room that could only 'antiquate' it, the mode of this presencing is critical. Pišta's claim to identity is quite precise, manifesting as his desire to become a *woman's woman*:

> When the psychiatrist asked me which sex attracts me, I said clearly: *female*. Though I was convinced that there is no female or male sex, but I didn't want to confuse him, I just wanted to make my wish come true. Of course, the psychiatrist's next question was: Why do you want to be a *woman* then? If you are attracted to women, you are a man. Precisely because of that, I answered, I want to be a woman's woman, because I am attracted to woman, I'm attracted to *femininity*, I desire a pure essential womanly love, men are sexually not interesting to me at all. I as a *woman's woman* need the tenderness of a *woman's woman*, nothing else. (Tišma, *Bernardijeva soba* 30)[24]

While the young woman from the past he 'encounters' in the car wreck and identifies with is a figure of this desire – desire as a 'flow,' a production (hence the Deleuze and Guattari term "desiring-production") – this longing would be *completed* once the protagonist leaves the wreck and heads towards a remote female commune, in which he would undergo a mysterious ritual indicating a sex transition. This (unexpected) epilogue of the novel helps resolve the puzzle around the protagonist's woman's woman identity, which before the closure seemed to be articulated solely as a desire. Part of an imagin-

---

23 "No, pitanje je šta sam ja u stvari želeo: nevinost ili krivnju? Izgleda da mi je ipak bila potrebna krivica da bih živeo i uživao, ali sa odstupnicom. Teško je živeti, još teže je uživati." (87)
    [But the question is what I really wanted: innocence or guilt? It seems I needed the guilt to be able to live and enjoy, but with an option to pull back. It's hard to live, even harder to enjoy.]
24 "Na pitanje psihijatra, koji me pol privlači, odgovorio sam kratko i jasno: *ženski*. Iako sam bio ubeđen da ne postoji nikakav ženski ili muški pol, ali nisam hteo da ga zbunjujem, na umu mi je bilo samo da ostvarim svoju želju. Naravno, psihijatrovo sledeće pitanje je bilo: A zašto onda želite da budete *žensko*? Ako vas privlače žene, vi ste muškarac. Upravo zato, bio je moj odgovor, želim da budem žena žene, jer me privlače žene, privlači me *ženskost*, želim čistu esencijalnu žensku ljubav, muškarci me u seksualnom smislu uopšte ne interesuju. Meni kao *ženi žene* potrebna je nežnost *žene žene*, ništa drugo."

able answer lays in the feminist revision of the very concept of the body without organs. Luce Irigaray interprets it as "a condition of dispossession of the bodily self, a structurally splintered position that is historically associated with femininity" (Braidotti 114). Moreover, Irigaray "points out that the emphasis on the machine like, the inorganic, as well as the notions of loss of self, dispersion, and fluidity are all too familiar to women" (116). She asks if the desiring machine does not "still partly take the place of woman or the feminine? Isn't it a sort of metaphor for her/it, that men can use?" (Irigaray 140–41). Likewise, Deleuze and Guattari's substantial concept of *becoming* – in which "becoming-woman" is a precondition of the whole process of transformation – has been demystified by a feminist re-examination as a concept in which the male is the "main referent for thinking subjectivity" (Braidotti 114), while woman remains the oppositional, dualistic other. Building on Irigaray's radical critique of the 'fantasmatic becoming-woman,' Braidotti further analyses the concept of *becoming* as amalgamating "men and women into a new, supposedly beyond gender, sexuality; [and] this is problematic, because it clashes with women's sense of their own historical struggles" (Braidotti 120), that is "undermining the feminist claims to a redefinition of the female subject" (116).

Hence, as suggested in the beginning, the process of *becoming* may alternatively be "sex-specific, sexually differentiated, and consequently [taking] different forms according to different gendered positions" (121). Pišta's 'taking-on' of the woman's woman identity is mimicking a problematic 'becoming-woman' process, for he does not experience a 'conventional' gender transition, but becomes, possibly counter-intuitively, a woman's woman. This special type of *becoming* raises the question of female genealogies – maternities (woman's woman) – but also female literary and artistic traditions which integrate issues of female difference. The protagonist's affection for this difference, his 'woman's womanliness' is exactly in the introduction quoted 'affirmation of the positivity of difference.' Unlike the body without organs that 'you can't reach but you forever attain it' (Deleuze and Guattari, *Plateaus* 150), his reaching of the female commune means attaining a woman's woman subjectivity (if not even the corporeality, for which a few clues have been offered in the final episode). Again, reaching of the female commune and what he experiences there is inseparable from the interdiscursive link the author establishes with another Yugoslav Neo-avantgardist author Judita Šalgo and her posthumously published novel *Put u Birobidžan* (The Journey to Birobidzhan, 1997). In this novel the (female) protagonist never reaches the desired destination, an imaginary 'female continent,' which is why Tišma's closure of the *Bernardi's Room* could be interpreted as an ending of the 'open-ended' journey in Šalgo's novel.[25] As it seems, the emptied place of the "no-body," which is how Rosi Braidotti defines the place of the 'feminine' (Braidotti 47) has over Tišma's 'interference' taken the contour of Judita Šalgo and her novel. The protagonist *has become* a woman's woman through the very process of writing one post-Yugoslav text against the late Yugoslav novel written by a woman author. Hence, the mode of 'presencing' the past is marked by this authorial and historical existence.

Finally, the joy, pleasure or at best translated *jouissance* that the protagonist refers to as "the only thing that mattered" (Tišma, *Bernardijeva soba* 56), goes beyond the 'immanence' of the body without organs that relates to the desire as a "process of production without reference to any exterior agency, whether it be a lack that hollows it out or a pleasure that fills it" (Deleuze and Guattari, *Plateaus* 154). In feminist psychoanalytical theory *jouissance* – an "orgasmic overflowing of female pleasure" (M. Eagleton 205) – is opposed to lack (Maccannell 85). In this sense, Pišta's physical lack – as an appropriation of the feminine position inside the psychoanalytical symbolisation process – is what qualified or even guaranteed the fulfilment of his wish in the first place.

The uselessness of the two 'non-objects' either assists in a Benjaminian 'traditionalization' – "that what makes tradition a tradition" (Brebanović 61) – or helps answering the question about the possible alternative 'use' of the work of art asked in the beginning of this paper. While the Bernardi's room stands for the first possibility, the Mercedes car wreck initiates the latter. Likewise, instead of fetishizing time, post-Yugoslav literary production is a machine of 'presencing': a woman author steps in with her "here and now" ('the Yugoslav' as time and space), thus 'repeating difference.' The *meaning* and *use* of *Bernardi's Room* as a post-Yugoslav 'writing machine' hence coincide when historized. The temporality of the late Yugoslav literature, its Neo-avantgardist and feminist spaces, appear to be critical in historizing the post-Yugoslav literary field. Nevertheless, this process is impossible without making an error in a (linear) temporality of a literary history. As Tišma puts it: "erring against oneself, always self-destructing. Otherwise, there is no jouissance, no existence" (Tišma, *Bernardijeva soba* 118).[26] This error sets off the impossible history of post-Yugoslav literature, for the "emergence of the machine marks a date, a change, different from a structural representation" (Dosse 127). Finally, this all

---

25   I wrote about this 'event' in detail in my article: "Neo-avantgarde and Feminist Underpinnings of Post-Yugoslav Literature and its Utopias: A Comparative Reading of Judita Šalgo and Slobodan Tišma." See References.

26   "grešiti spram samog sebe, stalno se samodestruirati. Bez toga nema u-žitka, nema postojanja."

was made possible because in and by this novel "the time variable [is crossed] with the other, just as powerful, variable of sexual difference" (Braidotti 121), thus releasing "the possibility of the genderization of both time and history" (ibid.).

3   Postscript: To Pry an Aura – "At a Speed Greater than Light"

The car wreck is a relic of a 'lived life,' both a body and a machine, dilapidated, and unlike the furniture, succumbing to the work of time. Alternately: from his present moment the protagonist penetrates the wreck, colliding with the past that is contained in it, or rather, that is activated by his intrusion: "Temporalization penetrates the machine on all sides and can be related to it only after the fashion of an event" (Guattari 112). The past which thereupon becomes present is the *event* as an outcome of this collision: "The purple-blue colour opens the box with scents which activate the impossible memories" (Tišma, *Bernardijeva soba* 7).[27] As it were, the impossible replaces likelihood, plausibility.

The car wreck is described as a shell, it shines, tastes and smells like salt or a wave (45). It brings Pišta in the proximity of the 'Ocean,' an important figure in the story: the car used to slide down the ocean shore (10). Its colour is also suggestive: "Now a dark purple shell shines on the parking lot like the shell of an Easter egg" (7).[28] Once again, the distant/distanced past is at hand *through* Pišta's intrusion into the car body shell: "To pry an object from its shell, to destroy its aura, is the mark of a perception whose 'sense of the universal equality of things' has increased to such a degree that it extracts it even from a unique object by means of reproduction" (Benjamin, "The Work of Art" 5). The effect routinely present in an auratic work of art which is namely "closing the distance in time between the painting of the picture and one's own act of looking at it" (Berger et al. 31)[29] is now available in a mechanically reproduced work. Though a mechanically reproduced object should by definition be deprived of an aura, the Mercedes car wreck *is* an aura, a shell of the "here and now" that Pišta puts on, penetrates.

---

27   "Ljubičastoplava boja otvara kutijicu s mirisima koji bude nemoguća sećanja."
28   "Sada se na parkingu sjaji samo tamnoljubičasta školjka kao ljuska uskršnjeg jajeta."
29   John Berger voiced a more vivid description of the phenomenon in his BBC TV series: the past offers moments of identification by being accessible through a temporal corridor that is "connecting the moment it represents with the moment at which you are looking at it, and something travels down that corridor at a speed greater than light, throwing into question a way of measuring time itself" (Berger, *Ways of Seeing*, ep. 1, 00:12:45).

While Bernardi's room's aura is an ironized veneration of aesthetics as an alienated projection of traditional, or bourgeois art, the car (wreck) is a 'mechanically reproduced' object replacing "an 'aura' of uniqueness, privilege, distance and permanence ... with a plurality of copies [allowing] the beholder to encounter the work in his own particular place and time" (T. Eagleton 58). To be able to do the same, we should recognise *Bernardi's Room's* 'materiality,' grounded in bringing one particular historical moment "literally there before our eyes" (Berger et al. 31). In his critique of the traditional aesthetics, Berger focused on the analysis of the visual arts, concluding that in this special sense of 'bringing a historical moment before our eyes' "all paintings are contemporary" (ibid.). Similarly, this novel produced its own and the contemporaneity of the Yugoslav literary past by, as Benjamin says, *seizing* that past.

References

Bakhtin, Mikhail. *The Dialogic Imagination: Four Essays*. University of Texas Press, 2004.

Benjamin, Walter. "The Work of Art in the Age of Its Technological Reproducibility: Second Version." *The Work of Art in the Age of Its Technological Reproducibility, and Other Writings on Media*. Edited by Jennings, Michael W. et al., Harvard University Press, 2008.

Benjamin, Walter. "The Interior, The Trace." *The Arcades Project*. The Belknap Press of Harvard University Press, 2002, pp. 212–227.

Benjamin, Walter. "The Work of Art in the Age of Mechanical Reproduction." *Illuminations: Essays and Reflections*, edited by Arendt, Hannah, Schocken Books, 1968, pp. 217–252.

Berger, John, et al. *Ways of Seeing*. British Broadcasting Corporation; Penguin Books, 1979.

Berger, John, et al. "Ways of Seeing." Episode 1. BBC, 1972. *YouTube*, 8 Oct. 2012, www.youtube.com/watch?v=0pDE4VX_9Kk.

Bogue, Ronald. "Deleuze and Literature." *The Cambridge Companion to Deleuze*, edited by Smith, Daniel W., and Henry Somers-Hall, Cambridge University Press, 2012. pp. 286–306.

Bourdieu, Pierre. *The Field of Cultural Production: Essays on Art and Literature*. Columbia University Press, 1993.

Braidotti, Rosi. *Nomadic Subjects: Embodiment and Sexual Difference in Contemporary Feminist Theory*. Columbia University Press, 1994.

Brebanović, Predrag. "Jugoslovenska književnost: stanovište sadašnjosti." *Tranzicija i kulturno pamćenje: Zbornik radova*, edited by Karlić, Virna et al., Srednja Europa, 2017, pp. 57–64.

Deleuze, Gilles. Interview by Toni Negri. "Contrôle et devenir." *le silence qui parle*, 7 May 2009, www.lesilencequiparle.unblog.fr/2009/03/07/controle-et-devenir-gilles-deleuze-entretien-avec-toni-negri/. Accessed 23 November 2019.

Deleuze, Gilles. *Proust and Signs*. Translated by Richard Howard, The Athlone Press, 2000.

Deleuze, Gilles. *Essays Critical and Clinical*. Translated by Daniel W. Smith and Michael A. Greco, Verso, 1998.

Deleuze, Gilles. *Negotiations, 1972–1990*. Translated by Martin Joughin, Columbia University Press, 1995.

Deleuze, Gilles, and Félix Guattari. *Capitalism and Schizophrenia. A Thousand Plateaus*. Translated by Brian Massumi, University of Minnesota Press, 2005.

Deleuze, Gilles, and Félix Guattari. *Kafka: Toward a Minor Literature*. Translated by Dana Polan, University of Minnesota Press, 2003.

Dosse, François. "Deleuze and structuralism." *The Cambridge Companion to Deleuze*, edited by Smith, Daniel W., and Henry Somers-Hall, Cambridge University Press, pp. 126–150.

Duda, Dean. "Prema genezi i strukturi postjugoslovenskog književnog polja." *Tranzicija i kulturno pamćenje: Zbornik radova*, pp. 45–56.

Eagleton, Mary. "Do Women Write Differently: Introduction." *Feminist Literary Theory: A Reader*, edited by Eagleton, Mary, Blackwell, 1990, pp. 200–207.

Eagleton, Terry. *Marxism and Literary Criticism*. Routledge, 2002.

Elster, Jon. *Karl Marx: A Reader*. Cambridge University Press, 1999.

Grosz, Elizabeth. *Space, Time, and Perversion: Essays on the Politics of Bodies*. Routledge, 1995.

Guattari, Félix. "Machine and Structure." *Molecular Revolution: Psychiatry and Politics*. Penguin Books, 1984, pp. 111–19.

Irigaray, Luce. *This Sex Which Is Not One*. Cornell University Press, 1985.

Kopicl, Vladimir. "Writings of Death and Entertainment: Textual Body and (De)composition of Meaning in Yugoslav Neo-avant-garde and Post-avant-garde Literature, 1968–1991." *Impossible Histories: Historical Avant-gardes, Neo-avant-gardes, and Post-avant-gardes in Yugoslavia, 1918–1991*, edited by Djurić, Dubravka, and Miško Šuvaković, The MIT Press, 2003, pp. 96–119.

Kreho, Dinko. "O čemu govorimo kada govorimo o postjugoslavenskoj književnosti?," on the radio emission *Pojmovnik postjugoslovenske književnosti*, Treći program Hrvatskog radija, 2015.

Lukić, Jasmina. "Rod i migracija u postjugoslovenskoj književnosti kao transnacionalnoj književnosti." *Reč*, vol. 87, no. 33, 2017, pp. 273–291.

Lukić, Jasmina. "Tijelo i tekst u feminističkoj vizuri," *Treća*, vol. 3, nos. 1–2, 2001, pp. 237–250.

Lukić, Jasmina."Žensko pisanje i žensko pismo u devedesetim godinama," *Sarajevkse sveske*, vol. 2, 2003, pp. 67–82.

Maccannell, Juliet Flower. "Jouissance." *Feminism and Psychoanalysis: A Critical Dictionary*, edited by Wright, Elizabeth, Blackwell, 1998, pp. 185–188.

Marčetić, Adrijana et al. editors. *Jugoslovenska književnost: sadašnjost, prošlost i budućnost jednog spornog pojma/Yugoslav Literature: The Past, Present and Future of a Contested Notion*. Čigoja štampa, 2019.

Matijević, Tijana. "Neo-avantgarde and Feminist Underpinnings of Post-Yugoslav Literature and its Utopias: A Comparative Reading of Judita Šalgo and Slobodan Tišma." *Feminisms in a Transnational Perspective*, edited by Renata Jambrešić Kirin, et al., Institute of Ethnology and Folklore Research, Zagreb/Università degli studi di Napoli "L'Orientale, 2019, pp. 325–338.

Osborne, Peter. *The Politics of Time: Modernity and Avant-Garde*. Verso, 1995.

Protevi, John. "Deleuze and Life." *The Cambridge Companion to Deleuze*, edited by Smith, Daniel W., and Henry Somers-Hall, Cambridge University Press, pp. 239–264.

Thiele, Kathrin. "Of Immanence and Becoming: Deleuze and Guattari's Philosophy and/as Relational Ontology." *Deleuze Studies* vol. 10, no. 1, 2016, pp. 117–134.

Tišma, Slobodan. *Velike misli malog Tišme*. Gradska narodna biblioteka "Žarko Zrenjanin," 2014.

Tišma, Slobodan. *Bernardijeva soba*. Kulturni centar Novog Sada, 2012.

Vidulić, Svjetlan Lacko. "Jugoslawische Literatur. Kurzer Abriss zur langen Geschichte eines produktiven Phantoms." *Traumata der Transition: Erfahrung und Reflexion des jugoslawischen Zerfalls*, edited by Boris Previšić and Svjetlan Lacko Vidulić, Francke-Verlag, 2015, pp. 161–182.

CHAPTER 3

Whose (Neo-)Avant-Garde? The Poetry of Josip Sever, Yugoslav Modernity, and the Problem of Mononational Literary History

Lujo Parežanin

As the supposedly highest expression of a national language and culture, literature is central to the process of cultural differentiation and appropriation[1] in the parts of former Yugoslavia where different varieties of Serbo-Croatian are used. More than any cultural practice (notwithstanding religion), it is the foundation upon which, for example, Croatian culture is constructed as being autonomous and distinct from Serbian. And as *the* mandatory school subject throughout primary and secondary education, it is the crucial means of the ideological reproduction of this distinction. From the moment they set foot into the educational system, pupils are taught a continuous line of Croatian literature from the 11th century onwards. Notions of national culture and literature are projected onto periods that predate the formation of nations by centuries and whose cultural geography is far removed from any trace of homogenization,[2] without any critical reflection on the ways national (literary) traditions are constructed.[3] From the other side of the cultural barricades, parts of the Serbian academia respond by proposing methodologically dubious and outdated "expansionist" claims regarding, for example, the literary

---

[1] I am not using this term in the sense of the current debates in the USA regarding minority cultures and their appropriation by the white American majority, but in the general sense of claiming cultural artefacts and phenomena as belonging to a national and ethnic group.

[2] The inability to project this totality is made visible from time to time in compromise solutions such as the notion of literary circles in Croatian baroque literature. One should add to this that such a projection is not in itself "right" or "wrong" – as Svetozar Petrović notices in his book *Priroda kritike* (*The Nature of Criticism*) (2003), indeed every construction of a literary tradition depends on it.

[3] Although recent changes to the national curriculum have somewhat done away with the linear paradigm, instead adopting the method of developing reading habits on contemporary works and then proceeding onto the "classics," the still-implied national model is not questioned. The public debate regarding the reading lists defined by the curriculum, however poorly informed, shows the ideological weight literature still surprisingly bears in the Croatian cultural-political field.

tradition of Dubrovnik, classifying writers such as Gundulić as Serbian on the basis of their writing in the Shtokavian dialect.[4]

As confusing as this is, this understanding of pre-19th century literature and culture is not an isolated conundrum. The central blind spot of Croatian (Serbian, Bosnian and Herzegovinian, etc.) literary and cultural histories, from which a distorted image is projected into the past, follows the consolidation of South Slavic nations in the second half of the 19th century. It is the problem of understanding the 20th century, dominated for the most part by two supranational entities – the two Yugoslavias, one bourgeois (1918–1941) and the other socialist (1945–1992).

1   Yugoslav State(s), National Literatures?

Much like the state – or instead, the idea – that gave it the name it never really bore, Yugoslav literature is by now no more than a specter.

Because of the insistence of socialist cultural policy on the autonomy of national cultures,[5] the notion of Yugoslav literature is thoroughly removed from the public and academic space, enclosed within the borders of the national(ist) model. Whereas the notion of Yugoslavia is an object of continuous scholarly interest, the notion of Yugoslav literature is seldom addressed in post-Yugoslav literary and cultural studies. However, Yugoslav literature is replaced with the concept of *post*-Yugoslav literature.[6] These concepts raise theoretical issues concerning their chronological and logical links. Yugoslav literature was apparently *before* post-Yugoslav literature, yet it is still uncertain whether these concepts are related as sequences or consequences. The conceptual triangle, comprising Yugoslavia, Yugoslav literature, and post-Yugoslav literature, entices ambiguity in what sense post-Yugoslav literature is post-*Yugoslav*, and what defines it as post-*Yugoslav literature*.

I will try to expound both theoretical and methodological quandaries of the concept post-Yugoslav literature, relying upon the discussion of Yugoslav

---

[4] For example, in the edition *Ten Centuries of Serbian Literature* published by Matica srpska.
[5] See Ahmad, 2000.
[6] See the important collection of (non-academic) essays by Boris Postnikov *Postjugoslavenska književnost?* (*Post-Yugoslav Literature?*), published in 2012. The book results from the author's program "Pojmovnik postjugoslavenske književnosti" ("The Glossary of Post-Yugoslav Literature"), broadcasted on the Croatian Radio 3, the national station specialized for the culture. The broadcasting of "Glossary" ceased in 2016 after the new right-wing management of the Croatian Radiotelevision purged the program of politically undesirable content.

literature as a historical concept proposed by Svetozar Petrović's book *Priroda kritike* (*The Nature of Criticism*).[7] It is a famous yet neglected book in the literary departments in Croatian, Serbian, or Bosnian universities. Could Petrović's position about a concept of Yugoslav literature be a reason for overlooking his book? It is not the only thing that made Petrović an academic eccentric regardless of the acceptance of his writing, with his still-relevant critique of the "immanent approach"[8] provoking debate in the academia during the 1960s and the 1970s,[9] the heyday of the Zagreb School of Literary Studies.

This ignorance is only to the detriment of our local academic communities, since the chapter "Filologija u vremenu" ("Philology in Time") of *Priroda kritike* remains as one of the most thoughtful and acute discussions of Yugoslav literary history/histories. Its relevance is recently revised by a study that bears the same polemical charge as Petrović's work, written by Predrag Brebanović, one of Petrović's students. Brebanović's book *Avangarda Krležiana: pismo ne o avangardi* (*Avant-Garde Krležiana: A Letter Not About the Avant-Garde*) (2016) is a radical intervention in the field of Krleža studies. It is radical in the sense that Marx ascribes to the word as an attempt to "grasp the root of the matter" (Marx 137). By reading Krleža as a *Yugoslav* writer whose work should be read as a continuous avant-garde *praxis* interwoven with the revolutionary *praxis* of the socialist project,[10] Brebanović reinstates methodological debates regarding the concept of Yugoslav literature. He shows the shortcomings of understanding literary histories confined to the horizon of the nation. On the contrary, Brebanović's book implies, literary history must include Yugoslavia into its analytical apparatus.

The crucial theoretical distinction in Petrović's argumentation is between the *standpoint of the present* and the *standpoint of the past* – the approach whereby the researcher observes the past from the perspective of her contemporary context and the one whereby she tries to recreate the observed object's original historical context. According to Petrović, we should not engage with the reconstruction of a particular historical moment but rather understand

---

7   Originally published in 1972. In this paper I refer to the 2003 edition.
8   Initially published in 1963 in the book *Kritika i djelo* (*Criticism and the Literary Work*) and included in the later book *Priroda kritike*.
9   Petrović went to Novi Sad in 1970 to teach at the local university. Afterward, he taught in Belgrade, never to return to Croatia. Petrović's "immanent approach" in literary criticism is connected to his conceptions of literary history and, consequentially, to the Yugoslav-national problem.
10 In this sense, as Brebanović proposes, even his work on the *Encyclopaedia of Yugoslavia* should be understood as part of this utopian project.

the past – and with it, literary phenomena – from the perspective of contemporaneity. "Literary history," he claims, "is a creative vision of the literary past" (Petrović 242). Yet, our perspective is determined by our social, political, and class conditions, and also by that which we could, recalling David Perkins' term, describe as "suprapersonal entities" (Perkins). It simultaneously considers national, East European, European, Western, etc., literary histories, all coexisting and mutually determined in complex ways.[11] As Petrović puts it, the literary text is delineated by a "plurality of contexts" (Petrović 246). This plurality includes the national context as crucial, but is in no way reducible to it.

The question is, then, how do we profit by making the Yugoslav context an integral layer of this plurality in the case of our literatures? Or, in Perkins' terms, can we justify a notion of Yugoslav literature(s) as one of the *necessary fictions* for our research? It is not only a methodological question but also a profoundly political one, taking into account the central role of language and literature in the construction of nationalist narratives, as pointed at the beginning of this discussion. Hence, Petrović's claim from *Priroda kritike* seems relevant today as it was a half-decade ago: "Whether or not can we imagine a Yugoslav literature as a supranational whole relies on the question of whether or not can we imagine a relevant standpoint regarding the unity of Yugoslav peoples that can reveal a meaningful perspective on the literary works of their past." (Petrović 248) The "unity of Yugoslav peoples" is, then, this "standpoint of the present." From this outlook, one envisions the cultural and literary community echoing both lost ties and the hope of regaining them in the future.

2 The National Avant-Garde as "Wooden Iron"

Although productive, Petrović's distinction between the standpoint of the present and the standpoint of the past lacks a crucial, final step. In his discussion, Petrović does not acknowledge that, whatever the strategy a historical discourse is employing, a literary historian *always* assumes a *standpoint of the present*. Take, for example, the following exchange between Faust and Wagner:

---

11 *Transnational turn* in the study of World Literature showcases that the modernist literature in the context of cultural systems goes beyond the national. Accordingly, the interaction (and competition) of national cultures in modernity structures the modernist literature (see, for example, Ramazani or Casanova).

WAGNER. Excuse me if I think it a great treat
to put oneself into the spirit of past ages;
we see how wise men thought before our time,
and to what splendid heights we have attained at last.

FAUST. Oh yes, we've reached the very stars!
My friend, for us the ages that are past
must be a book with seven seals.
What's called the spirit of an age
is in the end the spirit of you persons
in whom past ages are reflected. (Goethe 18, lines 570–579)

Reconstructing a historian's "standpoint of the present," his/her "spirit / in whom past ages are reflected," leads us to an understanding of the ideological implications of his/her arguments, as objective and impersonal as they may seem. It does not equate to reconstructing one's *intention*; instead, another name for this procedure, closer to a Marxist critical apparatus, would be – historicization.

If what we said about the misconceptions of Yugoslav literary histories is indeed true, then historicizing dominant interpretations that participate in this distortion is the prerequisite for a critical rewriting of these histories. It relates to the literary phenomena that seem deeply connected to the shared socio-cultural space of the two (radically different) Yugoslavias. If we speak of individual writers, none is more connected to that space than Miroslav Krleža, whose *oeuvre*, as Brebanović's research has shown, can fully be understood as an avant-garde project inextricable from the Yugoslav revolutionary project.

A crucial part of Brebanović's intervention is the critical examination of the ideological implications of various types of (primarily academic) readings of Krleža. Dissecting the works of several leading scholars such as Aleksandar Flaker, Stanko Lasić, Viktor Žmegač, and Dubravka Oraić Tolić, Brebanović reveals the politics of their historical classifications. Reading Krleža as a Croatian writer – something that is now as naturalized as the difference between "Croatian" and "Serbian" language – has a specific political effect, as well as describing his work in terms of the avant-garde.

A particular tension arises when these two levels intersect to raise the issue of the relationship between the national and the avant-garde. Commenting on Oraić Tolić's retaining of both of these categories in her reading of Krleža, Brebanović asks: "What if Krleža can be a Croatian avant-gardist only if we forget about Serbian surrealism, and Yugoslavia, and socialism? Or let us put it this way: what if Krleža became an avant-gardist in Oraić Tolić's interpretation so that he can remain a Croatian writer? Here, again, there is no need to be surprised, because the avant-gardization *à la Tolić* emerges in the middle of the 1990s as a part of a massive operation of severing Croatian from Serbian (not just avant-garde) culture" (125). According to Brebanović, this "avant-gardization" in the national key was not possible in Yugoslavia: "This begs the question: was not the main reason for this 'blindness' to Krleža's avant-gardism the fact that in the context of the existence of the Yugoslav state, the avant-garde could hardly be related to an exclusive notion of a Croatian literature?" (ibid.) For Brebanović, the avant-garde and the national are indeed mutually exclusive: "A national avant-garde is no more than wooden iron[12] [...] Why avant-garde if it is Croatian or Serbian? Why turn a volcano into an operetta?" (127). This operation, Brebanović claims, by which a writer such as Krleža is reduced to a national tradition, is nothing else than a dehistoricization masked as literary history. Its function is to serve the nationalist agenda (in this case, Croatian) in the negation of the historical experience of Yugoslavia, its culture, and its literature.

3   Josip Sever: Yugoslav Avant-Garde or Croatian Neo-Avant-Garde?

If, as Brebanović writes, the Croatian avant-garde is "wooden iron," the same should hold true for the artistic practices that can be seen as a reactivation, either affirmative or polemical, of avant-garde poetics in Yugoslavia from the 1950s onwards. In the field of literature, the critical example is the poet Josip Sever. His connection to local strains of the avant-garde tradition, as I attempted to show in my article "The Poetry of Josip Sever and the Problems

---

[12] The phrase "wooden iron" refers to the oxymoronic nature of the notion of a national avant-garde. It is an attitude I share with Predrag Brebanović, but also with Miklavž Komelj. In the article "Od nadrealističke do partizanske revolucije" ("From the Surrealist to the Partisan Revolution"), Komelj criticizes the attribution of a national (Serbian) character to the Belgrade Surrealists: "The term 'Serbian Surrealism' [...] seems highly problematic because it is based on the national that the Surrealist movement questions." Komelj even warns against designating Surrealism as Yugoslav: "However, Yugoslav Surrealists themselves spoke against the term 'Yugoslav Surrealism.' One can speak of Yugoslav Surrealists, but not about Yugoslav Surrealism. Just like we could not if we are to be truly consistent, speak of a French one" (48). The Yugoslav context showcases that the definition of the avant-garde in national categories (e.g., Croatian, Serbian) is both methodologically inappropriate and ideologically problematic. Similarly, the Yugoslav literature and culture elude from the limits of the national model. In studying Sever's poetry, I attempt to demonstrate both theses, the first regarding the avant-garde and the second regarding the Yugoslav literature.

of Studying Neo-avant-garde Literature" (2015), have been mostly ignored in the small but engaging body of academic research devoted to his work, to the detriment of theoretical and historical understanding of its complexity and the complexity of its literary-historical implications. Sever seems especially interesting in the context of Brebanović's discussion of Krleža presented above. Krelža is not only a crucial part of Sever's explicitly constructed avant-garde tradition (Parežanin, "Pjesništvo Josipa Severa"), but the same authors that Brebanović extensively criticizes in his book – Aleksandar Flaker and Dubravka Oraić Tolić – also prove to be crucial in the academic reception of Sever's poetry. Flaker and Oraić Tolić underscore Sever's relation to a particular national avant-garde tradition. Returning to Petrović's categories, what is then interesting is the implied *standpoints of the present* from which these authors proceed to situate Sever historically.

The title of Flaker's article is indicative: "Hrvatske inačice ine avangarde" ("Croatian Versions of an Other Avant-Garde") (1988). The article is published in *Suvremeno hrvatsko pjesništvo* (*Contemporary Croatian Poetry*), in which he analyses the work of Boro Pavlović, Radomir Venturin, Josip Sever, and Oraić Tolić, who, besides her scientific work, is also a neo-avant-garde poet.[13] In the article, Flaker writes: "The orientation [in Croatian post-war poetry] towards a foreign, other, non-Croatian avant-garde was introduced by Josip Sever, a translator of [Mayakovski's] *Lenin*, a reader of Kruchenykh, just returned from China" (254). Flaker's argument is based on two assumptions related to a specific, nationally inflected understanding of literary history. The first is that Sever is a *Croatian* version of Russian Futurism, the leading movement of the Russian avant-garde. The other is a specifically *Croatian* avant-garde tradition that, according to Flaker, Sever forecloses in favor of his Russian models – Mayakovski, Khlebnikov, and Kruchenykh. In short, Flaker establishes two crucial connections: 1) concerning the socio-cultural context, Sever is a Croatian writer; 2) concerning the avant-garde tradition, he is confined to Russian Futurism. By proclaiming Sever a Croatian writer, Flaker is occluding the Yugoslav context of his poetry in conformity with the implied methodological nationalism that Brebanović addresses in his book on Krleža. Second, by defining Sever as a local version of the Russian avant-garde, Flaker avoids the problem of acknowledging the local avant-garde tradition to which Sever explicitly responds – in line with his refusal to accept Krleža as an avant-gardist. Finally, closely related to the first objection, by claiming that Sever

---

13   For a basic discussion of her poem "Urlik Amerike" ("American Scream") in the context of avant-garde tradition, see Parežanin, "Reinterpretacija."

introduces an orientation towards a "non-Croatian" avant-garde, Flaker sticks to the "wooden iron" of a strictly national understanding of the avant-garde movements in Yugoslavia, even as he establishes Sever's divergence from them.

Nevertheless, Flaker provides valuable clues to draw the conclusions he avoids drawing. First of all, Flaker *does* mention a Croatian avant-gardist in his article on Sever – none other than Krleža. And as much as one can try to divorce Krleža from the avant-garde, not even schoolbooks – those pillars of today's cultural conservatism – deny that a significant part of his *oeuvre* undoubtedly belongs to it. Flaker excavates such a subtle connection between the theatricality of Sever's poem "Bitka" ("The Battle") and Krleža's poetics, but chooses to see this as a remote kinship and not a nod to the key figure of the local avant-garde tradition. Interestingly, one of Flaker's earlier books, *Književne poredbe* (*Literary Comparisons*), contains a detailed comparative analysis of Krleža and – Mayakovski! One can only be perplexed by the fact that Flaker fails to connect his conclusions when he references both of them in his reading of Sever, yet treats them as wholly unrelated. As I have already shown elsewhere,[14] to do this Flaker had to either miss or ignore Sever's May Day poems published in the journal *oko*, in which Sever explicitly treats both Mayakovski and Krleža as his own avant-garde tradition, along with other Futurists, but also August Cesarec and even Tin Ujević, a poet typically read as modernist. Flaker's notion of a "Croatian version of an other avant-garde" is distorting. It imposes the ideological basis of his *standpoint of the present*, which dictates the interpretation and contorts literary facts.

Flaker's focus on the relations between Sever's poetry and the Russian Futurists forms the basis of Dubravka Oraić Tolić's enticing yet also highly problematic article "Na kraju avangardnog raja" ("At the End of Avant-garde Eden"), published in the same collection. Oraić Tolić follows Flaker's method. She offers a compelling reading of Sever as an antiutopian, post-avant-garde/postmodernist poet who coevally subverts the Futurist tradition and the Yugoslav utopia. In constructing this double subversion during the death throes of Yugoslavia, Flaker and Oraić Tolić devise the Other of Croatian culture and literature.

Thus, the "other avant-garde" in Flaker's title acquires a psychoanalytical significance, for it points to an Other of both Flaker's and Oraić Tolić's interpretations – namely, Yugoslavia and the Yugoslav avant-garde. In order to avoid questioning their assumptions about Yugoslav and Croatian literary histories, Flaker and Oraić Tolić repudiate their previous research – as in

---

14   See Parežanin, "Pjesništvo Josipa Severa."

Flaker's case of Krleža and Mayakovski – and the empirically verifiable connections between Russian Futurism and "Croatian" avant-gardists such as the April-May 1923 issue of the Futurist journal *LEF*. They foreclose that Sever's May Day poems refer to this literary and cultural intertext. Flaker and Oraić Tolić exclude Sever's belonging to the revolutionary and literary tradition that includes Miroslav Krleža, August Cesarec, Tin Ujević, as well as Mayakovski and the Futurists.

While Flaker may not know about Sever's May Day poems, as they were not included in Sever's two collections, Oraić Tolić's academic denial of their existence is hard to understand. As the editor, she adds May Day poems in Sever's posthumous collection *Borealni konj* (*Boreal Horse*). In separating Sever from his literary predecessors, Oraić Tolić argues that "Sever doesn't need a tradition" (268). This claim is problematic not only because of the impossibility of escaping a relation with a literary tradition but also from the particular point of view of Sever's poems published in *OKO*. How should one understand these lines from the poem "Stilske vježbe V. Majakovskog i njegovog tima na temu 1-ga maja uz komentar J. Severa" ("Excercises in Style by V. Mayakovsky and His Team on the Subject of May Day with Commentary by J. Sever"):

> Ali imamo mi hrid
> Našega starca
> CESARCA
> Imamo KRLEŽU MIROSLAVA
> Njemu: mirovaja SLAVA
> Imamo naš prvi maj
> I prvomajsku poruku u stvari
> Kao korugvu.
> I kad nam ne "ćuhta":
> "Gremo mi puntari!" (Sever 171)

> (But we have our rock
> Our old man
> CESAREC
> We have KRLEŽA MIROSLAV
> To him: mirovaya SLAVA
> We have our May Day
> And the May Day message, in fact
> As a banner.
> And even when it's still:
> "On we go, we, rebels!")

The poem's intertext aligns Sever's national literary tradition (Krleža, Cesarec, Tin Ujević)[15] with the historical avant-garde International (puntari/rebels). Sever uses lines from Ujević's sonnet *Oproštaj* (*Farewell*), "ćuhtati" (waving banner) and "gremo mi puntari/on we go, we, rebels" to simultaneously link the discontinuity in the Croatian literary history (the breakup with the literary tradition) and continuity with the International avant-garde. He connects the Russian Futurists to their Yugoslav comrades – Krleža and Cesarec, who supported the revolutionary movement in Yugoslavia.

Why "Yugoslav" and not "Croatian"? The poem seemingly mentions only "Croatian" writers. If its horizon is Yugoslav, it would be expected to mention writers such as Koča Popović, Oskar Davičo, or Milan Dedinac. Sever's poem avoids referring even to Marko Ristić, Krleža's closest associate. Although Surrealists Koča Popović, Oskar Davičo, or Milan Dedinac had a significant impact on Yugoslav literature, their influence could not be compared to that of Krleža and Ujević. As much as the latter seems to be outside of the avant-garde, he had a profound impact on the development of Surrealism in Serbia – Belgrade Surrealists devoted to Ujević an entire issue of the journal *Svedočanstva* (*Testimonies*, 1924).

Sever's poem expunges Ujević's role in the construction of the Yugoslav avant-garde. The intertextual featuring of Krleža, Cesarec, and Ujević in the poem is significant. In the quoted lines, Krleža and Cesarec are referred to directly by mentioning their names. Ujević, on the contrary, is invoked by pasting from his sonnet *Oproštaj*. Note that Ujević uses the sonnet as a traditional form to bid his farewell to the literary tradition. He mimics the language of the literary predecessors to part with them. A newspaper article written by Zvonimir Milčec, and published in the Croatian daily *Večernji list* in 1978, sheds light on Sever's appreciation of Ujević and his influence on the entirety of Yugoslav literature and culture.[16] Milčec quotes Sever as claiming: "Tin is the greatest of all of them. The Serbs, the Croats, and the Muslims all agree: Tin is our Pushkin" (Milčec 5).

The question of "us" to whom Ujević belongs leads back to Sever's "Exercises in Style." It indicates that the context in which the poem should be read pertains to the domain of the poetic subject – who are these collective "we" that accept Krleža, Cesarec, and implicitly Ujević as their tradition? They are the "puntari" (rebels, revolutionaries) of the final verse – a direct quotation from

---

15   See my extended commentary on this and Sever's other May Day poems in Parežanin, "Pjesništvo Josipa Severa."
16   I am grateful to Mr. Saša Uzelac, Sever's nephew, for providing me with this article.

Ujević's famous poem "Oproštaj" ("Farewell"), but articulated in the context of May Day celebrations in a socialist state; in short, in a decidedly Yugoslav context.

From this perspective, it is hard to see just how Sever could be unequivocally read as a postmodernist or an anti-utopian poet. Contextualization of that supposed anti-utopianism or postmodernity of his writing is perplexing. For example, Oraić Tolić treats it as a cultural-literary abstraction by avoiding any specific commentary on the actual Yugoslav context that Sever is supposedly subverting. Similarly, Branimir Bošnjak in the book *Modeli moderniteta: Dekonstrukcija svijeta / jezika i postavangardni estetizam u poeziji Josipa Severa* (*Models of Modernity: Deconstruction of the World / Language and Post-avant-garde Aesthetism in the Poetry of Josip Sever*), published ten years after Oraić Tolić's article, takes Sever a step beyond the "end of the avant-garde Eden" and situates him into the post-avant-garde. Bošnjak also avoids proper social-historical contextualization (Parežanin, "Pjesništvo Josipa Severa"). The poet identified with anti-utopian poetics is detached from his utopian social context.

Sever's poetry links literary tradition, intertextual relations, the poetic subject, and national language. The strongest and, from the perspective of the linguistic and literal violence of the 1990s, a prophetic example is the poem "Balada o hrvatskom ili srpskom jeziku" ("The Ballad of Croatian or Serbian Language"). It relates to the politicization of the national languages in Yugoslavia during the late 1960s and 1970s. A line in the poem asks: "And when they finally slaughter, butcher in fact / one another, Serbian / and Croatian words. / What will then / remain?", proposing an answer: "Well, probably the language of the natural world."[17] After counting the many speakers of this peculiar language – birds, grass, trees, donkeys, children, and others – the poem unexpectedly turns to the "Rosy-fingered Dawn." It is a direct quote from Homer with a slight nod to the avant-garde: "That means / Croatian or / Serbian / language / will be spoken / by some people / just arriving / from Space" (Sever 178).

The poem refuses to side with the national(ist) attitudes of the 1970s – the tropes of the natural language, dawn, and people from space signaling their belonging to the utopian, avant-garde, Yugoslav horizon beyond the slaughterhouse of national distinctions. Along with "Exercises in Style," this poem

---

17 The original phrase "nemušti jezik," literally translated as "mute," "speechless" or "soundless language" and actually referring to an ability to communicate with animals and plants, is itself tied to the Serbian folk tradition – the "father of Serbian language" Vuk Stefanović Karadžić. *Serbian Folk Tales* (1853) includes a tale under the same title.

shows that the mystification of Sever's writing as a purely postmodernist, proto-deconstructivist indulging in the play of signifiers censors its ideological and social content. This content engenders the question of literary history on the levels of both tradition and language.[18]

4 The Significance of the Mundane

Returning to Petrović's challenge to imagine Yugoslavia as a starting point of our literary-historical research, the need for a Yugoslav perspective in understanding Sever's poetry becomes more and more evident. But where do we find such a perspective in this state of methodological blindness? Again, we should start by historicizing. Due to the denial of Yugoslav history, one should turn to the unexpected power of the mundane, of returning to historical facts. Instead of developing a theoretical understanding of the "Yugoslav modernity," we will try to catch a glimpse of its refractions in the seemingly basic facts of Sever's life.

The basic facts? History and archaeology both teach that there is no such thing – every fact carries in it the trace of an entire historical context of which it is a fragment. To grasp the context of Sever's poetry – of that which we named "Yugoslav modernity" – we can start with six seemingly self-evident and straightforward pieces of biographical information: Sever was born in Blinjski Kut on the periphery of Sisak, from where he came to Zagreb; he translated Mayakovski in high school; studied Russian language and literature under Aleksandar Flaker; went on a study trip to Russia in 1964; discussed the draft of his first collection *Diktator* (*Dictator*) in the flat of his friend Ludwig Bauer in Trnsko, a neighborhood in Novi Zagreb; he won the City of Zagreb Award for his second – and ultimately final – book of poems *Anarhokor* (*Anarchochorus*), published in 1977.

The question is this: what if we treat each of these facts as not at all as self-evident as they seem but ask ourselves how was it possible for Sever to come from a rural periphery to study literature in Zagreb? What did it mean to translate Mayakovski in the 1950s in Yugoslavia? How was it possible for Sever to study literature in a certain way, guided by Aleksandar Flaker? What made it possible for Sever to go to the USSR? How could he discuss his poetry in a

---

18   One could argue that even without these explicit remarks on "Croatian or Serbian language," it would be could be ask what does it mean to confine a writer deconstructively oriented towards language, this temple of national identity, to a national literary history.

flat in Trnsko in the 1960s? How could a supposedly anti-utopian poet win one of the most mainstream literary awards in 1977? Answering these questions endows us with the contours of the lost image of Yugoslav modernity.

Born in 1938 in Blinjski Kut near Sisak, Sever was a part of a generation whose high school years coincided with the substantial development of the Sisak urban area. By the middle of the 1950s, Sisak – or Veberland, as it was called in reference to the director of the famed local Iron and Steel Factory, Norbert Weber – experiences strong industrial development: in 1956, a new refinery is built which grows out of the resources of the Middle East countries orbiting the fledgling Non-aligned Movement[19] (especially Iraq), and by 1960 a new oil pipeline between Sisak and Stružac is built, further stimulating the growth of the oil industry. The Iron and Steel Factory becomes an integral economic factor, not just on the republic but on the federal level – during the 1960s, it employed around 6,000 workers. This process stimulates population growth in Sisak – from 1953 to 1961, it increased by 25%.

These conditions and widespread industrialization and urbanization in Yugoslavia increase the mobility of the population. Concomitantly, opportunities in culture and education improve for the youth in the wider Sisak area, especially for gymnasium graduates such as Sever. In his graduation year, he translated Mayakovski's poem "Vladimir Ilych Lenin." This translation will be, in the words of Aleksandar Flaker, "his passport to the land of the Cultural revolution" from where he returned "with some knowledge of the Chinese language and a great enthusiasm for Chinese culture" (Flaker, "Povratak Majakovskog").

In Zagreb, Sever attends the Slavic studies program at the Faculty of Humanities and Social Sciences, learning about avant-garde literature and literary theory. The modernization of literary studies accompanied the modernization of the cultural and literary field in socialist Yugoslavia during the 1950s. One crucial moment is the founding of the Croatian[20] Philological Society in 1950/51 that had a Section for the Theory of Literature and the Methodology of Literary History, founded in 1952. In 1955, the Section presented the results of its research in the publication *Pogledi 55*. The following year brought about the founding of the Department of Comparative Literature at the Faculty of Humanities and Social Sciences. At the same time, in 1957, the journal

---

19 The Brijuni Declaration was signed on July 19, 1956.
20 It would be interesting to ask nationalist historians why there was a *Croatian* Philological Society at the beginning of the 1950s if Croatian culture was systematically endangered by the communist regime.

Umjetnost riječi (*The Art of Words*) begins its publication. The journal introduces modernist and contemporary approaches to literary theory. It fosters a specialized discourse on literature relying upon the reception of stylistic criticism, Russian Formalism, and modernist New Criticism. It created the basis on which later theoretical influences such as structuralism and semiotics will be imported and participated in a modernist shift in understanding literary language. Literary works of neo-avant-garde germinated in this academic and scientific context.

A crucial protagonist of this process was Aleksandar Flaker. His academic beginnings are closely tied to the modernization of Yugoslavia's literary field and the shifts in Cold War politics that enabled academic exchange with the USSR. Whereas Flaker's doctoral thesis, defended in 1954, was devoted to the relation between the ideology of the Croatian Party of Rights and Russian literature, his subsequent research is turned toward the avant-garde. He enhances the reception of Russian Formalism. Flaker published the paper "Formalna metoda i njezina sudbina" ("The 'Formal Method' and Its Fate") in *Pogledi 55* (*Perspectives 55*). The first issue of *Art of Words* features his paper "Za potpuniju sliku sovjetske književnosti" ("Towards a Complete Picture of Soviet Literature"). It is followed with works such as "Cesarec i 'LEF'" ("Cesarec and 'LEF'"), together with the reprint of Cesarec's "LEF u Jugoslaviji" ("LEF in Yugoslavia"), "Boris Tomaševski" ("Boris Tomashevsky"), "Boris Mihajlovič Ejhenbaum (1886. – 1959.)" ("Boris Mikhailovich Eikhenbaum (1886 – 1959)." Flaker spends a part of this period in Russia at the Lomonosov State University. It indicates that the diffusion of Formalist Theory is enabled within geopolitical transformations that allowed for academic exchange between Yugoslavia and the USSR, especially the process of de-Stalinization under Khrushchev, which leads to the end of the Informbiro. On Tito's invitation, Khrushchev visited Belgrade in 1955, where they both signed the Belgrade Declaration that officially confirmed the thawing of Soviet politics, not only in relation to Yugoslavia. In April 1956, the Central Committees of the leading Communist Parties declared the end of the Informbiro. In June 1956, the Moscow Declaration will confirm the improvement of relations between Yugoslavia and the USSR.

In this context, not only does the academic and artistic exchange become possible, but it engenders a modernist turn in the understanding of the Russian avant-garde, especially its central persona, Vladimir Mayakovski. According to Flaker's analyses, Mayakovski was canonized in early post-war Yugoslavia as the greatest poet among the proponents of the revolution. The poet and prominent communist Radovan Zogović during the 1940s in the journal *Izraz* (*Expression*) formed the first model of Mayakovski's reception.

Zogović represents Mayakovski as a "strictly functional apologist of the revolution and post-revolutionary progress" (Flaker, "Hrvatske" 252). However, the change in the political and cultural climate after the Tito-Stalin split sprouts a different reception of Mayakovski's work and the entire avant-garde artistic and literary tradition.[21] Again, the space to turn away from Zogović was enticed by the shifts in the political context. In 1948, after the Tito-Stalin split, Zogović fell from favor as a Stalinist. Consequently, he was removed from all political and cultural positions. The first post-Zogović publication of Mayakovski's poetry in Zagreb was precisely Sever's translation of *Lenin*, edited by Flaker.[22]

This thawing of the political context will enable the first official student exchanges with the USSR, one of which will prove crucial to Sever's poetic development. In 1964 he and Ludwig Bauer will visit Moscow where Sever will, through the poet Gennadiy Aygi who worked at the Mayakovski Museum, meet Aleksey Kruchonykh, who lived in Kirov Street where some of the Futurists originally resided.[23] Hence, Flaker's description of Sever as merely a "Croatian version" of the Russian avant-garde is scrutinized. It shows that Sever's reception of Russian literature was not a spontaneous intra-literary process, but rather one entangled with the political, academic, and artistic temporal layers. Thereby, this reception withdraws from the monolithic national timeline.

The process of the literal, material formation of Sever's work, whose significant part is related to the subject of space, can also be linked to the modernization of real, urban space as the most recognizable aspect of Yugoslav modernity. According to Ludwig Bauer,[24] Sever's first collection *Diktator* (*Dictator*) drafts are partially formed during regular discussions of Sever's manuscripts in Bauer's apartment in Trnsko. The quarter of Trnsko was an integral part of Zagreb's spreading south of the river Sava. It implemented new standards in urbanism and architecture. Completed in 1962, Trnsko was the first

---

21   The appearance of the constructivist neo-avant-garde group Exat 51 a couple of years earlier could be understood as a sign of these developments.
22   It was published by Mladost in 1957 as part of the edition *Biblioteka Orion*. The first post-Zogović Mayakovski, regardless of the genre, was Flaker's translation of the play *Bathhouse*, published in 1953.
23   Its name during the 1920s was Myasnitskaya. Later it was renamed in honour of Sergey Kirov, whose assassination in 1934 served as the pretext for the purges of the 1930s. It bore Kirov's name until the dissolution of the USSR, when it became Myasnitskaya again.
24   See, for example, Bauer, "Josip Sever." I am also drawing from Bauer's comments on February 9 2019 as part of a literary manifestation Zagrebačke posvete (Zagreb Tributes). He explicitly referenced discussing *Dictator* with Sever in Trnsko. For the complete reference, see Bauer, public talk.

entire neighborhood to emerge across the river of Sava (Tatomir). The name Novi Zagreb (New Zagreb) – now designating that entire part of the city – was, according to Kristian Strukić (Strukić), first used as a part of Trnsko's original name *mikrorajon Novi Zagreb I i II* (*Microdistrict New Zagreb I and II*). Therefore, Zagreb's quarter of Trnsko was not only the setting of the composition of Sever's first volume of poetry. Trnsko metamorphoses into a synecdoche, referring to the urbanistic modernization of Zagreb and Yugoslavia.

Finally, how to use the fact that Sever's second collection of poetry *Anarhokor* (*Anarchochorus*) won him the City of Zagreb Award? Consider this passage from Oraić Tolić: "The dystopian semantic complex that in *Diktator* more often corresponds to the level of the signifier, liberated itself in *Anarhokor* from all relations. If Sever had still believed that in *Diktator* he could dictate a new, dystopian priority of sound over meaning [...], in *Anarhokor* he abandoned this and any other hope, and his poetry dissolved into *anarchy* of structure" (Oraić Tolić 271). Although *Anarhokor* supposedly exhibits an absolute rejection of hope and structure, propelling the creation beyond dystopia, the official literary-political system accepted the collection. That indeed says something about Sever's work, as well as about a system that shows itself to be capable of integrating his literary experiments. Artistic modernism is an inalienable part of Yugoslav cultural politics. Hence, depicting Sever as an oppositional writer is close to the revisionist type of discourse we are witnessing nowadays in projects such as *COURAGE – Understanding the Cultural Heritage of Dissent in the Former Socialist Countries*. This project lumps together far-right extremists, feminists, students' movements, and conceptual artists under the category of "cultural opposition" or "dissidence." These categories of revolt do not adhere to a Yugoslav context that systematically supported modernist and experimental artistic practices.

Both Sever's collections stem from *inside* the literary system, the first one being published by the Zagreb Student Centre as part of the *Razlog* edition. The first Sever's collection won the Zagreb City Award in 1972. Sever's work for *OKO*, where he published most of his writing outside the two volumes of poetry, must also be understood as part of the Yugoslav cultural mainstream. Therefore, Oraić Tolić's antiutopian reading is unacceptable – Sever maintained a continuous dialogue with the Yugoslav "optimal projection." Still, it is a complex interaction that is acknowledged by Yugoslav institutions and the literary system, confirmed by the City of Zagreb Award.

What does all this have to do with Sever's poetry from the perspective of literary history? It shows us that its context must be understood in terms of Yugoslav social, cultural, and literary modernization. Instead of simply being a Croatian poet or a "Croatian version" of some "other" avant-garde, Sever's work cannot be extricated from the interplay with the notion of Yugoslavia. He engages in the interplay even if one accepts the dubious interpretation of his poetry as anti-utopian or (proto)postmodern.

This supposed anti-utopianism does not develop as a generalized postmodern metanarrative but as entangled in the historical contradictions of Yugoslav reality. As much as a Croatian, therefore, Sever is a Yugoslav poet. From this perspective, we could proceed to speak of his two local protagonists, Krleža and Ujević. Is not Krleža a Yugoslav avant-gardist? Is not Ujević a Yugoslav modernist? Both are equally important to Belgrade's and Zagreb's literary circles. Reinscribing Sever in the modern Yugoslav literature and culture implies a rereading of Yugoslav literary and cultural history. Whereas Flaker's and Oraić Tolić's standpoints of present anticipated the nationalist destruction of the "unity of Yugoslav peoples," Petrović, on the other hand, took the unity as actuality. For Petrović, it is not that the "unity of Yugoslav people" exists, or does not exist, only viewed from the evershifting standpoint(s) of the present. Instead, he ascribed the role of the standpoint of the present to the already existing unity. In one historical moment, there *is* unity, despite its contingency and finitude. This temporal character of unity, its fortuitous and transitory character, opposes historical absolutism and relativism. Hence, one needs to reassess the role that academia plays in the history of the Yugoslav people.

5   Conclusion: From Neo- to Post- and Back

In discussing the dominant concepts of the theory of the avant-garde, one of the main problems is the misinterpretation of Peter Bürger's central category of the *historical avant-garde*. Instead of having an open, *relational* essence, it is defined as a closed historical category in the service of periodization in literary history. Thus, it is understood that by *historical avant-garde*, Bürger designates specific artistic phenomena that occurred during the early 20th century and largely ceased to exist due to the violent repression of progressive art in Soviet Russia and Nazi Germany during the 1930s. While this is the way Bürger historically defines the first phase of avant-garde artistic practices, it does not constitute the meaning of his widely misused term, whose crucial point of misunderstanding is the designation *historical*. By *historical* Bürger does not simply mean the *old* or the *first*. Instead, from the perspective of the "cognizing individual," the historical is that which came to its conclusion as a historical process. Hence, the avant-garde is a consequence of the historical process in the unfolding of the system of art. The notion of historical does not denote a *past event*. Instead, it is a varying complex of relations occurring in an epoch or a process of the present. This shift from chronology to temporality is announced in Bürger's comments of Adorno's definition of the avant-garde tradition:

> Through the avant-garde movements, the historical succession of techniques and styles has been transformed into a simultaneity of the radically disparate. The consequence is that no movement in the arts today can legitimately claim to be historically more advanced as art than any other. That the neo-avant-garde that makes it is least able to make good on this claim was explained in the preceding section. The time is gone when one could argue against the use of realistic techniques because the historical development had passed beyond them. To the degree Adorno does so, his theoretical position is itself part and parcel of the epoch of the historical avant-garde movements. That Adorno did not see the avant-garde movements as *historical* but as *still alive* in the present points to the same conclusion. (Bürger, *Theory* 63; emphasis added)

This distinction between what is "historical" and what is "still alive" pinpoints the processual and relational character of the notion of the historical avant-garde. Far from being a category of art history, the *historical avant-garde* describes the artistic present, which Bürger calls "the post-avant-garde phase" of Western art, and with it, the much-debated *neo-avant-garde*. From the perspective of these phases, Bürger understands the avant-gardes of the early 20th century as *historical* – this designation has no significance outside of the varying constellations.

The principal problem of the theory of the avant-garde and the potentials of neo-avant-garde practices is related to temporality, to the different ways in which the avant-garde reinstates (or not) the artistic, social, and political present. Deviation from Bürger's model implies treating the neo-avant-garde and the post-avant-garde as two different artistic phenomena that constitute different relations toward the avant-garde tradition.[25] Hence, they reveal themselves as two different *temporalities* of this tradition. As I have tried to demonstrate with the example of the Yugoslav artistic system in general, these two temporalities can be understood along the lines of Raymond Williams'

---

25 For Bürger, there is only the *post-avant-garde phase*, a post-stylistic period in the development of Western art, in which the neo-avant-garde is only one of many artistic formations. Therefore, any uncritical use of the term *post-avant-garde* in conjunction with the *historical avant-garde* for periodization represents a fundamental misunderstanding of Bürger's theory.

distinction between the *residual* and the *archaic* (Parežanin, "Within Reach"). Whereas the residual "has been effectively formed in the past, but it is still active in the cultural process – not only and often not at all as an element of the past, but as an effective element of the present," the archaic, on the other side, "is wholly organized as an element of the past, to be observed, to be examined, or even on occasion to be consciously 'revived,' in a deliberately specializing way." (22) The notion of the *residual* overcomes a one-dimensional description of the historicity of the avant-garde in Bürger's *Theory*.

The historicity of aesthetic categories establishes a link between Bürger, Benjamin, and Svetozar Petrović. In the article "Avant-garde and the Neo-avant-garde: An Attempt to Answer Certain Critics of Theory of the Avant-garde," Bürger elaborates on the importance of Benjamin's notion of the historical *constellation* in outlining the trajectory of avant-garde art from the beginning of the 20th century to the period of post-1968 disillusionment:

> I distinguished earlier between an unconscious, compulsive repetition and a conscious resumption. A third process needs to be distinguished from these two: return. A later event illuminates a previous one, without there being a demonstrable continuity between them. Here we are dealing with what Benjamin called a *constellation*. May 1968 made surrealism legible in a manner that it had not been legible previously. However, the connection between these two events cannot be understood according to the model of a repetition of which the subject is not aware or of a self-conscious resumption. In fact, it cannot be thought of in terms of a model derived from the subject at all: rather the second event, which possesses its own context of emergence, illuminates the first. This constellation underlies *Theory of the Avant-Garde*. From the standpoint of the utopia of 1968, whose failure was already unambiguously sketched out, the author read the historical avant-gardes and saw the failure of the May '68 movement prefigured in them. (Bürger, "Avant-garde" 711–712)

This understanding of historicity is grounded in Marx's *Grundrisse*, which contains a crucial methodological notion: not only is a "position that assumes it can understand past social formations without reference to the present of the researcher" impossible (Marx, as Bürger writes, does not even entertain the idea), but also the "progressive construction of history as the prehistory of the present" fails to grasp the entirety of a historical process (Bürger, *Theory* 20).

The prehistory of the present can be understood as a specific, dialectical understanding of the same problem Petrović addresses with his distinction between the *standpoint of the present* and the *standpoint of the past* discussed earlier in this chapter. If socialist Yugoslavia could be conceived as an avant-garde project realized on the level of society, then the question of understanding the temporality of the avant-garde, its historicity, is at the same time the central question of the post-socialist present and imagining of its alternatives. Literary studies in former Yugoslav countries can contribute to this emancipatory imagination by reinstating distinctions between *neo-* and *post-*, *residual* and *archaic*, "still alive" and "historical." As we have seen in studying the interplay between Sever's poetry and the Yugoslav project, reconsidering Yugoslav literature depends on the critical study of academic discourse. It turns Yugoslav literature into the means either of affirmation or negation of the Yugoslav project. From the standpoint of the present, the task is to examine whether such a disjunctive role is assigned to the post-Yugoslav literature.

References

Ahmad, Aijaz. "The Communist Manifesto and 'World Literature.'" *Social Scientist*, vol. 28, no. 7/8, 2000, pp. 3–30.

Bauer, Ludwig. "Josip Sever, život i poezija – Ako je ptica feniks doista ista." *Radio Gornji grad*, 2016, https://radiogornjigrad.wordpress.com/2016/11/01/ludwig-lujo-bauer-josip-sever-zivot-i-poezija-ako-je-ptica-feniks-doista-ista/.

Bauer, Ludwig. Public talk. *Zagrebačke posvete: Josip Sever / Između majmunskih zidova*. Pod starim krovovima. February 9, 2019.

Bošnjak, Branimir. *Modeli moderniteta: Dekonstrukcija svijeta / jezika i postavangardni estetizam u poeziji Josipa Severa*. Zagrebgrafo, 1998.

Brebanović, Predrag. *Avangarda Krležiana: pismo ne o avangardi*. Vuković & Runjić, Arkzin, 2016.

Bürger, Peter. *Theory of the Avant-garde*. Manchester University Press, 1984.

Bürger, Peter. "Avant-garde and Neo-avant-garde: an Attempt to Answer Certain Critics of Theory of the Avant-garde." *New Literary History*, no. 41, 2010, pp. 695–715.

Casanova, Pascale. *The World Republic of Letters*. Harvard University Press, 2007.

Flaker, Aleksandar. *Književne poredbe*. Naprijed, 1968.

Flaker, Aleksandar. "Hrvatske inačice ine avangarde." *Suvremeno hrvatsko pjesništvo*, edited by Ante Stamać. Zavod za znanost o književnosti Filozofskog fakulteta u Zagrebu, 1988.

Flaker, Aleksandar. "Povratak Majakovskog." *Matica hrvatska*, 2001 (Originally published in *Vijenac*, vol. IX, no. 198, pp. 20–21), http://www.matica.hr/vijenac/189/povratak-majakovskog-16467/.

Goethe, Johann W. von. *Faust I & II*, translation by Stuart Atkins. Princeton University Press, 2014.

Komelj, Miklavž. "Od nadrealističke do partizanske revolucije." *Lekcije o odbrani. Da li je moguće stvarati umetnost revolucionarno?*, edited by Miloš Miletić and Mirjana Radanović. Udruženje KURS, 2017.

Marx, Karl. *Critique of Hegel's "Philosophy of Right,"* translated by Annette Jolin and Joseph O'Malley. Cambridge University Press, 1970.

Milčec, Zvonimir. "Severova strana svijeta." *Večernji list*, May 20–21, p. 5, 1978.

Oraić, Dubravka. "Na kraju avangardnog raja." *Suvremeno hrvatsko pjesništvo*, edited by Ante Stamać. Zavod za znanost o književnosti Filozofskog fakulteta u Zagrebu, 1988.

Parežanin, Lujo. "Reinterpretacija avangardnih postupaka u pjesništvu Dubravke Oraić Tolić." *Književna smotra*, vol. 43, no. 159 (I), 2011, pp. 131–139.

Parežanin, Lujo. "Pjesništvo Josipa Severa i problemi proučavanja neoavangardne književnosti," *Umjetnost riječi*, vol. 59, no. 1–2, 2015, pp. 155–176.

Parežanin, Lujo. "Within Reach of the Optimal Projection: Yugoslavia and the General Theory of the Avant-garde." *5th Sarajevo Philology Meeting*. Filozofski fakultet, Sarajevo. September 21, 2018. Paper presentation.

Perkins, David. *Is Literary History Possible?* The Johns Hopkins University Press, 1992.

Petrović, Svetozar. *Priroda kritike*. Samizdat B92, 2003.

Postnikov, Boris. *Postjugoslavenska književnost?* Sandorf, 2012.

Ramazani, Jahan. *A Transnational Poetics*. University of Chicago Press, 2009.

Sever, Josip. *Borealni konj*. Mladost, 1989.

Strukić, Kristian. "Projekt 'Zagrebački kvartovi' Muzeja Grada Zagreba." *Muzej Grada Zagreba*, 2010, http://www.mgz.hr/UserFiles/file/Strukic%20Kristian%20-%20Zagrebacki%20kvartovi%20IM_41.pdf.

Tatomir, Vladimir. "Revalorizacija arhitektonske i urbanističke cjeline zagrebačkog naselja Zapruđe – istraživanje povijesnog, prostornog i društvenog naslijeđa kroz project Muzej Kvarta," graduate thesis. *Digitalni arhiv Filozofskog fakulteta Sveučilišta u Zagrebu*, 2016, http://darhiv.ffzg.unizg.hr/id/eprint/7070/1/ZAPRUDE_MUZEJ_KVARTA-VladimirTatomir_09062015.pdf.

Williams, Raymond. *Marxism and Literature*. Oxford University Press, 1978.

SECTION 2

From the Time That Belongs to No-One to Temporalities of Non-belonging

CHAPTER 4

The End of the World as We Know It? Anti-utopia in Post-Yugoslav Literature

Boris Postnikov

1 There Is an Alternative after All?

The breakup of the Socialist Federative Republic of Yugoslavia was an exceptional event in the context of the so-called Eastern European post-communist transition[1] due to – of course – its brutally violent character, as well as the highly specific position of former Yugoslavia as a non-aligned, relatively liberal socialist state that from the mid-60s onwards implemented workers' self-management and strong elements of the market economy. However, precisely because it was unique, it can be understood as crucial evidence of the uniformity of the overall post-communist 'transition' process – for no matter how idiosyncratic it was, the breakup of Yugoslavia ultimately led all post-Yugoslav countries towards the capitalist mode of production, multi-party systems, and the inevitable perspective of Euro-Atlantic integration. From the beginning, their destiny was framed within what Francis Fukuyama in the late 80s notoriously designated as "the end of history" (xi), the final global victory of capitalism and liberal democracy over their opponents. Fukuyama's words became the most emblematic proclamation of the neoliberal 'there is no alternative' doctrine, the motto of times in which – according to another already over-quoted sentence, usually attributed to Marxist scholar Fredric Jameson – it became "(…) easier to imagine the end of the world than to imagine the end of capitalism" (76).[2]

For the first time since this great historical triumph, the powerful global hegemony of neoliberal politics was strongly challenged, around 2008, when the financial crisis exploded and transformed itself into the worst economic

---

1   A persuasive critique of the concept of the 'post-communist transition' can be found in Boris Buden's essay "Children of Postcommunism."
2   Actually, Jameson himself attributed this sentence to an unknown author: "Someone once said that it is easier to imagine the end of the world than to imagine the end of capitalism" (76).

recession since the 1920s and 30s. On an ideological level, this was also the crisis of the legitimation of the global capitalist system – popular movements opposed the dominance of market relations, Marxist and socialist theories suddenly became influential again and the realization that, after all, there could be – and maybe should be – an alternative to capitalism worked its way through social and political field.[3]

This is, in brief, the wider context in which I would like to pose the central questions of this text: how did post-Yugoslav writers respond to the crisis of capitalism? Or, in other words: when Jameson's statement that it is "easier to imagine the end of world than to imagine the end capitalism" suddenly was not completely true anymore, how did post-Yugoslav writers try to imagine the end of the world? And how did they try to imagine – or failed to imagine – the end of capitalism?

I attempt to answer these questions through a brief comparative analysis of three novels: *Promijeni me* (*Change Me*) by Slovenian author Andrej Blatnik, *Planet Friedman* by Bosnian-Herzegovinian author Josip Mlakić, and *Lomljenje vjetra* (*Smashing the Wind*) by Croatian writer Edo Popović. Mlakić and Popović wrote their novels, respectively, in 2012 and 2011, when the economic crisis was at its peak, and Blatnik published *Promijeni me* in 2008 in the wake of the recession, so the context of global economic turmoil ultimately – although unexpectedly – influenced the reception of his work. None of these three novels had a major impact and none of them are considered a book for which the last decade or so of post-Yugoslav literary production will be remembered, but all of them enjoyed considerable success, making the shortlists of national and regional literary awards and getting predominately positive reviews, which – along with the fact that Blatnik, Mlakić, and Popović were already well-known and prominent figures in the post-Yugoslav literary field – allows us to read them as representative works of certain post-Yugoslav cultural and literary and tendencies in the years of economic recession.

One of these tendencies, for example, would be a shift towards themes related to the precarization of work, observable in the novels *Područje bez signala* (*No-Signal Area*) by Robert Perišić and *Ljubavni roman* (*Love Novel*) by Ivana Sajko, and short-story collections such as *Radnici i seljaci* (*Workers and Peasants*) by Viktor Ivančić or *O ljubavi, batinama i revoluciji* (*On Love, Beatings, and Revolution*) by Nora Verde (Postnikov). Another tendency, and

---

3 In the post-Yugoslav context, possibly the best example of this tendency is the formation of explicitly anti-capitalist political parties such as Slovenian Iniciativa za demokratični socializem (Initiative for Democratic Socialism, now part of Levica – The Left) or Croatian Radnička fronta (Workers' Front), both in 2014.

the one with which I will be dealing here, is a more formal one: the shift towards the dystopian and anti-utopian genre. Apart from Blatnik's, Mlakić's, and Popović's novels, books such as *Dolazak* (*The Coming*) and *Homo sucker* (*Homo Sucker*) by Andrej Nikolaidis, *Kriza* (*The Crisis*) by Tonći Kožul and Velimir Grgić, *2084: Kuća Velikog Jada* (*2084: The House of Great Misery*) by Ivo Balenović, *Razbijanje* (*Smashing*) by Miloš Živanović, *Neznanom junaku* (*To an Unknown Hero*) by Sreten Ugričić, or *NDH 2033* (*The Independent State of Croatia 2033*) by multiple authors, as well as theatrical pieces such as *Budućnost je sada* (*The Future is Now*) by the Montažstroj collective and movies such as *The Show Must Go On* by Nevio Marasović and *Ederlezi Rising* by Lazar Bodroža – all produced after the beginning of the crisis – testify to the strong shift towards dystopian and anti-utopian fiction among post-Yugoslav authors, most of whom previously had not shown an interest in these genres.[4] They use to write about the past and the present; now, suddenly, they turn their attention towards the future, opening up a completely new temporal dimension. This dimension is conceptualized as a consequential outcome of already-existing capitalistic tendencies and therefore provides us with a critical perspective on the socio-political system we live in. One could say that this dystopian/anti-utopian shift marks the end of 'the end of history' hypothesis. What was once understood as the end of history – the global victory of capitalism and liberal democracy over their opponents – now becomes, in a radical temporal turn, the beginning of a catastrophic future. However, Jameson sees the dystopian/anti-utopian genre as inherently reactionary, one that opposes and blocks visions of a post-capitalist utopian future. In *American Utopia* he states that "[t]he recrudescence and reflowering of dystopias in our present culture suggests deeply rooted anxieties (...)" (54) and "(...) the terror of the collective as such, the existential fear of losing our individuality in some vaster collective being" (54). The critical part of our task is therefore to answer the question: can contemporary post-Yugoslav literature challenge this view?

Before we proceed to examine the scope and implications of alternative fictional worlds created in post-Yugoslav dystopian and anti-utopian fiction as they are imagined in the three aforementioned novels, it is necessary to provide a few basic genre and sub-genre definitions. Here I rely on the work of Darko Suvin, who is considered one of the most influential science fiction the-

---

4   In his text "Trend distopijskog u suvremenoj hrvatskoj prozi" ("The Dystopian in Contemporary Croatian Prose") Igor Gajin already provided the basic theoretical mapping of this tendency. However – as is obvious from the title of his work – Gajin focused on contemporary Croatian literary production, leaving the broader post-Yugoslav context aside.

oreticians today and one of the most internationally prominent post-Yugoslav literary scholars.

2 Utopia, Eutopia, Dystopia, Anti-utopia

In his seminal book *Metamorphoses of Science Fiction* Suvin gives an almost classical definition of SF as the "literature of cognitive estrangement" (4), building upon the concepts of *ostranenie* by Russian formalists and *Verfremdungseffekt* by Bertolt Brecht. Consequently, utopia – understood as the sociopolitical subgenre of science fiction – is defined as "(...) the verbal construction of a particular quasi-human community where socio-political institutions, norms and individual relationships are organized according to a more perfect principle than in the author's community, this construction being based on estrangement arising out of an alternative historical hypothesis" (49). The advantage of this definition is at least twofold: on the one hand, it points out the strictly formal, literary aspect of the genre and, on the other, it emphasises its attempt to articulate a fictional critique of an actually existing society. In the essay "A Tractate on Dystopia 2001," Suvin proceeds to articulate a more detailed diversification of utopian sub-genres. Here he does not postulate utopia as a construction of a 'better' or 'ideal' world any more, but as "(...) the construction of a particular community where sociopolitical institutions, norms, and relationships between people are organized according to a *radically different principle* than in the author's community" (383). If this community is better than the existing one, we are dealing with *eutopia* (from Ancient Greek: 'a good place'). If it is worse, we are dealing with *dystopia*. There is one final division: dystopia then splits into *simple dystopia* – a plain structural inversion of eutopia – and an *anti-utopia* which "(...) is explicitly designed to refute a currently proposed eutopia. It is a pretended eutopia – a community whose hegemonic principles pretend to its being more perfectly organized than any thinkable alternative" (385), while it is in fact "significantly less perfect than an alternative, a polemic nightmare" (ibid.). Simply put, the anti-utopia is a fictional critique of an existing hegemony, an attack on the ideological claim that we live in the best of all possible worlds. Or – to put it another way – that we live at the end of history. Strictly speaking, all of our three novels – Blatnik's, Mlakić's and Popović's – qualify as anti-utopian prose.

Of course, in the context of Suvin's genre and sub-genre delineation, a question immediately arises: by what criteria do we consider one community 'better' or 'worse' than another? The answer is implicit: Suvin writes his essay from a Marxist position that is, of course, straightforwardly critical towards global capitalism and frequently invokes the perspective of ideologically dominated and economically exploited classes. The same, class-based criteria for the valuation of communities can be found more explicitly in Fredric Jameson's essay "The Politics of Utopia":

> The point about ideology is not a particularly complicated one: it sets out from the conviction that we are all ideologically situated, we are all shackled to an ideological subject-position, we are all determined by class and class history, even when we try to resist or escape it. And for those unfamiliar with this ideological perspectivism or class standpoint theory, it is perhaps necessary to add that it holds for everyone, left or right, progressive or reactionary, worker as well as boss, and underclasses, marginals, ethnic or gender victims, fully as much as for the ethnic, race or gender mainstreams. (46)

The consequence of this view, as Jameson underlines, is not only that all utopias spring from a specific class position, but that their fundamental thematization – the root-of-all-evil diagnosis in terms of which they are each framed – will also reflect a specific class-historical standpoint or perspective.

Here we can put aside the question of whether this bold hypothesis actually holds true and whether all dystopian and anti-utopian narratives ever constructed can be best understood through the class-theory lenses, because those we are dealing with evidently can – they are problematizing the actually existing capitalist system and therefore unsurprisingly rely on the vision of a class-divided society. Having detected the dystopian and anti-utopian tendencies of post-Yugoslav literature in the years of global economic crisis, and having suggested some basic insights into the nature of this literary genre and its socio-political implications, we can finally turn to our three post-Yugoslav anti-utopian novels. Let us start with a very short overview of their plots.

3 Anti-utopian Landscapes of Post-Yugoslav Literature

The story of Andrej Blatnik's *Promijeni me* is set in an undefined, yet evidently near future which in many ways resembles the present of Slovenia's post-socialist transition, slightly sharpening its consequences through a critique of commercialization, competition, social stratification and the ideology of consumerism.

It was a good time. People grew tired of wars, decided to give peace a chance, the moment of compromise arrived and the soldiers of once confronted sides sat together, violators and victims, and discussed how to split up the profits. The business went worldwide. It got accustomed to the state market. Where once was communism, now replaced by the more efficient capitalism, transformed communists took positions on supervisory boards, distributed the parade horses of the state-owned economy among themselves through privatization, and started sharing dividends, at the same time lamenting about the youth who still can't understand that the time of leisure is over, that everybody must be responsible for themselves, instead of requesting free education and free health insurance. (30)[5]

The story follows Borut, an extremely successful copywriter, who grows tired of his work, lifestyle, and the 'false values' he promotes through commercials, and decides to leave his career and his family. It is told from the interchangeable perspectives of Borut and his wife – while she manages the household and children, he starts searching for a more 'authentic' life. At one point, the omnipotent General Director of a megacorporation Borut worked for calls him back to create his biggest advertising campaign yet. Borut refuses, gets into a violent fight with the director and wounds him, but eventually decides not to kill him, explaining that even the murder of an evident first-class capitalist villain, responsible for the misery of many, would be immoral. "I won't kill. If you kill him, you become the same as he" (84). In the end, Borut comes home and his wife is now the one who goes away, leaving him with the children.

The story of Mlakić's *Planet Friedman* is set in a distant future, in a time after the great war between the so-called 'Friedmanists,' followers of the neoliberal guru Milton Friedman, and the 'Keynesianists,' followers of John Maynard Keynes, the proponent of a more socially sensible capitalism; two minor groups also took part in the war: the anarchists and the 'States.'[6] The Friedmanists are the ones who won and the planet Earth is now called Planet Friedman,

---

[5] Translations from the three novels are mine.
[6] This articulation of social antagonisms seems to be structured around two binary oppositions: economic (capitalism vs. anti-capitalism) and political (state control vs. individual freedom). Therefore, the 'Friedmanists' would be the proponents of individual freedom and free market capitalism (which ironically, but inevitably ends in the suppressing of individual freedoms by big corporations), The 'Keynesianists' would be proponents of state-controlled capitalism, the 'anarchists' are fighters against capitalism and state control and, finally, the 'States' want to supress individual freedom and control the market. It is interesting that only the fourth position is not occupied by some kind of grassroots social movement: where one

ruled by the rigorous principles of a neoliberal economy, profit-maximization, the complete absence of emotions from human relations, and the unprecedented power of big corporations. "One should be loyal to the market as an organism, corporations are the components of the perfect world. (...) Emotions are useless ballast" (10). Invoking the basic principles of world-systems theory, Planet Friedman is divided into zones – zone A for the privileged minority, zone B for the poor, zone C for the poorest of the poor – and the reader follows two main characters, Dr Gerhard Schmidt and athletic superstar Paula Bolt, while they travel through all three zones and discover the whole truth about Planet Friedman. Their mission is part of a complicated conspiracy that starts to unfold with the beginning of the war between the Friedmanists and the organization Blacktooth, a new radical paramilitary force that wants to overcome the rule of neoliberalism. Along the way, Gerhard realizes that the greed and insensitiveness of the Friedmanist free-market ideology and the fear and terror that Blacktooth terrorists bring are ultimately just two sides of the same coin. "Blacktooth doesn't need a Saviour (...). They want to break down that myth. There can be only one god on this planet: Blacktooth. Gods don't tolerate competition" (220). In the end, he, Paula and his son flee to a free space in a still uncontrolled zone.

Finally, the plot of Edo Popović's *Lomljenje vjetra* is set in Croatia in 2020: the country is divided into territory controlled by Holding – basically a conglomerate of a few relatively big cities protected by high walls where the rich minority lives – and the rest, populated by the poor. In these wastelands a terrorist group called Nejestivi (The Inedibles) kidnaps, tortures and kills high-profile managers of large corporations: the novel actually begins with a scene of abduction and execution followed by an argument between two Nejestivi members about the moral justification of murder.

> I can't believe you don't feel any remorse for what you're doing, Fractal Girl said.
> Remorse, he shrugged. We can't allow ourselves to be sceptical for one moment, let alone to feel remorse. And why should I feel anything for these bastards, anyway?
> Because they're human beings, for example.

---

would structurally anticipate the rebellious group of 'Marxists' or 'socialists' or 'radical leftists,' we find the ominous power of the state apparatus. This inconsistency, as we will see, is not symptomatic only of the shortcomings of Mlakić's fictional critique of the actually existing political and economic system, but also for the shortcomings of post-Yugoslav anti-utopian social critique *tout court*.

> Here you go again. The mere fact that they walk on two legs and talk, eat and defecate, doesn't make them human. As I see it, they are non-humans, and I sincerely don't understand why anyone would have mercy on them. Don't you understand that those people have that much only because others have nothing? And that they have that much not because they are more hard-working and more competent, but because they are greedier and thoughtless. (15)

After this quarrel, the story follows different characters through extensive prolepses and analepses – for example, we learn about the secret society of Dark Hoods, people who used to live in some sort of anti-consumerist heterotopia inside capitalist society, refusing to work for money and buy commodities. Finally, different storylines are resolved mostly in an escapist way: a character commits suicide after he kills a police officer, another finds peace in Spain working for a small shop-owner.

After briefly examining the major motifs and problems raised in the three post-Yugoslav anti-utopian novels, we encounter the central question of our research: how can they be read in light of Jameson's claim that it is easier to imagine the end of the world than to imagine the end of capitalism? First of all, it seems that this statement unfortunately still holds true. Although Blatnik's, Mlakić's and Popović's novels could be understood – at least at first glance – as highly critical towards the capitalist system, all of them evidently avoid articulating a systemic alternative to capitalism. Moreover, if read closely, they turn out to be not radical fictional critiques of capitalism, but rather critiques of capitalism's exaggerated 'malformations,' first of all neoliberalism. By attacking the unleashed, unrestrained, radically free-market system, they tacitly advocate for somewhat more controlled and more 'humane' capitalism. That is probably most obvious in the case of *Planet Friedman*, where – as we have already seen – the main opposition to the Friedmanists' ideology consists in Keynesianism, a view that promotes 'moderate capitalism.' Also, the case of Blacktooth movement shows that an alternative to the neoliberal system could be just as bad, or even worse. In Blatnik's novel, the main target of critique is the mere excessiveness of consumerism. One can find numerous passages that confirm this hypothesis, such as:

> Whenever he told them that there was no more fast food in the kitchen, his children would find a way to get it elsewhere. They would sign up for any known 'eat as much as you can' competition. (…) Borut never dared to forbid them to take part in public gluttony; he was afraid that information about him demotivating the children's competitiveness would get

to the school's advisory services and they would immediately send an emergency team to his house to take the kids away and put them in more socialized custody. (16–17)

There are extensive passages describing shopping practices:

> Children would stare at store windows with astonishment, looking at the shiniest things. They would spell out the bright labels and compete to be the first to see words such as CHEAP! OPPORTUNITY! and LAST DAY OF THE SALE! The logic was not clear at all. Immediately after the sale started and shoppers who had waited all night got out of their sleeping bags, rushing to get the objects of their desire with detailed lists in their hands, every retailer would follow their own strategy. Some would end the sale immediately, assuming the shoppers wouldn't notice, and even if they did, they'd still think their prices were the best. Others, having sold out the most wanted articles, would buy the same ones from other retailers, triple their prices, and then put them on a 50% discount. People would look at their contactor devices, check the prices, nod their heads, and fill their shopping carts with satisfaction. (127–128)

Apart from shopping practices, the repertoire of consumer society motifs in *Promijeni me* includes advertising (28–29, 113), the commercialization of the most intimate emotions such as romantic love (118–121) and a media-shaped reality (122).

In Popović's *Lomljenje vjetra*, on the other hand, we occasionally find parts that thematise the systemic problems of capitalism – for example, a short dialogue between the Nejestivi terrorist Gardener and his hostage, the high profile manager Milinović, in which questions of wage labour and commodity value are raised.

> Yesterday you took my wallet, said Milinović.
> The Gardener reached into his pocket, took the wallet out and showed it to him.
> Is this your wallet?
> Milinović nodded.
> The Gardener took the banknotes out of the wallet and threw them on the floor, keeping only twenty euros in his hand.
> What's this worth?
> Twenty euros, replied Milinović in confusion.
> Twenty euros, said the Gardener. And what are twenty euros worth?

> I don't get it, said Milinović.
> What is the worth of twenty euros' worth? explained the Gardener.
> I still don't get it, said Milinović. What you're saying is completely unintelligible.
> So you're not that smart after all. Just because you don't get something you say it's unintelligible. OK, let me try to explain it in another way. Let's say that you big shots who make decisions about everything and everyone got together and made a deal to pay a needlewoman two euros for an hour of work. (…) So, ten hours of her work are worth twenty euros. OK? In ten hours she can make a suit that, by the way, sells for a thousand euros. Let's put aside the question of who gets the difference in money for the moment. We can agree that the worth of twenty euros is one suit, is that right? So here's my question – what's your hourly wage? Somewhere around five hundred euros, I would say. And can you, my friend, make twenty five suits in an hour? (33)

This episode seems to articulate the basic principles of labour theory of value and exploitation of labour, which could be understood as theoretical cornerstones of a systemic critique of capitalism. Ultimately, however, it will provide a vision of capitalism being 'unjust' because of basic human moral flaws such as greed and the arrogance of the managers: "The main problem is that you and others like you started to believe that your blather is more important than someone's work (…) Scammers and jerks like you took over the world, don't you think?" (34). This view seems to obfuscate the systemic socio-economic relations set by the predominance of the market economy and commodity production. For at the level of systemic capitalist relations, as Karl Marx famously noted, "[t]he persons exist for one another merely as representatives of, and, therefore, as owners of commodities. In the course of our investigation we shall find, in general, that the characters who appear on the economic stage are but the personifications of the economic relations that exist between them" (85–86).

4   Anti-utopia and the (Lack of) Systemic Critique

The 'inadequacy' of the post-Yugoslav anti-utopian critique of capitalism developed here, which deals with its effects rather than its causes, has at least two interesting consequences. The first one is that all three authors tend to promote moral dilemmas as fundamental problems. When they write about the violence of the oppressed towards the oppressors, the question of its moral justification is inevitably put forward: the violence here does not have the political dimension of, let us say, the rebellion of the working class in class warfare, but instead becomes a question of personal choice. Second, the narrative resolution of all three novels is an escapist one: the escape of the main characters – in the form of suicide, fleeing to parts of the world still uncontrolled by political power, leaving their family or finding some sort of inner peace in a quiet, reclusive life – seems to be the only possible way of dealing with an unjust system. Both approaches – the moralization of the class conflict and escapism as the false resolution of that conflict – are fundamentally individualistic, which leads all three narratives into a deadlock of ideological contradiction. The neoliberal-capitalist system they are criticising is, of course, ultimately based on the ideology of individualism: "Neoliberalism is in the first instance a theory of political economic practices that proposes that human well-being can best be advanced by liberating individual entrepreneurial freedoms and skills within an institutional framework characterized by strong private property rights, free markets, and free trade" (Harvey 2). Yet, our three novels cannot find a way to strongly criticise the individualistic neoliberal ideology in any other manner than from the standpoint of 'methodological individualism.' If the possibility of collective resistance is given, it is almost immediately written off, as in the case of Mlakić's Blacktooth movement that spreads fear and terror or Popović's Nejestivi terrorist group that by the end of the novel falls apart. Therefore, these novels in no way challenge Jameson's view of anti-utopia as an inherently 'reactionary' genre. If anything, they provide us with new examples of his already quoted notion of "(...) the terror of the collective as such, the existential fear of losing our individuality in some vaster collective being" (54).

Of course, if we ascribe the critical shortcomings of these three post-Yugoslav anti-utopian novels to their authors' lack of political imagination, we would be only perpetuating the same mistake rooted in individualistic methodology. It is therefore more productive to read them as symptoms of a certain broader ideological and political context, one defined not only by the severe problems of the existing capitalist system, but also by the great historical defeat of anti-capitalist collective agents such as the Communist Party. Deprived of the plausible notion of a systemic anti-capitalist alternative articulated in some sort of strong collective political agency, these novels are inevitably condemned to a narrative perspective of the fictional characters' personal choices, therefore morally obscuring the political dimension of capitalism and fighting the omnipresent ideology of individualism from the methodologically individualistic positions in an already-lost war. Of course, none of this aims to deny them a certain imaginativeness, political impulse, or insightfulness in their fictional articulations of social conflicts. It merely means to point out how hard it is to imagine the end of capitalism even in the years of capitalism's most severe crisis.

References

Blatnik, Andrej. *Promijeni m*e. Translated by Jagna Pogačnik, EPH & Novi Liber, 2010.
Buden, Boris. "Children of Postcommunism." *Radical Philosophy*, no. 159, 2010, pp. 18–25.
Fukuyama, Francis. *End of History and the Last Man*. The Free Press, 1992.
Gajin, Igor. "Trend distopijskog u suvremenoj hrvatskoj prozi." *Anafora*, no. 3, 2015, pp. 41–58.
Harvey, David. *A Brief History of Neoliberalism*. Oxford University Press, 2007.
Jameson, Fredric. "Future City." *New Left Review*, no. 21, 2003, pp. 65–79.
Jameson, Fredric. "The Politics of Utopia." *New Left Review*, no. 25, 2004, pp. 35–54.
Jameson, Fredric. "An American Utopia." *An American Utopia. Dual Power and the Universal Army*, edited by Slavoj Žižek, Verso, 2016, pp. 1–96.
Marx, Karl. *Kapital. Kritika političke ekonomije*. Institut za izučavanje radničkog pokreta & Prosveta, 1974.
Mlakić, Josip. *Planet Friedman*. Fraktura, 2012.
Popović, Edo. *Lomljenje vjetra*. OceanMore, 2011.
Postnikov, Boris. "Povratak radnika. Književna reartikulacija klasnog antagonizma u postjugoslavenskom kontekstu." *Tranzicija i kulturno pamćenje*, edited by Virna Karlić, Sanja Šakić, and Dušan Marinković, Srednja Europa, 2017, pp. 187–196.
Suvin, Darko. *Metamorphoses of Science Fiction*. Yale University Press, 1979.
Suvin, Darko. *Defined by a Hollow*. Peter Lang AG, 2010.

CHAPTER 5

Post-Yugoslav Dystopian Dilemmas and Writing the History of the Future: Alternative Version or Parodic Subversion?

Miranda Levanat-Peričić

1   Millennial Endings and the Dystopian Turn to History

Although it seems contradictory, in portraying and writing about the future, utopian and dystopian thought always goes back to the past. This focus on the past, which narratives about the future are concerned with, has led G.S. Morson to base the difference between utopia and dystopia[1] precisely on their different relationship to history. "Whereas utopias describe an escape *from* history, these anti-utopias describe an escape or attempted escape, *to* history, which is to say, to the world of contingency, conflict, and uncertainty" (128).

Starting from this point, I will attempt to interpret the temporality of contemporary (new millennium) dystopian novels concerning their relationship to history. I assume that there are two fundamental directions in the dystopian evaluation of the past: an antimodernist trend, which affirms and supports tradition with particular regard to cultural and literary heritage, and a Menippean or satiric one, which works subversively with history and all canonized values, whether it be social, cultural, or artistic. First of all, the appearance of "new-millennium anti-modernism" is comparable to the features of anti-modernism that came into existence in the decades around the turn of the century. Then, due to sudden changes in social relations, there emerged conservative tendencies marked with a "pervasive sense of loss" (Jessup 3), a pessimism and criticism based on the belief that "civil society is a violent negation of previous epochs or primordial times" (Kravar 85). According to Lynda Jessup, that kind

---

[1] G.S. Morson uses the term *anti-utopia* instead of *dystopia*. Krishan Kumar also uses the term *anti-utopia* instead of dystopia, but he explicitly stresses that he uses these terms as synonyms ("Utopija i anti-utopija" 77). There are some approaches which insist on distinguishing between dystopia and anti-utopia, but for this work, this distinction is not relevant. Moreover, it is not easy to draw a sharp line even between utopia and anti-utopia/dystopia. Margaret Atwood has coined the word *ustopia* precisely to point out the mutual permeation of all these genres (66).

of tendency manifested "itself not only in the sense of alienation but also in a longing for the types of physical or spiritual experience in Utopian futures and imagined pasts. As such, it embraces what was then a desire for the type of 'authentic' experience supposedly embodied in preindustrial societies – in medieval communities or Oriental cultures, in the Primitive, the Traditional, or the Folk" (3). However, as the "pervasive sense of loss" connected with the decades around the turn of the century, anti-modernism can also be detected at the end of the 20th century as a reaction to the great social and political changes of that time. Actually, starting from "the awareness of decline" which is in the core of anti-modernism, Arthur Versluis suggested that "it is not until the beginning of the twenty-first century that we see a more general acknowledgement of pervasive, all-encompassing decline in all three areas of nature, culture, and religion" (98). Thus, while in the 19th century, enthusiasm about material progress was omnipresent, and accepted even among the socialists, who, as Jackson Lears noticed, "attacked the maldistribution of wealth, not the fundamental beneficence of economic growth," today this "late-nineteenth-century progressive faith" survives only "among real estate developers, corporate planners, and unreconstructed Keynesian economists" (7). The more industry and technology develop, the more increase in the sense of ecological, cultural and moral decline there is.

On the other hand, there is a specific natural or logical relationship between 'endism' as an idea of the end of history and the 'real' historical period of the millennial ending. As Krishan Kumar pointed out, "millennial endings even more than centurial ones give rise to millennial imagining" (63). Still, the most important event and the decisive impulse for a dystopian turn at the end of the first millennium, in Kumar's opinion, was the collapse of socialism: "Since socialism of one kind or another had become the central component of the modern utopia, the fate of socialism in the last part of our century must seem to bury utopia comprehensively" ("The End of Socialism?" 64). Thus, the end of the millennium and the fall of utopia could give a powerful boost to the development of an apocalyptic imagination.

2 Dystopian Anti-modernism and the Post-Yugoslav Dystopian Turn

As it has already been observed, contemporary Croatian literature in the first decade of the new millennium shows an evident "dystopian trend" (Gajin 42), which some critics interpreted as a non-literary confrontation with the crisis of the capitalistic system that had no alternative form after the decline of socialism. Moreover, this narrative turn toward the disastrous future can be read as an "anti-systemic message" (Postnikov 3). In post-Yugoslav circumstances specifically, the connection between the antimodernist mood and dystopian narratives can be regarded as a reaction to the collapse of the political community and the establishment of national states, which in Croatia was followed by war and economic transition accompanied by corrupt and uncontrolled privatization. According to this, the antimodernist belief about the end of the time, about the state immediately facing a catastrophe, has found its expression precisely in the endism of the dystopian narrative.

Although it can be connected with Sontag's "imagination of disaster" as a narrative of warning, dystopia is an ideal form of expression of antimodernist mood. In a general sense, a dystopian scenario points to a dark place where we will arrive if we continue to move the way we have already started. In that sense, the dystopian warning is mainly related to the undesirable side effects of 'progress,' and the content of the warning depends on the individual diagnosis of a social illness or aberration. The comparison between modernity and anti-modernism made by Arthur Versluis is based precisely on the contrast between the concepts of 'progress' and 'decline.' At the core of anti-modernism, he notices "the awareness of decline" and a belief "that technological-industrial development has destructive consequences in three primary and intertwined areas: nature, culture, and religion." (97) Narratives of natural, cultural, and religious decline will be analyzed separately as examples of the antimodernist core of the dystopian genre.

2.1   Narratives of Cultural and Natural Decline

Some of the already-mentioned new-millennial dystopian novels give their warnings in the spirit of anti-modernism, which means through antitheses such as nature/civilization, emotion/reason, or ideal/real, where the first member of the opposition is valued positively. From the antimodernist point of view, nature is a lost paradise, civilization is characterized by greed, and modern consumer society is an immoral society of the spectacle. In contemporary Croatian literature I have found three such examples – the novels by Edo Popović (*Lomljenje vjetra, Wind Breaking*, 2011) and Josip Mlakić (*Planet Friedman*, 2012), and then in a particular way the novel *Rat za peti okus* (*War for the Fifth Taste*, 2015) by Veljko Barbieri. Popović's and Mlakić's dystopias present very close worlds. Although Popović's dystopia is located in a future Croatia, and Mlakić's society is not specifically nationally marked, these two novels are comparable at the level of the type of warning they express and, accordingly, with regard to their diagnoses of social problems. In the center of Popović's and Mlakić's dystopic societies is the antithesis of the sick and healthy body, the human body that is the metonymy of the body of the planet and society as a whole. Mlakić' s Planet Friedman is a place governed by market greed, where earning profits has assumed religious dimensions. Accordingly, in a sacred book of so-called "Friedman's Sayings," one of them goes: "The market just has to remove its gangrenous tissue" (15).[2] This almost explicitly coincides with the situation in Popović's novel – thus, when the way of life advocated by the so-called Dark Hoods (a society of the unemployed who live on waste collection) is suddenly considered a "sick tissue" to be removed by the logic of the "healthy body" of a consumer society: The reasoning of the Croatian authorities at the beginning of the 21st century was: "We believe that consumer society is a bloodstream. Everything that is part of the system is excellent and healthy. What is not connected to the bloodstream is sick and needs to be removed" (Popović 55).

The antithesis of a sick and healthy society is also built on the plan of emotions. Namely, in both novels, suppressed emotions create a collective psychosis, and healing is achieved through art – Mlakić's hero finds sadness in Yeats' poetry, and Popović's hero in an unusual scene of an old man crying while listening to Janet Baker's arias. In both novels an antimodernist topic of 'paradise lost' is being developed in the form of nature that has withdrawn before the harmful influence of civilization, i.e., the consumer society that abuses natural resources. In Mlakić's novel, the space of infertile, 'dead land' spreads, glow-worms are extinct, cranes are exterminated, and dogs are infected with rabies. In Popović's novel, there is also the figure of the original noble savage, who lives with sheep on Velebit Mountain, gives names to the wolves, collects medicinal herbs, makes tea, and meditates. But his sheep and dogs get killed by Italian poachers.

2.2 Ecotopia as a Special Narrative Form of Natural Decline

During the 1970s and 1980s, ecology was the mainspring for alternative presentations of modern society. Then a new vision of a future society organized by ecological principles began to develop. After the title of Ernest Callenbach's novel *Ecotopia: The Notebooks and Reports of William Weston* (1975), this kind of futuristic vision was called "ecological utopia" or "ecotopia" (Kumar, "Utopija i antiutopija" 88). Since it is based on a criticism of technological progress, economic growth, and consumer mentality, the ecotopia can also be considered an antimodernist literary form. The structure of an environmentally conscious society in an ecotopia is constructed on the idea of respect for nature, i.e., a

---

2   The novels interpreted in this paper are not published in English translation, so all examples of translations from Croatian to English are mine.

life in harmony with nature based on traditional food cultivation and organic products.

Food is a frequent topic of dystopia, but it has a different meaning in the following two dystopian subgenres: it functions in a completely different way in antimodernist dystopian novels than in a Menippean dystopia, where it appears in the context of Bakhtin's "material-bodily principle of life" in the so-called "feasting pictures" which parody serious and spiritual themes. The best example of this is the dystopian Menippea of *The Slynx* (2000) by Tatyana Tolstaya, in which the changes of social status and the acquisition of political power by the main hero Benedikt Karpich are closely followed by the food he eats, which 'grows' in size from the scale of worms and mice into full-sized refined dishes of French cuisine.

The Croatian author who is unavoidable when it comes to food and dystopia is Veljko Barbieri. In his most famous "gastro-dystopia" from the Yugoslav period, *Epitaf za carskog gurmana* (*Epitaph for the Imperial Gourmand* 1983), food is a central semantic complex. Barbieri goes back to the theme of food in 2015 in the dystopian novel *Rat za peti okus* (*War for the Fifth Taste*). However, while in this dystopian Menippea a grotesque exaggeration of food in the style of Rabelais is typical, and the topic of table conversation is an ideal opportunity for rudeness, in Barbieri's novel, food catalogs and menus celebrate modesty, and consuming food nurtures the cult of good behavior at the table. Furthermore, in the novel *Rat za peti okus* (*War for the Fifth Taste*), in addition to the word 'food,' the most common word is 'tradition.' Food is not a side-effect with the function of a parody of serious topics, but an important topic understood as an identity marker in the relationship between 'our' (domestic) and 'their' (foreign) food. The war in the novel is fought between two gastronomic armies – an army gathered around the restaurant with the symbolic name of Arka (a clear allusion to Noah's Ark) is fighting for its native cuisine against the New World Intercontinental gastronomic army. The main goal of the New World is to overcome culinary differences and to create a global cuisine, destroying everything produced through natural cultivation – sowing, cropping, and reaping. Anti-modernism is manifested here in the form of 'passatistic regionalism,' a fear of losing one's identity and a conservative resistance to cosmopolitan endeavors. Zoran Kravar first noticed this kind of resistance to change in Croatian literature in the second half of the 19th century. At that time, the antithesis of "domestic tradition (threshold) – foreign new (today's age)" ran through the works of Josip Kozarac, Franjo Marković, and other writers (*Svjetonazorski separei* 87). In Barbieri's novel this antithesis appears in juxtaposing food from a domestic product grown in neighborhood gardens to genetically modified food from corporations which is sold cheaply in supermarkets. But in Barbieri's novel the antithesis of domestic/foreign also appears on the level of the (national) origin of the main characters. International cuisine is represented by a Japanese chef, who is always referred to as "a fake Japanese Yamamoto" (42). Namely, the local chef (also the autodiegetic narrator) constantly insists on his hybrid origin and says that Marshal Admiral Yamamoto was an unwanted child born out of wedlock from a Japanese girl and a domestic seaman. Whenever he is at the butcher's, Yamamoto reminds him of "the slanted, half-closed eyes on a pig's head" (16). Such racist essentialism in a surprising way connects this novel to the value system of Šufflay's novel *Na Pacifiku god. 2255* (1998) (*In the Pacific of 2255*). Following Spengler's predictions, in Šufflay's novel 'the decline of the West' is also seen as the downfall of the "white race" due to the supremacy of the "yellow race," especially because of the race-mixing and the degradation of the "great Nordic race" (194). His novel describes the ideal society of the future, whose values and laws are taken care of by the secret society of esoterics. At the top of that society is the Council of Twelve Sages led by Arhat, who is not only the wisest one but has an ideal "biological heritage" (Šufflay 96). The conflict between the two main characters in the Council, Cold and Heat, is also 'biologically' conditioned, as are all the other relationships between the characters in the novel. Cold is "a slender and blond, tall and handsome man, a pure member of Nordic race" (206). Heat's character is also described in terms of his origin. He is a descendant of an Englishman grandfather and a Malay grandmother from Pitcairn Island. At the beginning of the novel it is said that he become a member of the Council of the Twelve "despite of his grandparents" (27). In the value system that Šufflay builds in his novel, it is precisely this error of neglecting Heat's origins that will prove fatal. The utopia ends in disaster caused by Heat, and his action is explained by his origin, a temperament of the "half-breed" which he could not restrain when he realized that his wife Satya, a beautiful woman of the Nordic race, loves Cold, the perfect Nordic. Instead of allowing them to create the perfect descendant, he decided to destroy the whole world, all because of the "vanity of the Malays and the spleen of the English" which he could not control (233). Thus Šufflay's utopia has an apocalyptic end. It ends with destruction of a society conceived as ideal because it was built on eugenic principles. An apocalyptic event is the point where dystopia, as a post-apocalyptic narrative, usually begins. Therefore, the end of Šufflay's novel can be considered the beginning of dystopia, in line with Edward James's claim that the dystopian scenario is the logical outcome of realized utopia (224).

Šufflay's utopian vision is, in fact, the neuralgic panegyric of the 19th-century eugenics additionally driven by the spirit of the Völkisch ideology (Levanat-Peričić 316). However, his vision becomes less surprising when we place it in the context of his enthusiasm for Mussolini, which is often expressed in his essays about the 'biological roots of history.' Moreover, Šufflay expressed his admiration for fascism with an antimodernist discourse, emphasising that "fascism is not utopia," and that it is only possible "in the case of completely built, old nations" (*Svjetonazorski separei* 94). Šufflay's promoting the idea of fascism with the model of an ideal society or realizable utopia reminds us of the blurred limits between utopia and anti-utopia. In his review of ecotopias, Krishan Kumar warns exactly about this fact; utopia can easily cross into anti-utopia, and anti-utopia can be changed to utopia. Indeed, Kumar believes that an attempt to make an ecotopia can easily be transformed into an authoritarian society and even into an "eco-fascist" regime ("Utopija i antiutopija" 89).

2.3 Narratives of Religious Decline

As Zoran Kravar has already noted, anti-modernism is a worldview typical of the period after the 'death of God'; indeed, anti-modernism also recognizes this 'death' in the crisis of Christian religion and takes a negative attitude to the church, showing an indifference towards attempts to denounce Christianity as the culprit of the fall of pre-modern life and primordial harmony (*Antimodernizam* 14). However, Mlakić's and Popović's novels develop different and almost contradictory religious narratives. While in the center of Mlakić's novel there is a Christian belief in redemption based on the rebuilding of the bond between father and son, in Popović's novel the Church is just another corrupt corporations. But regardless of the differences, both novels describe not only a society without God, but also a society that lacks God after his 'death.' Mlakić's world of the future is ruled by greed, emotions are forbidden, and there is no faith because it is related to emotions. A return to emotions would mean a return to faith. There is also no God in Popović's world of the Croatian future because original faith has turned into a greedy institution. Both novels develop the kind of naive longing for lost harmony that can be restored only by sincere, uncorrupted faith and ideals of brotherhood and unity among people.

Mlakić's novel has a Christian proto-text in the form of belief in the redeeming power of the relationship between father and son, presented as the 'Saviour' and the 'Crucified.' At the end of the novel, the main character Gerhard Schmidt discovers a letter from his father, whom he had never met in his life. The letter is inserted between the pages of a Bible and, in the letter, his father interprets his view of the end of history: "In the past, we used to leave the world to our children, but that is not the case anymore (...) Fathers do not exist, and there are no sons. There is only naked greed, and a limited expiration date, the end of human history" (194). Furthermore, in his letter, the father admits that he "created a myth about his return" in which he embedded the myth of the resurrection of Jesus Christ. After he realized that his killers were approaching him, as a doctor who had the reputation of a Saviour because he created a myth about his resurrection to give hope to people who already had the Savior's reputation, he created a myth about his resurrection to give hope to people. He explained that he had done it because legends were the basis of all illusions about a better and more just world. While doing so, he took into account his great physical resemblance to his son Gerhard, thanks to which one day people would recognize Gerhard as his father, the Saviour. Since the relationship between father and son gains a dimension of religious redemption, after reading his father's letter, Gerhard decides to look for his own son because the bonding between fathers and sons is the only way to save the future world.

On the other hand, in Popović's novel, the Church is just one of the greedy corporations that cooperate with the ruling Holding – "It holds the right to the entire planet and has an agent in every remote spot" (44). Besides, it is incorporated into the market by organizing the sale of forgiveness; and with the purchase of forgiveness, there is also a "twenty per cent discount in White Angel Mall, right next to the cathedral" (68).

In both novels, the disrupted primordial harmony of the world is related to the future decline of religion. Popović's novel as a whole develops a more critical stance on this issue, insisting on current problems of Croatian society with regard to the problematic role of the Church in it. In this sense, he connects the Church with Holding, the governing corporation, which the contemporary reader can associate with a well-known real corporation Zagreb Holding.[3] But Popović goes on, linking the Church to worshiping crimes and criminals, since the Croatian society of the future in his novel has Crime Museums frequented by worshipers of crime and weirdness. This expresses a very sharp criticism addressed to the Croatian Catholic Church regarding the uncritical attitude towards crimes committed against members of other nations in all wars in Croatia. The healing of society (which, as in all dystopias, is sick and is looking

---

3 The company's website provides the following information: "Zagreb Holding was incorporated in 2007 in line with the Companies Act and is 100% owned by the City of Zagreb. It consists of 14 subsidiaries that have taken over the operations of the former city owned companies. Zagreb Holding also owns 8 companies and one institution and employs a total of about 7300 people (...)The Group provides a wide range of services that are grouped into business areas of utility, energy and market activities. It also provides services from the portfolio of public water supply and drainage and pharmacy activities" (https://www.zgh.hr/company-2245/profile-2250/2250).

for some way out) in Popović's novel is offered in the form of renewing Serbo-Croatian friendly relationships. As pointed out, in Mlakić's dystopian society, illness and decay result from repressed emotions. Although his novel offers a pragmatic interpretation of Christianity as a socially helpful illusion, he also expresses the belief that the redemption of humanity is based on the renewal of the father-son relationship, that is, the relationship between God and Man.

In conclusion, I would like to point out the values these two novels offer as compensation for the decline of religion in the dark world of a godless future – Mlakić's in turning to original Christianity, and Popović's in promoting the ideals of Brotherhood and Unity.

3 Dystopian Menippea

The fundamental difference between the previously analyzed type of anti-modernist dystopia and the dystopian Menippea lies in the representation of the past, especially in the way of evaluating tradition and the treatment of national and religious identities. In this respect, the identity topics in the novels of Borivoj Radaković *Što će biti s nama* (*What Will Happen to Us* 2015) and Ivo Balenović *2084. Kuća Velikog jada* (*2084. The House of Great Misery* 2012) become the subject of ridicule. These two novels belong to the type of dystopia which is associated with Menippean satire in several features that Bakhtin distinguished for that "carnivalised genre" which, as he suggested, "became one of the main carriers and channels for the carnival sense of the world in literature" ("The Serio-Comical Tradition of the Menippea" 189). At first sight, they are connected with Menippea through using an "inserted genre" and the "mixing of prose and poetic speech" in order to parody. As Bakhtin pointed out, the presence of these features contributes to the "multi-styled and multi-toned nature of menippea" (ibid. 192).

Also, these two novels abound with the features of the "grotesque realism" that Bakhtin observed in Rabelais's work, including "the language of the marketplace" (*Rabelais and His World* 145), "banquet imagery" (ibid. 278), "the grotesque image of the body" (ibid. 303), and "images of the bodily lower stratum" (ibid. 368). In addition to these elements of grotesque realism (which also include images of corporality, feast images, scandal scenes, inappropriate speeches and performances,), these two novels contain various procedures of *carnivalisation*, i.e. profanation of the high and the spiritual into the low and the corporal. Also, they are fraught with parodic rituals, curses, blasphemy, and radical black humor, as well as experimental fantasticality typical for Menippea (dream motives, insanity, traveling to the other world, etc.).

Both novels from Balenović and Radaković are set in a Zagreb of the future. Although the toponyms of the futuristic Zagreb point to the past, here, the future is an ironic subversion of the previously analyzed narratives of history. For example, in Balenović's Zagreb of 2084, the ideological confusion about the naming of the streets was sorted out by the Mayor, so that all the roads were named after him, e.g., the Street of the Most Beloved Mayor, the Boulevard of the Most Beloved Mayor and the Alley of the Most Beloved Mayor (18). However, Vladimir's grandfather remembers the time when the main square was called the Square of Brotherhood and Unity, and from it, "like the sun's rays," streets of "massive graves, Ethnic Cleansing, Concentration Camps" came out (19). Radaković's Zagreb toponyms are oxymorons that point out the strange idea of the reconciliation of the 'left' and 'right' political forces – "Square of the Stock Exchange and Erstwhile Poverty," "Street of the Social Revolution of King Zvonimir" (44), etc.

Radaković's novel is written in a partially versed prose, i.e., sentences in which internal rhyme is being sought. Nevertheless, this rhyme is irregular, so when the narrator needs a syllable, he changes the end of the word (he rhymes "Sartr" and "pas matr," "insan" and "Dasein," "gmail" and "znail"...). For this very reason, but also because of many neologisms such as "paljetkovati,"[4] it is complicated to translate or quote examples from the novel. Besides, the translation is made difficult because of inserted sonnets, descriptions of China in heroic decasyllable, Russian expressions written in Cyrillic, etc. The text is overwhelmed with quotations from literature and popular cultures that are ironic about each other. Thus, he will write the verse "Do you remember Lily, it was raining ceaselessly on Brest that day," mixing a popular hit from the eighties (a song by Srebrna krila) and Prevert's "Barbara." The main character is a professor of postmodernism at the Faculty of Philosophy in Zagreb, Tonći, who falls in love with Lili, the Tycoon's daughter, after a catastrophe that struck the capital. The disaster itself is a parody of a disaster – a water bomb dropped by a terrorist from a Canada Air flight onto The Zagreb Mosque, which injures "only" a Muslim priest (45).

Balenović's novel is, first, a parody of Orwell's dystopia – already with the title he hints at *1984*. Then the novel takes place in a reality show that is not a 'Big Brother House' but a 'Big Misery House.' The characters are Vladimir, who is also the autodiegetic narrator, then the General, the Tycoon, the Minister, the Blonde, Jesus, Milovan Ugor (the large intestine), Yersinia (a bacterium of

---

4 The phrase refers to the writer Luko Paljetak, and the verb "paljetkovati" is derived from his name and it could mean to "speak or write in Paljetak's style."

plague), Chebutykin (a character from a Chekhov drama), and Hitler's father Aloysius. While the characters of the General, Minister and Tycoon have the roles matched with expected satirical functions, the others participate in an unexpected travesty. The Blonde is the prophet Jeremiah (throughout the novel, she recites apocalyptic texts in the Old Testament style and hovers while doing it, although everyone perceives her as just a stupid blonde). The character of Jesus hides the prophet Muhammad, who signed up for the reality show jealous of his older brother Jesus because of his popularity. But eventually, no one there recognizes him as Jesus, and they accuse him of being a "fag," a Jew, and a drug addict, as well as being boring, "free of vice, plain, and sinless, and wrecking their viewer ratings" (24).

Furthermore, when the Minister, as a true believer and a family man planning to take his mistress to the quasi-religious site Međugorje for fasting and praying, the Tycoon suggests that Jesus should follow the Minister's example – to marry, find a job, and go regularly to church; even to take his mother (because Jesus has no mistress) on the trip to Međugorje. Jesus agrees to the proposal because (as he said) she had never been there (68). In the end, it turns out that the reality show is taking place in a mental hospital, which rounds out the metonymic image of the whole state.

As we can see from these examples, carnival laughter is radical, saves no one, but remains trapped in a world of a dark future from which there is no way out. As the inverse image of "this world," the image of the "other world" in dystopian Menippea is not conceived with the intention to repairing or altering anything in that world, merely to indicate its perversion. Accordingly, the aforementioned dystopian novels use adventure and fantastic narrative patterns in the way Bakhtin related these literary forms to Menippean satire, therefore, with the aim of "provoking and verifying the truth." Bakhtin explicitly pointed out that fantastic fiction in Menippean satire "serves not for the positive realization of truth, but as a mode for searching after the truth, provoking it, and, most important, testing it" (*Problems of Dostoevsky's Poetics* 114). That's why in the Menippea appears "a special type of *experimental fantasticality*" (116). Besides experimental fantastic, in the Menippea also appears "moral-psychological experimentation: a representation of the unusual, abnormal moral and psychic states of man – the insanity of all sorts (the theme of the maniac), split personality, unrestrained daydreaming, unusual dreams, passions bordering on madness, suicides, and so forth" (ibid.). Many of these examples of "moral-psychological experimentation" and "experimental fantasticality" typical for Menippea, appear also in Radaković's and Balenović's novels. According to Bakhtin, in Menippea these phenomena do not function narrowly "as mere themes, but have a formal generic significance," which is also the reason why we consider these novels Mennipean. Therefore, this leads us to the final consideration of the difference between dystopian Menippea and antimodernist dystopia, given their relationship to post-Yugoslav temporality.

4 Conclusion: Back to the History of the Future

In the novels that we have analyzed as examples of antimodernist dystopias, there are many recognizable hints to reality and known historical facts. In Popović's novel, for example, the case of the Zec family murder is mentioned, with the comment that it was a "trial balloon" for the beginning of a moral catastrophe because if the murder of a twelve-year-old girl "passed unpunished," then anything goes (38). But even though a concrete fact of history is noted, the part of history which invokes nostalgia is not, but it is set up through romantic passatism in an antimodernist way, as Kravar said – as a "desire for the restoration of primaeval beginnings" and a return to the "healthy state of the world" of the pre-civilization past (*Kad je svijet bio mlad*). Thus Popović's novel advocates an escape to Velebit Mountain, a return to the 'state of silence' in which Beethoven composed, back to the cultivation of land and the production of organic food in contrast to the banking economy.

On the other hand, the 'history of the future' in a dystopian Menippea is marked by Bakhtinian carnival laughter which has a regenerative effect but leaves no space for already-seen solutions. By contrast, dark anti-modernistic visions most often leave some room for the healing of society – in Mlakić's novel, these are emotions aroused by art, as well as the redeeming power of the relationship between father and son, which evokes an interpretation of Christianity as a socially useful illusion. On the other hand, the image of the future in a dystopian Menippea may best be illustrated with the words of Balenović's Vladimir: "It all started on the Plitvice Lake. It was at the time when the states existed. Now, fortunately, there are neither states nor Plitvice" (50). Of course, mentioning the Plitvice Lake where "it all started" is an allusion to the beginning of the Croatian war for an independent state. In the post-Yugoslav future, there will be no states nor lakes.

Although it seems that dystopia is a unique literary genre, after analyzing these contemporary examples, it seems that we are dealing with two opposed (sub)genres that have different formal, structural, and stylistic features. In the first place, these two subgenres derive from opposite literary traditions – antimodernist dystopias developed in the realm of 'serious' epic narrative with features of social and political criticism, and dystopian Menippea, which belong to the carnivalistic line of the novel developed in the Bakhtinian 'realm of the seriocomical.' After all, their fundamental difference lies in their evaluation of the past – while the antimodernist author chooses the traditional values that they intend to affirm in a dehumanized dystopic world, in the future of a Menippean society, there is no relevant past, and there are no values that can escape the radical laughter.

References

Atwood, Margaret. *In Other Worlds: SF and the Human Imagination*. Virago, 2011.
Bakhtin, Mihail. *Problems of Dostoevsky's Poetics*. Translated by Caryl Emerson. University of Minnesota Press, 1984.
Bakhtin, Mihail. *Rabelais and His World*. Translated by Helene Iswolsky. Indiana University Press, 1984.
Bakhtin, Mihail."The Serio-Comical Tradition of the Menippea," *The Bakhtin Reader. Selected Writings of Bakhtin, Medvedev, Voloshinov*, edited by Pam Morris, Arnold, 1994, pp. 187–193.
Balenović, Ivo. *2084. Kuća Velikog jada*. Jesenski i Turk, 2012.
Barbieri, Veljko. *Rat za peti okus*. Profil, 2015.
Booker. M. Keith. *The Dystopian Impulse in Modern Literature: Fiction as Social Criticism*. Greenwood Press, 1994.
Gajin, Igor. "Trend distopijskog u suvremenoj hrvatskoj prozi." *Anafora*, vol. 2, no. 3, 2015, pp. 41–58.
James, Edward. "Utopias and antiutopias." *The Cambridge Companion to Science Fiction*, edited by Ed Edward James and Farah Mendlesohn, 2003, pp. 219–229.
Jessup, Lynda, "Antimodernism and Artistic Experience: An Introduction." *Antimodernism and Artistic Experience: Policing the Boundaries of Modernity*, edited by Lynda Jessup, University of Toronto Press, 2001, pp. 3–12.
Kravar, Zoran. *Antimodernizam*. AGM, 2003.
Kravar, Zoran. *Kad je svijet bio mlad: visoka fantastika i doktrinarni antimodernizam*. Mentor, 2010.
Kravar, Zoran. *Svjetonazorski separei. Antimodernističke tendencije u hrvatskoj književnosti ranoga 20. stoljeća*. Golden Marketing, 2005.
Kumar, Krishan. "The End of Socialism? The End of Utopia? The End of History?" *Utopias and the Millenium*, edited by Krishan Kumar and Stephen Bann, Reaction Books, 1993, pp. 63–80.
Kumar, Krishan. "Utopija i antiutopija u dvadesetom stoljeću." *Diskrepancija*, vol. 2, no. 4, pp. 75–95.

Lears, T.J. Jackson. *No Place of Grace: Antimodernism and the Transformation of American Culture, 1880–1920*. Pantheon, 1981.

Levanat-Peričić, Miranda. "Metažanrovska obilježenost hrvatske spekulativne fikcije (od Šufflaya do Mlakića)." *Komparativna povijest hrvatske književnosti: "Fantastika: problem zbilje,"* edited by Cvijeta Pavlović, Vinka Glunčić-Bužančić, and Andrea Meyer-Fraatz, Književni krug Split – Odsjek za komparativnu književnost Filozofskoga fakulteta Sveučilišta u Zagrebu, 2016, pp. 307–318.

Mlakić, Josip. *Planet Friedman*. Fraktura, 2012.

Morris, Pam (ed.). *The Bakhtin Reader. Selected Writings of Bakhtin, Medvedev, Voloshinov*. London, Arnold, 1994.

Morson, Gary Soul. *The Boundaries of Genre: Dostoevsky's "Diary of a Writer" and the Traditions of Literary Utopia*. University of Texas Press, 1981.

Popović, Edo. *Lomljenje vjetra*. OceanMore, 2011.

Postnikov, Boris. "Imaginiranje sutrašnjice bez budućnosti." *Le Monde*, 2013, no. 10, pp. 3.

Radaković, Borivoj. *Što će biti s nama*. V.B.Z., 2015.

Sontag, Susan. "The Imagination of Disaster." *Connection*, Oct 1965, pp. 42–48.

Šufflay, Milan. *Na Pacifiku god. 2255. Metagenetički roman u četiri knjige*. Prosvjeta, 1998.

Versluis, Arthur. "Antimodernism." *Telos: Critical Theory of the Contemporary*, Winter 2006, pp. 96–130.

CHAPTER 6

Kant Has Some Relevance Here: On a Fictional Theory of Quentin Meillassoux and the Theoretical Fiction of Luka Bekavac

Ante Jerić

What is time?[1] There is a well-known passage in Kant's *Critique of Pure Reason* in which the philosopher delineates the positions which one can take with respect to the status of time and space: "Now what are space and time? Are they [1] actual entities? Are they only [2] determinations or relations of things, yet ones that would pertain to them even if they were not intuited, or are they [3] relations that only attach to the form of intuition alone, and thus to the subjective constitution of our mind, without which these predicates could not be ascribed to any thing at all?" (A23/B37–38, my enumeration). It is common to ascribe the first position – which takes time to be an actual entity – to Newton, the second position – which takes time to be determination or the relation of things – to Leibniz, and, finally, the third position – which takes time to be the basic form of intuition – to Kant himself. Time is then, according

---

1   This text is the middle part of a larger project which aims to examine the relationship between philosophy and literature or, which in the given context amounts to the same thing, theory and fiction. The project rests, in contradistinction to the work of Mark Fisher (155–156), on two claims:
   1)   Theory and fiction are separate discourses, and they remain separate even if one can be mistaken whether any particular text should be taken as a work of theory or fiction.
   2)   One discourse can be parasitic on the host of the other, and thus two interrelated cases immediately suggest themselves:
      a)   fictional theory (theory as fiction) – in this case we are dealing with works in which a theory is presented in the form of fiction. Nietzsche and Kierkegaard are the most prominent philosophers who were using fictional narratives to convey their theories;
      b)   theoretical fiction (fiction as theory) – in this case a work of fiction uses or incorporates theoretical forms and its conventions. Nabokov's chapter in *Ada*, "The Texture of Time," written as a treatise on the theory of time, or Reza Negarestani's novel *Cyclonopedia*, written as a series of theoretical texts, would be good examples of this tendency.
   The larger project rests on the two assertions, one prescriptive and one descriptive, which will be restated in the course of this text, but not thoroughly justified: not all theory is already literature and theory should not think of itself as literature.

to Kant, a basic feature of the human mind, a form of intuition in light of which all the matter we experience has for us temporal features, such as being simultaneous or successive. What is the position that Luka Bekavac takes vis-a vis time in his fictional oeuvre?

In their contribution to this volume, Jelača nad Ryznar argue that Bekavac's treatment of time is to be understood as a literary response to the philosophical problem that speculative realism placed back at the forefront of contemporary philosophical discussions – the possibility of knowledge of the world in itself, or a world independent from and indifferent to the human mind, thought, and knowledge. I wholeheartedly agree with their thesis, and I especially applaud their analysis of Bekavac's motif of "the archive" which indexes "the idea of nonhuman otherness – an other realm independent from and indifferent to human thought – precisely to a purely spatial configuration existing outside of time." The notion of the archive – which appears throughout Bekavac's fictional oeuvre – indicates that time in Bekavac's diegetic universe is taken to be a combination of [2] and [3]: there is really no such thing as time; what we call time is merely our misunderstanding of the relation between things, an illusion, a non-veridical form of our intuition that has no bearing on the world independent from and indifferent to us. This is certainly an unorthodox conception of time, and it does not correspond to any conception of time proposed by the philosophers we usually associate with speculative realism.

Quentin Meillassoux – the most prominent philosopher among the speculative realists – has proposed a truly novel conception of time that is incompatible with all of the positions delineated by Kant. Bekavac's and Meillassoux's views of time are radically different, they do not rhyme, and it is hard on the basis of their respective conceptions of time to claim that Meillassoux – as a speculative realist philosopher – has exerted significant influence on Bekavac's fiction writing. Nevertheless – as Jelača and Ryznar rightly claim – the problem of time in Bekavac's fiction should, in various ways, be understood in relation to speculative realism. In order to explicate this claim, the first part of this paper will introduce the work of Quentin Meillassoux and his thoughts on the "division of labor" between philosophy, science, and literature as separate discourses which can certainly be linked, but are ultimately irreducible to one another. The second part of the paper will present the basic features of Bekavac's diegetic universe and offer a brief interpretation of "Network" – one of the short stories from Bekavac's collection *The Gallery of Fine Arts in Osijek: Studies, Ruins* – which is intended to be understood against the background of Meillassoux's philosophy (not against the background of his conception of time *per se*, but by taking into account his divinology that nevertheless operates with the notion of nonlinear temporality). This interpretation aims to demonstrate just one among the myriad of ways in which Bekavac, after borrowing the notion from the domain of philosophy, uses nonlinear temporality. It is my contention that *In The Gallery of Fine Arts in Osijek* Bekavac deploys this notion in order to shape the story in which both the desire of (post-)Yugoslav writers to put their craft in the service of a critique of society, and certain aspects of Meillassoux's philosophical endeavour – in its most extravagant claims and pretensions – are simultaneously being parodied and satirized.

1 Fictional Theory: Quentin Meillassoux

Science, as conceived by 20th-century continental philosophy, proceeds on the basis of measurability and repeatability. It is fundamentally associated with calculating thinking, with the instrumental domination of the world.[2] Technology as calculating thinking is the condition for the inception and development of science and indeed takes part in its very nature. Within this picture, science, or technoscience, is somehow opposed to literature, and philosophy – which is there to think through their relation – is more often inspired by and allied with literature, especially poetry, than with science. Heidegger wants to 'speak' that which is 'poetic in poetry' by translating it in the language of philosophy. His own philosophy. If one does not accept the basic tenets of Heidegger's philosophy or one is simply unfamiliar with it, so that he misses the framework of this systematic and consequent line of thought, then it becomes increasingly difficult for him to accept the following opposition: calculability and control are on the side of science; play and freedom are on the side of literature, while philosophy, in its irreducibility to the either one of these domains, circulates in-between them and thinks through their relation.

Despite all of their respective differences, science, philosophy, and literature are similar because they share Fiction as their common ground. Fiction (with a capital F, not fiction as literature) is necessary for the execution of

---

2 In his study of the history of continental philosophy, Lee Braver names the latest phase of its development the "Heideggerian paradigm" (255–514). I argue that Heidegger's thinking of technoscience can be equated as the orienting presupposition that sets the starting point, basic assumptions, general outlook, and issues of relevance for the majority of continental philosophers in the second part of the 20th century. The respective philosophical projects of Gilles Deleuze and Alain Badiou, as an exception to this tendency, will not be addressed in the course of the text that follows.

emplotment, the formulation of a hypothesis that needs to be tested on empirical material and the development of ideas whose elaboration requires novel ways of argumentation.[3] It is not my ambition here to dwell on the common ground of these domains. On the contrary, I am going to try to increase the resolution of the image which shows the differences between them: I will try to give an account for some of the reasons of their delimitation and, in the end, I will sketch a different relation between them than the one proposed by post-Heideggerian philosophy by relying on the work of Quentin Meillassoux.

1.1 *Philosophy: Literature*

Let me first try to explain why the separation and delimitation between philosophy and literature comes to be. Does this question risk succumbing to anachronism? I do not think it does. I think it is a perennial question. One of the most vivid descriptions of the ur-scene of this separation and the most precise formulation of its origin was given by Barbara Cassin (45), who sees it as a consequence of Aristotle's refutation of the sophists. The categories she uses to give account of it are the binary opposition 'true-false' and 'existence.' The argument can be summarized in the following way: when one speaks, the meaning of the word expresses the essence of the thing. This is the case when the thing exists; the essence of entities is the meaning of the word that refers to it. Aristotle, faced with the sophist who put at risk ontology as a discourse on being *qua* being, responded in a novel way and in a manner that opened a radically new possibility for thinking. One is no longer forced to speak of something that exists in order to mean something; one can very well speak of nonexistent things without putting ontology at risk. "One can speak *nonbeing*," Cassin claims, "because one can *speak* nonbeing, because with the language of possibility comes a meaning that is no longer bound to reference" (37). The truth may be uttered when we speak about things that do not exist. Aristotelian semantics produces possible worlds in which true sentences assign nonexistent predicates to nonbeings – stemming not from the *false which is* but from the *true which is not*. By speaking of things that have no existence, by discarding any physical or phenomenal reference, one has opened up a possibility of promoting meaning alone, meaning itself, which is to say, literature

---

3 This claim is shared, and much better expressed, by Steven Shaviro: "Fictions and fabulations are often contrasted, or opposed, to scientific methods of understanding the world. But in fact, there are powerful resonances between them; they are both processes of *speculative extrapolation*. In other words, constructing and testing scientific hypotheses is not entirely different from constructing fictions and fabulations, and then testing to see whether they work or not, and what consequences follow from them" (11).

and the novel as literature's nascent paradigm. The novel is the way of speaking which does want to conform to the requirements of ontological adequation, it is a self-conscious *pseudo* which presents itself as such, it is a proud self-manifestation of speaking for the *pleasure of speaking*, a fiction which does not primarily want to capture reality even when it effectively does so.

I think of Aristotle's refutation of the sophist as a promising start for thinking of the reasons for the separation of philosophy from literature because it provides us with a firm grasp of the hierarchical relation which is established between the two domains: philosophy is deemed more worthy of the two because it is subjected to the pursuit of truth, while literature is subjected to the pursuit of pleasure. It is *legein logou kharin*, speaking for the pleasure of speaking, speaking for its own sake. From there on, the contact and exchange between philosophy and literature presumes the reactivation of silent, implicit, but nevertheless firmly established hierarchies: philosophy deals with ideas pertaining to reality, while literature can, in some cases, help it to convey these complex ideas in the form of a story and by doing so make them relatable to the nonphilosophers. As far as the matters of the truth of that which is, or the matters of reality, are concerned, literature can have, at best, a didactic function.

1.2   *Philosophy: Science*

The separation of science from philosophy, or at least of science from metaphysics, came about with a revolution in the methodology of thinking about reality. The backbone of that revolution was induction and the experiment. Science has repeatedly proven itself to be superior to metaphysics in discovering and explaining the fundamental elements of reality because it has given us new ways to rationally choose and privilege one hypothesis about the nature of reality over others. Kant's *First Critique* was, among other things, the acknowledgment and ratification of science's primacy over metaphysics as the first philosophy in the domain of knowledge. It was Kant who, without any hesitation and in a most thorough fashion, provided an account of the superiority of science over metaphysics: since Kant, metaphysics has been forced to revise its claim to be in possession of a theoretical knowledge of realities that are equal or even superior to those known by the sciences, and, since Kant, philosophers in general have become accustomed to the idea that science, and science alone, provides us with theoretical knowledge of nature, and – even more importantly – that metaphysics can no longer present itself as harbouring knowledge of a supposedly higher reality than the reality accessible to us by means of physics, or empirical science. The consequence of this succession was the pressing need to rethink the object and the tasks of philosophy. With regards to the positioning of philosophy vis-a-vis science, two different paths were taken:

a) Kant and his successors have inserted the transcendental subject into the emptied place of the object of philosophy. By doing so, they have taken on the task of exploring the conditions of the possibility of modern science, of its thinkability. Philosophy has changed its object: it could no longer talk about reality, but only about the conditions, grounds, methods, and implications of the sciences which study apparent, empirical reality. It is of less importance whether these conditions of the sciences are taken to be something dependent on the transcendental subject, language, the horizon of thinkability, their combination, or something else.

b) Some philosophers have not accepted the transcendental framework and have not taken part in the critique of metaphysics. Consequently, for them the object and the task of philosophy has not really changed. They have continued to build metaphysics, but now their thinking is informed and relies on scientific findings. That has proven itself to be a shaky ground. Science advances by devising hypotheses which are under a constant process of revision. They are all, sooner or later, modified, discarded, and forgotten, and, as a result, so are the metaphysics erected on their foundations. Maybe it is true that every metaphysics that was devised and advanced without taking an interest in the science of its time had to perish, but it is equally true to say that the same destiny awaits any metaphysics which grounds itself in the science of its day.

Quentin Meillassoux redefines the relationship between philosophy, science, and literature. In a very brief manner, I will present his understanding of the relations between these domains, starting from his account of the object and the task of philosophy. To put it briefly, Meillassoux (*Speculative Solution* 6) does not see philosophy as a kind of metadiscourse which comments upon other discourses and connects them with one another, but rather he is of the opinion that philosophy has its object which is the traditional object of metaphysics: the world independent from and indifferent to human mind, or simply the thing in itself. What is, in Meillassoux's account, the thing in itself? Let us start with some negative determinations.

According to Meillassoux ("Iteration" 136), the thing in itself is not [1] some fact, whether a thing or event, that we know is capable of not being; the thing in itself is also not [2] a fact whose not-being or its being-other we can conceive of, but of which we do not know whether it can actually be other than it is; and, last but not least, the thing in itself is not [3] a fact which we cannot, in any way, conceive of as being other than it is, or as not being, and whose necessity we nevertheless cannot prove. In the post-Kantian era, science has been dedicated to an analysis of the first two types of facts, those whose not-being we can at least conceive of, while philosophy has taken up the task of describing the facts that we cannot conceive of not being. Meillassoux proceeds by noticing the lack of reason for any fact, which is to say, the impossibility of giving an ultimate ground to the existence of facts and calls this lack of reason *facticity*. This lack of reason for any object – facticity – becomes the object of his philosophy. So, philosophy has an object that belongs exclusively to it. Meillassoux (*After Finitude* 80; "Iteration" 137) calls *factiality* facticity's property of not itself being factual. Factiality designates nonfacticity or, the absolute necessity, of facticity and of facticity alone. The task of philosophy becomes to think through the implications of factiality. Philosophy, by trying to think the thing in itself, becomes a discourse on factiality, which is to say a discourse on the necessity of contingency, a discourse dedicated to the precise deduction of the nontrivial consequences of that necessity.

We are now in the position to raise a question about the 'division of labour' between philosophy, science and literature. According to Meillassoux, these domains are irreducible, each of them has its own features and there is no hierarchy between them. Philosophy is interested in the non-empirical, in what may be, and not in what is. If one wants to think or know what is, one must pass by way of a certain regime of the empirical, understood in the broadest sense: scientific experimentation in the case of the natural sciences, and the experience of pure singularity in the case of literature.

What is meant here by pure singularity? Meillassoux does not elaborate on this notion, so one is obliged here to fill in the gap by proposing different solutions. Where are we to look for help? My provisional, tentative, revisable, and – let us admit it straightforwardly – probably misguided proposition is that we return to Kant. I am inclined to do so because it gives me a straightforward answer to the question about which Meillassoux remains silent: literary experience may be the experience of singularity, all well and good, but whose experience is it, who is the subject of that experience – the author of the literary work or its reader?

I am opting primarily for the reader. In the *Third Critique*, Kant defines aesthetic art as an art which prompts the animation of the senses and "intends directly to arouse the feeling of pleasure" (134). He then parses out two distinct categories of aesthetic art: the fine arts and the agreeable arts. The fine arts are distinguished by their communicability. The agreeable arts, on the other hand, are those whose purpose is 'merely' to please. Pleasure is the passive reception of some sensible object. It can be received by reading a good book or watching a football match. There is no assertion of universal validity when speaking of the agreeable. The same book can give one reader immense pleasure and leave another indifferent. All that is subsumed under the rubric of agreeable art is concerned with what is "of the moment, and not as a lasting matter to be made the subject of reflection or repetition" (135). Kant clearly values the fine arts more than the agreeable arts, he describes the latter using derogatory terms such as "mere."

For me there is nothing "mere" about the pleasure we obtain by encountering objects of agreeable art. If I decide, following Meillassoux, to think of literature as an experience of pure singularity, then I think of it first and foremost as an agreeable art. Aristotle's refutation of the sophist in the *Metaphysics* can, retrospectively, be read as the ur-scene of the separation of literature from philosophy. Sophists, the ones who speak for the pleasure of speaking, were banished from the philosophical community and they were consigned to literature. Literature and pleasure share an intimate link from the very start. There is nothing more singular or incommunicable than a pleasure, which is why I am equating it with the experience of pure singularity that Meillassoux mentions while discussing literature, but never elaborates upon.

Meillassoux does philosophy. If he decides to invoke literature, or science, in order to use their methods or results, then he is doing so for purely didactical purposes. This didacticism, despite his declarations otherwise ("Iteration" 144), activates old and well-known hierarchies. I will point out to the examples from his oeuvre that confirm this thesis.

My first example is concerned with the instrumentalization of the science of chronological dating within the debate on the arche-fossil in the first chapter of *After Finitude* (1–27). What is the purpose of bringing up the scientific results that point to the time anterior to the emergence of consciousness and human temporality? It is merely a propaedeutic tool that enables the uninitiated to get some sense of the necessity and relevance of his philosophical endeavour. Meillassoux only spoke of the science of dating and of the arche-fossil so as to awaken the reader's consciousness to the fact that Kant's transcendental philosophy, and phenomenology as its successor, had the rigorous consequence of making the discourse of science meaningless. The aporia of the arche-fossil culminated in the following proposition ("Iteration" 142): "the first condition of the thinkability of science turned out to be the abandonment of the very transcendental whose vocation was to investigate the conditions of the possibility of science." Meillassoux's readers thus learned that, far from being an intrinsically transcendental concept, the notion of a 'condition' could propel them to abandon the transcendental. What should not be left unnoticed is, as Meillassoux himself points out in the final chapter of *After Finitude* (113), that science could have discovered that, indeed, nothing actually precedes the emergence of consciousness. But it would not be of any importance. Meillassoux's work would not be in danger of collapsing nor would his project be any less needed. He would have lost one didactical tool, a powerful illustration, but nevertheless, only an illustration whose importance should not be overestimated. In this case, philosophical development does not depend on scientific discovery nor would a different scientific discovery made philosophy obsolete.

My second example is the instrumentalization of literature at work in the text called "Subtraction and Contraction" (72–118). In this interesting work, Meillassoux brackets the whole of Deleuze's oeuvre, invites us to do the same, and proceeds by imagining the world in which we would have at our disposal with only one remaining fragment of that oeuvre, taken from the book *What is Philosophy?*, that contains some rather cryptic remarks dedicated to the concept of immanence. There is no way for us to figure out what Deleuze invokes with the term immanence on the basis of that fragment alone. However, not all hope is lost: the fragment references Spinoza and Bergson as the two "princes of immanence" whose complete works have been saved. A close reading of Bergson, by the way of following Deleuze's remarks from the fragment, could navigate us toward a reconstruction of Deleuze's understanding of immanence. The clue that helps us the most is the fact that Deleuze tells exactly up until which point his understanding of immanence rhymes with Bergson's understanding, and where Bergson falters, thereby risking the collapse of his thought back into the transcendental philosophy he sought to render unnecessary. The game is set up so that the task of Meillassoux, and by proxy, his reader, is to correct Bergson's mistakes and proceed with caution toward the formulation of the theory of immanence. The final result would be neither Bergson's nor Deleuze's theory, but a new, fictional theory that should be in all of its essential elements similar to Deleuze's original theory.

Why does Meillassoux act like a writer? What is the point of imagining a world in which Delueze's oeuvre has been lost? Why is he incited to formulate a fictional theory when he already has at his disposal a rich and complete theory of immanence? The reasons for this undertaking are purely didactical in nature: it can help someone who is not familiar with Deleuze's theory of immanence to get a better grasp of the problem which provoked its inception, as well as the resolution of that problem. To truly understand the work of some philosophers requires, among other things, the ability to deduce their complete system from the central formula of that system captured in some significant fragment. Meillassoux's fictional theory that functions as a simplified model of Deleuze's original theory should shed light on the connection between many essential aspects of Deleuze's thinking and testify to its coherence.

2 Theoretical Fiction: Luka Bekavac

Meillassoux's didactics, when it comes to literature, are not always so inventive. He does not always build fictional theories, but simply borrows material from fiction in order to illustrate his theses. That is the case in his essay called *Science Fiction and Extro-Science Fiction*. Before I lay out the way in which Meillassoux uses the literature in that text, I again have to render Kant as his main dialogical partner and adversary. In the *Critique of Pure Reason*, Kant – while trying to answer Hume's sceptical challenge – claims that consciousness would not be possible without the order of appearances governed by a set of necessary laws. Kant, as Muhannad Hariri (195) puts it, wants to say that the conditions of the sciences and the conditions of consciousness are identical. We would surely not be able to conduct scientific experiments in the world if we were not conscious of it, but the crux of Kant's argument is located in the reversal of that claim: we would not be conscious if the world was not always already susceptible to scientific experimentation. Meillassoux (*Science Fiction* 36) takes issue with Kant and argues that there could be a world in which we would be conscious, but we could not practice science, since science as such would not be possible. He criticizes (31–32) Kant's conflation of the conditions of consciousness with the conditions of the sciences by arguing that Kant's implicit mathematical reasoning is flawed, in a way reminiscent of the fourth chapter of *After Finitude* (82–111). But, in doing so, Meillassoux does not simply repeat the older version of the argument but expands it by envisaging the existence of non-Kantian worlds outside science: extro-science worlds.

There are three types of worlds in which science ceases to be possible, of extro-science worlds, of non-Kantian worlds. The first type is one in which the contingency of natural laws is a rare occurrence of a local character and neither science nor consciousness is affected by what appear to be extremely occasional glitches in the fabric of reality. The paradigm of this kind of world would be a world in which something akin to a miracle occurred. The third type of world is not a world at all, it is a pure chaos, an entirely frenetic disorder in which nothing can subsist and in which consciousness, like science, would not be possible at all. These types of worlds offer little of interest to Meillassoux in his debate with Kant. They are also of a limited interest to the prospective writers. The plot in extro-science diegetic worlds of the first type would revolve around one and only one event which could not be inscribed in the causal order of events. All other strange occurrences within the worlds of this type could be explained by science, but the protagonist's credence in science would be seriously undermined and would change his worldview in some manner. Such is the case in Tom Perrotta's novel *The Leftovers*. The plot in extro-science diegetic worlds of the third type would be non-existent. Amidst the pure chaos no regularity could subsist, therefore there could be no narrator or the events worthy of narration.

The second type of non-Kantian world, an extro-science world, does seem promising. It is a type of world in which the contingency of natural laws is extreme enough to shake the scientific enterprise, but not the possibility of consciousness; in such a world, natural laws would take on the character of statistical trends and would totally lack the necessity that Kant has claimed for them. It is a type of world in which science seems obsolete and in which some consciousness experiences this obsoleteness and narrates about its consequences. This seems like a genuinely new horizon.

The second type of world in which science falters is Meillassoux's entry point into the domain of literary studies. By proposing extro-science fiction as a new category and in defining the criterion for its usage, he has shown that literary studies could find his philosophical work useful. A comparison of his procedure with the procedures at work within the founding texts of narratology reveals that he acted more like Roland Barthes than Vladimir Propp. Propp used the inductive method and moved from the particular to the general by way of extracting the simple and useful elements and regularities from the seemingly heterogeneous material within the corpus of fairy tales (Propp). Barthes, whose matter of inquiry were not the texts belonging to one genre but all narrative texts, had to act differently. He started with the general model (which he had borrowed from linguistics) and then proceeded to the analysis of the particular texts. By his account, it was necessary first to presuppose structural identity of the narrative texts, their hidden sameness, then to see if the general model corresponds to the particular empirical material, just in order to gradually rediscover the differences between the texts and to read them, once again, in their plurality (Barthes). Meillassoux, like Barthes, had started from an general model and then proceeded to see if it corresponded to a particular empirical material.

Meillassoux has offered this general model to literary typology and genre theory: he separates scientific worlds from extro-scientific worlds, and on that basis suggests the foundation of extro-science fiction as a new genre. Whether a literary work belongs to that genre will be determined by the features of its diegetic world: if the science in the world of the literary work is impossible, and not only unknown, then that work belongs within the confines of the genre of extro-science fiction. To conclude: "extro-science fiction," by Meillassoux's account (*Science Fiction* 5–6), "defines a particular regime of the imaginary in which structured – or rather destructured – worlds are conceived in such a way that experimental science cannot deploy its theories or constitute its objects within them." The scientific outlook in the real extro-science worlds, or the second type of non-Kantian worlds, remains necessary, but only as a negative which highlights the radical contingency and the unpredictability of the events within it.

The fictional work of Luka Bekavac so far includes three novels and one collection of stories.[4] All of these fictional works seem to belong to the same diegetic universe which is marked by weird occurrences: the flow of time is occasionally suspended, the arrow of time changes its direction, bioacoustical noise transmits messages from the "other side," and there is communication with worlds parallel to the diegetic world. This world, which is so far defined by a few real-world Slavonian-Baranian municipalities in northeast Croatia, is marked by the some kind of catastrophe which is destroying the biosphere, but whose nature and range is not at all clear to the characters in the novels, nor to the readers of the novels. There is also no clear articulation of the connection between this catastrophe and the strange occurrences, but the catastrophe has been theorized in all sorts of ways. Bekavac (*Drenje*) uses internally fixed focalization, and the character of professor Marković, who purportedly has the firmest grasp on the catastrophe and has developed a scientifically formalized description of it, is never used as a focalizer. What we know about him and his theories is only that what the other characters, who are biased in all sorts of ways, know. Under the guise and with the alibi of the bioacoustical project, Marković analyzes the strange noise. He considers this noise as a total archive "within which the stratification of the existence does not correspond to our living experience: within the human experience, 'here,' every moment is unique and we pass through it in a straight line and without the possibility of returning to the previous points. Over 'there,' figuratively speaking, every moment can be approached from multiple directions because it does not simply pass away. It does not come or pass at all, it just is" (144–145).

Marković's scientific apparatus, which he is trying to apply in the analysis of the recordings gathered at various Baranian locations in order to decrypt the 'messages' sent from some other frequency range, does not provide unambiguous results. One cannot determine the soundness of his theories and the characters of these novels and short stories have every right to find them dubious. An analytical, cold, and disinterested perspective is presented to us only in traces: in remarks, commentaries, scribbles, and indices of some

---

4 Novels: *Drenje* (2011), *Viljevo* (2013), *Policijski sat: slutnje, uspomene* (*Curfew: Premonitions, Recollections*, 2016); short story collection: *Galerija likovnih umjetnosti u Osijeku: studije, ruševine* (*The Gallery of Fine Arts in Osijek: Studies, Ruins*, 2017). All English translations are mine.

formalized theory, but never in its complete form or through the confirmation of its predictive power within the confines of the diegetic world. The value of Marković's theories within the larger diegetic universe remains dubious. Science, for all we can tell, could be impossible, and the theories could be illusions in a way that phenomenal experience of the characters is not and cannot be. It would make no sense to claim that their experience, taken as a quality or *what-it-is-likeness*, only *seem* to exist; phenomenal experience *is* a seeming; or, as John Searle put it, "where consciousness is concerned the existence of the appearance is the reality. If it seems to me exactly as if I am having conscious experiences, then I am having conscious experiences" (112).

Is the diegetic world that Bekavac has created an extro-science world within which the laws of nature are changing, or is it a scientific, Popperian world,[5] in which recent events have not been inscribed within the scientific order, but their inscription could be just a matter of time? I would be tempted to say it is an extro-diegetic world of the second type, but Bekavac's withdrawal of key pieces of information puts this thesis in question. Bekavac uses against my attempt at categorization the fact which Meillassoux recognized and aptly described:

> In truth, no manifest irregularity could ever suffice to demonstrate that a hidden law does not underlie the apparent disorder. Whatever the manifest disorder, we can always, as Bergson emphasized after Leibniz, detect an unknown order within it, or an order that does not correspond to the order we hoped for. In an extro-science world, we could thus always imagine a hidden law existing beneath the apparent disorder of natural chronicles. But in that world, those who persist in seeking such a secret law behind the absurd variations of nature would seem just as eccentric or vain as those who still try, in our own world, to find a quantitative law capable of explaining and predicting the course of human history. (*Science Fiction* 37)

Professor Marković fits the description of Meillassouxian eccentric, but he is an eccentric who may as well be right about the nature of his universe. Maybe his universe is a purely spatial configuration with features that, on the basic level, can be described without recourse to the notion of time. Bekavac's novels and stories look like they belong to the genre of extro-science fiction, but a

---

5 Meillassoux (*After Finitude* 85; 134) unequivocally states that Popper assumes the principle of the uniformity of nature, while Brassier (247–248) finds his assertion debatable.

critic – once again – must suspend the final verdict. I believe this is not a bug in my critique, but a feature of Bekavac's writing.

Do his texts belong to some specific genre at all? Before I answer that question, I have to say a little bit more about the work of Bekavac. So, by relying on the author as the principle of unification of the heterogeneous textual material, I will describe his work as contemporary and humorous. I will back up these mundane qualifications through the analysis of Bekavac's usage of metalepsis.

Bekavac is aware of the hierarchical relation which is established between philosophy and literature: philosophy has, let us recall the beginning of the text, casted literature as its other and deemed itself more worthy because it is subjected to the pursuit of truth, while literature is subjected to the pursuit of pleasure. The pursuit of knowledge and the pursuit of pleasure are very often intertwined and can be very dangerous. Bekavac takes up this old motive and uses it in a contemporary and humorous way which is reminiscent of Umberto Eco.

The Name of the Rose (1980) is the most famous text of Eco's. It is a novel in which the monks, hidden behind the walls of an abbey, read the second book of Aristotle's *Poetics*, which is dedicated to comedy. The monks do not know that the pages of the book have been impregnated with poison. The mechanics of reading looks like this: the monks automatically move their fingers towards their tongues, they soften them with their saliva, and then they return them to the book in order to turn its poisoned pages. The more time they spend reading the book, the more pleasure they obtain. It is this pleasure that is lethal. By reading the book, by laughing and enjoying themselves, they participate in their own undoing.

1) What do I mean when I describe Bekavac as a contemporary author? I mean primarily the fact that his work belongs to theoretical fiction, which could be a nascent genre. His writings are superior narratives which are made from a combination of elements taken from science fiction, horror, and thrillers, but which nevertheless stay irreducible to any of these genres and their patterns. It would seem imprudent to add to this list another genre label, especially the label of a genre which is not theoretically elaborated and whose definition has not yet been provided. I will describe Bekavac's fiction as theoretical fiction because I am of the opinion that this label could direct us toward a better understanding of his work. Let me first lay out my theoretical presuppositions. I approach this literary "genre," or orientation, from the standpoint of its reception. This approach takes a literary genre to be, to put it broadly, a classificatory category that is stabilized within some community after the sedimentation

of reading experiences and the implicit systematization of expectations from some literary work. The problem with any definition of a particular genre is its fluidity.

The definition changes with the changes of the works themselves and the readers' expectations from them. So, the definition of a genre given by the standards of classical logic, which would fix some necessary and sufficient conditions of a genre, is not to be expected here. As we have seen, science fiction in its current state would be a genre whose diegetic universe is built as an alternative to everyday affairs by way of introducing weird occurrences that can nevertheless be explained within the confines of the science of that diegetic universe. The diegetic world of Bekavac's novels has been marked with anomalies whose origins and nature continually evade the understanding of the inhabitants of that world. It is the impossibility of the scientific method to approach these anomalies and to give account of them that is forcing us to try to find a more suitable genre for these stories. After discarding science fiction, and extro-science fiction as well, as suitable frameworks for approaching Bekavac's novels, we could try to think of his writings as horror novels. This would make sense to do so because horror, as both the weird and the eerie, is the novels' *grundstimmung*. The feeling of uneasiness of the characters before the space-time anomaly is due to their failed attempts to connect their experiences to some conceptual order which is due to a lack of vocabulary to describe the catastrophe that is affecting them. Nevertheless, horror is really a secondary feature of the work. I find the fact that the characters are still continually attempting to analyze the cracks of their world and their strange predicament more pertinent than the fact that their attempts usually result in a failure which makes them terrified.

Therefore, my suggestion runs as follows: if this series of novels which share the same diegetic universe do not belong either to science fiction or to horror, then maybe we can recognize them as examples of theoretical fiction as a new genre. I described theoretical fiction earlier as a nascent genre. Every beginning is hard. To say that a genre is nascent, to claim that it is under construction, is a very problematic expression because it confronts us directly with Meno's paradox, which states the following: if we do not know what the object we are looking for looks like, then we will not recognize it when we encounter it; if, on the other hand, we know what the object looks like, then there is no need for us to look for it in the first place. In other words, without the possession of the operative concept of theoretical fiction, we would not be able to recognize some text as theoretical fiction; on the other hand, the possession of the concept of theoretical fiction renders reading and analyzing the various texts in order to determine the features of the genre unnecessary.

The only thing of concern in that case would be the correct application of the concept to the fictional material. So, how are we to start? The solution to our problem is the partiality of our knowledge which is accompanied by the partiality of the 'thing itself.' We do not know everything about the nascent genre, that is true, but that does not mean we know nothing about it. What we do know is the fact that the last decade has brought about the publication of several texts that do not fit existing categories and resemble each other to a degree which propels one to look for a new genre label under which they could be subsumed. This process has not yet ended. My bet is that Bekavac makes a conscious effort to influence and define, by way of his novelistic work, what could be assumed under that label in the future. It is an ambitious project: how many writers can say that they are trying to set a new task for literature, that they want to establish a new set of rules for their domain?

The basis of theoretical fiction is the relationship between literature and theory. At the moment literature has an instrumental relation toward theory. Theoretical fiction overturns this usual hierarchy between these two domains. It was philosophy, or theory, who usually used art as a mean of illustration of its theses, while in theoretical fiction the art of words uses philosophical and theoretical positions as material for the construction of a diegetic world as a frame in which the situations, characters, and relations between them can be seen as coexisting. Bekavac certainly proceeds in this way: his characters are laying out the rudiments of his theory in different formats, in some cases even as parts of something that seems like a complete and formalized theory; the narration is developed by their attempts to understand what was happening or is happening in the locations of Baranja; maybe *narration* is even too strong of a word because the story does not really progress by a narration of some sensical chain of events, but by a description of the defamiliarized world in which something is happening; although to say that *something happens* would also be too imprecise, because it is the possibility of the determination of the chronology of events, the fabula as the causal linkage of the events abstracted from the sujet, that now seems problematic, and maybe even impossible.

2) What do I mean when I say that Bekavac is humorous? The humour in his work is always in the background and it never undercuts horror as the dominant emotional tone. To get a joke in his work, you occasionally need to recognize that it belongs to the genre of theoretical fiction. *The Gallery of Fine Arts in Osijek: Studies, Ruins*, the collection of short stories, belongs to this genre and it seems that its author wants its reader to recognize this fact. The book is full of different references to writers who have been mentioned in the context of theoretical fiction. Three examples will suffice. The influence of Tom McCarthy is again on display here, although the resonances with

his work are weaker than in the last two novels where the ideas of radio emissions, instrumental transcommunication, and steganography were prominent. McCarthy and Bekavac share the same fascination with Cocteau: Cocteau's *Orpheus* has served as a kind of hypotext for both of them in their respective novels.

Reza Negarestani, the author of *Cyclonopedia*, the ur-text of theoretical fiction, is mentioned in the book by name. In one of the stories, and with a Ballardian undertone, the narrator describes a symposium organized to mark the twenty-year anniversary of the publication of Negarestani's book. In the near future of Bekavac's diegetic universe, theoretical fiction is established as a well-respected genre, and *Cyclonopedia* seems to be a classic whose eminence is so great that it is honoured even at the fringes of the academic world. One could claim that this is a kind of self-fulfilling prophecy.

This kind of prophecy will play an even more prominent role when Bekavac, this time without invoking any names, uses hyperstition. Unlike superstition, which is merely a false belief, hyperstition can be seen as a modern day self-fulfilling prophecy which functions causally to bring about its own reality. Here is an example: on the last pages of *Gallery*, in a story called "Network" (95–117), there is a scene set up in the future where The Faculty of Electrical Engineering changes its name to the Evangelical Theological Faculty. If Bekavac were a lesser writer, this would remain just an allusion to the current political climate in Croatia, or – if you like – a premonition of the ultimate consequences of the clericalization of public discourse and its infiltration in the sphere of public education; in any case, a marker of contemporaneity. However, the dean of this bastard faculty ends an address to his students with the following words: "The Messiah may be a machine, and we must build it, just as God is that which does not yet exist, but might emerge at some point in the future" (117).[6] This sentence still points to contemporariness, but it is a contemporariness that is not determined by the miserable state of Croatian public discourse. It points to a contemporariness whose horizon is defined by the peculiar reception of one particular philosopher. Bekavac does not hint at it in passing in order to please the few initiated readers. No, this sentence is in the service of Bekavac's killing joke, it is his closing word in the debate on whether literature should be socially 'engaged'[7] – which is an important theme in the debates concerning (post-)Yugoslav fiction – and a demonstration of the impact of that engagement by way of a satiric performative act. Bekavac instrumentalizes his own

---

[6] I thank Brian Willems for the translation of this sentence.
[7] Engaged literature is here taken in the Sartrean sense, as the responsibility of adapting freely made choices to socially useful ends.

literary creation for extra-literary purposes. He presupposes the complicity of his reader and tricks him by using a kind of ontological metalepsis, an act of "undermining the separation between narration and story," a "strange loop" in the structure of narrative levels or a "short circuit" between the "fictional world and the ontological level occupied by the author (Pier 190)."[8] Let me explain how he has been able to pull that off.

The Dean's sentence is an amalgam of two ideas worthy of a closer look. The second part of his sentence about the God who does not yet exist, but could come about, is a direct reference to Meillassoux and his thesis on the inexistent god. According to Meillassoux ("Excerpts" 215), we can be the condition of a world of justice, without being its cause. The advent of the Messiah as justice depends on us, but this dependence is not causal in nature: believers cannot do anything in order to provoke the advent of the Messiah, but only hope for his arrival. However, their hope is not simply worthless because it represents the formal condition for the advent of the world of justice. Believers have to expect the Messiah's glorious arrival and demand justice. Without their expectation, the coming of the Messiah would not mean a thing to anyone: justice that was not demanded would not be anything but a fortuitous occurrence, so it would not be justice at all. Meillassoux's divinology, one of the most bizarre parts of his philosophy, has become the dominant ecclesiastical idea in Bekavac's diegetic universe. However, the first part of the Dean's sentence shows that he has a rather interesting interpretation of it. The Dean talks about the possibility to act causally and to make a machinic Messiah. That looks very much like a hyperstitional argument according to which the existence of a belief in something is itself enough to bring about the contents of that belief.

This is the requisite for Bekavac's meta-literary commentary. His stories are usually full of technical nomenclature and his implicit reader is often confronted with very high demands. The standard demand of the work addressed to its implicit reader is to often look for references outside the work – such as the Schumann resonance, time-space prolapse, the Einstein-Rosen bridge, and others – which may or may not be helpful in the understanding of it. Confronted with this cryptic sentence in the Dean's address, which comes at the end of the book – structurally the most important place – the reader will probably want to trace its origins and, judging by my own exploratory experience, they will come to the encyclopedic entry "Roko's Basilisk."[9] This is

---

8 For a thorough exposition of the concept of ontological metalepsis, see the corresponding article in the *Handbook of Narratology* (Pier et al. 190–203).
9 Wikipedia has a very informative entry dedicated to this argument and its history. [URL: https://rationalwiki.org/wiki/Roko's_basilisk].

one of the most famous examples of hyperstitional fiction, a relatively interesting thought experiment, in essence a re-contextualized version of Pascal's wager and a thought experiment about the potential risks involved in developing artificial intelligence. The premise of the thought experiment is that an all-powerful artificial intelligence from the future could retroactively punish those who did not help bring about its existence, including those who merely knew about the possible development of such a being. It would do so – the theory goes – because one of its objectives would be to prevent existential risk – but it could do that most effectively not merely by preventing existential risk in its present, but by also by 'reaching back' into its past to punish people who were not effective altruists. The artificial intelligence and the person punished need have no causal interaction, and the punished individual may have died decades or centuries earlier. Instead, the AI could punish a *simulation* of the person, which it would construct by deduction from first principles. The moral imperative of the Basilisk is to punish you or your resurrected simulation because its fear of eventual punishment increases the chance that you will now, without hesitation, act to pave the way for an omnipotent intelligence which brings about the world of justice. The Messiah does not yet exist, but it could come about in the future and it makes more sense, as Pascal reasoned, to act like it will happen than to simply ignore that possibility. The machinic Messiah could come about. Bekavac knows that his reader would come to know the story about the advent of the machinic Messiah – also known as Basilisk – and, indeed, I came to know it. Not only that now I know it, but you – dear reader – know it too, and the Messiah could eventually know that you have known it. So, pave the way for his arrival or risk being tortured for all eternity. Bekavac's book is much more vicious than Eco's book. The latter told us a story about the dangers of taking pleasure in reading, while the former used our habit of taking pleasure in reading and put us in danger.

•••

Literature may be *pseudo*, but pleasure we take in it is never 'mere.'

References

Barthes, Roland. "Introduction to the Structural Analysis of Narrative." Image-Music-Text. Fontana Press, 1997, pp. 79–124.
Bekavac, Luka. *Galerija likovnih umjetnosti u Osijeku: studije, ruševine*. Fraktura, 2017.
Bekavac, Luka. *Policijski sat: slutnje, uspomene*. Fraktura, 2016.
Bekavac, Luka. *Viljevo*. Fraktura, 2013.

Bekavac, Luka. *Drenje*. Profil multimedia, 2011.
Brassier, Ray. *Nihil Unbound*. Palgrave McMillan, 2007.
Braver, Lee. *A Thing of This World: A History of Continental Anti-Realism*. Evanston, 2007.
Cassin, Barbara. *Sophistical Practice: Toward a Consistent Relativism*. Fordham, 2014.
Fisher, Mark. *Flatline Constructs: Gothic Materialism and Cybernetic Theory-Fiction*, Exmilitary Collective, 2018.
Hariri, Muhannad. "'It is not Until we Have Eaten the Apple': Forestalling the Necessity of Contingency." *The Legacy of Kant in Sellars and Meillassoux: Analytic and Continental Kantianism*, edited by Fabio Gironi, Routledge, 2018, pp. 179–200.
Harman, Graham. *Quentin Meillassoux: Philosophy in the Making*. Edinburgh University Press, 2011.
Kant, Immanuel. *Critique of Pure Reason, Cambridge University Press*, 1998.
Kant, Immanuel. *Critique of Judgement*. Oxford University Press, 2007.
Meillassoux, Quentin. "Subtraction and Contraction: Deleuze, Immanence and Matter and Memory." *Collapse*, no. 3, 2007, pp. 72–118.
Meillassoux, Quentin. *After Finitude: An Essay on the Necessity of Contingency*, Continuum, 2008.
Meillassoux, Quentin. "Excerpts from *L'inexistence divine*." Graham Harman, *Quentin Meillassoux: Philosophy in the Making*. Edinburgh University Press, 2011, pp. 175–237.
Meillassoux, Quentin. "Iteration, Reiteration, Repetition: A Speculative Analysis of the Sign Devoid of Meaning." *Genealogies of Speculation: Materialism and Subjectivity since Structuralism*, edited by Armen Avanessian and Suhail Malik, Bloomsbury, 2016, pp. 117–198.
Meillassoux, Quentin. *Science Fiction and Extro-Science Fiction*. Univocal, 2015.
Meillassoux, Quentin, Florian Hecker and Robin Mackay. *A Speculative Solution: Quentin Meillassoux and Florian Hecker Talk Hyperchaos*. Urbanomic, 2010.
Pier, John. "Metalepsis." *Handbook of Narratology*, edited by Peter Hühn et al., Walter de Gruyter GmbH & Co, 2009, pp. 190–203.
Propp, Vladimir. *Morphology of the Folktale*. American Folklore Society, 1968.
Searle, John. *The Mystery of Consciousness*, New York Review of Books, 1997.
Shaviro, Steven. *Discognition*. Repeater Books, 2015.

CHAPTER 7

The Narrative Out of Time: The Nonhuman World of Luka Bekavac's Fiction

Matija Jelača and Anera Ryznar

Croatian (post-)Yugoslav fiction has been essentially marked by its orientation towards the traumas of its immediate social and political contexts. Thus, it has been frequently labelled as realistic ("reality prose"), mimetic ("critical mimetism") and/or naturalistic ("new naturalism"). Igor Gajin's extensive study of contemporary Croatian literature (2020) explores the dynamics of Croatian sociocultural transformations in the post-socialist era, i.e. during the so-called period of transition, and he detects structural changes in the poetic identity of contemporary Croatian narratives, identifying causal links between the formative moments of the transitional project and Croatian literary practices. According to Gajin's analysis, the ideological discourse of the transition entails a teleological orientation towards two clearly set and predetermined goals – the establishment of 'real' or 'true' capitalism in the context of the long-awaited national state – which can only be achieved through linear, unidirectional progression from a gruesome but temporary present towards the promise of a future utopia. Suspended in this state of the anticipation of a future which does not seem to be arriving, the Croatian literary mainstream embraces the notion of temporality as teleology and structures neat, progressive linear plots which "integrate the dispersed reality by providing it with closed, clear-cut endings," be it "the wedding at the end of a love story or the discovery of the murderer at the end of a crime novel" (Gajin 204). In other words, Croatian mimetic fiction pursues teleological plots in order to establish sense and order where only chaos and disorder exist – primarily in the gruesome Croatian social and economic reality which mimetic fiction does not employ as its mere narrative setting but, more often than not, as its main topic and the object of its supposed critique. Nevertheless, even when mimetic narratives explicitly criticize the official ideology at the level of story, they nevertheless support it at the level of language and discourse by uncritically adopting its main regulatory principles – linearity, causality, rationality, denotation, and continuity – according to which we are purposefully plodding through historical time towards a better future. Gajin suggests that this type of dénouement, which conceives a future in terms of order rather than entropy, plays an important psychosocial role insomuch as it heals the trauma of transition and normalizes the pathologies and deviations of Croatian neoliberal discourse (205).

Luka Bekavac's impressive fictional *oeuvre* constitutes a decisive departure from the Croatian contemporary realistic-mimetic literary mainstream. Most notably, with regards to his treatment of temporality, Bekavac relinquishes mimetic teleology in favour of anomalous, impossible, and entropic timelines. However, while it might seem tempting to interpret such a move as a literary response to the bleak vicissitudes of Croatian post-transitional socio-political reality, this urge is to be resisted. Instead, our contention is twofold. First, what truly lies at the heart of Bekavac's fiction is the problem of time; and secondly, Bekavac's literary exploration of this problematic nexus is to be understood in relation to speculative realism, an important movement in contemporary continental philosophy that initiated the so called *speculative turn*[1] in the humanities. It will therefore be argued that Bekavac's fiction in general and his treatment of time in particular are to be understood as a literary response to a philosophical problem that speculative realism placed back at the forefront of contemporary continental philosophical discussions – the possibility of knowledge of the world in itself, or a world independent from and indifferent to human thought and knowledge. In order to explicate this claim the first part of the paper will provide a brief overview of speculative realism in general and its relation to literature in particular, with special emphasis being placed on H.P. Lovecraft's weird fiction and its relation to Bekavac's literary endeavour. The second part of the paper will then present a reading of the temporality of Bekavac's novels *Drenje* (2011), *Viljevo* (2013) and *The Curfew: Premonitions, Recollections* (2015) which will show that all of these novels deconstruct the classical notion of time on various different levels. Finally, the concluding part of the paper will bring these two strands of the discussion together in order to show the manner in which Bekavac's deconstruction of the classical notion of time is to be understood as a response to the challenge of constructing a literary work of art which would instantiate in the reader the experience of an encounter with a nonhuman object, a work of art utterly alien to human cognitive faculties.

---

1 This phrase was first used as the title of a collection of writings dedicated to this new tendency in continental philosophy (Bryant, Levi, et al., editors, *The Speculative Turn: Continental Materialism and Realism*, 2011), and in time it came to be used as the name of this tendency itself.

1 Speculative Realism, H.P. Lovecraft, and Luka Bekavac

In the beginning, speculative realism was merely the name of a one day workshop held at Goldsmiths College, University of London, in April 2007 which gathered four, at the time, relatively unknown philosophers: Ray Brassier, Quentin Meillassoux, Iain Hamilton Grant, and Graham Harman.[2] Given the major differences between their respective philosophical positions, the term 'speculative realism' was chosen as a compromise umbrella-term with which all four participants could agree upon, but with which none of them actually identified. As the ideas and themes of the Goldsmiths workshop disseminated across the humanities, eventually it came to be considered as the inaugural event of a new movement in continental philosophy, with speculative realism operating as its name. However, as the enthusiasm around speculative realism grew, the original Goldsmiths group began to dissipate, for it became obvious with time that the differences between the four were much greater than what they had in common. In the process, the very idea of speculative realism as a movement came into question, which culminated famously with Brassier proclaiming the whole thing "an online orgy of stupidity" (Erdem). However, while Brassier's harsh reaction was certainly understandable at the time given the circumstances, it is hard to deny that speculative realism did in fact denote, in continental philosophy, a real tendency away from what was perceived as the idealism of poststructuralism towards renewed attempts to articulate realist philosophical positions. To put it in the simplest possible terms, speculative realism can be construed as the attempt to pose anew the question of the possibility of knowledge of the world in itself, that is, of the world as independent from and indifferent to human thought and knowledge. While it could be argued that in some form or another this question is as old as philosophy, it was Kant's formulation of this problem and his solution to it that determined the philosophical landscape of the last two hundred years. As is well known, Kant gave a negative response to this question. Or to be more precise, Kant claims that our knowledge is limited to the world as it is for us, or the world as it is given to us in experience, and that therefore we cannot know the world as it is in itself. However, Kant also affirms our ability to *think* the world in itself.[3] In Meillassoux's influential interpretation, the two hundred years following Kant's injunction against the possibility of knowledge of the in itself

---

[2] The announcement for the workshop and the transcript of its proceedings can be found in Brassier et al.

[3] "...even if we cannot cognize these same objects as things in themselves we at least must be able to think them as things in themselves. For otherwise there would follow the absurd proposition that there is an appearance without anything that appears" (Kant, *Critique of Pure Reason* 115).

are nothing but a development and elaboration of this crucial Kantian insight. Meillassoux famously gives the name of *correlationism* to all post-Kantian philosophy, continental and analytic alike (5). At the heart of correlationism lies the affirmation of the idea "according to which we only ever have access to the correlation between thinking and being, and never to either term considered apart from the other" (5). Meillassoux's diagnosis of correlationism was the initial spark that ignited speculative realism, for this was precisely what brought together not only the four participants of the Goldsmiths event but also everyone else who enthusiastically followed along. The initial enthusiasm surrounding speculative realism was due to a sense of liberation from what was considered at the time a stifling state of continental philosophy and the humanities in general. Meillassoux's account of correlationism was seen as a perfect description of the logic responsible for this unfortunate state of things. But what was truly captivating about Meillassoux and the rest of the speculative realist philosophers was their belief that the correlationist circle could be broken out of, and that knowledge of the world in itself was indeed possible.[4] In fact, it could be argued that this was precisely the dividing line of philosophy before and after speculative realism. The question of the possibility of knowledge of the in itself was always at the centre of continental philosophy. But whereas most continental philosophers followed Kant's lead and addressed this question in negative terms, speculative realism was seen as opening an alternative affirmative path. Lee Braver has for the past few years been developing a reading of the history of continental philosophy along these very lines (2015). In his reading, at the heart of continental philosophy has always been the idea of "thinking the unthinkable" (Braver 11), "'grasping the ungraspable'" (Levinas in Braver 11) or "'experiencing the impossible'" (Derrida in Braver 13). Kant was again the one to have formulated this idea first. As it was already mentioned, Kant instituted a distinction between knowledge and thought. We cannot know the in itself but we can think it. This distinction is crucial not only for Kant's epistemology (and ontology) but for his aesthetics as well, in particular for his account of the sublime. In Kant, the sublime denotes an encounter with phenomena, which, by their magnitude or power, transcend our cognitive and physical faculties thereby making us feel small and weak in comparison. However, while these phenomena transcend our faculty of knowledge (understanding and sensibility), our faculty of thought (reason) transcends them as natural phenomena in turn. This is why, after an

---

4 Graham Harman is an obvious exception in this regard, for Kant's postulation of the unknowability of the thing in itself constitutes the basic tenet of his object-oriented philosophy.

initial feeling of pain and fear, the encounter with the sublime phenomena instils in us a sense of pleasure.[5]

According to Jean François Lyotard, "the aesthetic of the sublime is where modern art (including literature) finds its impetus and where the logic of the avant-garde finds its axioms" (77). As Lyotard further clarifies, the feeling of the sublime results from the conflict between "the faculty to conceive of something and the faculty to 'present' something. (...) We can conceive the infinitely great, the infinitely powerful, but every presentation of an object destined to 'make visible' this absolute greatness or power appears to us painfully inadequate" (77–78). These ideas "of which no presentation is possible" and which therefore "impart no knowledge about reality (experience)" are called by Lyotard "unpresentable" (78). In light of this, Lyotard argues that the essence of modern art consists in an attempt to "present the fact that the unpresentable exists. To make visible that there is something which can be conceived and which can neither be seen nor made visible: this is what is at stake in modern painting" (78). Lyotard further elaborates on this by claiming that in the case of painting, "it will 'present' something, though negatively; it will therefore avoid figuration or representation. It will be 'white' like one of Malevitch's squares; it will enable us to see only by making it impossible to see; it will please only by causing pain" (78). Concerning literature, Lyotard names Proust and Joyce as examples of the aesthetic of the sublime: "The works of Proust and Joyce both allude to something which does not allow itself to be made present. (...) In Proust, what is being eluded (...) is the identity of consciousness"; while in Joyce it is "the identity of writing" itself (80).

In contrast to Lyotard, who cites the greats of modernist literature as examples, speculative realism is usually associated with a writer of horror fiction, namely Howard Phillips Lovecraft. As Graham Harman famously suggested, besides the rejection of correlationism, the only thing all four members of the original speculative realism group had in common was a fascination with Lovecraft and his weird tales of cosmic horror (Harman 171). Lovecraft describes his ambitions in writing "weird fiction" thus:

> I wanted to achieve, momentarily, the illusion of some strange suspension or violation of the galling limitations of time, space, and natural law which for ever imprison us and frustrate our curiosity about the infinite cosmic spaces beyond the radius of our sight and analysis. These stories

---

5 Kant lays out his account of the sublime in the "Analytic of the Sublime" (pp. 128–159) of his *Critique of the Power of Judgment*.

frequently emphasize the element of horror because fear is our deepest and strongest emotion, and the one which best lends itself to the creation of nature-defying illusions. Horror and the unknown or the strange are always closely connected, so that it is hard to create a convincing picture of shattered natural law or cosmic alienage or "outsideness" without laying stress on the emotion of fear. (Lovecraft, "Notes")

On another occasion, Lovecraft states in the same vein "the crux of a weird tale is something which could not possibly happen" (Lovecraft, *Selected Letters* 434). Clearly, therefore, for Lovecraft, "the cosmic alienage," "the outsidedness," or "the unknown" are to be considered as synonymous with "the impossible." On yet another occasion Lovecraft writes about "the galling sense of *intolerable restraint* which all sensitive people (…) feel as they survey their natural limitations in time and space as scaled against the freedoms and expansions and comprehensions and adventurous expectancies which the mind can formulate as abstract conceptions" (295). What this last formulation reveals is that Lovecraft believed, like Kant, in the power of the mind to transcend human cognitive and physical limitations. However, it also reveals that Lovecraft went a step further than Kant, and believed in the capacity of the mind not only to think the impossible but also to imagine and represent it in literary form. Lovecraft's weird fiction constitutes precisely such an attempt to construct fictional narratives that purportedly depict the impossible or that which lies beyond human cognitive and physical faculties. The crucial place in these narratives, however, belongs to the human observer, that is to the characters, which encounter these impossible, nonhuman phenomena. It is the confrontation with these phenomena which transcend their cognitive and physical capabilities that engenders in these characters (and by proxy, supposedly, in readers themselves), the sense of cosmic horror constitutive of Lovecraft's weird fiction. Given that at the heart of Lovecraft's literary endeavour lies the idea of a nonhuman world, or a world independent from and indifferent to human thought, it should not be hard to comprehend the pride of place his weird fiction enjoys in speculative realist circles.

Now it is our contention that Bekavac's fiction can productively be read as a continuation of the tradition of weird fiction as initiated by Lovecraft and as reactualized in the contemporary philosophical context by speculative realism. Here it must be emphasized that this aspect of Bekavac's fiction, although essential in our view, is far from being everything there is to it. As is obvious to anyone even remotely familiar with this body of work, Bekavac's literature is rich and complex and it can certainly be interpreted in many different ways. But from the perspective of its main themes and ideas, as well as the affective responses it produces in its readers, it is hard to deny its Lovecraftian lineage. With regard to the former, the very notion of the world independent from and indifferent to human though and knowledge constitutes a vital part of Bekavac's fiction, and on many different levels. Indeed, how to create a literary nonhuman world constitutes a veritable problem for Bekavac, arguably one of the most important problems driving his entire literary endeavour. However, where Bekavac departs from Lovecraft is in regards to Lovecraft's conviction that this nonhuman world can be described, depicted, and represented in literary form. In contrast, Bekavac knows well that after the modernist revolution in literature there is no going back to a figurative, mimetic, or representational solution to this problem,[6] and it is precisely in this regard that Bekavac's fiction constitutes a significant advance over much of the tradition of weird fiction to date. Following the modernist cue, for Bekavac literature is nothing but a site of experimentation – experimentation with literary form itself and an exploration of the possibilities of literary discourse in general.[7] It is with regards to this that Bekavac's affinity for Lovecraft's attempts to present the unpresentable in literary form or narrate the impossible is to be understood.[8] As we have seen earlier, Lovecraft's weird tales depict his characters' encounters with impossible phenomena, which instil in them a sense of cosmic horror. The readers themselves are in turn supposed to experience the same sense of cosmic dread either by way of identification with the characters or by the purported monstrosity of the nonhuman phenomena described. Instead of trying to depict the characters' encounter with the impossible like Lovecraft has done, Bekavac explores the possibility of instantiating in the readers themselves the experience of an encounter with the impossible or the nonhuman. In order to achieve this, the literary text itself must become this impossible or nonhuman object which transcends the readers' cognitive faculties, making them thereby experience the sense of cosmic horror. While there

---

6 This claim and the following ones can be inferred from Bekavac's text itself and accordingly they are to be understood as referring to the implied author of these fictions. However, it is impossible to avoid mentioning that his real life counterpart indeed holds virtually the same views that is revealed by his various interviews, public appearances and scholarly work. For his most explicit and concise disavowal of mimetic-realist conception of literature see Bekavac as quoted in Mandić. For a similar yet more elaborate account on this same topic, see Bekavac, "Poruka ne postoji" and Bekavac, "Suvremena znanost."
7 For his views on literary experimentation see Bekavac, "Pet za pet."
8 Besides naming H.P. Lovecraft as one of his favourite horror writers (see Bekavac, "Poruka ne postoji"), Lovecraftian "cognitive horror" occupies an important place in Bekavac's scholarly work as well. See his articles "Teorijske fikcije: Ligotti, Negarestani i spekulativni realizam" (2016) and "Readability Thresholds – Xenography and Speculative Fiction" (2019).

are many different ways in which Bekavac attempts to realize this formidable task, experimentation with time constitutes its arguably most significant aspect. The next section presents a narratological reading of Bekavac's treatment of time which will enable us in turn to explicate this crucial point in the last section of the paper.

2   The Temporality of Bekavac's Novels

Over the last decade Bekavac has published three novels – *Drenje* (2011), *Viljevo* (2013) and *The Curfew: Premonitions, Recollections* (2015) – as well as the book titled *The Gallery of Fine Arts in Osijek: Studies, Ruins* (2017) which is connected to the novels but will not be included in the analysis since it is structured, very broadly speaking, as a collection of fictional essays.[9] The notion of time and the concept of temporality as such is not only important but constitutive for Bekavac's novels, which can truly be read as time-conscious novels or *Zeitromans* as Ricoeur put it, meaning they are both *tales of time* and *tales about time* (113). For example, the problem of time and its linearity precedes even the very act of reading Bekavac's novels; it springs up the moment we decide to approach these three novels as a single body of work or a novelistic trilogy. And there are reasons to do so – the novels branch out toward each other, forming links and connections, sometimes very clear and explicit, and sometimes subtle and contestable, open for interpretation on the part of the reader. To be more precise: even though each of these novels constructs its own storyworld, they simultaneously share the same diegetic universe, made coherent by the same characters, topics, events, and atmosphere. It is also worth noting that in an interview the author has insisted that he did not see these novels as a *series* or *sequence* of texts but rather as a *set* or *cluster* (without a beginning and an end), and that the reader could approach this cluster of texts from any given direction, read it in any given order, regardless of the date of their publication (Bekavac, "Nastavljam sličnim"). This constitutes the first temporal paradox, but not at all an innocent one, since it intervenes in the conventional reading order, particularly when it comes to reading thrillers, science fiction, and others genres that are structured around a mystery waiting to be solved, which typically occurs later on, at the end of the book or at the end of the trilogy.

---

9   This work from Bekavac is addressed in Ante Jerić's contribution to this collection, "Kant has Some Relevance Here: On a Fictional Theory of Quentin Meillassoux and the Theoretical Fiction of Luka Bekavac."

But, since Bekavac's novels do not adhere to the conventions of any particular genre, but rather combine the generic features of science fiction, speculative fiction, mystery, thriller, and theoretical fiction,[10] challenging and disputing these genres every step of the way, this disruption of the reading order, for example, the possibility of reading backwards from the last novel of the trilogy towards the first one, reorients the readers' generic expectations and prepares them for the deconstruction of the classical notion of temporality which takes place in the novels and affects almost every level of these narratives. Thus, by focusing on the specific treatment time has in these novels, we can set up a productive analytical perspective from which we can approach other aspects of this very complex fiction and interpret them in the context of speculative realism.

First and foremost, the notion of time is one of the main themes of these novels. It is elaborated extensively on the level of the story, experienced empirically by the characters and discussed theoretically among them: they constantly feel they are either behind or out of time, that they were born too late or too early, that time flows differently for them, that time has stretched and slowed down up to the point of completely stopping; they talk about different kinds of time (*standard time, lower time, new time*); they try to manipulate time and they often discard the notions of progression, causality, and order. Also, the scientific discourse which has been interpolated in the novels (Ryznar) contains a network of (para)scientific theories, real and mock scientific data and references in the field of theoretical physics, quantum ontology, and mathematics, which deal with the notion of spacetime and introduce in the novels concepts such as the Schumann resonance, time-space prolapse, singularity, the Einstein-Rosen bridge, and others. Basically, these are concepts which renounce the Newtonian idea of absolute time in favour of temporal relativity, simultaneity, and synchronicity. We believe it is safe to say that the novels take these theoretical concepts elaborated *in* the storylines and apply them *to* the very process of their narrativization, in order to break away from the imperative of the forward linearity of time. So, the novels employ various techniques to structure themselves as *antichronies, polichronies,* or *uchronias* which is a set of terms used by narratologists (Dannenberg; Herman) to describe metatemporal narratives or narratives which simultaneously invoke and resist temporal analysis due to the fact that they construct impossible, unusual, or anomalous timelines. But, according to Mark Currie (97), the fictional rejection of chronology often results in an affirmation of chronology on

---

10 See Jerić's contribution to this collection for a discussion of theoretical fiction in relation to Bekavac.

the part of the reader, since the forward linearity of time ranks among the very highest of absolute human predispositions and it is a cognitive prerequisite for the process of reading which heavily relies on the principle of chronology, intentionality, and causality. That is why the reader of Bekavac's trilogy, who tries to make sense of the story, tie up loose ends, and reconstruct disrupted timelines (and inevitably fails in doing so), paradoxically experiences the temporality of these novels as *entropic*,[11] meaning that with the progression of reading time, entropy (disorder, chaos) steadily increases and not decreases, which is what the reader expects when reading a book, for things to make sense in the end. We see this as the underlying paradox of these novels: that, while on the level of the story and its narration the books try to deconstruct the classical notion of temporality (the famous arrow of time), they simultaneously reaffirm that very notion on the part of the reader. So, in order to examine how this happens, we first must remind ourselves that narratology distinguishes three distinct levels or types of temporality in a narrative text:

a) The first one is *narrated time* or the time of the story (which in Bekavac's novels encompasses many different time levels and spans from the Second World War to the distant and dystopic future of the 22nd century).

b) The second one is *narrative time*, or the time of the narration (where we can observe different tactics used to disrupt the chronology, frequency, and duration of the narrated events and create a sense of temporal entropy).

c) The third one is *reading time*, or mental time required by the reader in order to make sense of the story, to reconstruct the disrupted timeline, and to finish flipping the pages of the book.

We will primarily focus on the interaction between narrative time (b) and reading time (c) and point out some narrative strategies used to produce a specific type of discursive temporality which we have called *entropic*.

The novel *Drenje* is narrated from the perspective of an omniscient third person narrator who partially focalizes the narrated events through the perspective of the main protagonist Marta, and thus it seems that in the respect of narration this is the most classically written of the three novels. It also seems that while the topic of time is extensively discussed on the level of the novel's story (through the motives of the *static noise* and the *archive* which introduce the notion of timelessness), the level of narration remains more or less unaffected by this temporal anomaly: events are narrated in a chronological order

---

11 We were inspired to use this term by Marie-Laure Ryan's article "Temporal Paradoxes in Narrative" (144).

with a few analepses which provide the reader with the necessary information about the characters' background and the history of the town Drenje. In other words, the narration does not disrupt the storyline in any of Genette's famous categories: order, duration, or frequency (25–34). Nevertheless, there are two aspects of the novel's discourse which draw attention to the position of the narratorial voice and which affect both narrative and reading time.

The first is *description*. The descriptive passages, which portray the physical properties of interior and exterior spaces, make up approximately one half of the novel. According to Seymour Chatman (31), the distinction between narration and description at the discourse level boils down to the fact that the narrative entails two time dimensions, *inner* or *story* duration, and *outer* or *discourse* duration, whereas description has no inner time dimension, however much time its actual transmission in a medium may require. In other words, long, painstakingly detailed, and often very artificial descriptions delivered by the novel's narrator do not affect the narrated time but do affect the reading time, which stretches significantly, in great part due to the way these descriptions are delivered. Descriptions also pose a question of the narrator's intent and position: why is he telling us all this, what is the purpose and function of these descriptions, what is their relevance to the story and why does the narrator, who we generally perceive as omniscient, suddenly behave as if he is visually limited by his own physical position and describing a video footage of the described scene? In other words, descriptions widen the diegetic gap between the narrator and the narrated world, a gap which will in the next example turn into an abyss.

A careful reader will notice that the opening descriptive paragraph of the novel is reproduced later on in two other instances. The first time it appears, it is at the very beginning, before the characters are introduced, and is therefore exclusively attributed to the narrator. Later on, when it is repeated for the first time, it is in the context of Marta's exploration of the countryside, which opens up the possibility that the point of view is in fact Marta's (Marta being the focalizer of that chapter). The third time it appears it is embedded deeply in the diegesis; namely, it is the text that the characters have extracted and deciphered from the static noise they recorded in the field. This is a typical case of what narratology calls the abyss structure (*mise en abyme*) and it is impossible not to notice that the name of this literary technique mirrors the name Bezdan (Abyss) which appears as an alternate word for the uncanny static noise the characters are studying but also as a mysterious toponym scattered throughout Bekavac's trilogy. According to Marcus Snow (140), in respect to the notion of temporality, the abyss structure (unlike, for example, a framed narrative) is intimated upwards, and we would suggest that this upward feel is because the abyss uses a different sense of temporality: it develops vertically (with its associated levels of hierarchy) rather than spilling out sideways. Its metaleptic verticality resists the putative linearity of a narrative and implies eternal looping and eternal regress. This process of mirroring, reflecting, and repetition further complicates the position of the narrator. The mechanic quality of his voice that we have earlier noticed from the technical jargon used in his descriptions suddenly coincides with the fact that in the abyss scene his own words are now produced by a converter, a mechanical apparatus the characters are using. So, when characters point out that "we use technical lingo to deanthropomorphisize things," (130) it truly can be read as a metanarrative commentary which describes the quality of the narrator's voice as mechanic and therefore inanimate. It is also a stylistic feature that contributes to the eerie effect of the novel.

The novel *Viljevo*, on the other hand, presents a kind of narratological conundrum in the sense that it is almost impossible to determine who (or what) its narrator is or whether, in fact, any narration is taking place at all. The three chapters of the novel are basically structured as three separate documents: a transcribed audio-diary, a revised transcript of a conversation, and a published scientific paper. One might think that the novel exploits the old technique of found or discovered documents but it still remains a mystery as to which higher instance is responsible for finding them, editing them, and binding them together to tell a story. So, the documents (or the chapters) are not mutually connected by a single narrative voice or an established chronology. What we in fact do have is a type of "narration" (or presentation, to be more accurate) which Genette (31) calls *repetitive* in the sense that a single event is presented from the perspective of three different characters participating in that same event. Furthermore, it is suggested that the characters occupy different temporal planes and that their accounts have been somehow tampered with (revised, rewritten, translated, transcribed) by known or unknown persons, which consequentially affects their reliability. So, with every new chapter, the reader is back at the beginning, reading different versions of the same event, but the contradictions that arise from the protagonists' testimonies prevent her from reconstructing a complete story. All this cancels out the idea of linear story progression as well as the strategies the reader must employ to reconstruct its basic elements. Therefore, the reading time is stretched to its limits since the reader is forced to move back and forth in the text and in time, searching for clues and trying to produce a coherent narrative. The discourse of the novel makes her job even harder and prolongs the reading process even more. Gaps and incomplete sentences, pages and pages of numerical sequences, words written in continuum, unseparated by blank spaces, dialogue written in separate columns and, on top of all that, dense and incomprehensible scientific discourse full of technical lingo, footnotes, and references – at this point we could quote the author once again and say that, if there *is* a narrator in this novel, he is undoubtedly a malevolent one (Bekavac, "Poruka ne postoji" 10).

Finally, the third novel *The Curfew* is the one which is most thoroughly immersed in the problem of temporality but shifts this problem to the level of personal or intimate time which it elaborates through the topic of memory and writing. The main diegesis is narrated from the perspective of an extremely self-conscious autodiegetic first-person narrator. It is a retrospective narration of his earlier life and the narrator uses this pseudoautobiographical discourse to open up problems that are inherent to it (such as the unreliability of memory, the incompatibility of intimate and monumental time, the problem of knowledge, the failure of logic and causality in this type of narrative, and so on).

As far as the temporality of the novel is concerned, its chronology has been disrupted both on the level of the story and on the level of narration, which is structured as circular or as a closed loop: retrospection is constantly being cut off by a series of interruptions and false starts, piled up notes and drafts, revisions and supplements. The main narrator is extremely time-conscious, we might even say he is 'stuck in time': he is unable to reconstruct past events but he is also unable to proceed, push his narration forward (for example, he announces the end of the story some 60 pages before it really ends). These mechanisms keep the reader trapped in a perpetual state of the anticipation of retrospection:[12] she keeps waiting for the events from the narrator's past to be transformed into her own reading present through the act of narration – an act which continually stumbles and misfires. It is also suggested on numerous occasions in the novel that, in order to make sense of the past events, the narrator must "forget oblivion" (Bekavac 164) which can only be achieved through the process of writing (by pressing the tip of the pen against the surface of the

---

12   One of Mark Currie's key concepts, inspired by Heidegger's and Derrida's understanding of temporality. The phrase refers to a temporal structure which "lies at the heart of the human experience of time but also at the heart of narrative (...) Narrative is generally retrospective in the sense that the teller is looking back on events and relating them in the past tense, but a reader or listener experiences these events for the first time, as quasi-present" (Currie 29–30). Or as Peter Brooks (23) puts it: "If the past is to be read as present, it is a curious present that we know to be past in relation to a future we know to be already in place, already in wait for us to reach it. Perhaps we would do best to speak of the anticipation of retrospection as our chief tool in making sense of narrative, the master trope of its strange logic."

paper). So, it is the materiality of the text which grants access to the timeless nature of existence, and this is the point where Bekavac's theoretical interest in Derrida comes into play[13] and opens this novel towards the genre of metafiction. Apart from the fact that the Derridean notion of the archive appears on numerous occasions in Bekavac's trilogy and presents one of its main motives (while preserving most of Derrida's intended meanings), the strange logic of this concept can be also observed on the level of the novels' discourse which seems to suffer from a strong case of "archive fever" in the sense that they paradoxically produce events as much as they record them. In other words, the temporal reach of Bekavac's story lines might encompass a period from the 1940s to some dystopian 22nd century, but we as readers are stuck in the novels' unbearable present, unable to reconstruct the narratives' past and to progress to their future(s).

3 The Narrative Out of Time

As we have seen, Bekavac's novels deconstruct the classical notion of the linearity of time on various levels. At the level of story, *Drenje* introduces the idea of "the archive" – a theme crucial in the other novels as well – denoting another realm, purely spatial and timeless, wherein everything that is, was, and will be exists simultaneously on the same plane. At the level of narration, all the novels employ various techniques to disrupt the chronology, frequency, and duration of the narrated events and thus construct impossible, unusual or anomalous timelines. Confronted with such disrupted, impossible timelines the reader attempts in vain to reconstruct them and tie all their loose ends together. In the process, the reading time is stretched to its limit, with the reader experiencing the temporality of these novels as entropic – instead of decreasing with (reading) time, their entropy increases. As a consequence, the reader is left overwhelmed and unable to make sense of the story as a unified, coherent whole. It is in this regard that Bekavac's novels can be said to be impossible, nonhuman objects, which, when encountered, instil in the reader the Lovecraftian sense of cosmic horror.

However, there is another, related sense in which Bekavac's treatment of time can be understood. This other sense is revealed by the opening line of *The Curfew* which states "There is no more time" (5). It is our contention that this statement, which is repeated various times throughout the novel both verba-

---

13 Bekavac is the author of the study on Derrida *Prema singularnosti: Derrida i književni tekst* (2015).

tim and with slight variations, is to be read not only in intradiegetic terms, but also as a metanarrative statement revealing an essential aspect of the novel itself and Bekavac's literary endeavour as a whole. This is to say that, in our reading, the crucial aspect of Bekavac's attempt to create a literary nonhuman world consists precisely in the idea of constructing a *narrative out of time* (to echo Lovecraft's similar formulations),[14] a narrative purportedly devoid of time. The motif of "the archive," which as we have seen appears throughout Bekavac's novels, indexes the idea of nonhuman otherness – an other realm independent from and indifferent to human thought – precisely to a purely spatial configuration purportedly existing outside of time. Bekavac's treatment of time outlined above can be read as an attempt to instantiate this very idea at the level of literary, narrative discourse as well. What this interpretation reveals is that the intent behind Bekavac's deconstruction of the linearity of time is not only to instantiate in the reader a Lovecraftian sense of cosmic horror but to challenge the conception of literature as essentially an art of time. By posing the problem of constructing a literary work of art as a nonhuman, impossible object, Bekavac draws attention to an obvious yet often overlooked proposition: What is a literary text in itself, independent from both its writer and its readers? Nothing but a material object and/or a spatial configuration existing outside of time. In other words, what Bekavac's fiction deconstructs is the duality of the materiality of (literary) texts/writing, which is spatial in nature, and the ideality of thought/reading which unfolds in time. While writing in general has traditionally been construed as merely a material representation of pure thought or intelligibility, here this binary is deconstructed and the materiality of writing is interpreted as the other of thought and as completely alien to it. To the extent that thought necessarily unfolds in time and a text exists as a material object in space, literary writing which pretends to the status of a nonhuman, impossible object is to be pursued by privileging the purely material, visual, graphic, or spatial aspects of writing.[15]

References

Bekavac, Luka. *Drenje*. Profil, 2011.

---

14 To name just the most obvious examples, two of the most famous Lovecraft's stories are titled "The Colour Out of Space" (1927) and "The Shadow Out of Time" (1936).
15 Interpreted in this way it is impossible to escape the reading of Bekavac's literary endeavour as a continuation of his theoretical pursuits and/or vice versa. Bekavac's paper "Readability Thresholds – Xenography and Speculative Fiction" constitutes his most explicit theoretical articulation of such a project to date.

Bekavac, Luka. "Poruka ne postoji izvan šuma (interview)." *Quorum*, vol. 27, no. 5/6, 2011, pp. 9–22.

Bekavac, Luka. *Viljevo*. Fraktura, 2013.

Bekavac, Luka. "Nastavljam sličnim, dakle drugačijim putem (interview)." *Portal Novosti*, 724, 30 Oct. 2013, http://arhiva.portalnovosti.com/2013/10/luka-bekavac-nastavljam-slicnim-dakle-drugacijim-putem/. Accessed 15 May 15 2019.

Bekavac, Luka. "Pet za pet – Luka Bekavac (interview)." *U carstvu melanholije*, 7 Jan. 2014, https://asjaba.com/2014/01/07/pet-za-pet-luka-bekavac/. Accessed 15 May 15 2019.

Bekavac, Luka. *The Curfew: Premonitions, Recollections* [*Policijski sat: slutnje, uspomene*]. Fraktura, 2015.

Bekavac, Luka. "Suvremena znanost uvijek je velika inspiracija (interview)." *Elektronske novine*, 20 Oct. 2015, http://www.e-novine.com/intervju/intervju-kultura/127126-Suvremena-znanost-uvijek-velika-inspiracija.html. Accessed 15 May 15 2019.

Bekavac, Luka. "Teorijske fikcije: Ligotti, Negarestani i spekulativni realizam." *Anafora*, vol. 3, no. 1, 2016, pp. 1–20.

Bekavac, Luka. "Readability Thresholds – Xenography and Speculative Fiction." *Cross-Cultural Studies Review*, vol. 1, no. 1–2, 2019, pp. 69–90.

Brassier, Ray et al. "Speculative Realism." *Collapse*, vol. 3, 2007, pp. 306–450.

Braver, Lee. "Thoughts on the Unthinkable." *Parrhesia: A journal of Critical Philosophy*, no. 24, 2015, pp. 1–16.

Brooks, Peter. *Reading for the Plot: Design and Intention in Narrative*. Harvard University Press, 1984.

Bryant, Levi, et al. (eds.). *The Speculative Turn: Continental Materialism and Realism*. Re.press, 2011.

Chatman, Seymoure. *Coming to Terms. The Rhetoric of Narrative in Fiction and Film*. Cornell University Press, 1990.

Currie, Mark. *About Time: Narrative, Fiction and the Philosophy of Time*. Edinburgh University Press, 2007.

Dannenberg, Hilary P. *Coincidence and Counterfactuality: Plotting Time and Space in Narrative Fiction*. University of Nebraska Press, 2008.

Derrida, Jacques. *Archive Fever: A Freudian Impression*. Translated by Eric Prenowitz, Chicago University Press, 1998.

Erdem, Cengiz. "Ray Brassier Interviewed by Marcin Rychter: 'I Am a Nihilist Because I Still Believe in Truth.'" *Senselogic*, 21 Aug. 2017, cengizerdem.wordpress.com/2011/03/05/ray-brassier-interviewed-by-marcin-rychte-r-i-am-a-nihilist-because-i-still-believe-in-truth/. Accessed 7 July 2019.

Gajin, Igor. *Lelek tranzicije: hrvatska književnost, kultura i mediji u razdoblju postsocijalizma*, Disput, 2020.

Genette, Gérard. "Order, Duration and Frequency." *Narrative Dynamics: Essays in Time, Plot, Closure and Frames*, edited by Brian Richardson, The Ohio State University Press, 2002, pp. 25–34.

Graham Harman, "The Road to Objects." *continent*, no. 3.1, 2011, pp. 171–179.

Herman, David. *Story Logic. Problems and Possibilities of Narrative*. University of Nebraska Press, 2002.

Kant, Immanuel. *Critique of Pure Reason*. Translated and edited by Paul Guyer and Allen W. Wood. Cambridge University Press, 1998.

Kant, Immanuel. *Critique of the Power of Judgment*. Translated by Paul Guyer and Eric Matthews. Cambridge University Press, 2000.

Lovecraft, Howard Phillips. "Notes on Writing Weird Fiction (1933)." *The H.P. Lovecraft Archive*, http://www.hplovecraft.com/writings/texts/essays/nwwf.aspx. Accessed 7 July, 2019.

Lovecraft, Howard Phillips. *Selected Letters 1929–1931, Vol. 3*. Arkham House Publishers, 1971.

Lyotard, Jean François. "Answering the Question: What is Postmodernism?" *The Postmodern Condition: A Report on Knowledge*. Translated by Régis Durand. Manchester University Press, 1984, pp. 71–82.

Mandić, Marko. "Bekavac: Ono što književnost može govoriti stvarno o stvarnosti, zapravo je laž i fikcija," in *Glas Slavonije*, 16. Feb. 2018, http://www.glas-slavonije.hr/356180/5/Bekavac-Ono-sto-knjizevnost-moze-govoriti-stvarno-o-stvarnosti-zapravo-je-laz-i-fikcija. Accessed 15 May 15 2019.

Meillassoux, Quentin. *After Finitude: an Essay on the Necessity of Contingency*. Continuum, 2008.

Ricoeur, Paul. *Time and Narrative, Vol. 2*. Translated by Kathleen Blamey and David Pellauer. University of Chicago Press, 1985.

Ryan, Marie-Laure. "Temporal Paradoxes in Narrative." *Style*, vol. 43, no. 2, Summer 2009, pp. 142–164.

Ryznar, Anera. "(Pseudo)znanstvena fantastika." *Suvremeni roman u raljama života: studija o interdiskurzivnosti*, Disput, 2017, pp. 223–242.

Snow, Marcus. *Into the Abyss: A Study of the* mise en abyme. 2016. London Metropolitan University, PhD dissertation. http://repository.londonmet.ac.uk/1106/1/SnowMarcus_IntoTheAbyss.pdf. Accessed 13 March 2019.

PART 2

Application(s) of/to (Post-)Yugoslav Time

∴

SECTION 1

Unhinging Memory and Space: Remembering (Post-)Yugoslav Time

CHAPTER 8

Re-reading/Writing Yugoslav Pasts and Presents in Post-Yugoslav Literature: Between (Yugo-)Nostalgia and "Lateral Networks"

Mirko Milivojević

As one of the dominant modes of remembering communism in Europe, along with melancholia, mourning, and disavowal (Scribner 12), nostalgia surely figures among the typical forms of remembering the Yugoslav socialist past after the breakup of the country in the early 1990s. The local coinage of 'Yugo-nostalgia' therefore is frequently used to designate various forms of affectionate and popular memory narratives addressing either the former socialist Yugoslav regime or various features belonging to the everyday life of the period in various post-Yugoslav discourses. It is starkly criticized either as a de-politicized or utopian form of memory and inappropriate discourse which relies primarily on consumerist products and the commodification of the past, thus disregarding the atrocities of the 1990s war period in Yugoslavia (Petrović; cf. Volčič; Luthar and Pušnik). Moreover, in underlining an ideologically polarized memory culture with a twofold structure in post-Yugoslav collective memories, many studies delineate 'Yugo-nostalgia' as being complementary to the hegemonic and institutional ethno-nationally driven narratives of historical revisionism, and therefore equally misrepresent multiple aspects attributed to Yugoslavia (cf. Luthar and Pušnik; Galijaš).

By focusing on literary texts by several post-Yugoslav authors belonging to different (post-)Yugoslav generations, Dubravka Ugrešić, Miljenko Jergović, and Aleksandar Hemon this essay argues against latter accounts and aims to examine rather different meanings and usages of nostalgia within the entangled post-socialist and post-war mnemonic landscape. This partially also includes re-examination of a context-specific phenomenon of 'Yugo-nostalgia' – for in challenging the ideological registers of the dominant memory narratives of competing nationalisms, and by dramatizing both personal and collective experiences related to the Yugoslav period – literary texts by these authors are frequently labeled 'Yugo-nostalgic.' Along the lines of more recent approaches which call attention to nostalgia's critical potential (cf. Velikonja 2009, Petrović 2012, Bošković 2013), this take highlights the dead end regarding the dominant discourse on (Yugo-) nostalgia, in which, as Petrović

(134) warns us, it is usually defined in general terms but is nevertheless frequently deconstructed according to a variety of its particular manifestations and narratives. In this respect, the discussion on nostalgia primarily goes along the lines of Svetlana Boym's re-conceptualization and distinctions between the 'restorative' and 'reflective' made in her seminal *The Future of Nostalgia* (2001). Taking this as a starting point, the essay argues that the representation of the Yugoslav past in these literary texts figures as an alternative, albeit already existing, mode within post-Yugoslav memory discourse. Thus, instead of starting from the assumption that nostalgia represents a typically unreflective form of memory, it should best be perceived as "a structure of relation to the past, not false or inauthentic in essence" (Bal xi). Moreover, conceptualized as a composite framing of loss, lack, and longing, which is attached to different temporal orders of the present and past, as Keightley and Pickering suggest (117), nostalgia is firmly engaged in negotiating between continuity and discontinuity (Atia and Davies 184). Therefore, such an approach to the very structure of nostalgic memory work can also be attributed to the particular usage of the prefix 'post' in 'post-Yugoslav,' as argued by Vladislav Beronja and Stijn Vervaet, namely by "mirroring both the break between socialist Yugoslavia and what came after it, as well as a certain continuity of its cultural, political or societal legacy" (5). It is thus taken similarly to the usage of 'post' in 'post-memory,' which highlights both the state of mutual dependence and ambivalent interaction between two temporal orders and instances (6).

On a similar note, by dramatizing the overall historical and societal entanglements of the Yugoslav past and present in their thematic scope, these texts are directed against amnesiac and hegemonic ethno-national memory narratives, and therefore also against political legitimizations of the dissolution of Yugoslavia in the 1990s. While performing nostalgic impulses in recollecting, remembering, and re-imagining both marginal as well as official events and symbols related to Yugoslav socialism, they do not aim at merely restoring the past but rather at reflecting on emblematic notions concerning Yugoslavia's dissolution, such as violent re-arrangements of identity and (collective) memory, traumas of displacement, and material losses. Moreover, viewed as reflecting on the "communality" and the "'past'" as two main traumatic points of "'Easterners,'" as highlighted in regard to post-socialist re-shaping of collective memories in Dubravka Ugrešić's seminal essay "The Confiscation of Memory," (Ugrešić, *The Culture of Lies* 221), the following accounts argue that nostalgia marks numerous complexities and alternative pathways related to both notions. In the same vein, it suggests that by antagonizing dominant memory narratives and in envisioning alternative pasts they also point to the dynamics and multidirectionality of cultural memory (cf. Erll and Rigney; Erll, "Travelling Memory"; Rothberg). In the last instance, they firmly engage in the possibilities of the articulation of collectivities which are grounded outside the boundaries of dominant (ethno-national) identities. It is in this sense that I deploy the term 'lateral networks,' in reference to the process of binding different social margins, i.e., subaltern subjectivities, which may not be readily apparent, as suggested by Lionnet and Shih in their conceptualization of "minor transnationalisms" (1). Namely, as Lionnet and Shih stress it rather as a starting point in re-shifting the theoretical framework, which is based on binaries of center/periphery and major/minor conceptions in their work, I appropriate the notion of lateral networks rather in order to tackle the more general terms and potentials of mapping and imagining foremostly new forms of subjectivity and different frameworks of collectivities as suggested in several post-Yugoslav literary works. However, as these may not be readily apparent, they can be viewed within as well as beyond the post-Yugoslav space, and in this regard, therefore, it calls for an open-ended character that can be viewed via the framework of multidirectionality of memory travels and dynamics.

1   Nostalgia Revisited – Svetlana Boym's Restorative and Reflective Nostalgia

The term *nostalgia* is a compound of the Greek *nostos* – to return home, and *algia* – a longing or sickness, and was first introduced by the Swiss student of medicine Johannes Hofer in 1688 who was interested in a 'disease' that spread among his countrymen while fighting away from their home, i.e. their home country (Boym 3–4; cf. Starobinski). As a cultural concept, it has undergone several semantic changes from diagnostics to metaphoric meanings and other multiple shifts throughout the last decades, and it has been treated differently within various disciplinary frameworks. Ewa Rychter thus notes that nostalgia can best be described as a "traveling concept" in Mieke Bal's use of the term (8). In the framework of memory studies, nostalgia is dominantly conceived as "longing for an idyllic past that never was," and often criticized as "unproductive, escapist and sentimental" or "regressive, romanticizing, the temporal equivalent of tourism and the search for the picturesque" (Bal xi). In this respect, Svetlana Boym's take on history and various transformations of nostalgic longing appears to be of crucial importance, for it is written in direct regard to the re-arrangements in post-communist memory politics which marked the turn of the millennium, as well as in terms of linking the concept to other critical accounts of cultural and collective memory. Boym defines nostalgia as "a yearning for a different time" and "the ache of temporal distance and displacement" (Boym xv), and she also describes it as a collective phenomenon, a "symptom of our age, a historical emotion" (xvi), which can be used differently depending on the particular context and on the particular uses by various agents. Unlike melancholia, therefore, in her view nostalgia is not necessarily oriented backwards, but can be equally prospective, oriented towards future or directed "sideways" as well (xvi–xvii).

One of the main features of Boym's re-conceptualization is a distinction made between two kinds of nostalgia, 'restorative' and 'reflective,' which delineate opposed narratives and potential political uses of the past, and characterize one's relationship to the past, i.e. to home or to particular imagined communities:

> Restorative nostalgia puts emphasis on *nostos* and proposes to rebuild the lost home and patch up the memory gaps. Reflective nostalgia dwells in *algia*, in longing and loss, the imperfect process of remembrance. The first category of nostalgics do not think of themselves as nostalgic; they believe that their projects is about truth. This kind of nostalgia characterizes national and nationalist revivals all over the world, which engage in the antimodern myth-making of history by means of return to national symbols and myths (...) Restorative nostalgia manifests itself in total reconstructions of monuments of the past, while reflective nostalgia lingers on ruins, the patina of time and history, in the dreams of another place and another time. (Boym 41)

Even though both types of nostalgia might use the same triggers of memory, they build different or even opposing narratives. In such regard, related to the notion of national memory and the re-construction of national identity, 'restorative' nostalgia is interested in a totalized or 'frozen' image of the past. In these narratives, the home ('nostos') is imagined and recalled as a place of origin, and thus remains intact over time. Such practices primarily aim at the homogenization of an 'imagined community' and operate via binary exclusion rather than affection (ibid). 'Reflective' nostalgia, on the other hand, "does not follow the single plot but explores ways of inhabiting many places at once and imagining different time zones" (Boym xviii). Opposed to strict national memory narrative-frameworks, it can also be understood as a form of social memory which, in Boym's understanding, "consists of collective frameworks that mark but do not define the individual memory" (ibid). Thus, relying on the fragments, details and leftovers of an official version of the past, it implies both a distance and a dialogical interaction between the past and present.

Characterized by the de-familiarization of past events, narratives of reflective nostalgia emphasize ambivalences and contradictions instead of suggesting a mere one-dimensionality or a unitary image of the past. Moreover, such works of nostalgia highlight the highly ambivalent function of remembering and thus can recall and criticize the past at the same time.

Although I am aware of the possible short-sightedness of this binary model proposed by Boym (cf. Keightley and Pickering 134–5), I nevertheless use it to underline its potentials of enabling a treatment beyond the assumptions of nostalgia necessarily operating as a typically unreflective form of memory. Rather, as Atia and Davies suggest, it "gives sensory depth to our awareness of the other places, times and possibilities that are at once integral to who we are and definitely alien to us" (184). Therefore, instead of applying Boym's twofold model to the larger corpus of 'Yugo-nostalgic' practices in diverse genres and medias, or even including conflicted institutional narratives which still occupy a dominant position within the post-Yugoslav mnemonic landscape, in what follows I will briefly look into several texts by Jergović, Ugrešić, and Hemon to examine the more critical and ambivalent use of post-Yugoslav pasts and presents as three authors who could easily serve as paradigmatic examples and as some critically acclaimed voices, and whose post-Yugoslav literary works deploy tonalities and topoi of nostalgia in dramatizing both the past period of socialist Yugoslavia and the post-war transition.[1] In this regard, I will primarily turn to Boym's notion of 'reflective' nostalgia in arguing for a more critical and inconclusive negotiation of such temporal instances, as well as a potentiality in negotiating multiple forms of communalities, i.e. collectivities that they equally propose through a combination of both affectionate recollection and reflexivity in approach. By challenging and affecting the dominant frameworks of collective memory, which are accepted "as a playground, not a graveyard of multiple individual recollections" (54), reflective nostalgia usually combines irony, parody, and similar narrative strategies in subverting the frameworks of official or national memory. In addition, the emotional topography of memory in these narratives opens a space for potential assemblages in the future. Namely, as Boym envisions reflective nostalgia with a clear "utopian dimension hat consists in the exploration of other potentialities" in regard to the possible temporal re-orientations, it can also "create a global diasporic solidarity based on the experience of immigration and internal multiculturalism" (342). It is in this regard that the function and structural aspect

---

[1] For two different ways of explicit applications of Boym's 'restorative' and 'reflective' nostalgia in regard to 'Yugo-nostalgia,' see: Lindstrom; Beganović.

of nostalgia also opens up to possible applications to more recent trends in approaches to cultural, i.e., collective memory, and which argue for the capacities of a dynamic of memories and transnational travels between different mnemonic contexts, i.e., spatio-temporal instances, media and genres, as well as arguing for multiple identities and networks apparent in the present or the future.[2]

Moreover, in the following analysis, I will also turn to two subcategories of reflective nostalgia – namely 'temporal' and 'topographic' nostalgia, as pointed out by Davor Beganović (151), underlining issues related to nostalgia and envisioning both potentially alternative Yugoslav past and communality. Following Beganović's suggested categorization, the temporal is particularly highlighted in narrative reconstructions of childhood years, while topographic nostalgia, on the other hand, stresses standardized tropes and narratives of displacement and exile. Hence, Jergović uses memory material linked to Yugo-nostalgic narratives in pursuing generational lenses for revising the past. On the other hand, Ugrešić instead turns to the concept of 'minors,' i.e., a 'minor transnationalism' in a post-socialist setting, building upon Deleuze and Guattari's model of "minor literature" (16–17). Lastly, in short *lieux* of conclusion, I will turn briefly to Hemon's work to point to the sum of both cases.

2   Reading/Writing History in Miljenko Jergović's *Historijska Čitanka*

The two volumes of Miljenko Jergović's *Historijska Čitanka* (*A History Reader*), first assembled in 2001 and 2004,[3] present a collection of short essayistic memory fragments published originally in the Bosnian weekly magazine *Dani* shortly after the war in Bosnia and the author's dislocation from besieged Sarajevo to Croatia in 1993. It focuses on events and phenomena that refer explicitly to the period of the 1970s and the 1980s in his native Sarajevo. Through a nostalgic recollection of the past via reminiscences of the author's childhood and teenage years, it serves as an alternative version of history. Jergović himself designates *Historijska Čitanka* as "neither history nor fiction," but "a catalog of that which exists as an inventory of an utterly subjective history of

---

2   For a recent theoretical conceptualization of (Yugo-)nostalgia in application to the frameworks of travelling and transnational memory in particular, see Popović. Similarly, for an overall re-conceptualization of post-Yugoslav cultural memory within the same theoretical frameworks, see Beronja and Vervaet.

3   In this analysis, I refer to the second edition of both volumes: *Historijska Čitanka 1* (2006), *Historijska Čitanka 2* (2008).

the city, state and the period" (Jergović *Historijska Čitanka 1* 9).⁴ Hence I do not read Jergović's memory essays as a memoir or an autobiographical story of his early life. Rather, by re-writing an intimate and collective past – highlighted dominantly by the emotional significance, it carries for both individual and collective identities – it offers a critical engagement in discussing different post-Yugoslav 'memory regimes' and institutionally imposed forgetting, and therefore also aims at introducing pluralities into ideological depictions of the Yugoslav past.

The term *'historijska čitanka'* in the collection's title derives from a specific supplementary textbook that was included in the educational curriculum in history classes during Yugoslavia's socialist period. This kind of text used to serve to complement the official historical narrative found in regular textbooks, and it contained anecdotes or memoirs related to particular emblematic figures, historical events, and collective subjects, as well as a variety of documentary and inter-medial material. However, while it certainly functions as a clear reference to the Yugoslav past, it also subverts the historical narratives which are used as one of the key elements in the process of the socialization and construction of national identities. Namely, in her examination of the construction of national identity based on the use of the past, Aleida Assmann emphasizes the importance of history in school curricula and textbooks in the following respect: "history automatically becomes applied history. It serves as the backbone for the nation-state and supports its values by constructing heroic and mobilizing patriotic narratives" (65). Set in the contemporary Bosnian/post-Yugoslav context, the dominant practice of historical revisionism is mainly achieved by constructing 'monumental' historical narratives in favor of the three competing ethnonational identities (cf. Kazaz, "The Poetics").⁵ Thus the composition of alternative and supplementary history texts, which primarily discuss everyday events and phenomena,

---

4 "(Historijska Čitanka) nije ni historija ni fikcija, nego je popis onoga što još uvijek postoji kao inventar jedne posve subjektivne povijesti grada, zemlje i vremena" (all translations from the two volumes of *Historijska Čitanka* are mine).
5 In the title, Jergović chooses a particular Bosnian word for 'history' in *Historijska Čitanka* – *'historija,'* instead of either Croatian (*'povijest'*) or Serbian (*'istorija'*) – and points to another issue regarding the conflict in memory/history that punctures post-Yugoslav nationalistic language policy. However, throughout the collection, in individual essays, he also uses both *'historija'* and *'povijest'* interchangeably. The very same issue is underlined also in the title of a documentary movie by Serbian director Željko Mirković *Dugo putovanje kroz istoriju, historiju i povijest Balkana* (*The Long Road Through Balkan History*, 2010) in which Jergović, together with Serbian author Marko Vidojković, plays one of the main roles. See also Zink and Simeunović.

when constructed from the 'bottom up' perspective by various marginal subjects and narrated via personalized voice, as Enver Kazaz further argues, can figure as an oppositional and subversive literary response to "the ideological postulate of grand narratives" and institutional historiography (163).

Along these lines, I argue that Jergović appropriates and mobilizes the supplementary notion of a 'history reader,' using it as a leading metaphor, as a conceptual and contextual framework for performing both the reading and writing of the history of the Yugoslav past. Hence, by highlighting memory material that was excluded from the regular and official (national) history records, Jergović produces an unofficial and 'subjective' version of the everyday history of Sarajevo, Bosnia, and Yugoslav socialism. By relying on subjective reflections which are firmly grounded in his personal biography and intimate memories, this work appears as an antidote to the grand historical narratives that stood behind the nationalist discourse. The work, therefore, aims to challenge not only hegemonic historical narratives but to equally question the legitimization of uniformity regarding the national identity of both the Yugoslav past and the post-Yugoslav present. In such a way, it engages with memory on two different levels: first, by re-evaluating the past and historical narratives, and secondly, by constructing an unofficial, alternative history of the everyday.

In regard to its thematic scope and the structural and formal aspects of narration, *Historijska Čitanka* appears similar to *Leksikon YU Mitologije* (*Lexicon of YU Mythology* 2004) – certainly one of the most critically discussed popular memory narratives reflecting on the Yugoslav past – primarily by highlighting the various features of everyday and popular culture.[6] However, in *Leksikon* the memory-material relates to the entire period of the socialist Yugoslav state, and its thread of entries also follows linearly in either a temporal or alphabetical order. Jergović's *Historijska Čitanka*, on the other hand, rejects any particular linear order, and by moving back and forth in time the essays are largely dedicated to various 'marginal' phenomena, objects, and events as well as both marginal and public individuals, concerning various facets of everyday life. These are primarily related to Sarajevo, but in numerous instances also to the overall Yugoslav space. A great number of them revisit local sub-cultural and public spaces, while others cover a wide range of popular culture, concerning music, sports, different media content (print, as well as radio and TV programs and personalities of the time), and include numer-

---

6   For a comparison of Miljenko Jergović's *Historijska Čitanka* and *Leksikon YU Mitologije*, especially regarding different versions and re-mediations of both texts, see Lešić-Thomas.

ous childhood games, gossip, virtually untranslatable local jokes, phrases, and urban/oral myths.

In recapturing joyful childhood memories, sensations, and affects, the essays also offer insightful comments and humoristic explanations that illustrate local mentalities, attitudes, and behaviors, as well as everyday rituals belonging to the late Yugoslav period. However, such depictions do not necessarily re-create an 'exotic' image of the Balkans, and they equally reject an idyllic image of Bosnian/Sarajevo's multiethnic and multinational past in any sense. Rather, such a take on past material reveals the complexity of societal relations and dynamics and points to inner contradictions and paradoxes inscribed into the socialist ideology of Yugoslavia. Thus, in numerous instances, the essays also capture a wider scope of publicly recognized symbols, slogans or rituals serving as memory sites connected to official discourses of the Yugoslav socialist state, as key political or socio-cultural events of the period intersect with marginalized and everyday phenomena. In this respect, as well, the text is by no means represented as a grand heroic story or idealization of the nation and ideological system, but it is dominantly viewed through arresting details, and underlining the author's personalized perspective, often combined with an ironic undertone as well. It is also in such a way that Jergović's the practice of reading/writing the intimate and collective past goes beyond the paradigm of "binary socialism" (Yurchak 4), which is often taken for granted and which relies on the essentializing dichotomies and divisions between 'us' and 'them.'

Through the introduction and epilogue sections added to the two volumes of the book version of the essays, Jergović provides the reader with a short commentary on his approach to memory and history via nostalgic recollection.[7] In the introduction to *Historijska Čitanka 1*, entitled "Zašto se sećati" ("Why Remember"), which begins by reflecting on complementary notions of forgetting and remembering, this becomes explicated through the acknowledgment of both notions as the necessarily constitutive parts of a memory process: "[F]orgetting doesn't hurt at all, but, still, it is good to remember. Remembering contains all the reasons both for joy and for sorrow, and they are often the same" (9).[8] What further remains essential – implicitly or explicitly – in almost every essay points also to an awareness of the very construc-

---

7 In the second volume of the collection, the author's epilogue is replaced by a section called "Bonus Tracks" which contains five additional essays.
8 "Zaborav nimalo ne boli, ali je ipak lijepo sjećati se. U sjećanju su svi razlozi, i za radost i za tugu, a oni su često isti."

tiveness of memory and history narratives, as Jergović shows a high level of (self-)reflexivity in the same regard. Namely, later in the introduction, Jergović makes clear that the content in the collection is not based on the 'real events' but rather on the "remembrance of real events and the strategy of forgetting," whereas "some names and dates have been remembered wrongly, some towns have been confused with others [...] There is probably a rule according to which one remembers and forgets, but since the narratives of memory are most often history or fiction, we avoid thinking of such rules" (ibid).[9] As suggested by Andrea Lešić-Thomas (434–435), on the one hand it "performs a seductive mythologization of the pre-war Sarajevo in particular, and on the other, its own doubting and self-conscious demythologizer, often talking with a sense of wonder or irony about things that in the past would have been considered as perfectly normal" (434). Similarly, when observed in terms of Astrid Erll's model of different rhetorical modes of memory, Jergović's introductory comment exemplifies a reflexive mode of remembering. According to Erll, it points to the way in which literary texts not only enact, perform or restage, but also observe and comment on content, mechanisms, and diverse issues of personal and collective memory registers ("Literature, Film" 391; cf. "Literatur als Medium," 269). It is in this sense, therefore, that via nostalgic recollection of a socialist past, or via a combination of 'experienced' and 'reflexive' mode of remembering – speaking in Erll's terms – the memory fragments in *Historijska Čitanka*, as well as the entries in *Leksikon YU Mitologije*, recover various cultural and material practices of everyday life, as well as provide a comment on the discourses that frame those practices, and thus negotiate their significance in constructing different frameworks of collective identities.

Moreover, by referring to the content as not meticulously fact-based, the text furthermore suggests a focus on the affective and emotional responses to these particular episodes of the past. In the epilogue section to the first part of the collection, entitled suggestively "Zlatne godine" ("Golden Years"), Jergović exemplifies how 'sentimental history' is constructed in both thematic and temporal aspects. Namely, through the inventory of pop-cultural and everyday phenomena, the text highlights what is personally and generationally significant. Starting with the first two football championship titles won by

---

9 "Ova knjiga ne govori o stvarnim događajima, nego o sjećanju na stvarne događaje i o strategiji zaboravljanja. U njoj postoje krivo zapamćena imena i godine, neki su gradovi postali drugim gradovima, (...) Vjerojatno postoji neko pravilo prema kojem čovjek pamti i zaboravlja, ali budući da su priče o sjećanju obično historija ili fikcija, izbjegavamo misliti o takvim pravilima."

teams from Sarajevo, the publication of a classic Bosnian/Yugoslav novel by Meša Selimović, followed by the release dates of key albums by local rock bands, and political scandals on a local scale, etc., Jergović foregrounds the emotional tonalities of nostalgic longing, displaying an ambiguous attitude towards history and memory which appears incompatible with any official and national grand narrative. The highlighting of an alternative lineage of socialist and Yugoslav history in Sarajevo is also resembled clearly in the sharp cut in the temporal setting of the project-column. However, as it suggests that reconstruction, i.e. the reading/writing of the past, should be embedded in a reflection on present losses, it conversely also facilitates the intertwinement of different frameworks of collective identities as well as the co-existence of different nostalgias implied by these phenomena. Namely, serving as sites of collective memory, the fragments of the past represented in the essays inspire not only a re-thinking of the overarching multinational identity of socialist Yugoslavia but also point to diverse (non-institutional) frameworks of collectivity which may be apparent primarily through the very content of this past material. Moreover, mostly told in the second-person singular ("You") or the first-person plural ("We"), and alternating between a child's and a teenager's narrative voice, the memory fragments also offer a 'cue' to the readers, provoking them to re-evaluate their own memories, and invite further possibilities for the applications of such memories and experiences as well. While the work refers to the potential co-witnesses of these phenomena, sites, and events, it also firmly relates to the last Yugoslav generation – namely the one whose formative period is embedded in the socialist past, but who was equally affected by the militant ruptures of everyday life and the existing communal imaginaries during the 1990s. Lastly, turning to an alternative network of collectivities, Jergović also suggests and reflects upon the possibility of further applications and travels for his essays – performed across media and geographic locations – which thus should be employed in facilitating new "sentimental and bootleg histories" in a variety of media and modes as well (Jergović *Historijska Čitanka* 2 8).

3 Coming to Terms with (Yugo-)Nostalgia in Dubravka Ugrešić's Novels

In contrast to Miljenko Jergović, in two post-Yugoslav novels, Dubravka Ugrešić combines the concepts of memory and exile as central topoi in negotiating and reflecting on both socialist and particularly Yugoslav legacies. Hence, as suggested by David Williams, Ugrešić's novels *The Museum of Unconditional*

Surrender (1996) and *The Ministry of Pain* (2004)[10] can be read as an unofficial "*diptych* on memory, displacement, melancholia and nostalgia" (70). Moreover, as both novels primarily reflect on the overwhelming traumatic losses following the fragmentation of Yugoslavia during the 1990s, Ugrešić explores multiple entanglements of these concepts and different modes of remembering which negotiate transnational identities as an alternative to the nationalist hegemony in the post-socialist setting.

The Museum, whose setting alternates between Berlin and Yugoslavia, largely engages with different practices, media, and metaphors that primarily highlight the politics behind the collective memories of the bygone communist past. In looking for different ways to re-configure identity ruptures in the post-communist present, the work of nostalgia is exemplified in the act of tracing and collecting a wide range of material objects linked to the past. According to Boym's reading of the novel *vis a vis* reflective nostalgia, such a nostalgic act exemplifies a substitute for the loss and the re-shaping of collective memory and serves as both the artistic and narrative device of deconstructing the linear coherence and totalized version of biography (Boym 210).[11]

Hence, next to the overarching trope of the museum suggested in the novel's title and prologue, and which covers a number of fragmented collections throughout the novel, Berlin also serves as one of the novel's central topoi of issues related to the re-construction of collective memory and nostalgia. Designated as "a mutant city" (Ugrešić, *The Museum* 104), "a non-place" (221), and both "a museum-city" and "a city of museums" (ibid.), Berlin is deployed in de-territorializing the institutionalized form of the museum and museum practice as well. It represents a platform for a dialogic mapping of various fragments and leftovers in negotiating the past and present, and both the narrator's personal and collective memories, as well as multilayered temporalities, of a Yugoslavia that is no more and the new order of European post-communism: "Berlin has its Western and its Eastern face: sometimes the western one appears in East Berlin, and the Eastern one in West Berlin. The

---

10   In this analysis, I refer to later editions of both novels: *The Museum* (1998), *The Ministry* (2005).

11   In her study on nostalgia, Boym takes both literary texts and works of architecture as occupying a central place of analysis. In same respect, the work of Dubravka Ugrešić, and especially the novel *Muzej bezuvjetne predaje*, plays a significant role in her argument for 'reflective' nostalgia. Similarly, it is Berlin – next to other urban environments in the post-soviet Russian context – that also serves as one of the key examples for negotiating between intentional and contingent monuments of the communist past in arguing between two types of nostalgia.

face of Berlin is criss-crossed by the hologram reflections of some other cities" (104). Furthermore, "as a city of potentialities" (Boym 197) and an accumulation of "transient epiphanies" (212), Berlin consists of a palimpsestic collection or compilation of literary and non-literary quotes and different takes on memory, i.e. (un)successful modes of remembering. Thus, by including intertextuality as a traditional literary approach to memory, Ugrešić relates to the longer list of exiles and nomads, both diachronically – referring to a number of exiled authors and artists particularly linked to Berlin, and synchronically – in numerous encounters with different migrant subjects from Yugoslavia or other post-communist European countries. Therefore, it is in this regard that Stijn Vervaet applies Michael Rothberg's notion of the "memory knot" to Berlin, namely serving as a memory trigger in several post-Yugoslav novels in which "different stories of extreme violence come together" (99). However, serving not only as the setting of a story about exile, the city also emerges as a paradigmatic reference point from where to approach the traumatic past of the Yugoslav 1990s, and as I would also add, to deal with uncertainties of the European post-socialist present (ibid).

In *The Ministry of Pain*, Ugrešić mainly looks at the ambivalent function of nostalgia and at 'Yugo-nostalgia' in particular. As the novel primarily reflects on the overwhelming traumatic losses inscribed in the fragmentation of Yugoslavia during the 1990s, and the sense of estrangement and exile in the post-Yugoslav context, her take on (Yugo-)nostalgia parallels Svetlana Boym's explorations of nostalgia by reflexively pointing to the ambivalence of being "homesick and sick of home" (Boym 50).

The story follows an immigrant, temporary university lecturer Tanja Lucić – also the novel's main narrative voice, and a group of Yugoslav exiles, immigrants, and refugees who are Tanja's students of *'Jugoslavistika'* in Amsterdam. The use of 'Yugo-nostalgia' again is firmly grounded in questioning the possibility of re-establishing a communality among exiled post-Yugoslav subjects under the conditions of transnational migrations and displacement. This is explicitly represented in the intersecting use of the narrated 'I' and 'we' throughout the novel. Namely, narrated dominantly by Tanja Lucić, the use of the first person singular 'I' in the narrative voice refers to her particular immigrant experience, but it also frequently transforms into the first person plural 'we' when it equates her own voice with that of her students. This is particularly prominent in those parts of the novel, which highlight the attempt of reconstructing notions and referential points of their mutual past and the aftermath of recent war events in Yugoslavia. Moreover, the narrative 'we' undergoes constant re-definitions in the novel, as it is applied to various identity-forms and subjectivities in different situations. Primarily referring to post-Yugoslav exiles and refugees, the 'non-adapters' of the exclusionist discursive practices of the newly established ethno-nationalisms in the post-Yugoslav space, it also suggests identification with other immigrants, nomads, and marginalized and displaced subjects mostly coming from the formerly communist countries in Europe. Tanja and her students frequently receive a number of derogatory labels and are subjected to stigmatizing stereotypes from their hosts in Amsterdam: "the beneficiaries of political asylum," "refugees," "children of post-Communism," "the fallout of Balkanisation," or "savages" (Ugrešić, *The Ministry* 52).

In the university class setting, Ugrešić points to the identity crisis resulting out of Yugoslav fragmentation as the text signals the fluid identity of post-Yugoslav subjects in numerous instances. In a number of cases, the former language of Yugoslavia is signified through a sense of intimacy but equally and neutrally as "our language," and in the same respect, the very signifier of 'Yugoslavia' becomes an object of multiple designations and re-compositions, such as "Yuga," "the former Yugoslavia" or "the former Yuga," "Titoland," or "Titanic" (13). Reflecting on her complicated position as a lecturer of a "subject that officially no longer existed" (34), and seeking "the common ground" (50) when confronted with the aftermath of post-Yugoslav fragmentations, Tanja stages a game of 'Yugo-nostalgia' to re-negotiate the coherence of 'ourness' through the joined therapeutic work of remembrance among the post-Yugoslav exiles.

Moreover, 'Yugo-nostalgia' can be described as a form of selective remembering and communicating various notions from the shared cultural and everyday space experienced in socialist Yugoslavia, and it also serves as a political counter-memory practice that recalls the tonality and argumentation of the 'confiscation of memory,' and which was underlined in Ugrešić's earlier writings as well as found in the novel:

> With the disappearance of the country came the feeling that the life lived in it must be erased. The politicians who came to power were not satisfied with power alone; they wanted their new countries to be populated by zombies, people with no memory. They pilloried their Yugoslav past and encouraged people to renounce their former lives and forget them. Literature, movies, pop music, jokes, television, newspapers, consumer goods, languages, people – we were supposed to forget them all. A lot of it ended up at the dump in the form of film stock and photographs, books and manuals, documents and monuments – "Yugonostalgia," the reminiscence of life in the ex-country, became another name for political subversion. (51–2)

This enables the victims and 'losers' to tell their stories about their own experiences of exclusion and memorization within the process of ideological re-arrangements which serve the nationalist narratives. Moreover, representing multiple reminiscences in the form of essayistic passages and prefaced by the name of each character among the exiled students, it also provides a multitude of narrative voices that intersect with Tanja's main narrative 'I.' Such a dialogical element in the novel furthermore performs the 'de-territorialization' of both 'Serbo-Croatian' and the ideologically 'cleansed' languages of new nations-states. Even more, the experimental 'Yugo-nostalgic' university class provides not only a critical contrast for the ethno-national boundaries in the collective Yugoslav identity and memory, but also subverts an institutional setting and canonized university curriculum which is based on the already ideologically contaminated language of Yugoslavia.

The entire Yugo-nostalgic recollection is represented symbolically and metonymically through "the plastic bag with the red, white and blue stripes" (47), which one of the students, Ana, delineates as her key memory-trigger regarding the Yugoslav past. It is also through Ana's elaboration on what should symbolically become a depository of the diverse topoi of Yugoslav everyday life and popular culture that the novel points to various notions attached not only to the Yugoslav past but also to issues of different components of post-Yugoslav subjectivity set in the present. Hence "the cheapest piece of hand luggage on earth" and "a proletarian swipe at Vuitton" (ibid), as Ana describes the bag, explicitly signifies the parody-version of the Yugoslav flag "minus the red star" (ibid). Further in her description, the plastic bag becomes the perfect symbol for a virtual museum not only for a Yugoslavia that once was but also for what it could have been and even for potentially different presents and futures, as it enables collective assemblages of "refugees and the homeless," since the bag also "made its way across East-Central Europe all the way to Russia and perhaps even farther – to India, China, America, all over the world" (48). Ana explains that the bag is mainly used by various categories of displaced and subaltern subjects, relating them to the 'red, white and blue stripes' of Yugoslavia as the transnational class of 'others,' minorities and Deleuze and Guattari's "minors."[12]

---

[12] According to Deleuze and Guattari (1986), the notion of "minor" is not necessarily equated with any ethnic or national minority, i.e. minority group. Similarly, it does not imply the question of major or minor numbers either, but it rather refers to subjects who do not occupy the position of power-structures, and who actually perform the acts of subversion to those very same instances and thereby challenge the "major" discourses, i.e. "major" language.

Other essayistic sections designated as virtual items of their "Yugonostalgic museum" (49) further exemplify Boym's reflective rather than restorative nostalgia. The evoked memories largely offer a carnivalistic image of multiple facets of the Yugoslav past, mapping essentially a stereotypical topography of "all manner of Yugogoods" (54), which were already included in the list of deprived notions in Tanja's reflection on the Yugoslav memory-conflict, and also resembles the mnemonic work presented in *Leksikon YU Mitologije*. Ugrešić's (Yugo-)nostalgia avoids an idealized or univocal image and does not aim at restoring the totality of either the past or the Yugoslav socialist system at any point. Instead, the polyphony of the text facilitates different tonalities and ambivalent takes on both the work of nostalgia and the depiction of a Yugoslav past. Similarly, the text displays various aspects suppressed by ideological taboos and personal traumas, including a series of stereotypes regarding the Yugoslav multicultural and multiethnic society, which in the end became fragile, and therefore also facilitated a wider range of negative effects and remembrances. Hence, it eventually fails to re-establish a unity based exclusively on the recollection of the very same elements of the former Yugoslav past and by ignoring the ruptures and entangled affects that followed or even those that were inscribed in it. Instead, it establishes an over-identification with different memory sites related and appropriated by combating nationalisms and further leads to a series of violent acts among the exiles themselves – reproducing the very outcome of Yugoslav fragmentation.

However, Ugrešić also employs reflective nostalgia when she points to a new articulation of nostalgic memory in both the present and future, which "opens up a multitude of potentialities, nonteleological possibilities of historical developments" and therefore, as Boym claims, is never finished (50). In several essayistic passages towards the end of the novel, the figuration of nostalgia negotiates the possibilities of new collective assemblages in both the present and the future, this time outside the exclusive binaries of past-present and beyond the frameworks of ethno-national memory and identities. Equally mirrored by the multidirectional travels of Ana's "plastic bag," it relates to diverse forms of the nomadic subjectivity of different political, i.e., mnemonic contexts.

Namely, towards the novel's ending and following Tanja's new status with a "low-life visa" in an Amsterdam-suburb symbolically named Little Casablanca and inhabited by various migrants, the two essayistic sections occupy different narrative voices. The first essay is narrated in the first person plural, designating the *"We"* of "barbarians," "losers," and "sleepers," representing "the false bottom of the perfect society" and "its ugly underside-its parallel world," "[T]he members of our tribe bear the invisible stamp of Columbus on their foreheads" (Ugrešić, *The Ministry* 225–228), and it highlights the entanglement of 'old' and already existing immigrant routes from various 'peripheries' towards the Western European centers. On the other hand, in a semi-ironic tone and referring explicitly to the post-socialist countries of Eastern Europe, the second passage envisions "the children of post-communism," a new generation of post-communist subjects, "transition mutants," and a "completely different tribe" yet to come, who, as the narrator informs us, will master the "multiple identities" and "be cosmopolitan, global, multicultural, nationalistic, ethnic, and diasporic all in one" (234–235).

Not unlikely to Ugrešić's previous novel, the new forms of identification follow the 'multidirectionality' of affective memory travels directed towards the "minor transnationalisms," as proposed by Lionnet and Shih. These are "found in unexpected and sometimes surprising places" and are created in "nonstandard languages, tonalities, and rhythms" in producing ways to "negotiate with national, ethnic, and cultural boundaries, thus allowing for the emergence of minor's inherent complexity and multiplicity" (Lionnet and Shih 8).[13] In Ugrešić's novels, such a shift tackles the potential of producing new forms of identification, foremostly by negotiating the entanglement between different, albeit transnational, frameworks of collectivity. In the same respect, it also displays different and multiple layers of (nostalgic) memory and temporality as it highlights the framework of (post-)communist (in *The Museum*) as well as post-communist and post-colonial (in *The Ministry*) heterogeneous collective subjectivities. In either case, however, as they are concerned with the issues of the past(s), they equally subvert governing discourses by underlining ruptures, errors, and pauses which invite us to re-think the linearity and the totality that such discourses propose.

4 Towards a Conclusion – Aleksandar Hemon's "Home-Comings" and "Departures"

In regard to the two subcategories of reflective nostalgia as suggested by Davor Beganović used in looking into nostalgia and memory in the texts by Jergović and Ugrešić, Aleksandar Hemon's work certainly covers and brings together both notions. Although at first sight Hemon's work can be seen primarily as

---

13 For more detailed theoretical application of the concept of minor transnationalism to the larger corpus of (post)Yugoslav literature, also featuring several authors mentioned in this chapter, see Lukić.

'Sarajevo-centered,' it traces and facilitates multiple cross-temporal and cross-spatial dimensions of memories and storylines in various ways, thereby joining different forms and frameworks of subjectivities that move beyond the exclusive (post-)Yugoslav context. Hence, in relation to 'temporal' nostalgia, Hemon offers a chronicle of Sarajevo, which is portrayed ambivalently in a number of his texts – primarily short stories and essays. And even though such a portrayal is highlighted through the combination of personal and national sites of memory, and it also stretches any clear generational characteristics and differences regarding the official discourse as embedded in the recollection of childhood and teenage memories, it still refuses to deliver an exclusively romanticized and uncritical image of the past. Instead, it becomes both the place of a nostalgic home and "the chronotope of crisis" (Zink). Similar to Miljenko Jergović in *Historijska Čitanka*, one part of Hemon's novel *Nowhere Man* (2002), entitled "Yesterday," which depicts Sarajevo in the 1970s and 1980s, the formative years of his central character Jozef Pronek is juxtaposed to the brutal destruction of the city in the following decade. Therefore, even when engaged with the tonalities and tropes of nostalgia, the work goes beyond a unilateral way of representing the past via essentializing tropes belonging to the socialist every day. Furthermore, what seems to be only suggested along the lines of generational disparities and conflicts in *Nowhere Man*, in "Islands" – the first short story in *The Question of Bruno* (2000) – the romanticized image of the childhood memories of the child protagonist and the story's narrator is silenced by the intersected voice of Uncle Julius, who constantly brings a load of his traumatic memories of Gulag to the surface as well, and thereby also juxtaposes two different temporalities and their affective components implied within.

On the other hand, Hemon's work explicitly embodies the dominant features of transnational literature and negotiates transnational and multiple (displaced and immigrant) identities. In so doing, it also allows for alternative routes, encounters, and detours to arise which oppose and present themselves beyond the trajectory, which sets the standard center-periphery link between Sarajevo/Bosnia and Chicago/USA. Therefore, re-drawing cartography, which includes Ukraine and other Eastern/European peripheries in the dominant Western centers primarily also enables the protagonists in his first two novels – *Nowhere Man* and *The Lazarus Project* (2008) respectively – to perform a constant re-negotiation of identities, as well as re-readings and subversions of nostalgia when confronted with personal, family, national, and transnational pasts. In this respect, by largely deploying figurations of displacement and exile, these texts also recall some of the topoi deployed in the two novels by Dubravka Ugrešić. Namely, they depict a variety of cross-spatial and -temporal relations with numerous places, characters, and identities around the world – as the protagonists in each of these narratives are represented as being constantly on the move and thus in an ongoing process of becoming and transforming – as well as putting the memories and experiences of Yugoslavia with other trans- and international pasts into various memory-constellations. In both novels, this is displayed not only thematically but also on the narrative and structural level. Namely, *The Lazarus Project* juxtaposes the brutal events of the Bosnian war with the story of Jewish pogroms in Kishinev in 1903 and the atmosphere of antisemitism in Chicago from the beginning of the twentieth century, but it also takes parallels to the USA post 9/11 as well as the overall (Eastern) European post-communist discourses. This is additionally highlighted via two parallel narrative and temporal lines, which alternate throughout the novel's chapters. The novel opens with the chapter/storyline of Lazarus' death in Chicago and following developments, which is narrated in the third person singular, but is followed/mirrored with the chapters with the first-person narrative by Vladimir Brik – a Bosnian-American – which traces the Lazarus' story one century later, as Brik takes the road trip from Chicago to Lviv and Kishinev and eventually his native Sarajevo with his compatriot and childhood friend Rora. In a similar vein, *Nowhere Man* offers several encounters of the main protagonist, Jozef Pronek, with multiple marginal characters, groups, and individuals who are predominantly circling Chicago, Sarajevo, Kiev and Shanghai. These relations and mutual influences are highlighted via fragmentary narration given through multiple narrative perspectives and temporal instances but are equally established through the list of well-known features of popular culture as well as a number of national and racial stereotypes. Hence, not unlike the negotiations made by Ugrešić, and also mirroring the traumatic memories of Uncle Julius as mentioned previously, these memory-constellations and encounters underlined in both Hemon's novels recall Rothberg's illustration of how "remembrance both cuts across and binds together diverse spatial, temporal and cultural sites" (8). The multidirectionality of these travels, therefore, also provides an alternative mapping of different and distant margins – both geographically and in societal terms – and point to lateral networks established through contingent and affective encounters, in which different and even opposed memory modes can also co-exist. But as they frequently point to societal ruptures and traumatic events, these multiple and multidirectional travels equally provide crucial insight to memories and memory battles that remain silenced and are still left to be preserved and/or re-activated. However, when seen through a nostalgic lens, it certainly clears the path for home-departures instead of homecomings.

The reading/writing of (Yugo-)nostalgia as analyzed in texts by Miljenko Jergović, Dubravka Ugrešić, and Aleksandar Hemon suggests that the work of nostalgic memory is not only directed to preserve or restore the past, but it potentially functions as an affective oppositional memory practice directed towards the present and even towards future imaginings as well. However, as its main interest does not necessarily lie in recovering the functionality of nostalgic memory – even within the politically tight context of post-Yugoslav memories – it highlights rather its capacity to indicate some of the vital components belonging to the overall literary and cultural discourses regarding the post-Yugoslav condition, as it remains one of the dominant features in post-Yugoslav literature. Therefore, the re-examination of (Yugo-)nostalgic memory provides a fruitful insight for the ongoing discourse on nostalgia within cultural memory, so this chapter can also serve as a productive analytical category for the highly important re-considerationof the entanglement and multidirectional framework of memories that puncture the post-Yugoslav context in general. In this regard, I suggest that the post-Yugoslav context is best approached in the terms proposed by Susannah Radstone, namely, "not as an end-point or theoretical home-coming but as a point of departure, opening out into those questions of knowledge, belief, temporal orientations and cultural, social and sexual politics that it condenses" (189). Similarly, as this series of lateral and multidirectional detours and encounters tends to show, it can also be useful as one possible starting point for tracing or turning to multiple and multilayered temporalities, which can be attributed to various frameworks of collectivities, as well as to co-existing and/or competing nostalgias and 'posts' in the theoretical and political re-orientation of the post-Yugoslav condition.

References

Adrić, Iris, Vladimir Arsenijević, and Đorđe Matić, (eds.). *Leksikon YU Mitologije*. Rende & Postscriptum, 2004.

Assmann, Aleida. "Transformation Between History and Memory." *Social Research: An International Quarterly*, vol. 75, no. 1, 2008, pp. 49–72.

Atia, Nadia and Jeremy Davies. "Nostalgia and the Shape of History." *Memory Studies*, vol. 3, no. 3, 2010, pp. 181–186.

Bal, Mieke, Jonathan Crewe, and Leo Spitzer (eds.). *Acts of Memory: Cultural Recall in the Present*. University Press of New England, 1999.

Beganović, Davor. "Reflective and Restorative Nostalgia: Two Types of Approaching Catastrophe in Contemporary Yugoslav Literature." *Balkan Memories: Media Constructions of National and Transnational History*, edited by Tanja Zimmermann, Transcript, 2012, pp. 147–154.

Beronja, Vlad and Stijn Vervaet (eds.). *Post-Yugoslav Constellations: Archive, Memory and Trauma in Contemporary Bosnian, Croatian and Serbian Literature and Culture*. De Gruyter, 2016.

Bošković, Aleksandar. "Yugonostalgia and Yugoslav Cultural Memory: Lexicon of Yu Mythology." *Slavic Review*, vol. 72, no. 1, 2013, pp. 54–78.

Boym, Svetlana. *The Future of Nostalgia*. Basic Books, 2001.

Deleuze, Gilles and Felix Guattari. *Kafka: Toward a Minor Literature*. University of Minnesota Press, 1986.

Erll, Astrid. "Literatur als Medium des Kollektiven Gedächtnisses." *Gedächtniskonzepte der Literaturwissenschaft: theoretische Grundlegung und Anwendungsperspektiven*, edited by Astrid Erll and Ansgar Nünning, de Gruyter, 2005, pp. 249–276.

Erll, Astrid. "Literature, Film, and the Mediality of Cultural Memory." *A Companion to Cultural Memory Studies*, edited by Astrid Erll and Ansgar Nünning, de Gruyter, 2008, pp. 389–398.

Erll, Astrid. "Travelling memory." *Parallax*, vol. 17, no. 4, 2011, pp. 4–18.

Erll, Astrid and Ann Rigney (eds.). *Mediation, Remediation, and the Dynamics of Cultural Memory*. De Gruyter, 2009.

Galijaš, Armina. "Nationalisten und Jugonostalgiker: Zerstörung der Erinnerungen, Umformung der Identitäten." *Traumata der Transition: Erfahrung und Reflexion des jugoslawischen Zerfalls*, edited by Boris Previšić and Svjetlan Lacko Vidulić, Francke, 2015, pp. 183–199.

Hemon, Aleksandar. *The Question of Bruno*. Picador, 2000.

Hemon, Aleksandar. *Nowhere Man*. Picador, 2003.

Hemon, Aleksandar, *The Lazarus Project*. Riverhead Books, 2008.

Jergović, Miljenko. *Historijska Čitanka 1*. VBZ, 2006.

Jergović, Miljenko. *Historijska Čitanka 2*. VBZ, 2008.

Kazaz, Enver. "Prizori uhodanog užasa." *Sarajevske Sveske*, no. 5, 2004, pp. 137–165.

Kazaz, Enver. "The Poetics of Testimony and Resistance: Anti-War Writing and Social Memory in Bosnia and Herzegovina After the 1992–1995 War," *Balkan Memories: Media Constructions of National and Transnational History*, edited by Tanja Zimmermann, Transcript, 2012, pp. 77–86.

Keightley, Emily and Michael Pickering. *The Mnemonic Imagination: Remembering as Creative Practice*. Palgrave Macmillan, 2012.

Lešić-Thomas, Andrea. "Miljenko Jergovic's Art of Memory: Lying, Imagining, and Forgetting in *Mama Leone* and *Historijska čitanka*." *Modern Language Review*, vol. 99, no. 2, Apr 2004, pp. 430–444.

Lindstrom, Nicole. "Yugonostalgia: Restorative and Reflective Nostalgia in Former Yugoslavia." *East Central Europe*, vol. 32, no. 1, 2005, pp. 227–237.

Lionnet, Francoise and Shih Shu-mei (eds.). *Minor Transnationalism*. Duke University Press, 2005.

Lukić, Jasmina. "Transnacionalni obrt, komparativna književnost i etika solidarnosti: Transnacionalna književnost iz rodnog ugla."*reč* no. 84, 2014, pp. 359–374.

Lukić, Jasmina. "Rod i migracija u postjugoslovenskoj književnosti kao transnacionalnoj književnosti." *reč* no. 87, 2017, pp. 273–291.

Luthar, Breda and Maruša Pušnik (eds.). *Remembering Utopia: The Culture of Everyday Life in Socialist Yugoslavia*. New Academia Publishing, 2010.

Petrović, Tanja. *YUROPA: Jugoslovensko nasleđe i politike budućnosti u postjugoslovenskim društvima*. Fabrika Knjiga, 2012.

Popović, Milica, "Yugonostalgia: The Meta-National Memory Narratives of the Last Pioneers." *"Nostalgia on the Move,"* edited by Mirjana Slavković and Marija Đorgović, The Museum of Yugoslavia, Belgrade, pp. 42–50.

Radstone, Susannah. "Nostalgia: Home-Comings and Departures." *Memory Studies*, vol. 3, no. 3, 2010, pp. 187–191.

Rothberg, Michael. *Multidirectional Memory: Remembering the Holocaust in the Age of Decolonization*. Stanford University Press, 2009.

Rychter, Ewa. "Nostalgia and its Manifold (Be)longings." *Annals of "1 Decembrie 1918" University of Alba Iulia – Philology (Annales Universitatis Apulensis. Series Philologica)*, vol.11, no. 2, 2010, pp. 7–24.

Scribner, Charity. *Requiem for Communism*. mit Press, 2003.

Starobinski, Jean. "The Idea of Nostalgia." *Diogenes*, vol. 54, 1966, pp. 81–103.

Ugrešić, Dubravka. *The Culture of Lies*. Phoenix, 1998.

Ugrešić, Dubravka. *The Museum of Unconditional Surrender*. Phoenix, 1998.

Ugrešić, Dubravka. *The Ministry of Pain*. Harper Collins, 2006.

Velikonja, Mitja. "Povratak otpisanih: Emancipatorski potencijali jugonostalgije." *Zid je mrtav, živeli zidovi! Pad Berlinskog zida i raspad Jugoslavije*, edited by Ivan Čolović, Biblioteka xx Vek, 2009, pp. 366–396.

Vervaet, Stijn. "Intersecting Memories in Post-Yugoslav Fiction: The Yugoslav Wars of the 1990s through the Lens of the Holocaust." *Post-Yugoslav Constellations: Archive, Memory and Trauma in Contemporary Bosnian, Croatian and Serbian Literature and Culture*, edited by Vlad Beronja and Stijn Vervaet, de Gruyter, 2016, pp. 99–126.

Volčič, Zala. "Yugo-nostalgia: Cultural Memory and Media in the Former Yugoslavia." *Critical Studies in Media Communication*, vol. 24, no.1, 2007, pp. 21–38.

Williams, David. *Writing Postcommunism: Towards the Literature of the East European Ruins*. Palgrave Macmillan, 2013.

Yurchak, Alexei. *Everything Was Forever, Until It Was No More: The Last Soviet Generation*. Princeton University Press, 2006.

Zink, Andrea. "Land in Bewegung: Die Imagination Jugoslawiens in Bosnisch-Kroatisch-Serbischen Literatur." *Erzählte Mobilität in östlichen Europa: (Post-)imperiale Räume zwischen Erfahrung und Imagination*, edited by Thomas Grob, Boris Previšić, and Andrea Zink, Francke Verlag, 2014, pp. 79–100.

Zink, Andrea and Tatjana Simeunović. "Verlorene Brüder? Miljenko Jergovićs jugoslawische Spurensuche." *Brüderlichkeit und Brüderzwist: mediale Inszenierungen des Aufbaus und des Niedergangs politischer Gemeinshcaften in Ost- und Südosteuropa*, edited by Tanja Zimmermann, V&R Unipress, 2014, pp. 519–542.

CHAPTER 9

Spaces of Memory in Dragan Velikić's Novel *Investigator*

Danijela Marot Kiš

1 Post-Yugoslav Temporalities

The disintegration of the Yugoslav state, the creation of new nation-states, and a turn from the communist regime and socialism to capitalism left a mark on the understanding of cause-and-effect relationships in (dis)continuity of past, present and future and affected the experience of the very structure of time. The tendency (or misconception) to explain current events and conditions (from war to economic collapse and social instability) by causes from the past or by the legacy of a failed regime has resulted in a peculiar experience of temporality that tends to break with the past while at the same time constantly renewing it. This understanding also influenced the meaning of the prefix post in the term post-Yugoslav, which does not imply a clear boundary between what was and what is, that is, it does not break with what was before, but arises from it and relies on it. The prefix post implies the constant inclusion (and even reliving) of the past in the present, with the past becoming the foundation of the present experience: it does not cease, it is not left behind, but mediated by memory lasts indefinitely. The past as an afterness that is not left behind but dominates the present (Brown 2010, 21) is woven into the literary narrative created after the breakup of Yugoslavia and is shaped as a material of memory ranging from (quasi) nostalgic recollection to criticism and irony. Through this renewal of the past as a material of individual and collective imagination, the category of narrative linearity was abolished and replaced by fragmentarity, which became one of the basic features of the post-Yugoslav narrative. The fragmentary experience of time, in which fragments of the past are preserved in memory or constructed by imagination projected into the present moment, is also reflected in the narrator's experience of the self. Like memory and time, the self is also fragmentary, so the subject is forced to retell itself over and over again, to compose an unreliable construct of the self through the shards of what once was. In this sense, the prefix post thus becomes a fundamental feature of time, narration, and identity in the context of the reality of the new nation-states in the former Yugoslavia.

2   An Intimate Tale on the Edge of History

Islednik (*The Investigator*), the 2015 novel by the Serbian writer Dragan Velikić, is a piece of (quasi)autobiographical prose[1] that offers an alternative history of the Yugoslav region. The writer's alternative approach to historical themes derives from a juxtaposition of personal and collective memory, where the 'ordinary person's' perspective is crucial for a rewriting of the larger historical story on the margins of historiography. The novel follows the unnamed narrator's exploration of history (childhood and youth) growing up in former Yugoslavia and intertwines the story of his life with the fragmentary biographies of several people who entered his life in different ways. The nonlinear narration focuses on several thematic points, ranging from the geography of memory, or the mnemonic reconstruction of personal histories against a backdrop of key historic events and a subtextual fear of forgetting (dementia), to an analysis of the relationship of the narrator with his mother.

Velikić describes his writing as similar to a bildungsroman, as "research of the self, which leads to the source, meaning the parents – in this case, the mother, all the way to revealing your own self in the very thing one turns their back on, from which one tries to escape" (Velikić, "Intervju"). The novel's themes, as described by the author, underline an intimate dimension of the narrative, stressing the relationship with his mother which defines the nature of his relationships with other people, other times, and the places he lives in. The key for narrators understanding of memory and temporality, as well as relation between the past and the present is inscribed in his relationship with his mother. The beginning of narration in the novel is marked by the mother's death. It's the point that represents the loss of the past, but also the possibility of its renewal and reconstruction. From that point of loss two different positions emerge from the narration: the position of the subject (the one who remembers) and the position of the object (the one who is the object of remembering). The mother's is the key role in this process of narrative dissociation: not only does her death initiate narrator's immersion in the past,

---

1   Based on De Man's aesthetic perspective on autobiography as "de-facement," Lejeune's pragmatic approach to the question whether a text can be regarded as autobiography or not, and Deleuze's and Guattari's thoughts on machines of faciality Diana Hitzke (198) offers a reading of post-Yugoslav literary prose (Albahari, Ćosić, Ugrešić) linking the meaning to a person's (author's) face. Such texts, claims Hitzke, cannot be categorized as autobiographies: they play with the question as to who actually speaks: the author, his literary alter ego or some fictional textual configuration? Velikić's writing in *Islednik* poses the same questions, following the resemblance between author, narrator and protagonist.

her presence becomes necessary for his understanding of identity as a temporal construction. Prolonged into the present, the mother's presence in the form of constant renewal of memories marks the simultaneity of the past and the present. Deleuze's and Guattari's concept of "body without organs" (BwO) represents the basis of this understanding of temporal simultaneity. In their interpretation of BwO the linearity of the causal link between the past (the parent) and the present (the child) is replaced by the simultaneity of their existence in the process of identity formation. Describing the BwO as a (potential) reality underlying some well-formed whole, Deleuze and Guattari deny the concept of linear temporality based on the terms "before" and "after" that is inscribed in the relation between mother and child, the past and the present:

> The BwO is not "before" the organism; it is adjacent to it and is continually in the process of constructing itself. If it is tied to childhood, it is not in the sense that the adult regresses to the child and the child to the Mother, but in the sense that the child, like the Dogon twin who takes a piece of the placenta with him, tears from the organic form of the Mother an intense and destratified matter that on the contrary constitutes his or her perpetual break with the past, his or her present experience, experimentation. The BwO is a childhood block, a becoming, the opposite of a childhood memory. It is not the child "before" the adult, or the mother "before" the child: it is the strict contemporaneousness of the adult, of the adult and the child, their map of comparative densities and intensities, and all of the variations on that map. (164)

The narrator's relationship with his mother in the form of remembrance marks the return of the past, but also the breakup with the past – not in the form of forgetting, but in the manner that includes the past in the present experience. It is the simultaneity of that what once was and of that what now is. The act of narration emerges from the temporary suspension of continuous process of dissociation and integration, de- and reconstruction of fragments of personal and collective experiences of temporality.

Apart from being an intimate confession, *Islednik* is also a fragmentary depiction of the period after the First World War, through the 50s and 60s in which the narrator's childhood and youth are set, all the way to the breakup of the Yugoslav republic and the present, located in several key places of one family's history.

Moving away from a firm point in the present in which he faces the fear of old age, meaning his experience of illness and death in his sixties, the narrator sketches out his childhood and adolescence, the relationship to his mother and her former neighbor and friend Lizeta Bizjak, and in doing so visits – be it in reality or through photographs and other people's stories – a series of cities and locations which have left their mark on these people's lives. Belgrade – the city of his early childhood, Pula – the place where he grew up, Rijeka – the unattainable place he longed for, as well as Rovinj, Vienna, Thessaloniki, and Trieste, introduced through Lizeta's stories, all of which are *topoi* in which the narrator's intimate history takes place against the backdrop of major historical events which affect and form the fates of the protagonists in various ways.

The description of the relationships within the family of four that often moves due to the nature of the father's job focuses on dissection of the narrator's relationship with the most important person of his childhood, his mother. The beginning of this reconstruction of the past is marked by a symbolic episode about the disappearance of the notebooks in which the mother kept track of all the hotels she had ever stayed at. For the mother, the loss of these notebooks represents a threat of erasing part of her memory: the information on those locations contained in the notebooks represents a guarantee of memory, the material evidence of the trajectories of a past life and a mnemonic trigger of memories. The character of the mother encapsulates a spatial relationship to the past and time mediated by memories inspired, in turn, by material evidence and witnesses of the experienced past (photographs, notebooks, diaries) and the physical and mental immersion into the spaces of one's former life (apartment buildings, city streets, beaches).

The intimate narration of memories, or more precisely, of the narrator's biography, is intertwined or at times merely crosses paths with the lives and stories of people who played a part in his life in different ways and locations, and in doing so sketches out the outlines of a time through the perspectives of different pasts. *Islednik* poses a question about the structure and nature of autobiographical stories through its description of the bond between the intimate and the collective, that which belongs to the personal account and all those stories that touch upon, influenced, or formed it at a certain point:

> All around he felt the invisible presence of others. Is he the owner of a single autobiography, or is he comprised of many? Whose lives is he living? Why does he experience events that have nothing to do with his life as part of his family history? Fixations and obsessions are harbingers of a seismic shift of consciousness that will, at a certain point, bring together the seemingly unrelatable. He can't shake off the words of his neuropsychiatrist friend: genetic identification takes into account, apart from the immediate family, everyone the individual and their closest rel-

atives ever attracted in love and friendship. Endless possibilities! (Velikić, *Islednik* 244)[2]

Velikić's approach to the main points of interest in contemporary post-Yugoslav literature – the narrative representation of the fragmentary nature of memory, questioning the generic limitations of fact and fiction, and descriptions of the obsessive relationship of a collector to the (material) remnants of a bygone time – is defined by predetermination, both within the context of family heritage (genetics) and the multiplicity of social and spatial conditions. The narrator's personal and intimate account of reality, strongly marked by the imposing presence and influence of his mother, seeps into stories and portraits of family friends and acquaintances, classmates, and the wider circle of people he had met and through which he came to know fragments of other personal histories. The fragmentary nature of remembering and narrating the past is not about coincidence and unpredictability, but rather a complex web of stories that cross paths and in doing so, permanently affect each other. Describing the literary (re)formation of memories into a story, the narrator criticizes the linear principle which he deems too close to historiography – "The monotonous accumulation of bare facts, without any analysis" (216), and instead opts for a fragmentary, multifaceted perspective, bringing together various personal accounts:

> He stopped reading the diary. He returned to the manuscript of his novel. He gave up on linearity in favour of multiple starting points. This is the first time he is writing in such a way. A special file folder for each of the characters. Somewhere along the way their paths will cross. His task is to follow his instinct. (218)

Strung together, the fragments of personal lives and family tales ranging from portrait sketches (OZNA chief Vasko Krmpotić, schoolmates Eugen Poropat, Marijan Milevoj, and Goran Ban, Radmila and various others) to chronicles grounded in verifiable facts (the Huttertoth family) and biographies (Lizeta Bizjak, Masleša the clockmaker…) create a networked perspective on the past as a story that is constantly changing, growing, and eventually disappearing into oblivion. The narrative becomes a metaphor for the perception of temporality, in which the imposed concept of linearity and wholeness is replaced by a fragmentary construction of accumulated time, and the past, present and

---

[2] All translations from the novel are by Katarina Reljić.

future exist all at once, intertwine and condition each other, just as shown in earlier described concept presented by Deleuze and Guattari. There is no lost unity of time which should be reconstructed by certain narrative, there is only a collectivity or multiplicity of stories and their internal contemporaneousness.

3   Tracking Time: Narration of Endless Temporality

The narrator's relationship to the past is characterised by a spatial structure of the lived experiences stored in memories. To confront the threat of oblivion and losing the continuity of the self, he builds a chronotope of the past through the abandoned spaces of his childhood and youth as well as through imagined reconstructions of places tied to other people's lives. The spatial perspective of remembering, as theoretically described by literature memory studies (Halbwachs, Whitehead, Neumann, Nora, Hansen) is the foundation of the narrative which recreates the memories inscribed into space, which is interpreted by Velikić's narrator through the metaphor of the door as an event boundary, a threshold that marks the liminal place between recalling and forgetting:

> It is scientifically proven that subjects are three times as likely to forget a task they were given if they had walked through the doors of a room before executing said task. That is because our brain regards the door as an event boundary and considers the decisions made in a room as stored inside it once we leave. Hence, we can recall them by returning to the room in question. (Velikić, *Islednik* 27)

The narrator's return to places from his past life is a crossing of the *event boundary*, an entrance into a space of the past defined by the topography of the cities he lived in or got to know through the stories of others. The process of returning, narratively formed as a series of episodes from different periods of his past and the pasts of other characters, intertwines the historical facts and personal accounts of marginal figures in history, always defined and evoked by spatial coordinates: all the stories that comprise the panorama of memories in *Islednik* are spatially motivated.

Within the problematics of collective memory, Maurice Halbwachs (*The Collective Memory* 139) contemplated its spatial characteristics, stressing the bond of a social group with the space it inhabits. Spatial coordinates – streets, buildings, neighbourhoods – stay permanently ingrained in one's consciousness, evoking memories and enabling navigation through the *space* of the past. Halbwachs interprets the spatiality of memory through a dichotomous relationship between the material object and its imprint on the collective consciousness: recorded empirical experience of a place (significant to the community) is crucial for the construction and restoration of a community's identity (139). Building on Halbwachs' interpretation, Anne Whitehead recognizes the psychological triggers of memories which are found in real places such as buildings and streets, and which can function as orientation maps, meaning as a means of navigating once-familiar places (11). The relationship between space and memory and the mnemonic function of material objects is also described by Birgit Neumann, Pierre Nora, Julie Hansen and Tadhg O'Keeffe. Their interpretations of the spatial nature of memory and the role of space in the organization and keeping of memories can be reduced to the paradigm of storing spatial coordinates in the collective and individual consciousness which produces links to a specific context of memory (which is akin to the psychological concept of contextual memory).

Islednik's narrator follows this theoretical paradigm of spatial memory, putting spatial coordinates before the unreliable mental mechanisms of memory. Fearing the oblivion that threatens to demolish the entirety of his personal experiences of the past, and by extension the wholeness of his own identity he finds a guarantee of the temporal continuity of identity based on memory in the bond between the space and the mind. By leaving the space in which meanings were created, the mind is exposed to the effects of oblivion and the synesthetic spatio-temporal status of memory is distorted. Like in the case of Proust's madeleine, a reunion with space that is abandoned and recorded in consciousness evokes memories associated with it, thus ensuring the (temporal) continuity of personal identity. Thus, the repetition or the eternal return is necessary for one's self understanding. But what does this repetition constitute? It is not a mere physical presence, a relation between the body and it's environment which triggers the process of remembering. Rather, as Deleuze (71) claims, the ideal constitution of repetition implies a kind of retroactive movement between two limits: the repetition in the object and the change in the subject. It is the movement in which the importance of imagination is confirmed: the cases contracted or grounded in the imagination remain no less distinct in the memory or in the understanding. Further, Deleuze states:

> Rather, on the basis of the qualitative impression in the imagination, memory reconstitutes the particular cases as distinct, conserving them in its own 'temporal space.' The past is then no longer the immediate past of retention but the reflexive past of representation, of reflected and reproduced particularity. (71)

Velikić's narration reflects this constant retroactive movement, shifting between the limits inscribed in the object and in the subject with the help of the imagination.

Opposite interpretations which see spatial memory purely through the mnemotechnical union between the mind and matter, Jacques Rancière attributes memory to objects themselves as its representations. Material markings such as buildings, tombstones, and memorials do not preserve the memory of the past, but rather create it. In dealing with issues of documentary fiction (as a film medium), Rancière stresses the fact – obviousness, as he calls it – that memory is not a set of recollections of a single mind (which is confirmed by the existence of collective memory): "Memory is an orderly collection, a certain arrangement of signs, traces, and monuments. The Great Pyramid, the tomb par excellence, doesn't keep Cheop's memory. It is that memory" (157).

Cancelling the concept of an individual consciousness as a depository of memory, Rancière moves the process of remembering to objects themselves, while labelling the mnemonic process resulting from the confrontation of the consciousness and the matter of remembering as fiction. Fiction is not interpreted as imagining, opposing or stepping away from reality, but rather as reorganizing and reimagining it, meaning that to understand the juxtaposition of reality and fiction does not rely on the concept of veracity and falsity, but a certain construction of meaning:

> But, in general, 'fiction' is not a pretty story or evil lie, the flipside of reality that people try to pass off for it. Originally, *fingere* doesn't mean 'to feign' but 'to forge.' Fiction means using the means of art to construct a 'system' of represented actions, assembled forms, and internally coherent signs. (158)

The narrative look into the past in *Islednik* embodies Rancière's concept of the fictionality of memory and its inscription into material objects. After years of absence, a visit to his childhood hometown of Pula marks for the narrator the starting point for the revelation and (re)design of the past and its narrative formation. His aim is to create a story that would be a representation of the past, its narrated memory:

> I won't make anything up, just discover things. (...) This is the first stop of the journey ahead. (...) Cruising through a town that turns into double vision. I am looking at what is. I am also seeing what once was.
>
> In the end a story will come of it, one that is not made up, a story mom would enjoy reading. (Velikić, *Islednik* 99)

The outline of the narrative structure the narrator creates explicates the experience of temporal simultaneity, the presence of the past in the present, while at the same time emphasizing the true nature of the fictionality of his endeavour – discovering and designing the past (memories) within space. The concept described is suggested by the novel's title, which designates the narrator as one who investigates (seeks out, finds) the past in the spaces of memory.

Facing an abandoned space again does not restore lost memories, but instead creates memory, meaning it rests on the (empirical) perception of space and its immediate experience. The interaction between consciousness and space as the carrier of (historical) meaning is the basis of the fictional process of (re)constructing the past.

The spatio-temporal concept of memory narratively formed in *Islednik* is not exhausted solely in the portrayal of the (re)presentational function of space in the construction of memory and the description of the mutual interconnectedness between space and remembering, but it also points to the spatial nature of the experience of time, meaning the narrative concept of time as space. The current moment of narration and the renewal of memories is described by the narrator as a place of simultaneous elimination and renewal of the past: everything that happened in the past also exists in this moment. The present has at its disposal a vast network of memories, spatially organized data on past events, places, and persons, whose junctions can activate and invoke a specific memory, linking it to another, more distant memory. Hence the function of the present is to rearticulate and reorganize the past, meaning not only, as Bergson claims, that there is no present, but also that in that elusive moment the past is reoccurring over and over again, always taking on a different form – or as Deleuze claims in his interpretation of Bergson, the present is what was, and the past is what is eternal and everlasting (Deleuze).

Similarly, Jelena Todorović (90) relates the cross-linked perspective of narrating space and time to *liminal spaces of memory*, in which various pasts are reconstructed in the present, creating a convoluted narrative with a distorted linear structure. According to Todorović, by escaping the exclusivity of being labelled autobiographical, *Islednik* combines the features of the novel, fictional memoir, essay, and philosophical debates on the nature of time:

> His narrator, (...) strives to account not only for his own past, but for time itself, longing to triumph over history, transience and oblivion. It is a book of accounts, of inventories, comprising a great atlas of the transient world of our recollections: a world that is insubstantial and ephemeral as life itself. (91)

In *Islednik*, Todorović recognizes a narrative concept of time which does not focus only on a single temporal fraction or a linear reconstruction of events, but instead possesses infinite potential temporality, compressing into a single narrative moment the fragments of different periods through multiple personal perspectives. "The past lives in the present. (…) The world is an endless amalgamation" (Velikić, *Islednik* 31–32), the narrator concludes while reminiscing about the streets, squares, and buildings of his childhood hometown and comparing his own perspective to the perspectives of those who walked those spaces before him. To Todorović, this style of narrating time is a legacy of the Baroque era, an attitude towards time based on the premise that it is possible to track it by collecting and renewing the remnants of the past buried in memories. *Islednik*'s narrative intervention into the reconstruction of missing pasts whose meanings constantly elude the present is described by Todorović in the following way:

> It belongs not just to one age, but carries within itself endless temporalities, in the same way that great Baroque works often did. Although composed as a series of reminiscences, its narration is not confined to one past and one present, but meanders between multitudes of pasts, together generating the present's metamorphic fabric. There is no finitude; nothing ever ceases to exist, but instead resides permanently on the edge of the present, intersecting with the times to come. Like notable writers of the Baroque, Velikić senses that *everything that ever was, exists eternally. It floats in the chasm of centuries*. (Todorović 91)

Islednik is a novel which narrates time and space by entwining them together through a concept based on the Bergsonian concept of duration, addressing human memory, and eventually the difference between the past and the present beyond the frame of linear succession. Velikić unites the memory of time and the memory of space in a series of non-successive narrative fragments linked to each other through the perspective of a present observer, and makes the past, renewed through memories, a part of the present. The narration of memories is not introduced as a (re)presentation of a missing past, one that no longer exists, but a reality which is still part of the present, which its contents supplements and confirms. This is the source of the narrator's immense fear of dementia: the loss of memory empties the present of the meaning given to it by renewals of the past and becomes reduced to the sheer empirical experience of one's surroundings – symbolized in the novel by the mother's vacant staring at the walls of the retirement home where she is spending her final days.

The narrative investigation of the past in *Islednik* correlates to Bergson's interpretation of the concept of time and the relationship between the past and the present: "The truth is that memory does not consist in a regression from the present to the past, but, on the contrary, in a progress from the past to the present" (260). Awareness of the past exists simultaneously with awareness of the present and becomes an integral part of it, meaning besides the present as the current horizon of the body and mind there is also presence as memory (Lošonc 94). *Islednik* addresses and narratively forms such a concept of time and, by dismissing the linearity of narration, creates its multiplied perspective in which what is experienced belongs not (only) to the past, but is also present in our current condition. The narrative now is always an echo of a past experience which is restored and continued through it: the past exists because of the present in which an awareness of past experiences is accumulated. The past which exists in the present, constantly reshaping the present and giving it meaning, is realized in the act of narration because we always also experience the present as the past, not in the sense of it linear (or even causal) succession, but of pure coexistence and contemporaneity (omnitemporality): "...stories have no beginning and no end, the only thing that exists is an eternal in medias res." (Velikić, *Islednik* 12) The narration of *Islednik* is a verbal conceptualization of such a contemporaneity: the events, experiences and persons described in the novel belong to the past as much as the present, existing mostly in a virtual dimension of memory that perpetually evades actualization. Because of its virtual nature, memory constantly regenerates in an infinity of presupposed scenarios which come to life by stringing together various perspectives. In that sense, the present is not an endpoint in which the memories are evoked and renewed, but a space of constant expansion, change and improvement.

4   Identity and the Repetition of Difference

By constructing a narrative of the past and the present out of fragments of the past which he constantly reshapes, reorganizes and polishes, the narrator of *Islednik* shapes his own life story and alongside it the life stories of a few family members, friends and acquaintances:

> To commune with the past is to constantly refine it, invoke it and be it, but since we *infer* it from the traces it left behind, and since those traces are dependent on coincidence, on the material used to communicate, fragile or not so fragile, on various events throughout time, that past is

therefore chaotic, accidental, fragmented... (...) writes in his diary Witold Gomborowicz. (Velikić, *Islednik* 77)

In this citation from the diary of Witold Gomborowicz, the narrator describes the arbitrariness and variability of the narrative construction of the past, while at the same time finding in this process of evocation and re-contextualisation the backbone of the existence in the present. The non-linear, fragmented structure of the novel in which a heterodiegetic narrative follows a homodiegetic one, and where the present point of view functions as a jumping board into different segments of the past, suggests that human existence is based on the constant reliving of variations of what had been, and is always dependent on certain changes in personal perspective. The originality of the present moment is thus suspended in favour of endless repetition and a renewal of the past, which becomes the basic principle of the functioning of the self and building one's personal identity. It is the repetition (eternal return) described by Deleuze as the prerequisite of identity as a difference, an identity that implies sameness arising from difference:

> The eternal return does not bring back 'the same,' but returning constitutes the only Same of that which becomes. Returning is the becoming-identical of becoming itself. Returning is thus the only identity, but identity as a secondary power; the identity of difference, the identical which belongs to the different, or turns around the different. Such an identity, produced by difference, is determined as 'repetition.' (Deleuze 41)

The narrative perspective of *Islednik* is reminiscent of Deleuze's theoretical paradigm of identity as eternal return, i.e. the repetition of difference, constructing the outlines of the self through a constant renewal, questioning and recontextualizing of memories. The narrator, as an observer or an active participant in events, attempts to articulate his present self by reconstructing and staging variants of his past self, contextually defined by the times and places he lived in. The difference invoked by this repetition is based on the temporal, is intrinsic by nature and does not include the empirical relationship between two things (before and after). The relationship between being *distinguished from* and *distinguishing itself* is described by Deleuze as follows: "instead of something distinguished from something else, imagine something which distinguishes itself – and yet that from which it distinguishes itself does not distinguish itself from it" (28). Distinguishing oneself as an intrinsic, temporal concept is a fragmentary, unstable, and contingent part of identity construction. Similarly, the identity of the narrator in *Islednik* is (re)constructed through the fragments of his memories which create an illusion of the continuity of the self by appearing in the present, while simultaneously confronting it with an awareness of the essential difference repetition inscribes into it.

5 Narrating Life in Reverse

Vital to the understanding of the narrative perspective of past in *Islednik* is the plurality of narrative positions based on the dichotomies of the experiencing and memorized subject and the narrating and recalling subject (Neumann 336) which comprises two perspectives: that of the young, growing-up narrator who is an active participant in events of the past, and that of an experienced, older narrator who recalls the past events and is afraid of memory loss. In terms of form, the novel is divided into three parts. The narrative perspective in the first (most comprehensive) part is that of an extradiegetic narrator who remembers his childhood after his mother's death while also making observations regarding his current state as an intradiegetic narrator. In the second part the narration is indirect, in the third person, exchanging these personal accounts for the fictional perspective of Lizeta Bizjak. In the third and final part of the novel, functioning as a sort of an afterword, the narrator directly addresses his mother (in a letter); it is an epilogue of his attempts to narratively shape a past connected to present observations. A nonlinear depiction of time where the past and present coexist and cross into each other is the result of a perpetual alternation of these changes in perspective, working to reinterpret history and the past, or more precisely to recreate them by connecting factual accounts and their material traces.

Prompted by the news of his mother's death and facing the growing suspicion of having inherited dementia from her, the narrator takes a journey – first through memories, later physically – to scenes of his early life, narrating a range of memories, from inarticulate impressions of his earliest childhood to very detailed accounts of scenes, episodes, and interactions. The three-part narrative structure characterized by the switch from first-person to a more distant, third-person narration way follows the stories of the three protagonists: the narrator, his mother and their neighbour and family friend, Lizeta. The narrator as the observer (the recalling subject) occasionally becomes the observed (the object of remembrance), and the intimate account of past events becomes a fragment of a complex, convoluted historical and familial story. In the metatextual final paragraphs of the novel's first part the narrator clearly explicates his part in the reconstruction of his family's history, declaring himself intent on continuing his mother's mission of carefully recording the past, only to become the protagonist of his own narrative construct in the introductory pages of the novel's second part:

> That morning the novel I was investigating appeared to me on the window of Hotel Skaleta. Everyone was there, standing in line: uncle Dragomir, the Huttertoths, Vesko Krmpotić, Count Milevski, Lizeta, Maleša the clockmaker, mother, sister, father... and I, continuing the story started in mother's notebook that went missing in Vinkovci. Where a life, predetermined and never fulfilled, was written down.
> (...)
> He was close to sixty when he realized there is such a thing as old age. Such familiarity with oneself! He finally found solid ground. No more before, or after; no fast, nor slow; no better, nor worse. Only the moment he was in.
> He fell in love with life backwards. (Velikić, *Islednik* 171–5)

Living life *backwards* from *the solid grounds of the present* is a paradigm that describes not only the temporal narration of the novel, but also a way of forming the self in the present moment. The concept of the self, based on the renewal of the past in the present, brings together the dual perspective of the one who observes and reconstructs the past with the one that is the product of such observation. It is a dichotomy the narrator describes as *closeness to oneself*, an acceptance of the external and fragmentary nature of one's identity and giving up on trying to force continuity and unity into one's own experience of self. Being close to oneself means to accept the difference which describes every attempt of defining personal identity as a temporal category, a difference which is realized through the juxtaposition of perspectives within the narrative. According to Deleuze, this is why eternal return does not appear second or come after, but is already present in every metamorphosis, contemporaneous with that which it causes to return. Eternal return relates to a world of differences implicated one in the other, as a complicated, properly chaotic world without identity. [...] Thus, the circle of eternal return, difference and repetition (which undoes that of the identical and the contradictory) is a tortuous circle in which sameness is said only of that which differs." (57)

The difference, which is an emblem of the anti-essentialist concept of identity as a place of divergence and change, is integral to the relationship of the subject who remembers and the object of remembrance and subject and object of past events. The narrative "I" is, much like the concept of personal identity, constructed between the "view from within," the individual's self-awareness, and the observational "exterior view" of his social designation. Both positions involve a moment of change in time (akin to Paul Ricoeur's concept of *idem* identity), and only their overlapping in the present forms the difference which begins to suggest the answer to the question *who am I*?

The shift in the narrative perspective highlights the unreliability and fragmentation of memory as well as the dichotomy of the experiencing/memorized "I" and the narrating/recalling "I" in the autodiegetic form (Neumann 336) as opposed to the heterodiegetic form. The dialectics of the experiencing "I" as an active participant in past events and the recalling "I" which reinterprets and reimagines past events has been replaced by a heterodiegetic form, aiming to create a collective, fragmentary perspective of memory. The meaning of this narrative twist is explained in the final part of the novel, in which the metatextual comments on the nature of narration are inserted between fragments of the narrator's, his mother's and Lizeta's stories:

> He was, at the same time, the observer and the observed. [...]
> Every story exists in as many versions as there were participants, main or supporting roles, silent witnessed on the side, or obsessive narrators colluding with prior events. (Velikić, *Islednik* 248)

Islednik presents its story as a number of fragments which do not function like a mosaic in which each piece has its predetermined place – they are more like a sand mandala which will not be finished until it is destroyed. That is why the narrator's restoration of the past is haunted by the spectre of oblivion as the final act of reconstructing the story of a life.

6   Between Fact and Fiction

The panoramic view of growing up, told by an adult on the threshold of old age faced with the possibility of permanently losing his past due to "the gentle touch of dementia," is formed by two crucial relationships: that of the narrator and his mother, and that of the narrator and their neighbour Lizeta. The troubled relationship between the strict, obsessive, *petit-bourgeois* mother and her son finds a counterpoint in his short-lived interaction with the free-spirited, uninhibited Lizeta. In the final part of the novel the story of Lizeta changes from the realistic into a hypothetical narrative perspective of her life, created by the narrator from a series of gathered facts and second-hand accounts of her life.

The relationship with the mother is represented through a solid bond with places, items, names and persons, realized as a geography of memory in which memories are stored in order to ensure the meaning of personal identity:

> Mother exercised her memory every day. The notion of boredom was incomprehensible to her. She would take one of the boxes brimming with photographs, and slowly moving from one image to another, she would try to not only recall the names of individual persons, but also contextualize them in several sentences – determine their roles in the infinite universe of the past.
>
> Or she'd go through the closet and the drawers for hours. The discovery of an item she had completely forgotten about would cheer her up. To her, a whole episode of her life would be saved from oblivion because of that object. She had an obsessive desire to have the entirety of her experience at her disposal, at all times. That is why it was necessary to constantly relive the past, to carefully establish rule over the vast territory of memory. Without constant looking back at the road already taken, life would lose meaning. (Velikić, *Islednik* 49)

The same attitude towards memory is seen in his relationship with Lizeta, but it now takes up much broader coordinates which translates the real context of memory ingrained in objects and locations into a space of possibilities and imagination and alternative personal history, as a counterpoint to the fact-based nature of his mother's story. Mother and Lizeta are exercising their memory trying to repeat the past in order to prolong the sameness of their identity, using their imagination in this process of recreation of meanings and falling into the paradox of repetition that, according to Deleuze, lies in the fact that one can speak of repetition only by virtue of the change or difference that it introduces into the mind which contemplates it (70). Instead of sameness, they prolong only the difference that is inscribed in the repetition of their stories.

Upon his return to Pula, the narrator relives memories and emotions linked to them, drawn from his childhood: insecurities, conflicts, and traumas embedded in his relationship with his mother. On the other hand, Rovinj, Trieste, Vienna and Thessaloniki – the places where Lizeta had lived at various times in her life and which the narrator comes to know through her stories and later complements with fragments of other people's accounts, factual data, and his own imagination – represent an alternative topoi of memory, a counterbalance to a life saved in the material remnants of the past. The mother's obsessive-compulsive, deterministic and Lizeta's observational stance towards the past create the factual versus imaginary memory dynamic within the novel's fragmentary, nonlinear narrative as an autobiographical account of a life that has, and/or could (not) have happened. That dynamic is realized in the constant presence of the fear of forgetting, dementia, and the inability to relive as the endpoint of the chaos of the modern times.

The narration of the past in Velikić's novel reflects an effort to counter the nonchalance of oblivion as a characteristic of the modern age which, along with patterns of selective memorization, constitutes what is fundamentally a relationship to the past:

> It's time to report to my mother.
> The people from the beach have taken over the world. You remember those kind-hearted hillbillies stepping on our towels at Stoja and Valkane? They laugh, they yell, they put out cigarette butts in rock cracks. They nibble on seeds and talk loudly in the cinema. Relaxed and mindless in the eternity of the present. In the frantic chase of pleasure and luxuries, the world was perverted by abundance. The past is gone. Nobody remembers anything anymore. Speed has eliminated memory. Desire is a weakness. Remembering is defeat. It's shameful to have unfulfilled desires. Carelessness is in oblivion. [...]
> That afternoon on the terrace of the *Negroponte* restaurant, I decided to listen to my mother's advice, to go *there*. To witness.
> I can only stand up to the people from the beach with the help of my memories. (Velikić, *Islednik* 94)

The narrator's attempt of dealing with the chaos of oblivion has a dual nature and refers to the oblivion of the society, a symptom of focusing obsessively on the eternal present, and the oblivion of an individual, consequential to the degenerative memory loss condemning one to eternally repeat the present. The concept of oblivion – presented by the narrator as the consequence of high-speed modern life and the abundance of the modern world – is essential to understanding the fiction of memory as the issue at the heart of the novel. Here it is necessary to return to Rancière's interpretation of documentary fiction, which is the result of juxtaposing two basic regimes of memory: the first one, which is stored in the material representations of the past (monuments) and the memory of the modern world, and the other – that which is characterized precisely by the degeneration that has emerged from the overabundance of information to which *Islednik* alludes. Rancière emphasizes that the abundance of information characteristic for modern life does not correspond to an abundance of memory:

Information isn't memory, and it does not accumulate and store for memory's sake. It works exclusively for its own profit, which depends on the prompt forgetfulness of everything that clears the way for the sole, and abstract, truth of the present to assert itself and for information to cement its claim to being alone adequate to that truth. As the abundance of facts grows, so grows also the sense of their indifferent equivalence and the capacity to make of their interminable juxtaposition the impossibility of ever reaching a conclusion, of ever being able to read, in the facts and their juxtaposition, the meaning of one *story*. (157)

Rancière concludes that memory must combat the abundance of information as well as a lack thereof, it must be "constructed as the liaison between the account of the events and traces of actions" (158) as a plot or fiction. The conception of memory in *Islednik* follows Rancière's ideas closely. It questions the status of information/facts in the construction of historical and personal stories by addressing the personal and collective oblivion and memory which bridges the gap between fiction and fact. In the abundance of information, i.e. the hoarding of reality, Velikić discovers the roots of oblivion (the mother's perspective of the past), juxtaposing it with the observer who remembers by creating links between "facts and traces of events" (Lizeta's perspective of the past). In this regard, *Islednik* is indeed a work of documentary fiction which is stripped down by an artistic process of (re)shaping a past reality, dismantling the story into fragments, stretching out and condensing time, reaching for different voices and perspectives, scenes, images, and topographical markings, observing and recollecting at the same time. *Islednik* is a novel of excessive memory, a synthesis of temporal accounts that achieves its meaning by finding a balance in the abundance of data deprived of meaning, and with it a reference to the reality and a fictional undertaking that will give back meaning to such an abstract reality by fighting the indifference and pointlessness.

References

Bergson, Anri. *Materija i pamćenje*. Translated by Olja Petrović. Fedon, 2013.
Brown, Wendy. *Walled States, Waning Sovereignty*. The MIT Press, 2010.
Deleuze, Gilles. *Difference and Repetition*. Translated by Paul Patton. Columbia University Press, 1994.
Deleuze, Gilles and Guattari, Felix. *A Thousand Plateaus. Capitalism and Schizophrenia*. Translated by Brian Massumi. University of Minnesota Press, 2005.
Halbwachs, Maurice. *On Collective Memory*. The University of Chicago Press, 1992.

Halbwachs, Maurice. *The Collective Memory*. Harper Colophon Books, 1980.
Hitzke, Diana. "Between De-Facement and Machines of Faciality: On the Violence of Autobiographical Reading." *Serbian Studies Research*, vol. 6, no. 1, 2015, pp. 197–223.
Lošonc, Mark. *Pojam vremena u Bergsonovoj i Husserlovoj filozofiji* (doctoral dissertation). Novi Sad, 2017.
Neumann, Birgit. "The Literary Representation of Memory." *Media and Cultural Memory*, edited by Astrid Erll and Ansgar Nünning, Walter de Gruyter, 2008, pp. 333–343.
Rancière, Jacques. *Talking Images*. Translated by Emiliano Battista, Berg, 2006.
Todorović, Jelena. *Hidden Legacies of Baroque Thought in Contemporary Literature: The Realms of Eternal Present*. Cambridge Scholars Publishing, 2017.
Velikić, Dragan. *Islednik*. Laguna, 2015.
Velikić, Dragan. "Intervju: Dragan Velikić za *Express*." *Meandar*. By Sanja Baković. Mar 14, 2018. https://www.meandar.hr/intervju-dragan-velikic-za-express/.
Whitehead, Anne. *Memory*. Routledge, 2009.

CHAPTER 10

In Search of Home Time

Kujtim Rrahmani

> La délicatesse poëtique ne signifiera jamais l'amour propre d'un Poëte, mais la délicatesse de la poësie. J'aimerois autant appeler la maison, l'habit, la chemise d'un Poëte, une maison poëtique, un habit poëtique, une chemise poëtique ; c'est à quoi mene le style pincé & étudié.
>
> PIERRE-FRANÇOIS BIANCOLELLI, *Agnès de Chaillot*

∴

1   Life Is Elsewhere

Life is elsewhere. Yes, this sounds like a very old literary and social formula. *Home* also seems to follow this lifeline. Life is hidden in time: in a time that is *elsewhere, missing,* or *home.*

What is the time-space of home? Usually, the paradigm *life is elsewhere* depicts a utopian home time versus *life is home* and *house is home.* Elsewhere remains a space of an imagined home without a house, and this is why home is always coming back to the house.

Life and home time transcendence become more vibrant in the contemporary fictional landscape of the authors Dubravka Ugrešić (Croatia) and Zejnullah Rrahmani (Kosovo). After an *elsewhere* literature, their *back home* fiction turns toward its home sense of time through experiences of homeward journeys, recognizing emotional ties to different time frames and ideologemes. Their new personal fictional space of *home literature* is derived through *le temps retrouvé*, as a nexus between the *literature of consequence* and *Opfernarrative* delivered through an inner emotional spectrum and perspective of loss and memory, embodied in a *confessional* fiction. House-and-home, in short, becomes emotion; the return home distills the home time of *yesterday* in *today* and vice-versa.

Through the ages, *home* and *home time* have become ideologically colored entities. For centuries, conflicting ideological mappings motivated by divergent ethnic narratives have held the South-eastern European literary imagination ransom. This ethnic and ideological polarization – in addition to the religious clashes – has permeated the entire literature, from poetry and fiction to historical genres. "As an interface between competing religions and cultural-literary ideologies, East-Central Europe has often felt the pressure to redefine itself by streamlining its past and integrating its ethnic complexities into some coherent concept of regionalism or Europeanism" (Cornis-Pope 2).

As a part of this thinking, the South-eastern European literary cosmology was inclined to walk the avenue of occidental conceptuality, as well as the occidental meaning of home. However, during this phase, "all literary creativity was channeled through a prism of ethnicity; all writing was subordinated to the struggle for national and ethnic survival" (Elsie 301); the home that was envisaged was associated with *home feelings*. The Balkan has and still wanders across this avenue. Post-1989, different actors from different political backgrounds are merely brought to the subsequent acts of renegotiation. In a word, literature remains in the *cage* of lost poetics and lost home and time, a promised poetic and promised home, between *elsewhere, somewhere, nowhere, here*, and *there*. Between yesterday, today and tomorrow. Between desiring presence and languishing in absence. A dozen authors "in many of their novels and short stories, either the (pseudo-autobiographical) narrator or the main characters are migrants from the former Yugoslavia who try to find their place in Western Europe or in the US" (Vervaet 164–165); the psychology of migration and exile is deeply imbued with meaning-making in both the home space and time.

I begin with a personal story of mine to suggest some views on the perspective of *elsewhere*. By the very end of the 1980s, I read *Life is Elsewhere* by Milan Kundera, an exemplary novel of life as utopia, life as a projection into another space and time. Kundera's second novel was first published in French as *La vie est ailleurs* in 1973, and then in Czech as *Život je jinde*, in 1979. It was also published in Croatian in the same year, and I was lucky to read it with during the fall of the Iron Curtain (1989). It is worth noting that soon this metaphor prompted a literary culture of different (mis)readings and interpretations, most deriving from the political horizon of major events.

At that time, as a student of literature, I became obsessed with literary forms through authors such as Danilo Kiš and Anton Pashku. Kundera's novel woke me up to the relation between politics and aesthetics or between poetics and the politics of time. *Life is Elsewhere* cut straight to the point. Jaromil, the hero artist, was implicated in the political mechanisms of his era. This fictional story became a real political projection for Kundera, who, in exile in France, distanced himself politically from the regime.

Back in 1990, I wondered whether France was the very space and time of *elsewhere*, the dreamed home for Kundera, especially when the communist regime in Albania came to an end, and, paradoxically, when the Albanian writer Ismail Kadare went into exile in France. At the very end of the oppressive regime in Albania, he envisaged his life happening *elsewhere*! In that spirit, life *elsewhere* had become a *utopian* formula for a better life for many inhabitants from Central and South-eastern Europe. For them, *elsewhere* would reappear as a promised land, a perfect new home, and *home time*.

Consequently, a utopian quest for a lost dreamed home, or even an unreachable life, punctuated this sense of poetics. Moreover, after the 1999 bombardments in Kosovo, and as a sequel to the Balkan drama like in other post-Yugoslavian spaces (Croatia, Bosna and Herzegovina, Serbia), the literary imaginary was fragmented, thematically and as a sensibility. Its narratives turned to the lost subject, exiled in lament for a lost life under the ruins of the past or a quest for the lost/unknown human endeavor. On the one hand, home and life were lost and conserved as meaning under the ruins of past life, though ideological shadows were there. On the other hand, life was not simply happening due to various absences. In this way, the spirit of any fictional confession became a journey to a missing home as a possible dwelling space. And any confession was personal and communal at the same time. A new wave of memory spaces, literary ethnographies, and *mythologiques* turned into mythopoetic tales from the Eastern flow streams (see: Drascek) along the shores of a literary Adriatic and its hinterland. Wars and migration brought to this literature themes of clashing meanings, time, and space. Yesterday's *life elsewhere* underwent new, lived, and literary experiences.

2 Life Is Missing

If yesterday's life was elsewhere, in the wake of the struggles and wars of the last decades, life as a personal experience has been postponed to *another time*. In other words, life *here* and *now* was missing. The post-Yugoslavian literary imagination in the newly independent states was rebuilding a literary sensibility. A new (post)national mindset began dwelling within *our* past, today and tomorrow. New auto/biographical spaces were reshaping the fictional world. Often, the literary imaginary is turned into a subject without main narratives and lost in fragmentation, exiled in the theme of lament for the loss under the ruins of the past. However, the inner emotional and intellectual coherence of this imaginary will take place. Perhaps David Albahari's novel *Mamac* (*Bait*), written in 1994, after he moved to Canada, and published in 1996, is one of the cornerstones of *nostalgic* fiction, deployed after the *breakup of Yugoslavia*. Consequently, this tale of a man who *left without a mother* is extrapolated into a literary sensitivity.

At first glance, it may seem that the post-1989 period unlocked the literary imagination from modern ideological polarisations. However, a new *wasteland* of literary space, populated by ancient political spirits, has reappeared. One way or another, an ethnic landscape has influenced the philosophy of literary motifs. Even personal narratives are deeply imbued in ethnopolitical disputes and derived from major events. *Exile literature* became one of the literary *discoveries* of the Balkan literatures.

In order to offer an exemplifying paradigm of this phenomenon, at least in the post-war era in the Balkans (from 1999 onwards), two authors will be analyzed here as representatives of exile and *homeward* literary journeys. To read the literary cosmology of Dubravka Ugrešić and Zejnullah Rrahmani is to experience homeward journeys and wanderings, to recognize the emotions of *literature in a cage* when it comes to *the dangerous liaisons* between poetics and politics on the one hand and the discovery of new emotional and intellectual perspectives of exiled fiction on the other. The exile of their literature affirms *life missing* from a wasteland that they want to break away from, affirming the *home space* and trusting that "recollection becomes freedom of the past" (Blanchot 26) by forging a past space within a current home space and time in a permanent search for *une chemise poétique*. This is how the lost time of a lost poetics forges a new literary space and home time.

Ugrešić, who lives mainly in Amsterdam, and Rrahmani, a Kosovo novelist who lives between Canada and Kosovo, were hostages of conflicting mappings transferred into literary stories. With a special focus on the project of nation-state building, the major national narratives re-emerge in the background of their fictional stories. Yet, their literary perspectives manage to turn the topic around. Emotional-intellectual feelings appear first, followed by a national background as the generator of all events. They manage to employ a narrative artistic strategy to tell a personal tale that stems from ideological consequences. In telling small personal stories, they convey larger stories as well. They have gone into exile and are still wandering. Their journeys make sense in the context of literature that tends to be deeply personal and *confessional*.

Ugrešić's novels *Lisica* (*The Fox*, 2017) and *Muzej bezuvjetne predaje* (*The Museum of Unconditional Surrender*, 2002) and Rrahmani's last short stories and novel (2006–2015) evoke great events through microhistories. These events are presented as a part of a thematic and narrative structure and pretend to be singularized narratives. Their fragmentary nature calls for an entirety, as a memory at least. Their literary form is derived from authorial experiences and theoretical positions alike; this is how they see the world after their past, after the many stories of their lives.

In contrast to earlier thematic focalizations through a specific historical and cultural history, now their literary fantasy will be be identified with different micro-narratives on the subject. Auto/biographical and other extra-literary dimensions from the past will be reframed only inasmuch as they enter personal literary projections and experiences by turning the author's life into a vivid source of literature. From this perspective, new perceptions about the past arise.

Unlike the historical novel, the prose of Rrahmani and Ugrešić design a structure based on the shape of the current situation to rebuild what is lost. Their heroes have lost their former sanguinary lust to new personal circumstances, and they struggle on a homeward journey, despite, perhaps, an absent/evaporated home. All of that is embodied in the experience of writing as a wandering around the world and as a crucial preoccupation of identity: Where to stay, where to go? This Hamletian dilemma has become a thematic point for this kind of literature. A wandering-around-space/time identity is evident in *The Fox* (Ugrešić) and *The Beggar and Sophie* (Rrahmani). Neither author is theoretically obsessed with the form of their prose. This could be a spontaneous dimension of their narration wherein, above all, the *what* matters most.

In her first novel *Forsiranje romane reke*, (*Fording the Stream of Consciousness*, 1989), Ugrešić affirms her devotion to literary procedures by being incarnated in the skin of a writer. In a departure from this pursuit of poetry through literary form, in *Fox*, she embarks on a search for poetry as a life experience of the beauty and pain of human stories. In fact, Ugrešić opens this novel by wondering *how stories are made*. It depicts her journey as a constant quest for the nature of a literary and poetic tone, but her continued walk takes her down other paths. She shows an authorial face as a protagonist of events and as a protagonist that has gone into exile and returned home. Now, great ideological accounts only gain heft through personal experience. She works hard on the foundations of her home and home time. If the return home in old myths and tales means the end of the adventure (see: Campbell), for her, this return becomes a call to adventure, of facing *yesterday* and *today*. The skin of the fox as a literary figure and the mini-stories of Fox itself constitute a dimension of the hero's home. However, the personal experiences of the *fox*-character that are limited to a trauma become a substantial confession, especially in the micro-story about the beginning of the war, when the author/hero flees into exile:

> When at one point in my life I found myself in a situation in which the city sounded the alarm (a message I couldn't comprehend at first), radio and TV and our nearest neighbours cautioned me, with panic, to rush and carry the bag with *the necessary things* down to the basement, I didn't know that that phrase, which belongs to the war dictionary, would announce a radical change in my life. I first racked my brain over the content of the bag with *the necessary things* only quickly to realize that such content did not exist. (Ugrešić, *Lisica* 123)[1]

The entire story speaks about those *necessary things (najnužnim stvarima)*, the things she could not understand as long as she was losing everything, being forced to leave home. This episode deploys home time into the scene of carrying the bag with the *necessary things* to the basement, where the concept of linear time is transcended into a concept of momentum's forever echoing time, like a frozen idea and perception of home time.

As a *literature of consequence* and a sort of *Opfernarrative*, composed of many micro-stories on the fox and other reminiscences and situations, the literary texture of this novel, displays an echoing personal *Erlebnis* and life story, more than "playful characteristics typically associated with postmodernism" (Obradović 28) – typical for some of the author's other pieces. The *necessary things* in *the frozen time* scene that she has taken with her have forever generated frozen emotions throughout the entire subject. This scene initiates a distinctive echoing voice of the house by becoming a suppressed house voice *incarnated* into home-and-house time. This complexity is mostly a result of seeing life from an exiled perspective as a search for the lost world transcended into a new home time which eclipses the post-modern interplay of fragments with narrative time effects. Here the theme becomes tone and home time, a structural constancy of the novel.

Home is lost. New York or Amsterdam are not substitutes. But home must be somewhere, and the idea of never turning the head towards the lost home remains wrong.

> And there I realized that the advice that I had given to myself – after the experience with the bag with the necessary things – to never ever want a home again, was simply untenable; that the desire for a home is strong, that it has a power of primary instincts; […] house seems to be the greatest achievement of any emigrant; it turns out that emigrants,

---

[1] All translations from this text are mine.

many of them risking their own lives, flee their own countries just to buy a house, sooner or later, and celebrate the flag of the country in which they have stopped; moreover, many of them spend all their lives in two houses, one in the country which they have abandoned, the other in the country in which they have stopped, just so as not to suffer the traumatic loss of one or both of them. (Ugrešić, *Lisica* 125)

This is the *bad time* of a home imaginary and experiences, of home fear and home fire. Utopian time projected into the retrospective sentence *never want a home again* is immediately rearranged as an awareness of *now* in [*this*] *was simply untenable*. While home fear pushed her away, the home fire memory calls her back. *Home time* becomes a hostage between home fear and home fire. Indeed, the home fire's voice is stronger and prevails the time imaginary.

It is the very strong desire compared to the *power of primary instincts* that make the author-hero go even decades back. And here she is, back home:

My re-examination started from the moment I landed in Zagreb with the intention of finally seeing that house. Had I not catapulted myself out twenty-two years ago, without thinking, even for a moment, what would happen to me, where would I be heading and how would I be going any farther now? Didn't I leave then, abandoning my home and the fallen homeland, because of the air that was so dense with hatred that one could not even breathe, and now, look at me, standing still in front of the same old mousetrap? Have I lost my mind?! Home? What home?! Well, I have a home, don't I, in Amsterdam?! Friends? What friends? Didn't my friends, staring silently at the community playing cat and mouse with me, write me off with an indifference that froze the blood in my veins? (132)

The first was the act of leaving, and the second is of coming back home, where no one is waiting for you. This is not an adventure of life *elsewhere* or *at another time*, but of *life nowhere* and of the lost-and-found home-and-house as home time, now supposed to be *everywhere*, or at least in two geographic points, in exile and *here*. She did all of this without silencing the traumatic and nostalgic voices (see: Denić-Grabić, 155–162) by enlarging her emotional spectrum and the narrative architecture of home within the autobiographical narrative discourse.

The author Zejnullah Rrahmani changes his earlier avenue of searching for home under the shadow of ethnicity and the nation-state, as he did in his first novel *The Lost Vowels* (1974). At the same time, this new perception of the home appears together with new narrative techniques and literary forms. In 1999, Kosovo's waves of war threw Rrahmani to the shores of Canada. Ever since, living between Kosovo and Canada, he became an author associated with the psychology of exile and wandering narrative. The year 1999 was a watershed moment for his work, in which his literary subject and style transformed. The most notable change came with the novella *99 Emerald Rosaries* (2006), which was enriched by the *Ballovc Stories* (2008) and the fictional confession called *Illumination* (2008), as well as the narrative and spiritual wanderings of *The Beggar and Sophia* (2011) and *Five Prayers* (2013).

In these books, Rrahmani's previous thematic focus on ethnicity has returned to himself and to his relationship with the world, with life, and with love. Returning to oneself as the first and last home becomes a narrative cosmology and a passion for the author. He articulates the feeling of turning to oneself explicitly in one of the passages of *Illumination*, entitled "Back to Oneself":

> "– Get back to Yourself!"
> It was the voice of the Lord. There was no doubt. But then he plunged into thoughts, because the road could not be seen anywhere…
> (Rrahmani, *Iluminacione* 96)[2]

If the road could not be seen anywhere, the hero had to create it, namely, to find it. The road and the roaming had become his home, his home time also. The search would become a passion for Zena, the hero of the story, and he would be asking himself:

> Listen, Zena, why are you in a foreign country? Why did you leave the fount of wisdom? (Rrahmani, *99 rruzare* 260).

It is this self-reproach that keeps him searching. Indeed, he is just a homeless beggar searching for his home and inner spiritual time, as can be seen in the following passage of *99 Rosaries*, a mini-story titled "The Journey":

> As far back as he could remember, travelling was in his blood. […] He abandoned home with just a flask on his arm and a long stick in his hand. He would eat whatever people would give him and sleep in train stations, mosque porticoes or wherever they would allow him to, in inns, stables.

---

2 All translations of Rrahmani's texts are my own.

> The summer had seen him among the shepherds, far off across mountains. They said he had befriended the wolf and the bear, the rabbit at the gorge, and the fleet-footed dear. Then his roads became longer and longer. They said they had seen him all around the Balkans, Italy, Europe. [...] He has travelled across oceans and seas ... until one day the road brought him back to Albania, again.
>
> An olive grove on the seashore ...surrounded by cliffs and stones...
>
> ... For a while, and the magic was gone: Kosovo was beyond the mountains, wild and nefarious, and, yet, he could not do without her. (370)

Though in love with traveling, Rrahmani's wanderer feels inextricably tied to his homeland. But now, as a place that generates memories of love, the concept of home that gives peace of mind in the first place generates intensive emotional bonds with *the final stop*. In other stories of the collection *The Beggar and Sophia* (2011), the walls of the house are identified with the long journey in the world. The beggar keeps dreaming and seeking, translating thus Sophia's character into ancient Greek wisdom or prudence.

Indeed, the author-character that often refers to himself in his books as a hero named Zena (a diminutive of the author's name, Zejnullah) embarks on Zen Buddhist's path a hermit who announces the quest for love and recognition as final virtues. This narrative spiritual journey begins with the poetry of the Near East, categories of the marvel and admiration for the beauties of mysteries and wanderings, and walks towards the magic of images in line with the poetics of the Far East, from Zen Buddhist tones to the dramatic images of Japanese haiku.

In the case of both authors, personal experiences are turned into personal literature shaped as *episodic memories*. Usually, the storyteller begins to identify with the author/real character. The story gains plausibility in the autobiographical genre. The narrator becomes a self-referee/author-narrator, bringing together the literary and the non-literary. This transition from a story about others into a personal confession renders *life transcription* into a literary home and a spiritual home time. This is transcended, *à la* old Greek, from *Chronos* into *Kairos*, from clock-based timekeeping into the eternal time of momentum. In brief, both authors promote a kind of *confessional prose*, distinct from post-modern tempers.

The author-heroes, through an autobiographical tone, also provide historical evidence and documentation on political and artistic movements, adding historical, documentary, and even archival levels to the story. However, while Rrahmani begins his story on a personal note and recreates his imaginary journey, Ugrešić constantly turns the story towards an autobiographical, testimonial account. Exactly because of this, Ugrešić's literary memory assumes traumatic tones and the story depicts life as a consequence of this. Within the author's imagination, one comes across the tones of past writings from the literary discourse of Danilo Kiš. But here, fiction and facts turn into a narrative literary culture of a quest for a poetic home. For both of them, seen *à la* Bachelard, the oneiric house-home remains rooted in the house-home of memory (see: Levillain 2005). Thus, historical time which is developed as a cumulative time of personal experiences, is turned into narrative poetic time and tone.

3 Life Is Home Time

But can a human being have two homes? Are both authors lost in a struggle against losing any of their homes? Is there an asylum-seeker who does not dream of a primordial, irreplaceable, and unchangeable home? Though either the *other home* changes and is reconstructed gradually, without being noticed, or both collapse gradually. Can wandering become a substitute for a home supposed to be somewhere and the time-space of home? Ugrešić's and Rrahmani's literature is closely related to these topics, and they enrich the archery of such tonalities and topics in South-eastern European letters. The personal space of their autobiographical heroes affirms solitude to be a yearning for a home-space-time that is the basis for the meaning of life.

In Ugrešić's writings, this home space begins with the perception of home as a cosmos or world and continues with the perception of the palpable walls of the house. Hence the perception of space oscillates between an intangible and tangible concept of the home/house. Home becomes house and vice versa. All these fragmented forms of home/house are reanimated as the heroes' personal experiences, and emotions are identified as a kind of nostalgia, while "nostalgia (from *nostos* – return home, and *algia* – longing) is a longing for a home that no longer exists or has never existed" (Boym xiv) at least as a material house. A strong nostalgia preserves and creates the home-space-time indefinitely, while "nostalgia is a sentiment of loss and displacement, but it is also a romance with one's own fantasy" (ibid.).

This *home* literature, promoted by Rrahmani and Ugrešić, motivated and built within the cosmology of home-house-émigré poetic sensitivity, as a sort of *confessional* fiction, insists on telling the story in the first-person singular as a literature about *us*. The mark of this writing abounds in the heroes' strong emotions throughout their wanderings. Life experienced, turned into literature through personal perspectives and narrative point of views, differs from many contemporary constructions, at least in the distance it creates from the events that belong to a third person. The literary pattern delivered from the inner emotional-observational narrative world remains a crucial trait of this fictional ink, percolated with loss and nostalgia.

The recent works of Rrahmani and Ugrešić promote a literary homeward journey and wandering by ignoring the still-encaged ideological perspectives in the region. Perhaps this literature does nothing but record an *absent life* through the emotional memories for *then* and the emotion of loss and emptiness for *now*, beyond the *important* events and happenings, more often than not as a comeback to *small things*, to solitude as a consequence more than an experiencing poetic space. Absence forges a strong sense of house-home, which "assumes the physical and moral energies of a human body" (Bachelard 57). In addition, absence prompts the adventure of (re) building the home/house and home time.

Finally, the literary philosophy of home as inter-time and inter-space converted into literature of crossways and cross-poetics seems to be recycling the South-eastern European poetic mind, but somehow beyond the already stereotypical divisions or mergers of the global-local. A new relationship with the history of a community and *my history* are being settled by turning past historical narrative into the *narrative about history* (see: Richter and Beyer), about the self through these historical events and boundaries, converting earlier metaphorical discourse into a metonymical fictional discourse (see: Hamiti), all of which is in favor of the *domestication of fiction*. In addition, the metaphoric home seems to be in search of its metonymical location.

Authors like Ugrešić and Rrahmani know to focus the literary discourse towards *the necessary things* as marks of time-and-space domestication, envisaged as absence or presence, as physics or metaphysics. At the end of the day, what should literature do, if not that?

The literature of any era always finds a way to create its home poetics as a part of its perspective of *humanitas*.

Life is home. And home time. This sounds as old as the human literary and social imagination itself.

References

Bachelard, Gaston. *La poétique de l'espace*. PUF, 2004.
Blanchot, Maurice. *L'espace littéraire*. Gallimard, 1955.
Boym, Svetlana. *The Future of Nostalgia*. Basic Books, 2001.
Campbell, Joseph. *The Hero with a Thousand Faces*. Fontana Press, 1993.

Cornis-Pope, Marcel. "Introduction: Mapping the Literary Interfaces of East-Central Europe." *History of the Literary Cultures of East-Central Europe*, vol. 2, edited by Marcel Cornis-Pope and John Neubauer, John Benjamins Publishing Company, 2004. pp. 1–8.

Denić-Grabić, Alma. *The Narrativization of Memories. Trauma and Nostalgia in the* The Museum of Unconditional Surrender *by Dubravka Ugresić and* Frost and Ash *by Jasna Samić. Balkan Memories*, edited by Tanja Zimmermann, Transcript Verlag, 2012. pp. 155–162.

Drascek, Daniel (ed.). *Kulturvergleichende Perspektiven auf das östliche Europa*. Hubert & Co., Waxmann Verlag, GmbH, 2017.

Elsie, Robert. "The Hybrid Soil of the Balkans: A Topography of Albanian Literature." *History of the Literary Cultures of East-Central Europe*, vol. 2, edited by Marcel Cornis-Pope and John Neubauer, John Benjamins Publishing Company, 2006. pp. 232–301.

Hamiti, Sabri. *Studime letrare*, Prishtinë: ASHAK, 2003.

Kundera, Milan. *Život je negdje drugdje*. Znanje, 1979.Obradović, Dragana. *Literature, Postmodernism, and the Ethics of Representation*. University of Toronto Press, 2016.

Levillain, Henritte. *Poètique de la maison*. Paris: Presses de l'Université Paris-Sorbonne, 2005.

Richter, Angela and Beyer Barbara (eds.). *Geschichte (ge-)brauchen. Literatur und Geschichtskultur im Staatssozialismus: Jugoslavien und Bulgarien*. Frank & Timme Verlag, 2006.

Rrahmani, Zejnullah. *99 rruzare preg smeragdi*. Prishtina Faik Konica, 2006.

Rrahmani, Zejnullah. *Iluminacione*. Prishtina Faik Konica, 2008.

Rrahmani, Zejnullah. *Lypësi dhe Sofia*. Prishtina: Faik Konica, 2011.

Ugrešić, Dubravka. *Forsiranje romane reke*. August Cesarec. 1989.

Ugrešić, Dubravka. *Muzej bezuvjetne predaje*. Konzor, 2002.

Ugrešić, Dubravka. *Lisica*. -Fraktura, 2017.

Vervaet, Stijn. "Ugrešić, Hemon, and the Paradoxes of Literary Cosmopolitanism: Or How to World (Post-) Yugoslav Literature in the Age of Globalization." *Komparativna književnost: teorija, tumačenja, perspektive. Encompassing Comparative Literature: Theory, Interpretation, Perspectives*, edited by Adrijana Marčetić, Zorica Bečanović-Nikolić and Vesna Elez, Faculty of Philology, 2016, pp. 161–169.

SECTION 2

*De-composing Broken Bonds: The Culture of
Non-relational Relation*

∴

CHAPTER 11

Transition, Trauma, and Culture in Croatia (Notes on Post-war Literature and Film)

Saša Stanić and Marina Biti

> Whatever safety democracy and individuality may muster depends not on fighting the endemic contingency and uncertainty of human condition, but on recognizing it and facing its consequences point-blank.
> ZYGMUNT BAUMAN, *Liquid Modernity*

∴

1   Aporias of the 'Transition'

The word 'transition' (from the Latin verb 'transire,' which means 'to go over' or 'to cross' – presumably, from one point in space/time to another) entered the political discourse in the late nineteen-sixties and the early nineteen-seventies to denote and to a certain degree also to explain changes ('cross-overs') of regimes in the countries of South America and Europe. Extracted from sociological narratives on big social turns referred to as "great transitions" – the first, related to industrialization; the second, related to computerization; and the third, related to globalization (Sztompka 2004: 155) – the word was reforged into a political term in the late nineteen-eighties, at the time of disintegration of the former Soviet Union and Yugoslavia, and used to refer to changes taking place in the countries of Central, Eastern and Southeastern Europe, including, of course, Croatia.

The Croatian secession from Yugoslavia in 1991 was a symbolic act that was interpreted and broadly acclaimed as the fulfillment of Croatia's centennial urge to achieve its independence. In Croatian public discourse, this year became a synonym to the ending of a long history of national oppression and the beginning of a new era of freedom, its meaning charged with expectations of oncoming democratic, economic, and cultural benefits for the Croatian people. Difficulties were expected yet considered surmountable as the new goals appeared to be clear and achievable, no longer hindered by historic obstacles. Whatever may still have had remained in the way of a better future was expected to be resolved quickly and efficiently, and, if not immediately, then at least at the point in which Croatia would finally become a fully-fledged equal among equals, a member state of the European Union. The period needed to achieve that final political target came to be referred to as the 'transition.'

However, by the year 2013, when Croatia was finally admitted into the European Union, it became obvious that the concept of transition, defined by a beginning (1991) and leading, by the logic of linear progression, to an expected ending (2013), had been used to denote romantic desires, and that symbolic delimitation of timelines had little to do with actual effects the actions of the period had brought onto and into the Croatian society. As the hopes for a better future began to give way to doubt and pessimism, the word 'transition,' in public discourse, assumed the traits of a euphemism and came to be used to justify or conceal disorderly or deviant political, economic, and cultural practices. Rather than to come to a halt in 1991 or 2013 and give way to palpable democratic changes, the continuation of ill-designed practices, many of them linked to the process of privatization, gradually pushed society into frustration over its social, economic, and cultural issues.

In 2013, if not even earlier, it would have been more beneficial for the society to face the fact that "major social change, developmental or progressive in some respects" also incurs "grave social costs" and "that change itself, irrespective of the domain it touches, the groups it affects, and even irrespective of its content, may have adverse effects, bring shocks and wounds to the social and cultural tissue" (Sztompka 2004: 156). However, the idea of 'transition' and its connotation of the inescapability of progress proved to be much more appealing than the notion of crisis, or trauma. Its continued usage allowed for the hope that the problems on the road to a better future were minor and temporary, and that it took only (more) patience to overcome obstacles and achieve the ever-expected better outcomes. Hence, it became easy to overlook what was in fact "a contradictory development of the system" (Gramsci, via Filippini and Barr 88), and the inability of the system, and of the subjects within that system, to confront challenges, and to resolve them.

Even if contradictory developments were to be detected, it would, on the other hand, not have been popular in the nineties to predict that the Croatian 'transition' would fail to evolve in the desired direction and that the state of crisis caused by the sudden change was likely to stretch into the indefinite future rather than end with a particular event, linked to a predefined political goal. Hegemonic discourse, historically based and politically operated, has been known to step in, not only in totalitarian societies but also in Western democracies, to silence timely critical intervention, as to 'protect the order' and reaffirm the official policies of the state. It is along these lines that, in the nineties, the criticism was silenced or ignored, giving way to reductive interpretations, symbolically charged narratives, and myths, inducing compliance with the official policies rather than promoting dialogue that might have been corrective to the country's course. Such discourse proved to be seductive also to many a historian, as well as social or political scientist, leading them to succumb to the celebratory rhetoric of the post-war period rather than to submit it to corrective questioning.

It is certainly no novelty that national discourses go hand in hand with myths, which is why some Croatian historians see the year(s) 1990(1) not only as the very beginning of the process of Croatian transition towards democracy but also as the absolute beginning of Croatian modern history. Paraphrasing a former Croatian minister of culture, historian Zlatko Hasanbegović, this year was to be understood as the 'Year Zero' that marks the beginning of the present-day Republic of Croatia. Beyond this date, according to Hasanbegović, history, in the full sense of the word, ceases to exist, as the previous event(s) can only pertain to "historiography, family memories, informal narrative" (direktno.hr). Irrational as such an approach may seem, there is also a rational dimension to it since its mythological frame enables the hegemonic appropriation of freedom to disengage from the inconvenience of a past that might not fit the present or the future picture that politicians wish to draw for the people. A contemporary state is, as Jacques Derrida would put it, a "state of the debt" (Derrida 1994), and such a state naturally aspires to be released of its burdens, and especially of its debts to history and culture that would have preceded its existence. So, it takes a new beginning, the Year Zero, to start everything anew – to produce a new national history, to overwrite traditions, and even religions if deemed necessary. A new state wants and needs an all-new identity, and, in starting over, confiscates memories of lives once lived (Ugrešić 101). This amounted to the discarding of memories of the once-celebrated Second World War for the sake of celebrating the more recent war and linking it to the idea of the mythical beginning of all history.

One might, however, wonder if it was 'identity' what came across via such narratives, or perhaps the loss of it? Can identity be replaced, past amputated, memories deleted? Anyone who has ever tried 'to start over' would certainly have learned that a future can only be constructed upon facing, questioning, reinterpreting – coming to terms – with the past and that it is only via a reconfirmation of the past self that the self can also be embraced in the present and find its direction into the future. In Ricœur's terms, this is a matter of "permanence in time" (Ricœur 116) related to what he refers to as *idem*-identity, i.e., "the uninterrupted continuity between the first and the last stage in the development" (Ricœur 117). In a ricœurian perspective, the consciously articulated 'what' that refers to selfhood in terms of what we believe we are or perhaps what we may aspire to become, seeks harmonization with the uniqueness of who we are – our *ipse*. The notion *of ipse* points to the unchangeable self of an individual, or indeed to the common core of a nation, and an all-new 'what' cannot emerge without cost to the balance. When a disruptive event separates the past from the present, it disturbs the very permanence that the relational construct known as 'identity' relies on if it is to be at all. Some level of crisis, or trauma, regardless of approval or disapproval of the disruption itself, becomes inevitable. If speaking of collective identity, the disruption is likely to be caused by some widely and deeply felt historical turn, that can be welcomed by some or feel forced upon by others. While manifestations of traumatized states may range from ecstatic to mournful, from euphoric to depressive, and from aggressive to withdrawn, the shattered sense of permanence is still common to all. A loss of the past is – a loss, and the experience is traumatizing, even if some choose to interpret is as gain.

If history is to be revisited rather than dismissed for a present to find its way to the future, for the identity to be reaffirmed and for dialogue to start spreading in a society, what possible links could be discovered between the Croatian pre-war history, the post-war change, and the country's targeted new future? Some analysts did indeed posit the question and justifiably argued that the changes which led to the democratic turn were rooted in the fifties of the past century (Živković 53–54), within a particular layer of history that the politicians of the new era largely preferred to ignore. It was during the fifties and on the former Yugoslav soil that the postulates of private ownership and the open market gained popularity, carving the pathway to the future downfall of the socialist project, and building up into an outcry for democracy. This was also the time when the famous 'confrontation on the literary left' stirred up the discipline of the post-WWII mindset: the famous lecture that Miroslav Krleža delivered at the Third Congress of Yugoslav Writers in 1952 made way for the new freedoms of artistic expression and helped set aside the formerly nurtured values of the so-called social realism. Whilst the Croatian Independence War did indeed lead to an indisputable symbolic cut – political, economic, and cultural – from the precedent regime, triggering a chain of very real repercussions, it is also justified to assume that such a turn would not have been achievable had not the liberating processes, initiated decades earlier, sufficiently matured as to enable changes to grow into a force that would redirect the course of history. Bearing such examples in mind, one cannot but wonder if the symbolic 'cut' should have been defined perhaps more flexibly, in a way more inviting of critical revisitation, requestioning, and reinterpretation of history, especially concerning the traditions that could arguably be sustained to have helped open the paths to the occurrence of that 'cut' itself.

Yet, the official narrative remained focused not on the events that preceded, but on the ones that followed the 1990 elections: the constitution of parliamentary democracy, Croatia's declaration of independence, the international recognition of the new Croatian state, the Croatian admission to the UN and, at a later point, also to the EU. All these acts were interpreted, for the most part, independently of modern Croatian history and came to be viewed as reflections of 'the ancient Croatian drive for independence' that would somehow have disappeared into obscurity for most of the 20th century only to re-emerge in the last decade of this century. It hence appears that it was the shift in the official ideology that came to count as a measure of all history, rather than open-minded critical observation. As the new political elites assumed legitimacy to depict the entire pre-war period in a black-and-white technique, declaring it essentially irrelevant to the Croatian identity, almost a century of Croatian memory – decades of it actively remembered by the living, present-day citizens – got simply sucked under. This discontinuity grew into a cognitive problem since the burden of the denial of the relationship between the self and the memory of past selfhood proved to be an obstacle to the nation's ability to effectively assume the new identity that was forged for them and to move forward. The disruption and the void that it had produced could maybe have suited the opportunists who were quick to change their ideological colours after the war, and, to a degree, also those who genuinely experienced hardships during the past regime and who may have believed their trauma would disappear in being passed on to others, deserving, in their view, of collective punishment. The loss of productive points of reference to the more immediate past was however most directly felt by citizens who felt and interpreted that past as their own for the simple fact of having lived it, and these were deprived of legitimacy concerning any kind of publicly acceptable identity related to their previous existence. The lack of organized public dialogue that might have played a mollifying role came to be replaced by a chaotic debate that switched to the publicly less exposed levels of the society, and all kind of interpretations of that missing part of the past began circulating. This informal debate continues to this day, largely across social networks and comments that track the texts in the media, giving rise to mutual accusations and disagreement that, rather than contributing to a resolution of tensions, appear to contribute to a collective psychosis, thus also pointing to an overall inability of the Croatians, regardless of their ideological preferences, to assume a productive stance towards their future.

Other than the widely acknowledged political cut with the past, a different kind of directly experienced change was also felt in the field of economy. This came with the official acceptance of the capitalist model of trading, and with the process of privatization that, unfortunately, "largely enabled the rise of the grey economy" (Čučković 247) rather than the desired development of a free-market economy based on equal opportunities and the implementation of the rule of law. Changes were also extensively felt in the cultural field where the process was, first and foremost, manifested in language policies, with the primary focus on defining the uniqueness of the Croatian language as opposed to the highly similar 'langues' of other former Yugoslav republics (Serbia, Bosnia and Herzegovina, Montenegro). A new cultural space was also created, exposing Croatian art to the processes of redefining (most obviously, via the changed literary curricula in primary and secondary education) as cultural bonds to former Yugoslav republics were broken.

With all the complexities in mind that affected the core of the Croatian sense of identity, are we then to speak of the traumatizing impact of the social changes that had befallen Croatia, rather than of 'transition'? The topic is not to be taken lightly, as "saying simply that social change produces trauma" would indeed be "a gross simplification" (Sztompka 2004: 158), just as it would be inadmissible not to consider the possibility. The four traits that give rise to circumstances under which social trauma is likely to occur have to do with the nature of change: its speed (suddenness); scope (comprehensiveness); substance (its relatedness to the core aspects of the social life/personal fates of the citizens), and with the mental frame with which the change is faced – typically, that of disbelief that a change of such speed, scope and substance can be happening at all (158–159). A "breakdown of the political and economic regime" (160) certainly fulfills all four conditions, not to mention the augmenting effects on all the traits when such a breakdown was preceded by war, as in Croatia indeed it was.

While the Croatian public was made aware of the traumatizing impact of war on its direct victims and participants, and the shocking experience that affected the lives of the general population was acknowledged, the traumatizing potential of the political, economic, and cultural change that began to take place at an accelerated speed in the war's aftermath was hardly discussed at all. While the media handling of the devastating impact of war-related change may be criticized for sometimes selective treatment of the victims (e.g. Silvana Menđušić's 2016 documentary series *Rat za portun / The Gateway War*, on evictions of former Yugoslav Army families from their apartments during the nineties in Split, testifies to that) the omission to address the traumatogenic issues related to the all-encompassing nature of political, economic, and cultural post-war changes, made almost everyone a potential victim of trauma. Though these changes could have been identified as alarmingly traumatogenic for their speediness, scope, depth, and effects, the negative consequences were, at best, discussed in terms of collateral damage to the process of 'transition,' i.e., as irregularities that would somehow disappear by themselves.

With numerous anomalies emerging and multiplying rather than disappearing, it soon became obvious that it was one thing to declare a new era of democracy and order, and quite another to see the idea through. The understanding of transition as "an interval between two political regimes" (Sørberg 31–62) was certainly not intended for misuse, yet misused it was in more than one way. In early times, this concept would have been well adjusted to wishful thinkers, and later to the authorities in need of an excuse for their lack of direction or corrective action. The idea that there was a 'transition' under way offered false solace to some, and alibi to others, allowing the traumatic consequences of the war to mutate to an all-new level with the nation's exposure to the multiplication of traumatizing effects of the gravely unattended peace. In arriving at the inevitable question: *Can the causes be traced, and consequences repaired?* – there can therefore be no simple, or single answer, but only an attempt to shed light on the complexities that require addressing and to procure a sense of direction for the many steps that still need to be taken.

1.1 *'Transition' Traced, Revisited*

According to Sørberg, there were three major stages of the transitional process in Croatia. The first stage, the period between the years 1989 and 1995, was marked by the rise to power of the Croatian Democratic Community (HDZ),[1] by the country's struggle for statehood, its declaration of independence, and by the Croatian Independence War. During this period matters related to statehood had priority over democracy and reforms. The second stage, from 1995 to 1999, was the post-war stage, which was also the time of the signing of the Dayton Agreement on December 14, 1995, which symbolically ended with the death of the first Croatian president, Franjo Tuđman, on December 10, 1999. This should have been a time of post-war normalization, and the accelerated development of democratic culture in the broadest sense of the term. However, this did not happen, and the rigidity of the former period merely

---

1 HDZ stands for *Hrvatska demokratska zajednica*, which means: Croatian Democratic Community.

continued. It is worth mentioning that there were tensions between Croatia and the USA during this period, due to Operation Storm in 1995, which was not supported by the Americans. Authentic political statements that testified to this were, interestingly, documented in the BBC's documentary series *The Death of Yugoslavia, 1995–1996*. The series was then used as the base for the book bearing the same title, authored by journalists Laura Silber and Allan Little.[2] During the third stage, the opposition rose to power for the first time (January 3, 2000), and this brought about some positive changes in democratic standards and international relations. However, this was also a time when the biggest opportunity for normalization was missed, as corruptive practices, unaddressed by the government, began to take their toll. The leftist government failed to stay in power beyond a single mandate, and by 2003 HDZ was back, now with Ivo Sanader as the prime minister. Under Sanader's lead, HDZ moved beyond the narrow frame of nationalist policies, which helped open Croatia to the processes of Europeanization. Many sustain, that this was – despite later controversies over Sanader – the most positive period in the entire history of Croatian independence. However, the impression that things were getting better, and that 'real' democracy was underway, did not last.

The hope that perhaps culture could deliver a transformative impact, even when it became obvious that the so-called transitional process was failing to move "beyond the post-war transition paradigm," may have risen in 2010 when Ivo Josipović, jurist and composer, was elected to the presidency (Jović and Lamont 1609). That hope, however, practically dried out by 2014 when Josipović lost his seat to Kolinda Grabar-Kitarović and more-or-less vanished with the parliamentary elections of 2015 when the new HDZ government was formed by Tihomir Orešković, and the ultraconservative historian Zlatko Hasanbegović was appointed as the minister of culture. In Croatia, up to now, experience tells us that the negative bonds between politics, economy, and culture are hard to break, and positive influences – if, and when they do occur – tend to be incidental, incomplete, and usually too frail to last.

Seeing that the 'transition' – acknowledging that such a process was once set to a start – appears not to have led to expected outcomes, are we to assume that perhaps it still lasts? If this were the case, additional stages would need to be added to Sørberg's timeline. The beginning of the next stage – the fourth – would then coincide with Ivo Sanader's unexpected and, to the date, unexplained resignation from the position of prime minister in July 2009. The

---

[2] Soon after that, in course of the same year, the Croatian translation of Silber's and Little's book was also published.

post-Sanader period gave way to processes of post-ideological escalation, during which the two leading parties, the rightist HDZ and the leftist SDP,[3] despite their differences at the symbolic level, adopted similar techniques in competing for public appraisal, largely at the cost of their moral credibility. Even though Croatia managed to achieve its main strategic goal, admission into the EU, during this period, the general outlook was not that of greater clarity, but rather that of rising confusion and eroded values, contaminated with corruption across the public sphere that led to the loss of citizens' faith in political institutions and the government. No less impactful was the fact that, for the first time in post-WWII history, Croatia found itself without a firm authoritarian lead. The Big Leader position was vacated after decades of Tito's, Tuđman's, and Sanader's rules, and this vacancy provided new space for questionable political practices behind the curtains of the officially proclaimed democratic values.

The recent Croatian president, Kolinda Grabar Kitarović, stepped into office on February 19, 2015, thus marking the beginning of the possible fifth extension to the Croatian transition. The reappropriation of the Big Leader model of governing was quite obviously a part of her agenda, but she proved unable to impose the needed level of authority to achieve such a goal. Among other things, she failed to implement the discourse of unity that she advocated during her campaign. Instead of adopting a moral standpoint, she furthermore engaged in populist gestures and opened the door to ever more present attempts of historical revisionism which seeks to rehabilitate the shameful parts of Croatian history at the cost of its anti-fascist tradition. The period was that of a general downfall of moral standards in politics, which particularly affected the sphere of culture which was transformed into a direct battleground between politically/ideologically opposed sides, with the left-wing finding itself on the losing side, especially after the Ministry of Culture adopted strategies to reduce or even deny public funding to programmes and activities proposed and/or practiced by 'leftist' artists and NGOs. The effect of this was the marginalization of their public impact that had a negative reflection on the social perception of values in general.

If we were to succumb to the logic of postponement and extend this description to include the current or the hypothetical sixth transitional stage, only to point to the seventh, if not also to an eighth stage or more, this would only emphasize that the concept of 'transition' has already been stretched *ad absurdum*, covering a myriad of mutated forms of the previously unresolved

---

3 SDP stands for *Socijaldemokratska partija* which means: Social Democratic Party.

problems and allowing them to deepen and multiply over time. As new aporias emerge and the expectations of a future-to-be repeatedly regress into the repetitive mode of the ever-troubled present, it rather appears that Croatia's 'transition' was headed, from the point in time in which it was presumably initiated, for a historical blind spot. That historical standstill (sometimes labeled by yet another euphemism, the so-called 'post-transition') is all too plainly evidenced by the country's underachievement across a broad range of statistically measurable categories such as investments in science and technology, culture, healthcare, social care, etc., and perhaps most shockingly by its low rating when it comes to the citizens' perception of their quality of life, as shown by the Eurostat's Life satisfaction in the EU Member States survey where Croatia's ranking in 2018 was second-lowest, negatively outranked only by Bulgaria which was listed at the very bottom. All this needs to be taken for what it is, rather than be disguised under one label or another if it is to be overcome at all.

1.2   *Red Flags*

The problematic and rather arbitrary disposition of the Croatian 'transition' can be said to correspond with the notion of the so-called "fifth risk," though only to point to a rather peculiar, inverse Croatian version of the phenomenon. This term, coined by Michael Lewis (2018) refers to the misgivings caused by the lack of "well-organized government in place to respond to /.../ contingencies when they hit." However, the Croatian lack of organization – a typical manifestation of the so-called 'structural trauma' (Sztompka 2004: 161) reflected in the government's inability to adequately react to contingencies – was not caused by unfilled positions in the governmental administration, as in America under Trump (which was discussed by Lewis in his book), but by a trend quite opposite to that. Stage after stage, and government after government, the devaluation of professionalism was enforced thanks to the multiplication, rather than reduction of positions of political and social influence, within the governmental administration and beyond. This surplus soon became a problem, seeing that such positions were filled to satisfy short-term political agendas, following ideological and political criteria, regardless of interests – economic, cultural, or other – of the broader public that paid for them, and of the country itself. The multiplication of positions, therefore, led to more cost and less profit for the country and the people; to a loss of vision concerning possible solutions; and, above all, to the general obscuration of responsibility concerning any given problem that may need to be solved. The mere semblance of activity of the inactive yet ever-spreading threads of power therefore became the measure of all activity across the public sphere, as it found its way into social services, educational and public health institutions, and more, masking or providing excuses and alibis to different forms of inadequacy, or even failure.

When contingencies hit, yet remain unresolved, and the same scenario hits, again and again, the citizens tend to lose faith in the country's governing bodies and institutions. This appears to be much more the case in post-communist societies than in Western democracies, as shown by research carried out by Mishler and Rose (1997), Sztompka (1998), Catterberg and Moreno (2006), and others. The 'distrust syndrome' (Sztompka 2004: 178) appears to be particularly at work when it comes to the Croatians' lack of faith in their political institutions, as shown by Sekulić and Šporer (2010). This syndrome is also reflected in Croatia's alarmingly negative demographic trends, documented in data regularly updated by the Croatian Bureau of Statistics (Državni zavod za statistiku). Numbers speak for themselves, and they reveal constantly lowering birth-rate (most recently set at 1.47, which is significantly more distant from the 2.1-threshold than in many European countries, including the Czech Republic, as an example of a country on a post-communist path) and a steady increase of the death rate, alongside a growing tendency of young and largely highly educated people to leave Croatia for better opportunities elsewhere. This is reflected in a negative ratio between the working population and. that of the retirees, and negatively affects the country's GDP, and the economy in general. Hence, the further loss of faith in the institutions that gives rise to general dissatisfaction occurs causing the traumatizing continuation of the vicious circle to become unstoppable.

So, how do the Croatians cope? Numerous adaptive strategies are at work, more notably negative than positive ones. The political elites come and go, but their activity remains directed at the preservation of their power statuses, masked – at best – by meagre reforms that fail to address any complex issue or produce the needed and life-felt curative effect. These are usually publicly presented, in one form or another, as "innovative strategies" (Sztompka 2004: 184) but tend to come closer to "illegitimate adaptations" (184). These can primarily be found on the side of the public sector but are often also adopted by citizens inclined to search for systemic loopholes that might aid them in overcoming hardships. Numerous "retreatist adaptations" are also at work, and these tend to take the form of "passivism, resignation, and marginalization," but also of "the craving for paternalistic care, a strong ruler, and simple solutions to economic problems" to which "all kinds of populists and demagogues" (186) are more than happy to respond. Demagogy lives off insecurity that also leads to the formation of "group egoism or factionalism." The groups that gather around demagogical figures usually seek to fortify their public standing by assuming "system-blame" attitudes: either by placing blame on "the past and seek the sources of present troubles in the days of communism, and the villains of present traumas among former communist" or on capitalism itself, while exhibiting "nostalgic cravings for the past" (187).

The feelings of pessimism, cynicism, and anger are often narrativized in columns and commentaries published in the Croatian media, finding their way into a verbal conflict between groups of citizens ('blame-groups') who voice themselves via social networks. For the lack of possibilities to fight objective hardships, they tend to weaponize language which they use to demean, humiliate, and disgrace the ever-needed "enemy" – the ideologically differing 'other.' Sensationalist media headings and populist content, all too easily shareable across social media, add to frustrations and disillusionment, causing the psychotic[4] pursuit of culprits to continue. While the loss of certainty, typical of modernity, may have caused people around the world to fall prey to similar feelings of fear and anger, the added issue of a lost past reflected in the unresolved sense of the present and stained with ever-present hypervigilance to perceived future threats, equivalent to an overall sense of displacement in time and space, as parts of the psychotic equation, make the Croatian case appear even more alarming, and that much more needy of curative action.

2   Reflections on Culture

Let us start this part of the discussion by pointing out that the term 'culture' will be primarily used to denote cultural production, i.e., "the social processes involved in the generation and circulation of cultural forms, practices, values, and shared understandings" (Chandler and Munday 2020). We will narrow this focus down further and observe cultural production through the prisms of literature and film, seeing that these artistic forms more directly than others contribute to the narrativization of history, identity, and trauma, which have so far been accentuated as relevant to this discussion. Besides their narrativity, an additional reason to link literature and film is derived from the similarities in their susceptibility and/or resistance to processes that envelop and sometimes penetrate the field of cultural production from sources pertaining to the broader cultural background. Finally, the third reason to observe the two

---

4 "When delusions are shared on a mass scale, they can be hard to recognize. In fact, individuals who share the mass delusion may not be psychotic, themselves; what they embrace, is" (LaBier 2010).

modes together, which is largely technical, is that in the contemporary technological era writers often revert to scriptwriting and vice versa, and the two modes often tend to cross paths on the Internet.

Since cultural forms do not only inhabit the area of life directly related to cultural production but also to the totality of circumstances that shape what is usually referred to as a nation's way of life, that totality – when contextually required – will also be referred to as 'culture.' In such cases, 'culture' will be understood in terms of "place and /.../ nationalism and the domain of the nation-state" (Barker 66) and observed from the perspective of its exposure to the powers of "tradition and social reproduction" as well as those that shape themselves into a call for "creativity and change" (68). Such forces are at work in all societies, yet they can clash or unite in ways that are unique to each constellation, leaving imprints of values and creating time-space patterns within and across the society. These are sometimes also referred to as trends that testify to values related to specific constellations of power, subordination, and cultural influence typical of particular social environments and historical timeframes. Hence, we will discuss the three trends that can be identified in the Croatian society of the post-war period – that of ideologization, commodification, and resistance – and point to how film and literature may be affected by sets of values pertaining to the broader cultural context, or perhaps how they may affect these values and provide corrective input that the literary forms, when or if socially empowered, have been known to achieve.

In tracing the trends, our overview of culture will furthermore be guided by our interest in the relationship between cultural production and culture in general, specifically concerning issues of memory/history, identity, and trauma that have been recognized as crucial to the aporias of the 'transition' that appear to be keeping Croatia's 'history of the future' in a deadlock, and its future postponed. In embracing the view that it is primarily through the creation of literary narratives that the suppressed 'memory residues' can be enabled to "appear in public life" (Alexander 6) and that "literary interpretation, with its hermeneutic approach to symbolic patterns" can act as "a kind of academic counterpart to the psychoanalytic intervention," then an interpretation of narrative forms that seek to tear down the barriers which keep the post-war trauma in a state of denial, may be said to constitute a modest attempt at that kind of intervention. It will therefore be via the exposure of a broader range of cultural synergies that this analysis will aspire to point to narrative models that open up the paths to a rediscovery of selfhood based on the "(re)construction of solidary relationships" by which "societies expand the circle of the we" (5), as to restore "the collectivity's identity, its stability in terms of meaning" (10), which is crucial to the restoration of the society's deeply divided and yet unhealed core. If it is furthermore true that "for the wider audience to become persuaded that they, too, have become traumatized /.../, the carrier group needs to engage in successful meaning work" (15), then perhaps the carrier group of the very best of writers and film narrators may arrive at being only just sufficiently empowered to enable such meanings to penetrate the dormant zones of the collective consciousness, and – in the best possible scenario – act as trigger to its activation.

2.1 *Ideologization*

During the early nineties, the old value system came under revision, and a new system, more adapted to changed circumstances, began taking shape. This brought about a new beginning in the sphere of cultural production as well as the creation of a new artistic canon. Literary figures – appreciated or even unquestioned during the former system (such as Miroslav Krleža) – come under strict scrutiny, and attempts were undertaken to marginalize their cultural relevance and replace them with new icons (such as Ivan Aralica). It was, to a degree, expected that the authors who had previously expressed their commitment to the former regime might come under review, yet many changes that took place seem to have escaped expectations. Former advocates of communism and its party members were quick in their transformation into apologists of the new democracy and supporters of a nationalist political agenda, while those who consistently criticized the former society found themselves on the margins once more. An example of such practice is the case of the playwright Ivo Brešan (1936–2017). A fierce critic of the former socialist set-up and a talented writer, Brešan – one might think, rather surprisingly – received little or no acknowledgment from the new state. The reason, most likely, was his continued interest in social malformations – an attitude which he practiced in his new circumstances much like in the old ones. From this standpoint, his dramatic opus dating from the Yugoslav era is comparable to his work from the nineties and until his death. Before and after, he persisted in unveiling primitivism and corruption through satire. His work thus remains open for future research which is likely to expose the extent to which a genuine critical attitude works against one's broader recognition and seems not to be a valid ticket into national history. The same irony applies to Feral Tribune which, during the eighties, existed as a satirical supplement to the newspaper Nedjeljna Dalmacija, and was at that time praised by Franjo Tuđman for its criticism of communism and Serbian nationalism. However, once Franjo Tuđman became president of the newly founded state of Croatia, he seemed to lose his appreciation of satire and viewed the paper's criticism of the new circumstances as destructive and hostile to the establishment.

The Croatian Democratic Union (HDZ) won elections in the spring of 1990, presenting itself as a millenaristic movement (Abercrombie, Hill and Turner 251) and asserting itself as a symbol of victory and freedom for the Croatian people, while the presidency of Franjo Tuđman was viewed as the peak of a tradition of Croatian kings, viceroys, and aristocracy. Tuđman, furthermore, came to be compared with saints and religious icons, not excluding Jesus Christ. The cultural arena was expected to match such assumptions and it was therefore cleansed of any component that might have posed a threat to the promoted concepts of Croatianism. Three myths, supported by the mechanisms of the state, were given precedence over all other topics: the statehood myth, the myth of the Croatian Independence War, and that of a deep interconnectedness between the Croatian people and the Catholic Church (Markovina 142). Croatian culture thus ended up being subdued within the state-generated mythology, with the result of having its value measured on the base of its mythological relevance. Barthes' observations regarding the ability of myths to aid the process of naturalization (Barthes) may prove to be useful in understanding the period since the mythologization of reality enables an artificially created state to appear as natural, and the values on which such a state is based to be accepted as socially and politically unquestionable.

Thus, the entire cultural production of the nineties came to be filtered through the national myth, which largely gave way to a victimological discourse that found its expression across all public discourses and different genres. This resulted in contradictions between the popular victorious and no less popular victimological approaches, and the films produced during this period testify to this discrepancy. The victorious sentiment, therefore, came through in a declarative rather than in an emotionally convincing manner that the best of the Yugoslav films about the Second World War and the people's liberation movement once succeeded in expressing. The directors of the nineties seemed trapped between the topics of victory and loss, between the commemorative approach linked to Vukovar and the celebratory one linked to Knin, and this discrepancy between lamentation and celebration marked the entire social sphere, especially on dates such as August 5th (the liberation of Knin) and November 18th (the fall of Vukovar) which provided quite different grounds for the polarization of the public sphere.

Admittedly, the subordination of culture to the ideology of the state has become somewhat less intense with the passage of time, yet it never disappeared. The persisting steadiness of this phenomenon can well be illustrated by the postponement of the European Theatre Night from the 18th to the 25th of November 2017 due to the protest of the war veterans' associations against the manifestation being held on the same date that also marked the fall of

Vukovar. Suspending an international theatrical manifestation under the pressure of any social group is a clear sign of a tendency to reduce rather than to expand the scope of cultural life, and to narrow it down to nationally relevant topics. This is also an indication of how such tendencies undermine efforts not only to accept but also to produce an open culture that could not only attract a broader international audience but also address the Croatian society from diverse perspectives help heal the nation deeply shattered by the events in its recent history, and its aftermath.

When HDZ won the elections in 2015, causing the former coalition led by the social democrats (SDP) to step down from power, culture suddenly became a topic of central interest to the media, which was without precedent in recent Croatian history. The reasons, however, for the sudden focus on culture had more to do with the further downfall of values than with actual cultural achievements. Conservative reactions to theatre plays and films came to be voiced in the form of public protests and demands to include certain authors into the literary curricula in schools were heard from all sides. The culture was generally used to express political views, and numerous associations demonstrated their political inclinations by expressing attitudes on various cultural topics. After the period during which cultural topics were used to create support for the project of the state itself, and after the period that saw the rise of commodification, Croatia reverted, more openly and more strongly than before, to institutional interventionism that aspired to a strong reconfirmation of the ideology of the national state, but also to defining desirable or undesirable values in the field of culture. This was usually achieved by providing, or denying, institutional legitimacy to cultural activity. Two examples, amongst many of this period, are illustrative of such institutional action – that of Tanja Belobrajdić and Jakov Sedlar.

Tanja Belobrajdić presented herself to the Croatian readership in 2015 with her debut novel *Crni kaput / Black Coat*. The novel depicts the sufferings of Croatian defenders in a Serbian camp in Vukovar, and as such, it soon acquired the attribute of anti-war prose. Soon, the author was doubly awarded for her manuscript: in Vinkovci she received the Josip & Ivan Kozarac Award for a debut writer, and the Society of Croatian Writers awarded her with the Slavić Award for the best debut novel in 2015. The public interest in Tanja Belobrajdić escalated when it became known that she was the former wife of Tomislav Duić who, during the war, acted as commander of the Military Centre of Investigation Lora, in Split. After the war, Tomislav Duić was sentenced to eight years imprisonment for charges that included war crimes, the illegal capturing and torturing of civilians (mainly of Serbian nationality), and murders that took place within Lora. In 2009, his wife Tanja, formerly Duić, was also charged for criminal offenses by the Dalmatian Committee for Human Rights for activities undertaken while she was a member of the 72nd Batallion of Military Police and coordinator of calls to active duty in Lora. The charges against her were based on 24 testimonies which identified her as a participant in the torture and degradation of prisoners. The scenes described in her novel hold an unusual resemblance to the content of the testimonies against her, documented in the case files, the key difference being the inversion of roles: Serbian victims from the testimonies act as Croatian victims in Belobrajdić's novel, and Croatian torturers are replaced by Serbian torturers. The media found plenty of material to indicate that the novel comes close to being an actual admission of crimes, in reversed optics, all of which resulted in Tanja Belobrajdić filing charges against *N1* and *Novosti*, i.e., it resulted in a judicial process that ended in penalties for the media for tarnishing the reputation of the author. Even though the lawyers who represented the media requested that the witnesses who testified against Belobrajdić in the previous proceedings be heard once more, the court declined their request. Belobrajdić's guilt remains unproven, but the suspicion, driven by the court's rejection of witnesses, lingers on, and thus the case remains controversial. This controversy, however, did not affect the decision of the Ministry of Culture to appoint Tanja Belobrajdić as a member of the Committee for Assigning Financial Support to writers in 2017. It needs to be said that unproven charges cannot be used as an argument against someone's institutional advancement, but on the other hand the published novel disqualifies the author in yet one more way since this manuscript – even though it may be praised for its anti-war dimension if the broader context is unknown or rejected – abounds in obvious grammatical and stylistic errors and gives reason to question the level of literacy expected from a writer. Paradoxically, Tanja Belobrajdić, despite her lack of writing skills and other controversies, gained final and official recognition thanks to her involvement in the work of the Committee which assigns support to professional writers and evaluates their work. The case is scandalous in more than one way, and it deepened the lack of faith in the Ministry of Culture and other institutions, causing many writers to abstain from demanding support, though this moral gesture was undertaken not only against their financial interests but also with no effect on how the Ministry operates.

Among other examples of the strange criteria at work is the case of Jakov Sedlar who won the Award of the City of Zagreb in 2017 for directing the film *Jasenovac: Istina / Jasenovac: The Truth* (2016). However, it was soon out in the open that the film, which emphatically proclaimed to speak the truth, was based on inaccurate data and forged documents. The Antifascist League of the Republic of Croatia filed criminal charges against the author, and Sedlar himself admitted to having illegally obtained the documents he used (which were no longer in his possession, hence he could not show them to the press), stating that he had honestly believed his sources to be genuine (Benačić). Cases like these are usually euphemistically referred to as 'controversial,' although this particular case raises questions of a more serious nature, such as that of deception and unprofessionalism. The award, however, was never withdrawn.

Hence institutional awards, as signs of cultural value that tend to dominate over the field of culture, have been compromised, both in the case of Belobrajdić and in the case of Sedlar, which are far from being the only two examples to inspire doubt in the value criteria propagated by official bodies at different institutional levels. While providing legitimacy to questionable cultural products and inviting negative reproduction (Giddens 1012), Croatia's battle over values came to be even more deeply entangled in political issues, and the cultural field even more tightly constrained by the overpowering effects of ever-interfering political influences.

2.2   *Commodification*

Due to the disintegration of Yugoslavia, the former market based on 22 million citizens/consumers suddenly shrank to approximately four million consumers, i.e., to the number of actual citizens of the Republic of Croatia. Apart from the physical reduction to an even smaller number of people who can be said to be potential consumers of cultural products, the change itself also brought about a crisis in the criteria used to observe and evaluate the cultural scene, both production-wise and reception-wise. In popular music, the so-called *turbo-folk* and *pop-folk*[5] assumed the cohesive role between the former Yugoslav republics, and the rise in popularity of these genres largely revealed the nature of cultural inclinations which reflect the taste of vast portions of the public in different spaces of the former state, Croatia included.[6] The case invites further discussion of the thesis that the so-called field of 'low' culture

---

5 The mentioned phenomena in the field of music are discussed in the following books: *Sounds of the Borderland: Popular Music, War and Nationalism in Croatia Since 1991* by Catherine Baker and *Balkan: od geografije do fantazije* (the last chapter) by Katarina Luketić.

6 This view is reflected in a book written by a musical critic, Ante Perković: *Sedma republika: pop kultura u YU raspadu* (*The Seventh Republic: Pop Culture within The YU Dissolution*), published in 2011. Perković sees the music of the period as a separate cultural entity that once connected and still connects the six republics of the former Yugoslavia. The book was subsequently used in the filming of a documentary serial directed by Brankica Drašković and entitled *Borderland Soundtrack*. Both the book and the serial (filmed in 2016 and 2017, released in 2018) stress the function of music as that of popular resistance that defied political processes of dissolution of the former state.

finds ways to incorporate resistance to political change while, paradoxically, individual consumer groups of that very same cultural product use it to send political messages and distinguish themselves from other groups in a rather tribal manner that manifests itself in heated antagonisms. This 'short circuit' between a lost 'sameness' and a newly found 'difference' does not arise independently of the overall clash between nationally supported cultural values and the taste of the public which tends to override national boundaries.

A literal definition of 'value' points to "a property of a commodity that makes it exchangeable for another commodity or for money," which is only a step away from a broader definition of values as "a property of that which is valuable," not only in the material sense of the word but also morally and spiritually (Anić 40). In other words, the concept of value is established contextually, between and among people, and requires temporal and spatial framing. "What individuals value is strongly influenced by the specific culture in which they happen to live", said Giddens (Giddens 1039), i.e. by the systems of reproduction that are affected by the ideological underpinnings of the state within which they operate. As Herbert Marcuse said in *One-Dimensional Man*: cultural values are incorporated into "the established order, through their reproduction and display on a massive scale" (Marcuse 60). In other words, cultural values are defined in much the same way as any other human attitude is defined. The process includes what Edward S. Herman and Noam Chomsky referred to as "manufacturing consent" (in *Manufacturing Consent*, 1988) largely under the influence of the mainstream media and the governing politics which promote state-preferred values. Occasional discrepancies do occur, and even those, often, are given space only to maintain the illusion of plurality, rather than to invite an actual interplay of differences.

That lack of plurality was very much felt in Croatia, especially in the early stages, when the processes of economic restructuring inhibited production, distribution, and reception of cultural products, thus causing the artistic production to stagnate. For example, in 1994, only a single full-length film, produced during the precedent year, was shown at the Pula Film Festival. During the first half of the decade, the number of novels annually published was under 10, which is a meagre number that speaks for itself.[7] Numerous other productive mechanisms also came to a downfall – e.g., book publishers perished, as well as Jadran Film which was once the leader in film production – and the distribution of what was produced was not even intended for a

---

[7] The data is listed with precision in Krešimir Nemec's book *Povijest hrvatskoga romana od 1945. do 2000.* (pp. 442–447).

broader, still uninformed, audience. All this gave rise to a system of values that gave precedence to ideology over culture and made the economy and culture appear as mutually unrelated, even though ideology had already become their common denominator.

A notable turn, however, started taking place around the year 2000 when the notion of the market rose to the position of a new arbitrator of cultural values. A single date can almost be pinpointed, since the change coincides with the elections held on January 3, 2000, as well as with the appearance of FAK (Festival alternativne književnosti / Festival of Alternative Literature) on the literary scene. The group of writers within the FAK initially presented themselves as a phenomenon of popular culture, but thanks to high media coverage it soon assumed dominance and presented itself as a new form of the mainstream. This group of writers openly advocated commercial success as the new measure of literary relevance, and their joint appearances, as well as their writing, showed a tendency to distance themselves from the practices of the previous period.

The reviews discussing the poetics of FAK usually stressed that these writers were distinguishable by their realistic procédé, and hence their prose was referred to as "the prose of reality." The FAK writers were quite clearly open to Anglophone influences (the *New Puritans*, Raymond Carver, Charles Bukowski, etc.), but also to domestic literary models from the sixties, the so-called "jeans prose" as it was termed by Aleksandar Flaker (1924–2010) in 1976. What seems more important than any of this, and seems to have passed largely unnoticed, is that the FAK writers chose realism to contrast and oppose the mythical discourse of the nineties. This might have something to do with the generational shift and with the classical antagonism between the 'young' and the 'old,' but it is, in any case, a clear sign of rejection when it comes to the models dictated by institutional authorities in different fields, including that of culture. FAK deserves credit for revitalizing the literary scene and, no less importantly, for attracting the media which once more began to take interest in culture. FAK introduced public readings of literary works which helped popularize domestic literary production. Publishing companies began to develop and prosper at about the same time (Celeber, Hena com, V.B.Z.), and some of the FAK writers also took part in the production of films. For instance, books and/or scenarios by Jurica Pavičić, Ante Tomić, and Miljenko Jergović were used in the production of good quality films (*Svjedoci / The Witnesses*, Vinko Brešan, 2003; *Što je muškarac bez brkova? / What Is a Man Without a Moustache?*, Hrvoje Hribar, 2005; *Karaula / The Border Post*, Rajko Grlić, 2006; *Buick Riviera*, Goran Rušinović, 2008) that were well-received by critics and by the public. However, the criterion of commercial success which was, thanks to the FAK writers, soon accepted as the criterion of artistic value, soon flew against those very writers who propagated it.

The dissolution of FAK was triggered by a discussion on the literary value concerning two popular female authors, Vedrana Rudan and Arijana Čulina, whose sales figures significantly topped those of the most outstanding FAK authors – Ante Tomić, Miljenko Jergović, and Zoran Ferić. The discussion was initiated by Borivoj Radaković who disqualified the work of Rudan and Čulina under a title-statement: "I Can't Stand This To Be Referred to as Literature" (Radaković 2003), in an article published in Jutarnji list. In his critical review of Rudan's novel *Ljubav na posljednji pogled / Love at The Last Glance* which he judged to be artistically worthless, at the same time disregarding his own publicly propagated views on market as arbiter to value, when he ridiculed books written to suit the taste of two or three university professors, as opposed to those embraced by a broader audience (Dragojević 2003). Radaković's outburst led to the reaction of another member of the FAK group, Kruno Lokotar, who was, incidentally, the editor of Rudan's book. This caused the initial FAK trio (Lokotar, Radaković, and Rizvanović) to find themselves on different sides and led not only to the dissolution of the festival but also to a state of collision with the criteria which they had fought to affirm. While they were successful in overriding the older generation of writers with their own sales figures, the view that they did so due to being more progressive than the writers before, but not less worthy in the artistic sense of the word, fell apart as the new popular writers, better attuned to the taste of the public and unconcerned with the notion of artistic value, emerged.

Another case that revealed the existence of loopholes in the market approach to culture was that of Nives Celzijus (Drpić) who won the prestigious Kiklop award in 2008 for her book *Gola istina / The Naked Truth* in the best-selling category named "The Hit of The Year." The Kiklop award existed between 2004 and 2014, previously honouring Dan Brown, Paulo Coelho, Ante Tomić and Slavenka Drakulić, while the category "The Hit of The Year" was revoked in 2008, as was the award won by Nives Celzijus, who subsequently won it back through court proceedings in 2013. This scandal over the well-known Croatian starlet winning the prestigious book award on the grounds of sales figures rather than literary value led to even more scandalous aftermath as the members of the awarding committee came face to face with the workings of their criteria and revealed not only their general disorientation concerning value definitions but also a willingness of cultural elites to step over the lines of legality when attempting to save face. It is also relevant to point out that this award was initiated upon the dissolution of FAK, which was conclusive to the restructuring of the literary scene. The FAK writers had by then established their positions: Kruno Lokotar as an editor, Borivoj Radaković as author and translator, Miljenko Jergović as a distinguished prose writer who was about to take over the leading role in the literary field, previously filled by Ivan Aralica. The generational turn also coincided with the founding of the Society of The Croatian Writers (2002) – a new writers' association with a leftist outlook on society, in contrast to the older association which practiced more traditional, rightist views.

The market-turn and the democratization of artistic production, viewed through the prism of commercial success and general popularity of certain authors and titles, show that the process gained its momentum in the early years of the second millennium, rather than in the nineties. The delay is largely owed to the fact that the culture in Croatia rather heavily depends on the goodwill of politics, and that it took a certain time to commodify cultural products and build the audience that would enable their spreading across the market. The timing, furthermore, coincides with the spreading of communication technologies which enabled writers, as well as filmmakers, to obtain more direct modes of accessing their readers and viewers, and provided them with numerous new possibilities of using media platforms. This gave them a greater level of control of their public image and enabled them to communicate their ideological positions directly to the audience, via day-to-day topics rather than via cultural products. Hence, social engagement that too often comes in the form of ideological preaching appears to have become a widely used self-marketing tool, which brought the relations between culture, ideology, and market practices to an all-new level of inseparability.

2.3 Resistance

The Croatian culture of the post-war period has seen a quantitative growth both in literature and in film, yet the evaluation of cultural content, overly burdened by the ideological dimension of communication within and beyond the cultural field, can be said to have resulted in an overall crisis of values. The downfall of criteria was largely induced by the general perishing – shutting down or, in some cases, slowing down – of literary/cultural journals, such as Godine nove and Torpedo (the initial platforms of the later-to-become FAK writers), Nomad, Novi Kamov, Zarez, Libra libera, Gordogan, Europski glasnik…, coinciding with the gradual withdrawal of the older generation of literary and cultural critics such as Branimir Donat, Igor Mandić, Velimir Visković, and Zdravko Zima, whose influence has not been matched, let alone surpassed, by the critics of the newer generation. The critics of the younger generation have mostly found new niches on the Internet, and partly on the radio, the best examples being Booksa.hr and Bibliovizor edited by Gordana Crnković Raunić on the Croatian Radio. Literary blogs have also become sites of critical evaluation of literary and cultural processes, though these are often unedited, and vary in quality. Again, some positive examples need to be pointed out, such as Knjiški moljac (The Bookworm), started by Božidar Alajbegović in 2004, who also published critical texts in printed media, such as Vijenac, Književna Rijeka, Val, Nova Istra, etc. While individuals such as Alajbegović were ridiculed for their persistence in retaining an unbiased approach and lack of will to advertise the more influential publishers, many other critics succumbed to the dictate of the market or perhaps kept their positions in the printed media yielding to political, social and financial pressures that accompany the activities of the printed news publishing in Croatia.

The general crisis of values can also be related to the cultural space being suddenly swamped with genres such as the soap opera and reality TV, which have contributed to an overall preference for easy reads and popular topics, their value measurable in terms of commercial success, often causing authors to feel constrained to abide by such preferences. Besides, audiovisual production often recruits authors who started as writers with serious literary aspirations, yet induces them, at least to some degree, to let go of them. Vlado Bulić was, for example, initially praised for his debut novel *Putovanje u srce hrvatskog sna / A Journey into The Heart of The Croatian Dream* (2006), but he soon became involved in scriptwriting for the television, which was existentially a more lucrative choice that somewhat garnished his literary standing. On the other hand, Velimir Grgić, a film producer and a scriptwriter, moved in the opposite direction, and he now writes books on topics initially conceived for the film industry. On top of all, writers are often invited to write columns and commentaries for the media, and this tends to interfere with their literary endeavors. A firmer correlation between writers and the media was established by FAK writers who gained a lot of public attention thanks to their engagement in newspapers, but their focus on often petty day-to-day topics and surrender to the call of popularity appears to have prevented them from developing their full literary potential.

The doings of the market, however, need not be entirely negative, and some of the critics argued in favour of the market approach seeing it as a way to defeat ideologization. Even Igor Mandić, a well-known Croatian writer, literary critic, columnist, and essayist, for much the same reasons as the FAK writers in their beginnings, expressed his belief that the valid awards are only those which can be expressed in terms of the market (Mandić 183). However, the experience of the period usually referred to as the 'Croatian transition' reveals that this view, focused on the notion of the commensurability between cultural value and commercial success, is as faulty as the view that it justifiably contests. There is, in fact, a common denominator to both approaches: the depletion of the intermediary role of professional and unbiased literary and film criticism that, unburdened by ideology but also insubordinate to the commercial indicators of value, that both tendencies appear to have contributed to. With this, both tendencies also contributed to the lack of a qualified readership, which remains a problem insufficiently addressed by society in general, and, more specifically, by the Croatian system of education. A variety of factors have led to a deficiency of will and/or ability to socially reaffirm the unbiased professional judgment and procure it with a position of adequate cultural influence, such an outcome coming at the cost of cultural values in general.

Hence, we read about institutionally backed-up artists and those who, for one reason or another, succeeded in obtaining popular attention, yet at the same time we are likely to have little or no insight into neglected artistic and cultural products, or those that may not even have had the opportunity to see the light of day due to the lack of their adherence to ideological or popular market criteria. An example that can be pointed out is that of Aljoša Antunac (1967–2011) who was, according to Boris Postnikov "too critical, too real and too resistant" and whose writing, therefore, represents "the very boundary that could not be crossed, topic-wise or problem-wise, by the writers of the first decade of the twenty-first century, without losing its media acceptability" (Postnikov 37). Antunac wrote his prose (*Poslije zabave* / *The Afterparty*, 2007; *Neka vrsta ljubavi* / *Some Kind of Love*, 2007; *Tamo gore, iznad, tamo su šine* / *Up There, Above, That's Where the Rails Are*, 2011) around the same time when the FAK writers caught public attention, but he failed to be recognized by the media due to his much more radical approach to writing. He did not aspire to make reading "easy," language-wise, or content-wise, which is why his work has remained largely unknown, to the date, to the broader literary audience. There are, of course, other writers besides Antunac who produced prose of literary relevance but passed largely unnoticed for their lack of media exposure, such as Snježana Bilić, Darko Desnica, Zoran Roško, and others, posing a task to literary critics yet to be fulfilled.

This is not, however, to say that aesthetic niches do not exist within the Croatian cultural space and that writers and film directors who do not shy away from investigative challenges and are indeed both inclined and able to confront the ideological barrier and/or challenge popular tastes, pass completely unnoticed. It does, on the other hand, appear, that recognition for such work is more easily received at home when preceded by international praise. Such is certainly the case of the UK-based Croatian writer, Tena Štivičić, and her drama *Three Winters* that was initially written in English, to be subsequently translated into Croatian by the author herself under the title *Tri zime*. This is a story of a world "torn down and re-erected, then torn down again"[8] that seriously deals with issues of identity. The plot revolves around family relationships that are traced across four generations and through three stages of Croatian history – namely, the years 1945, 1990, and 2011 – and it unveils the intimate histories of people caught up in the web of historical events that caused them to assume new roles and social positions under the burden of numerous contradictory social and intimate effects of the different Croatian 'befores' and 'afters.' Praised for her profound approach to the topic, and especially for her insightful portrayal of the roles of women, Štivičić's play received critical acclaim upon having been staged at the National Theatre in London in 2014, and upon receiving the prestigious Susan Smith Blackburn Prize for the year 2015. This also led to the publication of *Tri zime* in Croatia, to its staging at the Croatian National Theatre in Zagreb (2016), and to the award that the author received at Marulićevi dani Festival in Split in 2017, which officially sealed Štivičić's status of a prominent Croatian playwright.

It was also via international appraisal – although in a thornier scenario – rather than thanks to the reception in Croatia that Dubravka Ugrešić came to be acknowledged as perhaps the most distinguished living Croatian writer. Though awarded with the NIN prize for her novel *Forsiranje romana reke / Forcing the Stream of Consciousness* (1988), judged to have been the best new Yugoslav novel of the year 1988, the literary standing that she had obtained during the former regime proved to be no bullet-proof vest against the numerous public attacks that she experienced in 1991 after she had spoken out against the war and assumed a firm anti-nationalist stand. She would most likely have had great difficulties in recovering a position of influence in Croatia had she not left the country in 1993 to teach at European and American universities. Having established her new home in Amsterdam, and evolving in her "post-Yugoslav, transnational, or /.../ postnational"[9] identity, she has also developed into an internationally renowned writer, and became the winner of numerous literary prizes, known for her distinctly postmodern literary collages created from fragments that she extracts from reality and from fiction, as well as from different genres and discourses, in order to question the aporias of modern-day humanity. Her interest in characters who lost their future

---

8 These words are Tena Štivičić's, extracted from an interview for bbc.com, by Vincent Dowd: "Croatian play 3 Winters has female soul" (Dowd 2014).

9 The statement is from the speech the author delivered upon receiving the 2016 Neustadt International Prize for Literature; see: Dubravka Ugrešić, "Who am I, Where am I, and Whose am I?" (2016).

for having lost their base in the past (as in her novel *Muzej bezuvjetne predaje / The Museum of Unconditional Surrender*, 1997), in the topic of human displacement (as in *Ministarstvo boli / Ministry of Pain*, 2004), and in the everlasting process of creating meaning (in *Lisica / The Fox*, 2017), is also closely knit with her Croatian (Yugoslav and post-Yugoslav) experience and with her experience of living in exile, and it testifies – in a ricœurian sense of the word (Ricœur 1992: 159) – to history as a phenomenon to be narrated if it is to be understood at all, and if it is to remove itself from the enslaving influence of dominant narratives.

Hence, it appears that the best of Croatian literary production arrives on the Croatian cultural scene via international backroads and that it is generally deeply immersed in the topic of identity and historical trauma. While questioning history, it also appears to engage itself in an active dialogue with the lived reality that is used as grounds for fictionalization, motioning the perpetual interplay between faction and fiction that enables one to be mirrored in the other, and calling for the (re)identification of readers' real selves via the fictionalized constructs that point back to the real ones. Such narratives can be said to assume a therapeutic mission, inviting the literary audience – via semblances of their own 'selves'– to identify and to confront the state of in-betweenness that, in real-life contexts much like in literary settings, keeps their collective identity detained and in a scrambled state within the growing gap between their past and their future.

The hybridity of forms, i.e., the ficto-factual nature of modern literary expression allows for excursions in either of the two directions. Just as it may open the doors to imaginative journeys, as in Ugrešić's *Baba Jaga je snijela jaje / Baba Yaga Laid an Egg* (2007), where a modern fairy tale based on a mythological figure aims at the reality of gender discrimination, it can also be based on a documentary approach, enriched with fictional elements. Such a facto-fictional – rather than ficto-factual – approach is often perceived as exclusive to film, largely due to the increase in presence and popularity of creative documentary films (a trend perhaps best represented by Dario Juričan's trilogy: *Gazda*, 2016; *Gazda: Početak*, 2018; *Kumek*, 2020, and most successfully applied to the last of the three titles), that is parallel to quite an opposite trend in written documentary production that appears to have moved away from the older traditions of artistically marked feuilletons and travelogues, rather than being inclined to explore new challenges concerning the possibilities of rhetorical interaction between journalism and literature. Exceptions, however, do exist, and an impressive one is certainly that of Viktor Ivančić, writer and journalist.

Ivančić is perhaps best known for his long-lasting column, *The Robi K. Notebook / Bilježnica Robija K.*, that he started in 1984 and which is still published to the present day. In this endless series of texts or, rather, stories, Ivančić juxtaposes the changes that took place over a significant period of Croatian history against the steady presence of a never-aging nine-year-old named Robi K. Robi K. appears in the role of narrator, but also that of a character surrounded by other characters (family members, a teacher, schoolmates) across the entire series of *The Robi K. Notebook* texts. The infantile perspective that the author adopts is as multi-edged as it is taboo-proof, and it involves the ever-present bluntly direct questioning of the social, political, and psychological set-up of the world of the grown-ups. As the stories of Robi K. accumulated over time, they were also compiled into a 2,700 page-long publication that (so far) encompasses five published volumes. With the publication of this book, all the pieces of the lengthy narrative fell into place, thus avoiding the risk of a possible loss of its significant parts to generational shifts of its followers, and perhaps also the (un)traceability of all the parts of the whole across different publishers who acted as hosts to the column at different points in time (FESB, *Nedjeljna Dalmacija, Feral Tribune, T-portal, Peščanik*). Born out of an outstandingly enduring journalistic endeavor, the newly shaped collage revealed a synergy between all its disparate yet interconnected parts, along with a postmodernist spirit that can be mainly attributed to the fictionalization that takes place at fiction's very edge. As a book on history that questions history, consistent throughout in its focus on the countless paradoxes that challenge the meanings of the lives that were lived both in the pre-war past and in the present, *The Robi K. Notebook* might perhaps be best classified as 'counterhistory': a deconstruction of the real that establishes links between the realities of the "before" and the "after," that laughingly yet seriously resists their separation and reweaves scattered parts into a whole.

3   'L'Avenir'

We have been arguing against the political uses of the word 'transition,' yet this is not to say that transitions do not occur. A transformation of one state into another of any given phenomenon is indeed a process that involves time, as well as change – in substance and form. Transitioning – whether triggered by natural causes, or by human action, or as in most cases, by a combination of both – does indeed occur whether we know it or not, whether we control it or not, and regardless of the degree to which we may control it. We cannot but be in the process of becoming. It is the issue of control over that process that is crucial to our debate, and it involves yet another temporal category: the future.

The understanding of transition that has been contested in this discussion is one that involves an inflexible approach to predictability and is based on pre-conceived views of the nature of change. It cannot ever precisely be known what course some process of change might take, nor is it possible to foresee all the factors that can affect that change and perhaps set it in a new direction, nor can the completion of that process depend on anyone's formal decision. While it is legitimate to set targets and oversee them with corrective action, it is not legitimate, and indeed does not lead to appropriate corrective action, to misuse language to falsify the reality of the process, be it because of wishful thinking, or false representation. A lie is a lie, regardless of motivation, and regardless of any awareness that may or may not be attached to it. When lies are disseminated from levels of legitimacy over the truths of a nation, they can only lead to more lies and their speedier spreading, while the psychotic effects that are likely to emerge make lies undistinguishable from the truths which can truly drive that nation's history into a blindspot.

Errors do occur and may be fixable, yet one cannot fix them without acknowledging them. It is the very refusal to acknowledge erroneous deeds that leads to further erroneous action that comes about to justify rather than alter what was misguidedly done before, until a point is reached in which the failed outcomes of a projected future are so burdened with lies that they bounce back on and into the present – with inevitably stifling effects. Derrida is decidedly right in affirming that "the trauma remains traumatizing and incurable because it comes from the future" (Derrida 2005: 104), and that "its temporalization proceeds from the to-come" (105). It is always the fear of something worse that could happen in the future that prevents us from overcoming the meaning of an earlier traumatizing event, rather than that event itself, and it is that future-oriented fear which is likely to lead further away from the declared goals, rather than make them happen. "Bad things happened to us, so the bad things we do for the best and worst of reasons and call them good to prevent worse things from happening while expecting good outcomes to be reached" is, more or less, the formula, based on a false logic that motivates the nauseating temporal circle, and, proverbially, also a vicious one: it causes the present to suffocate under the pressure of the misrepresentations of the unfulfilled expectations of the future that were ignited by goals which were set in the past.

We also spoke of trauma and of how it succeeds in separating subjects from their past, and of the turmoil that it causes to the human sense of identity. We pointed to the war as the primary cause of trauma in Croatia, but also to the traumatizing impact of the switch from the socialist to the capitalist economy and of the rearticulation of the cultural sphere in the post-war reality of the

Croatian people as the secondary source of trauma. The horrors of the experience of war and its traumatic effects were probably why the meanings related to the primary source overshadowed the potential traumatizing impact of the secondary source, and why the post-war dimensions of change were mainly seen as curative – since they would enable society to transition into a future of greater prosperity, based on the rule of law and democratic values – and not as a yet another potentially traumatic development. Yet the fear of something worse that could happen remained, and it appears to have marked the so-called 'transition' every step of the way, causing it to backfire on its noble goals. This is how language also separated from reality: it came to be used to write off any deviation as incidental and irrelevant to the course; to minorize corruption and theft rather than to present and resolve any particular case; to verbally condemn the rising criminality of the powerful, yet only to ascribe the phenomenon to some 'other side' of the political spectrum, while allowing 'one's own' to enjoy the protection of the state; to be used as a weapon for assigning blame by almost everyone, that weapon pointed at the ever-blameful 'other' – 'the Ustasha' or 'the Nazi' if 'the other' is on the right, 'the Chetnik' or 'the Serb' if 'the other' is on the left. Assuming responsibility for one's share of the blame was never to become a part of that discourse, the 'we' and the betterment forever postponed.

So, we are where we are, the wounds of the past yet unhealed, in the history of the future that appears to have backfired on its goals, causing new wounds. This state is referred to as 'the present.' Whatever may feel wrong in that wounded present has in the meantime interwoven itself with new misgivings that enabled blame to move away from those who are, or were, directly responsible for the country's well-being – the governments. The alibis that they use are as real as they are false in relation to the core issue – that of the inadequacy in dealing with the forces of the unexpected, while at the same time expecting other preconceived outcomes, prevented from happening by that very attitude. The contingencies of the period ranged from the global economic crisis of 2008 to the floods in the east of the country in 2014 and the European migrant crisis of 2015, more recently they include the COVID-pandemic crisis of 2020, the earthquake that hit Zagreb, and the one that followed at an even greater magnitude and hit Sisak-Moslavina County – all in the same year. This is 'the present' that lasts and has been witnessed throughout the years of the so-called 'transition' that somehow also led to the idea of 'post-transition,' as if to re-seal itself by the term. There is, by now, a lot of past accumulated even in that narrow historical framing of the Croatian present, so far not learned from as to alter the attitude towards the future.

What is it like to be immersed in 'the present'? The topic found its way into a documentary narrative, entitled *Djeca tranzicije / Children of Transition* (2014), written and directed by Matija Vukšić. This film is, as the title suggests, about children, bearing, however, much broader implications relevant to the experience of 'transition' as 'the present.' Vukšić presents four individual cases of children, all of them born into the 'transition': they have no memories of the war, and they do not know what life was like during the era of socialism. Whatever they know, and are, is derived from the world of the grown-ups and reflected in the relations among the children, which makes them, in every sense of the word, epitomes of the present. They represent 'the now,' and the picture of that 'now' is devastating. One of these children is eight-year-old David, "Messi from Slavonski Brod" – an outstanding football player: his story is one of bitter disappointment after failing to receive a promised invitation to play for a prestigious international football club, topped by more of the same for the lack of his father's social influence to assure him entrance into the junior league of a Croatian club in Zagreb. Another is Natalija, who comes from a background of poverty and is bullied at school for not keeping up with the trends, these being largely related to smartphones and clothing; she changes schools. As opposed to this, we also meet six-year-old Lana who dresses extravagantly and changes outfits many times a day, visits hair stylists, wears makeup, and spends the rest of her time playing with her smartphone. Finally, we learn of yet another case of peer bullying, Internet-related, over a boyfriend issue that leads fifteen-year-old Marta, too fragile to bear the pressure, to take her own life. She speaks, eerily, "from the grave," i.e., via the traces found on her phone and via the words from her diary, while all the other children speak directly into the camera. Vukšić collages all four destinies into a coarsely painful narrative in which he, as narrator, remains below the radar. It is the children who speak, epitomizing the sadly futureless voice of 'today.'

The inescapable question is: how can the traumatized world of today find its way into a more productive future if we are all pushed into the history of our trauma, that which can be "referential precisely to the extent that it is not fully perceived as it occurs" (Caruth 18), and therefore experienced only as perpetual, hurtful 'present'? Whatever the answer, it requires the trauma to be acknowledged and faced, in order to reconceptualize, both socially and individually, and revive the 'self,' across all temporal categories, enveloping its 'coming-to-be,' 'being,' and 'be-coming.' It is primarily the past that must be readdressed for a more empathetic and socially productive collective identity, 'the we,' to emerge. However, the process also depends on a reconceptualization of the future and needs to be liberated "from the value of 'horizon' that traditionally has been attached to it – a horizon being /.../ a limit from which I pre-comprehend the future" (Derrida 2001, 20). This requirement is also highlighted by Bauman, who takes it a step further in saying: "Whatever safety democracy and individuality may muster depends not on fighting the endemic contingency and uncertainty of human condition, but on recognizing it and facing its consequences point-blank" (Bauman 213). Seeing that the present, much like the words we exchange with others, "to be understood /.../ has to transform the context in which it is inscribed" (Derrida 2005: 20), the creation of a transformative opening, or openings of and within that context, is needed for the future to be faced, and for contingencies to be overcome rather succumbed to. It is only by the state-of-mind transformation within the present context that the "future [*a l'avenir*]," as "the coming of the other, /.../ the coming of what does not depend on me" (Derrida 2005: 60), can occur in a way productive of outcomes.

Understanding the future as 'l'avenir,' as 'to-come,' or as an event to be faced "that can break into the present unexpectedly at any moment" (Hoy 163), depends indeed on the existence of that very openness to face it. It is on the optimistic side to state that such openings can be found in the work of some of the authors already mentioned, and others (such as Daša Drndić, Slobodan Šnajder, Slavenka Drakulić – in literature, or Rajko Grlić, Dalibor Matanić, Dana Budisavljević – in film) whose narratives, when combined, represent the memory of the past and the present, that which "transcends the individual's lifetime" (Gross 539), while providing grounds for the value-driven readiness for 'l'avenir.' This comes with a demand for an "active and interminable critique" (86), not merely to be used as a "weapon against despair" (Hoy 170), but also as a tool to guard value: if the noise of misused language is to be silenced, it is the voices that speak up from within literary narratives, from the clearest and the best of them, that can lead the way.

References

Abercrombie, Nicholas, Hill, Stephen, Turner, Bryan S. *The Penguin Dictionary of Sociology* (Fifth Edition). Penguin Books, 2006.
Alexander, Jeffrey C. "Toward a Theory of Cultural Trauma." *Cultural Trauma and Collective Identity*. Jeffrey C. Alexander, Ron Eyerman, Bernard Giesen, Neil J. Smelser, and Piotr Sztompka. University of California Press, 2004, pp. 1–30.
Anić, Vladimir et al. *Hrvatski enciklopedijski rječnik*, vol. 12. EPH and Novi Liber, 2004.
Baker, Catherine. *Sounds of the Borderland: Popular Music, War and Nationalism in Croatia since 1991*. Routledge, 2010.
Barker, Chris. *Making Sense of Cultural Studies*. SAGE Publications, 2002.

Barthes, Roland. *Mythologies*. Farrar, Straus and Giroux, 1972.
Bauman, Zygmunt. *Liquid Modernity*. Polity Press in association with Blackwell Publishing Ltd, 2000.
Caruth, Cathy. *Unclaimed Experience. Trauma, Narrative and History*. John Hopkins University Press, Baltimore, and London, 1996.
Catterberg, Gabriela and Moreno, Alejandro. "The Individual Bases of Institutional Trust: Trends in New and Established Democracies." *International Journal of Public Opinion Research*, 18 (1), 2006, pp. 31–48.
Čučković, Nevenka, *Siva ekonomija i proces privatizacije u Hrvatskoj, 1997–2001*. Financijska teorija i praksa 26 (1), 2002, pp. 245–271.
Derrida, Jacques. *Rogues: Two Essays on Reason*. Translated by Pascale-Anne Brault and Michael Naas. Stanford University Press, 2005.
Derrida, Jacques. *Specters of Marx. The State of the Debt, the Work of Mourning and the New International*. Routledge, 1994.
Derrida, Jacques and Ferraris, Maurizio. *A Taste for the Secret*. Polity Press, 2001.
Dragojević, Rade. "Kad su autorice u pitanju." *Novi list*, 8. Dec. 2003, pp. 23.
Filippini, Michele and Barr, Patrick J. *Using Gramsci: A New Approach*. Pluto Press, 2017.
Flaker, Aleksandar. *Proza u trapericama*. Sveučilišna naklada Liber, 1976.
Giddens, Anthony. *Sociology*. Polity Press, 2006.
Gross, David. "Temporality and the Modern State." *Theory and Society*, vol. 14, no. 1. Jan. 1985, pp. 53–82.
Herman, Edward S. and Chomsky, Noam. *Manufacturing Consent*. Pantheon Books, 1988.
Hoy, David Couzens. *The Time of Our Lives: A Critical History of Temporality*. The MIT Press, 2009.
Jović, Dejan and Lamont, Christopher K. *Croatia after Tudman: Encounters with the Consequences of Conflict and Authoritarianism*. Europe-Asia Studies, vol. 62, no. 10, Dec. 2010, pp. 1609–1620.
Lewis, Michael. *The Fifth Risk*. W. W. Norton & Company, 2018.
Little, Allan and Silber, Laura. *The Death of Yugoslavia*. Penguin, 1996.
Luketić, Katarina. *Balkan: od geografije do fantazije*. Algoritam, 2013.
Mandić, Igor. *Oklop od papira. Autobiografski saldakonti 1966.–2013*. V.B.Z., 2014.
Marcuse, Herbert. *One-Dimensional Man. Studies in the Ideology of Advanced Industrial Society*. Routledge, 2006.
Markovina, Dragan. *Između crvenog i crnog: Split i Mostar u kulturi sjećanja*. Plejada, University Press, 2014.
Mishler, William and Rose, Richard. "What Are the Origins of Political Trust? Testing Institutional and Cultural Theories in Post-Communist Societies." *Comparative Political Studies*, 34(1), 2001, pp. 30–62.
Nemec, Krešimir. *Povijest hrvatskog romana od 1945. do 2000*. Školska knjiga, 2003.

Oraić Tolić, Dubravka. *Paradigme 20. stoljeća. Avangarda i postmoderna.* Zavod za znanost o književnosti Filozofskog fakulteta Sveučilišta u Zagrebu, 1996.

Perković, Ante, *Sedma republika: pop kultura u YU raspadu.* Novi Liber – Službeni glasnik, Zagreb – Beograd, 2011.

Postnikov, Boris, *Postjugoslavenska književnost?*, Sandorf, Zagreb, 2012.

Radaković, Borivoj, "Ne mogu više podnijeti da to zovu literaturom." *Jutarnji list*, 6 Dec. 2003, pp. 42.

Ricœur, Paul. *Oneself as Another.* The University of Chicago Press, 1992.

Sekulić, Duško and Šporer, Željka. "Gubimo li povjerenje u institucije?" J. Kregar, D. Sekulić i Ž. Šporer (ur), *Korupcija i povjerenje.* Centar za demokraciju i pravo Miko Tripalo i Pravni fakultet Sveučilišta u Zagrebu, pp. 71–117.

Sørberg, Marius, "Croatia since 1989: The HDZ and the Politics of Transition." *Democratic Transition in Croatia: Value Transformation, Education, and Media.* Edited by Ramet, Sabrina P. and Matić, Davorka. Texas A&M University Press, 2007, pp. 31–62.

Sztompka, Piotr. "The Trauma of Social Change. A Case of Postcommunist Societies." *Cultural Trauma and Collective Identity.* Jeffrey C. Alexander, Ron Eyerman, Bernard Giesen, Neil J. Smelser, and Piotr Sztompka. University of California Press, 2004, pp. 155–195.

Sztompka, P. Trust, "Distrust and Two Paradoxes of Democracy." *European Journal of Social Theory*, 1 (1), 1998, 19–32.

Turković, Hrvoje and Majcen, Vjekoslav. *Hrvatska kinematografija. Povijesne značajke, suvremeno stanje, filmografija (1991–2002).* Ministarstvo kulture Republike Hrvatske, 2003.

Ugrešić, Dubravka, *Kultura laži*, Konzor, Zagreb – Samizdat B92, 2002.

Živković, Andreja, "From the Market… to the Market: The Debt Economy After Yugoslavia." *Welcome to the Desert of Post-Socialism: Radical Politics after Yugoslavia.* Edited by Horvat, Srećko and Štiks, Igor, Verso Press, 2015, pp. 51–66.

Online Sources

Benačić, Ana. "Sedlar u intervjuu za N1 opovrgava korištenje fotomontaže." *N1*, 8 Apr. 2016, hr.n1info.com/a115889/Vijesti/Sedlar-u-intervjuu-za-N1-opovrgava-koristenje-fotomontaze.html. Accessed 10 Oct. 2019.

Blasdale, Alex. "Michael Lewis: *The Big Short* author on How Trump is Gambling with Nuclear Disaster." *The Guardian*, 22 Sep. 2018. www.theguardian.com/books/2018/sep/22/michael-lewis-trump-gambling-america. Accessed 10 Oct. 2019.

Chandler, Daniel and Munday, Rod. "A Dictionary of Media and Communication." 3rd edition. Oxford University Press. *Oxford Reference*, https://www.oxfordreference.com/view/10.1093/oi/authority.20110803095652897. Accessed 5 Jan. 2020.

Dowd, Vincent. "Croatian play 3 Winters has female soul." *BBC*, 3. Dec. 2014, https://www.bbc.com/news/entertainment-arts-30122217. Accessed 4 Jan. 2021.

"EU in Figures." *European Union*, europa.eu/european-union/about-eu/figures/living_en. Accessed 20 Oct. 2019.

"Hasanbegović: 30. svibnja 1990. treba biti jedna vrsta nulte godine." *Direktno.hr*, 6 Mar. 2016, direktno.hr/direkt/hasanbegovic-30-svibnja-1990-treba-biti-jedna-vrsta-nulte-godine-41148/. Accessed 10 Oct. 2019.

LaBier, Douglas. "A Growing 'Social Psychosis' Clashes With Serving The Common Good." *Pyschology Today*, 3 Oct. 2010, https://www.psychologytoday.com/us/blog/the-new-resilience/201010/growing-social-psychosis-clashes-serving-the-common-good. Accessed 31 Dec. 2020.

"PISA 2015 – Results in Focus," www.oecd.org/pisa/pisa-2015-results-in-focus.pdf. Accessed 20 Oct. 2019.

Ugrešić, Dubravka. "Who Am I, Where Am I, and Whose Am I?" *Literary Hub*, 10. Nov. 2016, https://lithub.com/dubravka-ugresic-who-am-i-where-am-i-and-whose-am-i/. Accessed 5 Jan. 2021.

CHAPTER 12

Writing against the Code and Fitting in with the Code: Reading Dubravka Ugrešić in the Context of the International Literary Field

Iva Kosmos

Dubravka Ugrešić is an internationally acclaimed author.[1] She is primarily established in international literary circles as an exile writer who left Croatia in 1993, in the middle of the war (1991–1995) that occurred during the breakup of Yugoslavia. She was severely attacked and publicly disgraced in the Croatian media because of her essays on political and social topics that challenged and contradicted the dominant nationalist rhetoric of the newly formed national state (Ožegović; Williams, *Writing Postcommunism*). While rejected at home, she gained recognition in the international field as a politically engaged and highly critical author, a cultural interpreter of the Balkans and a prolific essayist who always questioned established assumptions.

Apart from being recognized in media and literary circles, she has been the subject of wide-ranging research in both post-Yugoslav and international academia. Her essayistic and literary work is mostly understood in terms of a mode of resistance to dominant discursive codes. Her texts are read as a rejection and subversion of primarily nationalist, xenophobic, patriarchal Croatian and other post-Yugoslav ideologies (Obradović; Jambrešić Kirin; Williams, *Writing Postcommunism*; Lukić), yet also as a critique of a neoliberal European discourse and of a European chauvinism (Kovačević, "Storming the EU Fortress"; Williams, "Europeans"; Karpinski), as well as mainstream westernized discourse on the Balkans (Kovačević, *Narrating Post/Communism*; Vervaet, "Ugrešić"). Simultaneously, her resistance to national ideologies and identities is understood as a new form of transnational identity and literature (Cornis-Pope, Marcel; Young; Anderson). She has also been studied as an author preserving a complex memory of a denounced Yugoslav socialism (Seccardini; Vervaet, "Whose Museum?"; Beronja). In short, both in the media

---

1 The author acknowledges financial support by the Slovenian Research agency for the research program "Historical Interpretations of the 20th Century" (P6-0347) and for the postdoctoral research project "Cultural Memory in Post-Yugoslav Theatre" (Z7-8281).

and in academia she is understood as an author who is always questioning different aspects of Croatian, post-Yugoslav or European dominant ideologies.

In this chapter I would like to pose a slightly different approach to her work and authorial persona. I will question whether we might analyze her narratives not solely through their mode of resistance to dominant discursive codes, but also as a set of narratives that fit in with dominant discursive codes of Western self-perception in the international literary field.[2] On the one hand, I wish to ask whether her narratives fit in with a Westernized imagining of the Balkans and of an East/West divide that indirectly and implicitly confirms a Western self-imagining. On the other hand, I wish to examine how her narratives correlate with other discourses that support the self-imagining and self-justification of the West as a place of democracy – discourses such as individualism, free speech, and free market rhetoric.

There are two reasons why I aim to analyze narratives of Ugrešić in the context of the international literary field and in relation to Western discursive codes. Ugrešić is firmly established as an international writer who publishes simultaneously in several "literary centers," from Amsterdam and Berlin to London and New York, in different languages and at renowned publishing houses. Considering her firm rootedness in the international literary field (see Casanova), I will analyze how the author communicates with the expectations and requirements that are articulated in that field. I start here from Bourdieu's thesis that every literary field offers a "space of possibles, a system of different position-takings in relation to which each must be defined" (Bourdieu 200), a space "including potential courses of action and works which were never in fact realized" (Speller, chap. 2). According to this approach, every literary position sets certain systemic requirements and expectations of authors that want to claim that position. The authors can answer these expectations in different ways, with different strategies, but it is almost impossible to ignore expectations connected with their position(s). Ugrešić assumes (at least) two positions

---

[2] In this article I will use the East/West dichotomy from the point of view of symbolic geography and unstable, constantly shifting borders. The "West" roughly correlates with USA and Western Europe, and has a legacy of liberal democracy and capitalist economy. It also represents the superior part of the dominant dichotomy. With the term East, I encompass both Eastern Europe and the Balkans, as they both function as the subordinate part of this dichotomy. However, there is a distinction between these two terms, as Eastern Europe is a wider concept and includes the Balkans, but also other designations, such as Central Europe. The difference is again in the symbolic value, as Central Europe discursively functions as a Western oriented, lighter version of Eastern Europe or as a "redeemable" Eastern Europe, while the Balkans is an "irredeemable, extreme, and problematic Eastern Europe" (Kovačević, *Narrating Post/Communism* 10).

in the international literary and cultural field: the position of an exile, and of a translated author. Both of these positions require that the authors concerned act as so-called cultural translators or cultural brokers. To fulfill this role and to communicate with their public, they need to articulate themselves in a cultural code known to the international public. In other words, they need to refer to the already existing knowledge of their public, communicate with dominant discourses and confirm at least some expectations of their public, while simultaneously offering new and unpredicted cultural or literary elements (Pisac, *Trusted Tales*; Kovačević, *Narrating Post/Communism*). Because of this dynamic, which is dictated by the literary field, it seems logical that every author who gains public recognition to a certain extent communicates using dominant discursive codes, and responds to some expectations. My goal is to evaluate the work of Ugrešić in relation to this dynamic.

With this introduction, my intention has been to note that a literary opus, and even an author, can simultaneously exist in different cultural and social frameworks which are bound up in different temporalities and with different discourses attached to them. In so doing, I follow this book's main thread, recognizing that literature is simultaneously part of multiplying and heterogenous chronologies and temporalities. As there are different post-Yugoslav literatures and cultures, we can play with the idea that there are different Dubravka Ugrešićs and their literary works. First, there is the Ugrešić in the Croatian national chronology, an author who is half-hidden, half-ignored by some parts of society, including the older cultural elite, while newly appreciated (or "discovered") by a younger generation's critical voices. Then, there is the Ugrešić considered from a post-Yugoslav temporal perspective, recognized as one of the main authors of the post-Yugoslav literary canon, a position that has been especially established by post-Yugoslav and other researchers living abroad, working in Western academia. Thirdly, there is Ugrešić on the international literary market, who publishes her cultural and political essays in major international newspapers, is a relevant name to a number of international readers without a Yugoslav background, and who represents an exile writer from a faraway and foreign country. These are only three typical possibilities, and there could be even more Ugrešićs that perhaps recognize the differences between her positions in different international circles, for example German- or French-speaking circles. All these cultural and literary fields, various literary circles and markets exist simultaneously, as well as different temporalities intertwined with them, creating a setting best described as an a-chronological multiplicity of coexisting temporal and social frames. The example of Ugrešić reveals the heterogeneity of the temporal frames. While a lot of research has been completed examining Ugrešić's work in relation to the dominant Croatian and post-Yugoslav fields, this article will center specifically on the position of Ugrešić within the international literary field, meaning English-speaking literary centers, and her communication with the dominant discursive codes of that field. As already said, Ugrešić is perceived in the international field as an exile writer and translated author. Let us, then, briefly examine the structural expectations of exile and translated writers.

Although the geopolitical conditions that enabled the phenomenon of Eastern European exiles are long gone, the story of Ugrešić's exile was and is still crucial for her positioning in the literary field. For example, her publishers and promotors define her exile as a central part of her biography in their press releases, presentations and other forms of promotional biographies, while seven out of eight reviews of her newest novel *Fox* (2018)[3] still introduce the author through the story of her exile from Croatia. In being perceived as an exile, Ugrešić is linked to a long tradition of Eastern European writers living and writing in the international field, such as Brodski, Kundera, and Nabokov. These dissidents are part of a much wider socio-political and cultural context, tied to foreign policy, diplomatic relations, and knowledge production in the time of the Cold War. Writers and artists in this specific period played a role as "foot soldiers in a global *Kulturkampf*" (Hammond, "On the Frontlines" 3). In other words, they were included, willingly or unwillingly, intentionally or unintentionally, in the production of a specific vision of the world in the international context. Sometimes, these authors' writings would be used by their countries to confirm their ideological position, while on other occasions to subvert bipolar visions of the world (Hammond, "On the Frontlines"). Some authors also expressed severe criticism of their own states – which could then be used by the "other" side to confirm their own vision of the world. Eastern European exiles were traditionally accepted into the international literary field as cultural translators, social commentators and informants who would explain the unknown "East," while also confirming certain Western stereotypes about the region, invoking old orientalist stereotypes and endorsing a Western self-image. This dynamic was analyzed by Nataša Kovačević who has shown that Eastern European dissidents' criticisms of their own countries would often fit in neatly with the specific vision of the world that suited their hosts: it supported dominant ideological currents, Western images of itself, and the superiority of Western values. Kovačević showed that authors like Brodski and Nabokov would self-fashion themselves in accordance with dominant

---

3   Reviews of the novel *Fox* are available on the author's webpage dubravkaugresic.com, as of November 2018.

discourses, and that their "othering" of communist regimes would simultaneously reproduce geographical divisions "which cast the East as immutably totalitarian – whether monarchic or communist – against the West as progressive, politically fluid and respectful of human rights" (Kovačević, *Narrating Post/Communism* 7). Although the Cold War is over, many authors argue that Cold War rhetoric is relevant today, as it survives in the form of an East/West divide, orientalist stereotypes, and especially the demonization of historical socialism, which positions capitalism as the relatively mild alternative to the inherently bad system (Juraga and Booker; Kovačević, *Narrating Post/Communism*). While Kovačević positions Ugrešić as an exile writer who manages to overthrow and subvert the dominant Western discourse on the Yugoslav wars, I still want to examine whether Ugrešić's writing aligns with other elements of the dominant discourse. Or, in other words, is it possible that Ugrešić's writing simultaneously is aligned with several discourses, intertwined with several coexisting temporalities, engaged in both the subversion of a certain discourse, but also the reproduction of another, coexisting dominant rhetoric.

The second reason to observe how Ugrešić's narratives relate to the dominant codes is by tracing the general position of authors from the global periphery in the international field, both those who write in English and those who are translated. These authors' literature is often presented as an ethnography or as a source of information on remote spaces (Huggan; Pisac, "Emerging Politics"). For example, David Williams, in his articles (for example, "Europeans without Euros" 5) and in his monograph *Writing Postcommunism* (2013) treats Ugrešić's biography, her literary novels, and his own ethnographic experience as equal sources of knowledge about the post-socialist condition. He does not differentiate between his ethnography and her literature. This approach is not exactly new, as translated or world literature traditionally acted as a "window on the world" and as a path to understanding foreign cultures (Damrosch). However, what might be specific to the contemporary literary field is a set of tendencies to translate those literary works that adapt to the dominant conventions and values of the wider social project that justify Western self-perceptions and a *status quo* embodied in global pluralism and neoliberal democracy (Pisac, "An Anthropology"; Pisac, *Trusted Tales*; Huggan; Brennan *At Home in the World*, 38–44). This means that the works of foreign authors are often presented through a paradigm of protecting free speech, individual freedom, or advocating universal human rights. Pisac explains the literary translation of small and unknown nations as being part of a bigger global and political project of "helping" underdeveloped nations, which simultaneously confirms Western superiority, justifies its interventionism, confirms a

Western value system, and also confirms the Western economic and social system. For example, Pisac says that the project of protecting free speech and helping persecuted authors is "the product of a Western liberal individualism connected to capitalism and the accumulation of wealth," as it "belongs to a neoliberal discourse of aid and development. It not only assumes the difference between 'them' and 'us' [...], but further objectifies any kind of knowledge that can 'liberate' the 'underdeveloped' [...]" (Pisac, *Trusted Tales* 92). Bearing this in mind, Pisac concludes that both the authorial persona and textual narratives of Ugrešić – as well as those of other successful writers from the global periphery – becomes a part of the project of validating and protecting the contemporary *status quo*, embodied in neoliberal democracy (Pisac, *Trusted Tales* 266–67). To investigate this claim, I will firstly focus on the messages and meanings relating to Ugrešić's biographical narrative, followed by a focus on Ugrešić's earlier political essays, and finally on her later essays that deal with the cultural mentality of her "countrymen."

1   Reading Dubravka Ugrešić's Biographical Narrative

Ugrešić's life story is a widely known and strongly codified narrative that has been repeated numerous times across different media: autobiographical essays, public performances at literary festivals and readings, interviews, media profiles, book reviews, biographical notes, etc. The biography's narrative fits the conventions of Eastern European dissidence that were established in the twentieth century, with the core elements of political persecution, the author's resistance, and a final flight undertaken by a highly sophisticated intellectual. One of the reasons why Ugrešić's life story is so valuable and highly convincing is that it structurally fits the already existing pattern of other dissidents' stories. In several of her essays, she cites the insults she received from her country, and they are regularly repeated in the international press.[4]

---

4   Examples include the biographical essay "A Question of Perspective" from the book *Karaoke Culture* (Ugrešić *Karaoke Culture*) and the essay "Writer in Exile" from the book *Thank You for Not Reading* (Ugrešić, *Thank You for Not Reading*). In the latter example, Ugrešić criticizes the international field as pushing exiles to fit in with the expected image of a persecuted writer, but simultaneously serves the same pattern as she cites a list of attacks she received: "The surroundings they have abandoned rarely forgive exiled writers. The fact that, before he left, they had burned him in effigy, spat in his face, attacked them publicly, made normal life impossible for him, threatened him, called him in the middle of the night to drive him out of the country, published his phone number in the papers that others could do the

However, this narrative pattern does not encapsulate the author's personal, individual story alone: it also supports a very specific vision of the world, made up of two opposites, East and West. The place of exile is a place of oppression and backwardness, a place of brutality and stupidity implicitly posed as a counterpart to the guest-country, which consequently seems better than this radically negative place. The introductory section to Ugrešić's profile in the *Guardian* describes her home-country in the following way:

> During the breakup of Yugoslavia in the 1990s, Dubravka Ugresic was denounced, she says, as "a whore, a witch and a traitor." A reluctant citizen of newly independent Croatia, she took a stand against nationalism "and all its perversities," and like many people became a target. As the Balkan wars escalated, she found herself the victim of a "collective paranoia: people rushed to be willing executioners. Nobody forced them to kill, spit on and humiliate others – but they did. It became acceptable. It was like being marked with a yellow star." (Jaggi)

In this context the West is not necessarily praised, but it does implicitly take the role of the persecuted writer's savior. Western society and Western papers are those that are welcoming, "saving," understanding and even celebrating the oppressed writer. By this I am not suggesting that Ugrešić as an author uncritically supports an East/West divide, quite the opposite, as in some of her essays she critically reflects on this. However, her life story, as told in the international media, by publishers and by the author herself, simultaneously supports this vision of the world, made up of two opposites. The focus is on the East, depicted as radically collectivist, violent, oppressive, and homogenous, which indirectly posits the West as the "lesser evil," a society that might have its own problems, yet is still sane enough to critically reflect on and differ from the maladies of the East.

To depict what kind of stories the international literary field recognizes as convincing and authentic, we can tell a story of a certain motif in Ugrešić's biography. In the international media (Jaggi; Evans), publishers' web pages (General Information) and even academic texts (Beronja 110; Williams, "Europeans" 2) there is a specific phrasing describing Ugrešić's exile. They state that

---

same (and others did, with gusto), the fact that they erased him from public life, put him on blacklists, prevented him from publishing, that they publicly humiliated him, excluded him from their ranks, threw his books out of public libraries and school curricula [...] (all of which, incidentally, happened to me) [...] (Ugrešić, *Thank You for Not Reading* 138).

Ugrešić left her native land when the Croatian president at that time, Franjo Tuđman, proclaimed that Croatia had become a "paradise on Earth." In the Croatian context, this phrase is not known as Tuđman's, but as a national tourist slogan from 1997. In one of her essays, "Writer in Exile," Ugrešić does place this slogan in Tuđman's mouth. Playing with the biblical symbolism of (forbidden) independence and knowledge, she writes: "That's why when the Croatian president euphorically proclaimed Croatia 'paradise on earth' in the early 1990s, I knew what I had to do. I took an apple and got on the first train leaving the country" (Ugrešić, *Thank You* 148). Because of the nature of her imaginative, playful literary style, it is not clear whether "paradise on earth" was an actual statement uttered by the Croatian president, or a playful metaphor encapsulating Tuđman's national view, or even a popular tourist slogan, which in a purely fictional game ended up as Tuđman's own words in Ugrešić's essay. However, despite this vagueness, the international press, publishers, and academia automatically reproduced this motif as having been a publicly known statement made by Tuđman and used it as a key motif in Ugrešić's biography. Why did they take up this information without any fact checking? There are reasons to believe that the international field accepted this detail as it fits well into the standard narrative of the crazy dictator in the East and the writer on the run to the West. Individual narrations that have a good fit with already existing and socially confirmed narrative patterns appear reliable.

A special element of Ugrešić's life narrative is also an underlined motif of self-chosen exile. A traditional exile narrative stresses coercion as the main reason for exile. However, in Ugrešić's version, the author was not only forced to leave due to social pressure, but she also willingly chose to leave because of moral principles, in order to gain freedom, independence and autonomy of thought and action:

> The exile ought to remember that with his departure he has rated individualism higher than collectivism, that he has preferred a "fundamentally discontinuous state of being" (Said) to a false national continuity, that he has therefore, preferred the freedom of rootlessness to "roots" and "cradles" [...], that he has, therefore, of his own free will, abandoned the stubborn, exclusive, self-intoxicated, aggressive noise of the isolated tribe ready to throw stones at the first person who is different from them. (139)

Ugrešić constantly keeps choosing exile as a moral principle, for there is no legal obstacle surrounding her return to the country. Exile thus becomes a free choice enabling freedom, but necessarily sacrificing a "normal" life that offers stability and collective interconnectedness: "The exiled writer finds himself in a snare of intoxicating and frightening freedom. That freedom implies acceptance of marginality and isolation. In choosing exile, he has chosen loneliness" (146). As is often implied in Ugrešić's essays, life in a community correlates with conformism and adaptation to lower moral standards. This kind of "collective life" is an antidote to exile and serves to underline the specificity of exile, which becomes a state of radical personal autonomy, with the possibility of almost complete freedom, choice, action and thought. In an interview from 2015, Ugrešić confirms her choice of radical freedom:

> [I] would always be an outsider in a national, but also in any bigger, literary game. Above all because I am a woman: a woman writer working in a small language and coming from a part of the world where literature and culture were never priorities. Do I complain because of such major handicaps? Perhaps. But, as an outsider I was free to shape my own literary taste, to pick my own literary traditions, to build my own system of literary values. I was free to disregard expectations, and fully aware that I would not be at the center of things or quickly canonized. So there was nothing to worry about. (Ugrešić, "A Conversation" 213)

Ugrešić was often branded by journalists with names implying individual heroism, such as a "Balkan warrior" (Jaggi) or "born rebel" (Levy). Both these titles, as well as the described biographical narrative, heavily emphasize individualism as a positive value, which is counterposed to collective conformity. However, the notion of individual autonomy and independence can be read at least in two different ways, and in two different contexts. If we place the call for individual autonomy inside the temporal framework of Tudman's ideology, it surely functioned as a call against the installation of nationalism, collective compliance and ideological uniformity. However, the same story in the temporal framework of the international global neoliberal *status quo* may function differently. Namely it can fit in with the prevailing cultural idea of individualism,[5] which supports the current economic and social order.

---

5 The "myth of individualism" is broadly defined a "belief system that privileges the individual over the group, private life over public life, and personal expression over social experience; it is a worldview where autonomy, independence, and self-reliance are highly valued and thought to be natural; and it is an ideology based on self-determination, where free actors are assumed to make choices that have direct consequences for their own unique destiny" (Callero 17).

Although, historically, individualism has had the emancipatory effect of abandoning the restrictions of old social strata, today it functions differently. "The artificial separation of the self from society, and the belief in the primacy and superiority of the autonomous actor" (Callero 29), in combination with other ideas such as freedom, radical self-responsibility, and self-choice are closely related to the dominant open-market philosophy. Individualism and the belief that an individual is not preconditioned by society, is alone responsible for their faith and hence can act completely autonomously, aligns with the fundamental values of liberal capitalist democracies. Although in some of her essays Ugrešić might have worked on debunking the myth of the self's separation from society, her biographical narrative does not operate in that way. The excessive emphasis on her autonomy fits the notion of an atomized individual acting against a repressive society exclusively by the power of her will. Her biography also avoids a discussion of the social conditions that enable her to be publicly heard as an author. This includes the privilege of having a specific academic and cultural background enabling her to claim the role of an exile in the international literary field, which is laden with symbolic value and grants public visibility.

On the other hand, Kovačević promotes Ugrešić exactly as the type of writer who differs from other exiles reproducing an East/West divide. Kovačević builds this argument on Ugrešić's essayistic criticism of the European Union, multiculturalism, and the politics of identity, all of which hide other structural inequalities. Here we encounter a complex dynamic: although Kovačević is right and Ugrešić criticizes the West and the main tenets of its dominant discourse in her essays, this does not mean that her life story and the way it is narrated – both by the author and by other actors – does not reproduce the tenets of the same discourse the author criticizes in the aforementioned essays. Her life story as an exile, as argued above, implies East/West dichotomies and reproduces Western images of the oppressive Balkans and Western ideals of individual autonomy. While these can function as social criticism in the Croatian or post-Yugoslav context, internationally they fit in with dominant discourses. The international and Croatian/post-Yugoslav contexts belong to different, but intertwined temporalities. On the one hand, the exile narrative fits in with orientalism and Balkanism, which have a long continuity in Western and international cultural frameworks. On the other hand, the exile narrative aligns with the contemporary free market and free speech rhetoric. The same narrative correlates with two different sets of meanings, which coexist in the same social and cultural context, but belong to different temporal frameworks.

2   Essays as Documentary Literature and Academic References

The related question of how the context, the temporal framework, and the social use of a text impact its meaning is present in reading Ugrešić's essays. I will claim that some of her essays reproduce an East/West divide as well as orientalist or Balkanist stereotypes. However, this reading depends on her texts' specific use and the cultural broker role that the author performs in the international field.

The Culture of Lies is Ugrešić's best known collection of essays, which includes critical texts written in the nineties that inspired attacks on the author that resulted in her leaving Croatia. These essays are sharp, bitter and focused on Croatian political barbarity and the brutal nationalistic ideology. It focuses on a kitsch and aesthetic debasement, which function as a reflection of the moral and political corruption of the newly established Croatian society (cf. Obradović). Although Ugrešić writes about Croatia, she often stresses that the situation is no better in Serbia (or Slovenia, or Bosnia, etc.), as all post-Yugoslav societies are built on nationalism, nepotism, and corruption and are reflections of each other. Again, we can approach these texts from different social and cultural contexts and temporal frameworks. In the context of Croatia, this was read as a subversion of the newly established national discourse, which also provoked a strong and violent response from the cultural elite. Still, these essays were also published in the international press, in the international cultural and social field, which is based on different values, assumptions, and relations. What was their reading?

In Kovačević's opinion, Ugrešić's early essays actually subverted the international discursive code. Kovačević reads Ugrešić's earlier collection *Have a Nice Day*, published in English in 1994, through the context of the international discourse on the war in the nineties, which defined the conflict through an ethnic perspective. The conservative media spoke of eternal ethnic hatred and essentialized the conflict; left-liberals called for international intervention based on a story of a conflict between the good (Croats) and the bad (Serbs), engaging Western forces (once again) in the role of saviors (Kovačević, *Narrating Post/Communism*; see also Longinović). In this context, Ugrešić's essays, with a critique of the nationalism of her own "tribe" (Crnković 545), were set against the dominant discourse of the war's ethnicization. They subverted the established narrative of the battle between good and evil, presented the complexity of the situation, and offered an alternative position; that of someone who does not identify with any ethnic side (Kovačević, *Narrating Post/Communism*). I believe the same reading could be applied to *The Culture of Lies*, as Ugrešić continues to reject an identification with ethnicity and with ethnic perspectives. However, while criticizing "her own tribe" – which is exactly what breaks the dominant discourse on the war – Ugrešić also uses Balkanist images through an assembly of homogenous, manly, robust, violent and unsophisticated characters. There are leaders on all ethnic sides who are equally brutally vulgar in their appearance and behavior, intellectuals who are equally amoral in changing their principles according to their leaders, and everyday people, who are either victims or equally frightening hordes. And they are all, more or less, the same, as in her famous description of the Yugo-man:

> Yugo-man, the male inhabitant of the former Yugoslavia, hardly exists in the singular. He is rarely an isolated instance, a person, an individual, he is most frequently a group of men. Yugo-man is brought up in a group, he grows up in a group, he lives in a group, he dies in a group. [...] And that's why contemporary supporters of masculinism, in their search for a lost male identity, need not travel to New Guinea. Tried and tested male identity is here, right in front of them. (Ugrešić, *The Culture of Lies* 114)

With a focus on the kitsch, grotesque, and the barbarity of the new national realities, these essays criticize both national and international discourses of idealized nationalism and essentialized ethnicity. However, at the same time they also reproduce general stereotypes of the Balkans as being a wild region and a powder keg, full of uncivilized authoritarians. The international reader is thus served an image of the Balkans as created through centuries of Western textual production: a repository of negative images about a wild, violent, corrupted and authoritarian European "Other" (Todorova).

While Ugrešić reproduces some of this negative imagery relating to the Balkans, these images and motifs are not the only elements that impact on this kind of interpretation. As some authors have argued, the interpretation of Ugrešić's essays also depends on the specific literary style employed within; a style that appeared in newspapers, which again signals a different type of reading. Gordana Crnković, in her review of *The Culture of Lies* from 1999, sees generalizations as "one of the main traits of Ugrešić's literary writing – a technique whereby characters are constructed as well-known types rather than as unpredictable individuals" (Crnković 545). For Crnković, this might function well in essays that are concerned with literary topics or are focused on a writer's personal experiences. On the other hand, she is critical of those essays that try to resemble cultural or socio-political analysis. The problem is, Crnković states, that Ugrešić's literary style – especially her use of generalizations – reduces the people she tries to present to homogenous categories, such as all men as "chauvinists," all countrymen as "frenzied nationalists," etc.

(ibid). "Such typification is not always successful in more referential essayistic discourse, as it presents the author's disinterest in the people she writes about and neglects factual 'details' that do not fit the general type" (ibid). In other words, these generalizations function differently when they are not employed in literature, but rather in a text that acts – as stated by Ugrešić herself – "as a translator of [her] own reality and the reality of [her] own country into a language comprehensible to West European readers" (Ugrešić in Crnković 545; Ugrešić, *The Culture of Lies* 169).

On the other hand, in her detailed study of *The Culture of Lies*, Obradović rejects this and similar criticism, saying that it "subsume[s] [Ugrešić's texts] into journalism," while they should be understood and read as essays (Obradović 72). Obradović reminds us of these essays' characteristics: subjectivity and a lack of formal structure, established conventions, systematic expressions and established methodologies, such as those pursued in academic writing (ibid). Here I would add other qualities of Ugrešić's essayistic literary style, such as the usage of hyperbole, satire, irony and, as already said, deliberate generalizations and simplifications in order to highlight certain problems and make clearer points. Obradović continues to say that these mentioned "instabilities" obscure the essay's contribution to the social debate in this particular historical situation. She therefore proposes that *The Culture of Lies* should be read as a period piece, "read and quoted by scholars when they need a dash of local color to enrich their descriptions of the early Tuđman years" (73).

I understand Obradović's proposition as an attempt to return *The Culture of Lies* to its original context, temporal framework, and social role. In the context of the Croatian and post-Yugoslav social debate of the nineties, these essays unquestionably provided a much-needed voice articulating social opposition. However, texts travel, and they change their role in different places and periods. The central issue is that *The Culture of Lies*, along with other essays in the international context, are not read as a "period piece," but as a cultural translation. There are a number of reasons for this that we have already mentioned: translated literature has traditionally acted as a "window to the world" (Damrosch), Eastern European exiles acted as representatives of their societies (Hammond, *Global Cold War Literature*), texts from the so-called global periphery are traditionally read as ethnography (Huggan). All these traditions unavoidably frame the process of reading and understanding Ugrešić's narratives and texts. However, it seems that the international reception of her work is truly exceptional, as *The Culture of Lies* and some other works are not only metaphorically understood as cultural translators, but literally read as ethnography, documentary literature and as a factual source of information on the Balkans. Some of the best examples of these uses of Ugrešić's work are to be found in academic writing, as certain researchers use Ugrešić's essays as academic references. Researchers who write about political changes in the nineties, nationalism, political transition, and cultural memory in post-Yugoslav space often refer to *The Culture of Lies*, especially to one of the essays from the same collection, "The Confiscation of Memory," which was published in *New Left Review* and thus attracted additional visibility. This does not mean that these researchers use some of Ugrešić's anecdotes or popular and well-pointed terms, such as "the confiscation of memory" to enrich their writing, quite the opposite. They often use Ugrešić's essays as a primary source of information in academic writing. I will name a couple of individual examples so as to demonstrate this wider phenomenon.

Dominik Bartmanski, a researcher from Yale, has written about nostalgia in Poland for the academic journal *Acta Sociologica*; he has compared it with similar phenomena in the Balkans, citing *The Confiscation of Memory* as the only source (Bartmanski 2011). German theater scholar Alexandra Portman has written about nostalgia in post-Yugoslav theater; in her introduction she briefly presents the social context and different politics of remembrance, while also referring to *The Culture of Lies* as her only source (Portmann 2017). The best example of replacing literary discourse with an academic one is Zala Volčič's article "Yugo-Nostalgia: Cultural Memory and Media in the Former Yugoslavia," published in *Critical Studies in Media Communication* (Volčič). Volčič refers to *The Confiscation of Memory* when writing about the social transition and national identification in Yugoslavia. Following this, she describes the ideological transition from socialism to capitalism and the conception of nostalgia as a productive relation with the past, while referring to the novel *Ministry of Pain*. These examples do not analyze Ugrešić's work, nor do they use it to add a "dash of local color." They cite it as a source of information.

I am citing these examples as they point to the special status and use of Ugrešić's texts, especially *The Culture of Lies*. The fact that her texts are used as an academic source reveal that there is a tendency to read her literary texts, essays, and even novels, as documentary, factual, and analytical texts. Her texts, as already pointed out by both Crnković and Obradović, include social, cultural, and political analysis, but they are also characterized by a specific literary style and approach to the subject. If we read these essays as an ethnography or as academic literature, is it possible to assume that some of the mentioned characteristics, such as hyperbole or generalizations, will be taken for granted? Although I cannot provide a clear answer to this question, it is not unreasonable to speculate that using essayistic texts with sharpened views and a satirical approach to reality, as documentary and academic representations of the Balkans, could reinforce stereotypical imagery relating to this region.

3   Essays on the Unchangeable Nature of "Countrymen"

While *The Culture of Lies* invites different readings which arise from different uses of the book and their placing in different contexts and temporal frameworks, links with Balkanism are more obvious in Ugrešić's later essays. The earlier essays, such as those in *The Culture of Lies*, are clearly set in a particular time and space: Croatia during Tuđman's rule. The later essays often provide general cultural depictions of the mentality, habits and customs of her "former countrymen," which are often depicted through an essentialist view as unchangeable.

Essays on mentality prevail, for example, in the collection *Nobody's Home*, published in Croatian in 2005, and translated to English in 2007. The collection features essays on cultural phenomena which are arbitrarily interpreted and mostly negatively evaluated. A personal understanding of cultural phenomena, often without analysis and argumentation, serves to prove the same point – that "countrymen" are full of a superficial vanity and unfaltering belief in their own geopolitical importance, which is reflected in their cultural habits. For example, in the short essay "Shit," Ugrešić satirizes the typical Eastern European cultural habit of ritualistic negative criticism, here ascribed specifically to former Yugoslavs. This cultural code is illustrated by a habit of ex-Yugoslavs to describe every novel, movie, or performance as "shit." The satirical approach goes together with a kind of typification, which goes hand in hand with an erasure of the differences between the characters that form a unified collective body. Another rhetorical device is hyperbole, or exaggeration, as it is claimed that literally everything is evaluated as "shit." Proclaiming everything as "shit" functions as a metonymic device describing the general approach of Ugrešić's "countrymen" to the world. In other words, "shit" becomes a metonym for the national character of former Yugoslavs. This typified image serves the function of simultaneously mocking and criticizing the author's countrymen, as this cultural habit is revealed as a sign of fake pride and as an attempt by the countrymen to humiliate other people in order to make themselves feel better. A common denominator in this and in Ugrešić's other essays on her "countrymen" is the message that in Croatian, Serbian, or any other post-Yugoslav and Balkan society nothing can change and nothing has changed. This message is reproduced both in the essays on cultural mentality and in the comments on the political and social situation.

In "A Short Contribution to the History of a National Literature" from the collection *Thank You for Not Reading*, published in 2001, and translated in 2003, Ugrešić mercilessly mocks the discourse of Croatian national pride and ironically describes the main reasons why it is better to be a Croatian writer. She ironically cites machismo, male dominance, absolute state control over literary production, along with the cleansing of libraries from books by Serbian writers with "schoolchildren [...] [who had] sometimes been recruited to help librarians carry the books out to the trash" (Ugrešić, *Thank You for Not Reading* 118) as good reasons for being a Croatian writer. Her statements are often edgy and deliberately provocative, and leave no place for nuance. For example, she states: "It is sufficient, for example, for the minister of culture to announce publicly that he does not care for this or that writer and that writer is all but banned. Fellow writers gladly assist in this process of changing their colleagues' biographies. This is exceptionally thrilling and rejuvenating for the writers themselves" (ibid.). She also picks and emphasizes the most bizarre and grotesque statements from the Croatian media, such as the following statement by an unnamed "prominent Croatian intellectual": "Just as a mother, almost invariably, prefers her backward child, fragile, weak, sickly, and placed in special classes, so to I, often, not always, favor Croatian literature over the Himalayas to which I am directed by duty, intellect and spirit" (120).

Because of her literary style, it is again impossible (and unnecessary) to evaluate which elements are factual, and which motifs are stylistically over-exaggerated or simply invented in order to make the point clearer or the narrative episode more vivid. The essay was written in 2001, according to the Croatian edition, or in 2000, according to the US edition. This is a period of political change in Croatia, which after Tuđman's death in 1999 gained its first left-liberal social-democratic government. In Croatia, this period was marked by an atmosphere of opening up and of social change. The essay does not note such a change, but rather projects the message that "nothing has changed." As such, in the local context, this essay can point to the continual ideological misuses of literature that still need to be revised, and it can function as a reminder of the continuous presence of negative social phenomena. However, the question remains of the role of this and similar essays in an international context, where they act as cultural translators. Depictions of post-Yugoslav societies as unalterable societies that have not changed in the slightest over the last ten or so years align in the international context with already existing expectations of the static, unchangeable, and half-civilized Balkans, forever frozen in a state of semi-barbarity.

The same feeling of a "cursed present" and frozen temporality is also to be found in the collection *Europe in Sepia*, published in 2013 and translated in 2014. In "The Croatian Fairy," Ugrešić portrays her evening train travels to Croatia as an entrance into a space "lost in the murky black" (Ugrešić, *Europe in Sepia* 54). She also repeats a motif of frozen time: "In Zagreb it's as if all clocks stop" (48). On another occasion the clock goes back to the authoritarian past and freezes there: "The clock was violently wound back twenty years ago. Franjo Tuđman was the first to mess with its hands, successfully erasing fifty years of Yugoslav social life and state sovereignty, grafting his Croatia onto the Ustasha puppet state of the Second World War" (66). And again, although this statement could be read as social criticism in the Croatian context, it simultaneously produces an image of the unchangeable, authoritarian Balkans, frozen in the past.

Although Ugrešić's essays capture twenty-five years of social and political reality, they do not record changes, negotiations, political or cultural struggles in post-Yugoslav societies. In her essays, Ugrešić almost never discusses strongholds of resistance in Croatian or other post-Yugoslav societies; she also does not discuss negotiations and competition between different ideological options. This is a legitimate essayistic strategy, as the essays are often written to provoke a public debate, not give a balanced portrait of a society. In the Croatian context this could function as a criticism of the continuity of nationalism and other unresolved issues, although the strong message of "eternal recurrence" closes the possibility of imagining any alternative. On the other hand, her insistence on the unchangeable character of the Balkans comes close to essentialization and orientalization, especially if read through the context of the international imagining of tribal Balkan struggles transmitted across the centuries.

I do not intend to claim that Ugrešić is or is not correct in her social portraits. To the contrary, I am trying to show that the same narratives can have different functions, interpretations, and meanings in different contexts and temporal frameworks. A portrait of a corrupted social reality functions differently in the society critiqued than in an international context unacquainted with the object of criticism and which reads those essays as information on a foreign land. While a sharpened portrait of political barbarity can function as a criticism of unresolved political problems in the post-Yugoslav or Croatian context, the same portrait in the international context may align with Balkanist stereotypes and Eurocentric prejudices. Ugrešić's narratives can thus be read in at least two ways: as a critique of a socio-political reality, but also as the reproduction of a dominant code relating to the Balkans.

4 Conclusion

Ugrešić's narratives and texts should not be read apart from the contexts in which they are operationalized – including the different discursive and cultural codes with which they communicate and the author's different positions in the literary field. In the post-Yugoslav or Croatian context, some of these texts can be read as satire, as social and political criticism pinpointing a continuity of certain social problems and problematic narratives. However, when these narratives are produced and published in the international context, where they act as cultural brokers and translators, they perform different roles and connect to different cultural codes and discourses. In this specific context, Ugrešić's narratives sometimes align with dominant discursive codes in terms of confirming stereotypes of the authoritarian and unalterable East, which implicitly reproduces an East/West divide. They especially reproduce the imaginary of the Balkans as authoritarian, wild, uncivilized and essentially corrupted.

On the other hand, her appraisal of liberal values, such as individuality, freedom, and individual autonomy, which are counterpoised to Croatian and post-Yugoslav collectivism, nationalism, and authoritarianism, also resonates with the dominant discursive code of (neo)liberal democracy. While the insistence on individualism could have had a subversive effect in Tuđman's 90s, this is less so in the context of the international literary field. The correlation between individualism and the dominant ideology again depends on the international context, in which individualism aligns with Western rhetoric of free speech and free markets.

While reproducing some parts of what can be called contemporary Cold War rhetoric it needs to be underlined that Ugrešić does not demonize, ridicule, or reject socialism, strategies that are central to the contemporary construction of the East/West dichotomy. Ugrešić's texts are set against "the confiscation of memory," and reclaim memory relating to Yugoslav everyday life and the positive legacy of the socialist system (Seccardini; Vervaet, "Whose Museum?"; Vervaet, "Ugresic, Hemon"; Beronja). However, it also seems that it is exactly those texts that somehow pass under the radar of international readership outside of academia. While her exile and biography are still at the forefront of international attention, not even one of the texts in the issues of *World Literature Today* (2016) and *Music & Literature* (2015), both dedicated to her opus, tackled her writing on socialism, nostalgia, or memory. It is possible to assume that this is the case as her biography better resonates with authoritative narratives on the East and West than her writing on socialism, which little aligns with those narratives.

Finally, how can these alignments with dominant discursive codes be understood in the wider context of Ugrešić's work, which is otherwise established as being unconventional and subversive? Do they function as a deviation in her work, or do they resonate with the position that she occupies in the international field? Firstly, I argue that this is not a deviation, but an element both expected and preconditioned by the role she occupies in the literary field. From exile writers – especially those linked to the tradition of Eastern European writers writing during the Cold War – it is expected that they represent their cultures and states and that they do so in a specific way. It is expected that they are politically active and oppressed or persecuted in their home countries, the governments of which are then posed as oppressive counterparts to the liberal West. Both Ugrešić's biography, its discursive organization, and some of her essays confirm this narrative and, consequently, audiences' expectations.

On the other hand, these expectations are not only connected with exile writers, but with translated authors in general. For successful communication between a translated author and an international public, it is crucial that they speak the same cultural code. Repeating the same pattern of exile narratives, as created along the East/West divide, Ugrešić forms the basis for successful communication with her international audience. Images of the uncivilized East confirm that both the author and their public share the same knowledge, which is then easily embellished with additional locally specific details provided by the author. This does not mean that Ugrešić glorifies Western values, liberal democracy, or the capitalist system – quite the opposite, as the author has criticized all of these in several of her essays. Despite this, the image of the brutal and primitive Balkans, established through Ugrešić's life story and essays, implicitly confirms Western superiority.

Secondly, this type of orientalism or Balkanism reaffirms Ugrešić's role as an exile, which springs from the aforementioned link between her role as an exile and as a cultural translator. The author's life story confirms that she has had an authentic experience of a certain culture, which authorizes her role as a cultural translator. However, there is also a reverse process: the author's role as a cultural broker and her criticism of her home country legitimizes her role as an exile, not only during the 90s, but also after that period. If her home country and home region remain the same repressive and authoritarian place, this means that the social situation that made her go into exile has not changed. A dark picture of the Balkans structurally provides the necessary conditions for her position as an exile. If her home country remains and always will be a place of totalitarianism and oppression, her exile position and situation is constantly reproduced and confirmed.

The reading process not only concerns the text, but also the context and temporal framework – this might ring especially true in the case of those writers who are perceived as exiles. Their narratives and narratives about them can change their meaning, considering their role, use, and function on the literary and cultural fields, as well their interaction with other dominant cultural codes in a specific field. Once the text has played a role as an act of political criticism it can slide into the role of cultural translator or even become an academic reference, its meaning changing in this process.

In the end, this analysis serves to illustrate the complexity of meaning-making processes, depending on the use of texts and the context of reading. Considering this, we can state that Ugrešić's essays simultaneously communicate with several contexts, temporal frameworks, and discourses. In the Croatian context they functioned subversively, and it should perhaps be underlined that it is not necessary to question the significance of Ugrešić's essays in the Croatian context to raise questions about their different uses and meanings in the international context. In the international context her texts can both subvert the dominant ethnicization of the war in the media, but also reinforce certain stereotypical imagery of the Balkans and reproduce the ideas and ideologies of (neo)liberal democracies, such as the myth of individualism. While acknowledging this vast diversity and different readings of Ugrešić's work, I have primarily tried to recognize those narratives that align with dominant codes in the international cultural field and their specific temporal framework. It could be concluded that by confirming some of these dominant discursive codes, the author has gained visibility in the international field, and in so doing, has also gained the opportunity to question certain other discursive codes.

References

Anderson, Alison. "Dubravka Ugrešić and Contemporary European Literature Along the Path to Transnational Literature." *World Literature Today*, vol. 91, no. 1, 2017, pp. 61–63.

Beronja, Vladislav. *History and Remembrance in Three Post-Yugoslav Authors: Dubravka Ugrešić, Daša Drndić, and Aleksandar Zograf*. University of Michigan, 2014.

Bourdieu, Pierre. *The Rules of Art: Genesis and Structure of the Literary Field*. Stanford University Press, 1996.

Brennan, Timothy. *At Home in the World*. Harvard University Press, 1997.

Callero, Peter L. *The Myth of Individualism: How Social Forces Shape Our Lives*. Rowman & Littlefield Publishers, 2009.

Casanova, Pascale. *The World Republic of Letters*. Harvard University Press, 2004.

Cornis-Pope, Marcel. "East-Central Europe and the Search for a Literature of the 'Third Way.'" *Global Cold War Literature*, edited by Andrew Hammond, Routledge, 2012, pp. 199–211.

Crnković, Gordana P., et al. "The Culture of Lies: Antipolitical Essays by Dubravka Ugrešić; Celia Hawkesworth; Thomas Cushman." *Slavic and East European Journal*, vol. 43, no. 3, 1999, pp. 544–46.

Damrosch, David. *What Is World Literature?* Princeton University Press, 2003.

Evans, Julian. "Joan Collins and the Decline of the West." *The Guardian*, 8 May 2004, https://www.theguardian.com/books/2004/may/08/highereducation.news #maincontent. Accessed 14 January 2020.

General Information on Authors. *Saqi*. Saqi Books. https://saqibooks.com/author/ugresic-dubravka/.

Hammond, Andrew (ed.). *Global Cold War Literature: Western, Eastern and Postcolonial Perspectives*. Routledge, 2011.

Hammond, Andrew. "On the Frontlines of Writing: Introducing the Literary Cold War." *Global Cold War Literature: Western, Eastern and Postcolonial Perspectives*, edited by Andrew Hammond, Routledge, 2012, pp. 1–16.

Huggan, Graham. *The Postcolonial Exotic: Marketing the Margins*. Psychology Press, 2001.

Jaggi, Maya. "Novelist Dubravka Ugresic talks about why she fears for Kosovo's future." *The Guardian*, 23 Feb. 2008, www.theguardian.com/books/2008/feb/23/politics2. Accessed 2 January 2020.

Jambrešić Kirin, Renata. "Prognanice u nacionalnom kanonu: o egzilnoj ženskoj književnosti." *Dom i svijet: o ženskoj kulturi pamćenja*. Centar za ženske studije, 2015, pp. 125–164.

Juraga, Dubravka, and Keith Booker. "Introduction." *Socialist Cultures East and West: A Post-Cold War Reassessment*. Praeger, 2002, pp. 1–10.

Karpinski, Eva. "Postcards from Europe: Dubravka Ugrešić as a Transnational Public Intellectual, or Life Writing in Fragments." *European Journal of Life Writing*, vol. 2, 2013, pp. 42–60.

Kovačević, Nataša. *Narrating Post/Communism: Colonial Discourse and Europe's Borderline Civilization*. Routledge, 2008.

Kovačević, Nataša. "Storming the EU Fortress: Communities of Disagreement in Dubravka Ugrešić." *Cultural Critique*, vol. 83, 2013, pp. 63–86.

Levy, Michele. "*Europe in Sepia* by Dubravka Ugresic." *World Literature Today*, 26 February 2014, http://www.worldliteraturetoday.org/2014/march/europe-sepia-dubravka-ugresic#.U_utIPldVsk. Accessed 2 January 2020.

Longinović, Tomislav. *Vampire Nation. Violence as Cultural Imaginary*. Duke University Press, 2011.

Lukić, Jasmina. "Pisanje Kao Antipolitika." *Reč*, vol. 10, no. 64, December 2010, pp. 72–102.

Obradović, Dragana. *Writing the Yugoslav Wars: Literature, Postmodernism, and the Ethics of Representation*. University of Toronto Press, 2016.

Ožegović, Nina. *Medijska Reprezentacija Kulturne Proizvodnje u Hrvatskoj Od 1991. Do 2005*. 2013. University of Zagreb, Faculty of Humanities and Social Sciences, PhD dissertation.

Pisac, Andrea. "An Anthropology of Literary Success. 'Hits,' 'near-Misses' and 'Failures' from Ex-Yugoslavia." *Wasafiri*, vol. 29, no. 2, 2014, pp. 58–64.

Pisac, Andrea. "Emerging Politics of Authorship: Recovering Collectivity, Negotiating the Risk." [sic] – *A Journal of Literature, Culture and Literary Translation*, vol. 3, 2011, https://www.sic-journal.org/ArticleView.aspx?aid=122. Accessed 2 January 2020.

Pisac, Andrea. *Trusted Tales: Creating Authenticity in Literary Representations from Ex-Yugoslavia*. 2010. Goldsmiths, University of London, PhD Dissertation.

Seccardini, Gabriela. "Life with an Adaptor, So We Don't Burn Ourselves: The Book, Memory, and the Museum in Dubravka Ugrešić's Poetics of Exile." *Anglistica: An Interdisciplinary Journal*, vol. 17, no. 1, 2013, pp. 69–77.

Speller, John. *R.W. Bourdieu and Literature. E-Book, Mobi*. Open Book Publishers, 2011.

Todorova, Maria. *Imaginarij Balkana*. Inštitut za civilizacijo in kulturo-ICK, 2001.

Ugrešić, Dubravka. "A Conversation with Dubravka Ugrešić." *Music & Literature*, no. 6, 2015, pp. 209–225.

Ugrešić, Dubravka. *Europe in Sepia*. Open Letter, 2014.

Ugrešić, Dubravka. *Karaoke Culture*. Open Letter, 2011.

Ugrešić, Dubravka. *Thank You for Not Reading*. Dalkey Archive Press Book, 2003.

Ugrešić, Dubravka. *The Culture of Lies*. Phoenix House, 1998.

Vervaet, Stijn. "Ugrešić, Hemon and the Paradoxes of Literary Cosmopolitanis: Or How to 'World' (Post-) Yugoslav Literature in the Age of Globalization." *Komparativna književnost: teorija, tumačenja, perspektive*. University of Belgrade, Faculty of Philology, pp. 161–69.

Vervaet, Stijn. "Whose Museum? Whose History? Whose Memories? Remembering in the Work of Dubravka Ugrešić." *Comparative Critical Studies*, vol. 8, no. 2–3, 2011, pp. 295–306.

Volčič, Zala. "Yugo-Nostalgia: Cultural Memory and Media in the Former Yugoslavia." *Critical Studies in Media Communication*, vol. 24, no. 1, Mar. 2007, pp. 21–38.

Williams, David. "'Europeans without Euros': Alternative Narratives of Europe's New Happiness." *Australian and New Zealand Journal of European Studies*, vol. 2, no. 1, 2010, pp. 57–71.

Williams, David. *Writing Postcommunism: Towards a Literature of the East European Ruins*. Palgrave Macmillan, 2013.

Young, Stephenie. "Transnational Memories and A Post-Yugoslav Writer." *Transnationalism and Resistance: Experience and Experiment in Women's Writing*. Rodopi, 2013, pp. 159–182.

CHAPTER 13

Narrations of Lost and Found: The Twists and Turns of the Friendship Discourse in the (Post-)Yugoslav Environment

Zala Pavšič

1   Theoretical Starting Points

The said paper sheds light on the dynamics of the discourse of friendship in the former Yugoslavia as traced from the late 1980s to examples that are more contemporary. Such a complex task requires a complex theoretical framework based not only on the works of regional researchers in the Balkans but also on the philosophical starting points by Jacques Derrida.

In his seminar *The Politics of Friendship* and the homonymous book published in 1994, Derrida points out that the greatest canonical meditations on friendships (Cicero's and Montaigne's, for example) relate to the experience of the loss or death of a friend. Thus, commemorative discourse on the death (or loss) of a friend is the discourse, which permits public mourning or public expression of love of a late friend, i.e., to express emotions which are a perhaps part of our personal narratives, but which otherwise have little room in public discourse – hence, "[i]t is thanks to death that the friendship can then be declared" (qtd. in Kaplan 131).

Moreover, Derrida opens both the seminar and the book by maintaining that friendship (at least the most perfect of its kind) does not exist and cannot exist. The only kinds of friendships that do exist are human, which are inevitably flawed. For this reason, Derrida describes friendship as a category that is yet to come, a category of the future that "belongs to the experience of expectation, promise or engagement" (236).

Finally, he formulates his thesis around the question of when will humanity be ready to embrace democracy that will not ridicule friendship or, rather, when will humanity be ready to experience equality. To put it more accurately, the crucial form of inequality, which Derrida points to, is the exclusion of women, not only from the discourse of politics and the discourse of philosophy but from the discourse of friendship as well (see footnote in chapter 4).

2 Narratives of Loss in the Disintegrating Yugoslavia

The war in Yugoslavia and its disintegration led to the formation of several types of narratives of loss that relate to the lost homeland (or the state, as people knew it) and the lost way of life people knew before the war. In her article "The Lost Way of Life" (1996), Natalija Vrečer describes the results she obtained from interviews with refugees in Celje, for whom the war was a traumatic experience because they had "lost their way of life, their country, home, relatives, neighbours, job, belongings, etc." (132). Lost ties (with friends, relatives, and neighbours) within the context of the lost "normality" of living are also at the centre of Ivana Maček's reflections in her paper "Imitation of Life" (2007), in which she describes how everyone in wartime Sarajevo faced the loss of a relative or neighbour, either because they had left the city or because they had died. She, likewise, notes that new friendships were formed even during the war: as an anonymous female inhabitant of Sarajevo indicates in the article, friendships were considerably different and more short-lived than those made during peacetime. "But perhaps just because of the sharing of the most difficult moments they are as strong as the old ones" (54).

The significance of the given narrative was also pointed out by Alenka Bartulović (2013), who in her research pairs narratives of a lost home with narratives of a lost city (Sarajevo) and understands both as one of the variants of the anti-nationalist discourse in post-war Sarajevo. Characteristically, "Sarajevo has over the recent years become a space that many of its inhabitants no longer find recognizable" (248).

Scholars dealing with the (post-)Yugoslav environment have dedicated much less attention to the question of friendship than, for instance, to the loss of the *komšiluk* (neighbourhood) or the dissolution of ethnically mixed marriages. Hence, I chose to focus more on friendship as friendship in itself, without the adjective 'lost' or without a specific environment in which it is explored, conveys strong theoretical and metaphorical implications.

3 The Metaphorization of Our Experiencing the World

The academic literature on the Balkans in general is replete with metaphor. As observed by the collection of essays *Balkan kao metafora* (*Balkan as Metaphor*, 2003), the notion of the Balkans itself is charged with a certain idiomatic meaning: it inherently connotes inferiority, backwardness, and barbarianism. According to the editors of the above mentioned volume, the collection of essays has been created precisely with the aim of shattering the continuous image of the "wild" Balkans (as implied by the popular metaphor of the Balkans as a "powder keg") as construed from the outside.

On the other hand, the strategic position of the Balkans is conveyed by the metaphor of a crossroads or bridge (between the East and the West). The context of the latter is described in detail in a collection of essays which, likewise, takes its title from a metaphor for the fragmentation of Bosnia – *The New Bosnian Mosaic* (2007). The metaphor of the bridge in the same collection is set in correlation with the destruction of the bridge in Mostar on 9 November 1993, while its reconstruction in 2004 is perceived as a symbol of the accord reached among the Bosniaks, Serbs, and Muslims.

The usage of metaphor during the war (but especially its pitfalls and dangers) is also examined by Dubravka Ugrešić in her essay "The Realization of a Metaphor," which she starts with the thesis that the war in the Balkans can only be read as a literary text, where a host of "stylistic devices, tropes and figures" (57) are at work. She points to the danger of blurring the boundary between a word (metaphor) and reality or, rather, the moment when a metaphor becomes real. In her reflections, she follows Russian structural linguist Roman Jakobson, who describes the realization of a trope as "the projection of a literary device into artistic reality, the turning of a poetic trope into a poetic fact, into a plot element" (qtd. in ibid.). In such a sequence of events, a metaphor in a text on war, whether spoken or written, has developed further and became a reality.

In another essay published within the classical collection *The Culture of Lies*, Ugrešić takes friendship as a fitting template to outline the disintegration of Yugoslavia (a template because nation-states envisage a new type of friendship that caters to the newly developed ideology of nation) when describing her conversation with a literary editor who wanted her to write "a novel about a little Serb and a little Croat to show, through an account of their growing-up together: a) the origins of Yugoslavia; b) the history of the break-up of Yugoslavia; c) the essence of the bloody conflict in the Balkans" (168).

However, researchers should keep in mind "that metaphors are often misleading, as much in our self-conceptions as in our perceptions regarding other cultures" (Bartulović 89). In the course of their research, they should therefore also note the difference between the metaphors that the inhabitants of a certain area use for themselves rather than metaphors that have been created from the outside.

In my research, I was analysing the way friendship (in this respect especially lost friendship) appeared as a metaphor for the disintegration of Yugoslavia. The said metaphor suggests that there is most likely some kind of analogy between the processes of losing friends and the disintegration of the state, with the ensuing war that allows us to bring both phenomena into a metaphorical relationship. It is the analogy between individuals' personal lives and global events: according to this equation, the fragmentation of the state into six republics would be followed by the parting between friends of different nationalities. While in real life, socio-political events affect individuals' lives, metaphorization follows a trajectory in the reverse direction: interpersonal contacts and the destinies of individuals metaphorize events on a global level.

The metaphor of friendship may be classified as an active one, particularly in view of the recent (or even current) production of works (especially documentaries) using the relationship between two or more friends as a metaphor for the disintegration of the state. In the course of my research, I also discovered that the narratives of lost friendship belong to the field of both metaphors coming from outside and metaphors people use to verbalize their experiences. For this reason, certain sources should be read with a great amount of caution.

The activeness of the chosen metaphor is also evident when taking into account its evolution from the end of the eighties onward: in the former Yugoslavia, there was a special policy, known as *the idea of brotherhood and unity*. It was introduced as a means of bonding the six republics. For that very same purpose, the government systematically encouraged the experience of multi-ethnic friendships, which was especially evident in the case of obligatory military service for generations of men from all over the country. Moreover, the policy encompassed the highlighting of examples of multi-ethnic friendship through friend duos, one of the most well-known example being the actors Boris Dvornik and Bata Živojinović. They performed together in cult Yugoslav films such as *Most* (*The Bridge*), *Bitka na Neretvi* (*The Battle of Neretva*), and *Sutjeska* (*The Battle of Neretva*).

In the decade after the death of Josip Broz Tito, Yugoslavia is faced with a political as well as an economic crisis resulting in a growing gap between the Yugoslav republics. In addition, in the late 80s, the image of the harmonious Yugoslav brotherhood is slowly being replaced by narratives of overwhelming closeness. Moreover, the notion of brotherhood becomes associated with exploitation, mistrust and threats. The relationship between brothers is no longer marked by their unity but by their differences, a state where one of the brothers is more equal than the other. It is a form of Orientalism which Milica Bakić-Hayden describes as a "nesting of Orientalisms" (917) and which implies that the states of former Yugoslavia have developed their own respective variants of Orientalist conceptions of one another. One of the most evident examples of the discourse of friendship and brotherhood being associated not with unity but with individualism (and therefore, with independence) is the correspondence that the Slovenian intellectual Taras Kermauner had with many high standing Serbian public figures. He published some of these letters under the title *Letters to a Serbian Friend*.

The correspondence aimed toward discussing public matters and the relations between the Yugoslavian republics, especially Slovenia and Serbia. These relations became highly strained after the wave of Serbian nationalism became evident in their address of the Kosovo issue. Matters got worse after the publication of the Serbian National Academy Memorandum in 1986, which Serbian intellectuals wrote in order to save the Serbian question inside the existing Socialist Federative Republic of Yugoslavia. The document had far-reaching consequences for Serbian politics, especially for the formation of the nationalist movement inside the Serbian League of Communists and the rise of Slobodan Milošević. The chain of events only made the divisions between the Yugoslav republics greater: Slovenia started to entertain the idea of leaving Yugoslavia and joining the European Union, while Serbia thought that the issue of Kosovo could only be resolved if the country stayed united.

4 Friendship Impossible

After Slovenia and Croatia declared their independence, the military sanctions of the Yugoslavian National Army began.[1] In much the same way as the deaths on the front, the grievances of women, and the war rapes, friendship, too, became a platform for mobilizing national emotions. This brings us to the example I mentioned above: the case of Boris Dvornik and Bata Živojinović. The duo appeared together in several Yugoslavian movies. In *Bitka na Neretvi*, for example, they actually played two partisans fighting side by side against

---

1 The paragraphs on Bata Živojinović and Boris Dvornik are based on my paper "The Discourse of Friendship, Discourse of War: a Gendered Perspective of the Disintegration of Yugoslavia," presented at the Feminisms in Transnational Perspective Conference at IUC Dubrovnik in 2017. The paper follows Derrida's conclusion on the phallogocentric nature of the friendship discourse and provides an in-depth analysis of friendship discourse as found in wartime works and contacts between female writers, scholars, and anti-war activists who were not exposed as the messengers of the needs and demands of their nation-states: rather, they were marked as public enemies for their antinationalist and antiwar stances and engagement. Moreover, their wartime texts and activities challenge the narrative of "friendship lost" by consciously promoting multinational friendship and the need to stay in touch with their friends from other republics of Yugoslavia even when infrastructural connections were broken. Hence, in order to gain a more holistic picture of all possible spectra of friendship discourse, I thus refer the reader to a parallel reading of the mentioned text, which will give a more complex picture of the problem and a more gender-balanced presentation of the matter.

the Germans. When one of them is wounded in combat, the other carries him on his back to find help, but the friend ends up dying in his arms.

One year before the war, both actors met at the Festival of Performing Acts in Niš. It was already evident that Yugoslavia was coming apart, and the actors joked about it, saying that they might be the only hope to hold the country together (Čikeš). Soon after, Živojinović became a member of Milošević's party and, for a short period, Dvornik was politically engaged in the Croatian Democratic Union. Dvornik decided to break with Živojinović publicly and did this by reading an open letter addressed to him. It was broadcasted by Croatian National Television (HRT). In it, Dvornik accused Živojinović of being a Serbian nationalist and of having called for the death of all Croats in the Serbian parliament. He also referred to the times when they performed together in films and reminded him that the situation was no longer a film, but a real battlefield. "We built bridges, Bata," he reminds him, "tracks, barricades, we killed many enemies, but all that was just a film. We did that to warn generations, to prevent it from ever happening again" (Dvornik, "Boris Dvornik Bati Živojinoviću" 4:52–5:05).

It soon became evident that this was not simply a communication between Boris and Bata, but above all a communication between a representative of the Serbian nation and a representative of the Croatian nation. And when Croatia proclaimed its independence, which was followed by Serbian aggression against the country, it became impossible for public figures to maintain their relationships with representatives of other nations, especially those of the invading country. Such examples were also evident in popular music, in songs such as "E moj druže zagrebački" ("Oh, My Zagreb Friend") by Bora Đorđević and "E moj druže beogradski" ("Oh, My Belgrade Friend") by Jura Stublić. While the latter was often understood as an anti-war song, it nevertheless implies that multi-ethnic friendship is lost or no longer possible.

5 Reconciliation Emerging: Negotiating Different Perspectives

In the beginning of the 21st century the discourse of friendship has been given a new impetus with a shift towards narratives of reconciliation. Moreover, this shift does not only include transformations of narrative but also genre: public letters and letter correspondences are replaced by TV broadcasts and especially documentary movies. In 2006, the Croatian commercial television Nova TV broadcasted what seemed to be a reconciliation between Bata Živojinović and Boris Dvornik via computer connection Beograd-Split. At the time, Živojinović was lying in a hospital in Belgrade, waiting for a heart operation, and wanted his family and Dvornik to be with him in this difficult time.

Živojinović said that it was time they made up, and that their reunion had a symbolic meaning for both the Croatian and the Serbian nation. Soon after, Dvornik died. Živojinović did not attend the funeral. When the journalists who interviewed him for Croatian Television asked him why, he replied that he had heard that Croats punctured the tires of cars with Serbian registration plates (B.M.).

Their public communication is, as a consequence, the kind of communication that serves propaganda purposes, but that has lost its edge in the post-war years. While Dvornik's open letter was broadcast on national television in order to rouse national sentiments, their subsequent reconciliation was broadcast as a piece of infotainment at the end of the news programme. Especially because it was fairly unconvincing: while Živojinović did most of the talking on the show, Dvornik appeared gloomy and uncomfortable, and the entire footage looked feigned. Their reconciliation seemed all the more disingenuous after reading the above mentioned interview in which Živojinović justified his absence from his friend's funeral with his Serbian descent.

Recent years have also led to the popularization of the motif of friendship on the big screen: in documentaries filmed over the last decade, a special emphasis on reconciliation could be found in movies funded by the Institute for War and Peace Reporting (IWPR). This fact is not irrelevant, since it is obvious from the Institute's name that it is an organization that finances efforts aimed at achieving peace and reconciliation. Their frequent collaborator, film director Ada Sokolović, has filmed two documentaries which both take place in Bosnia and Herzegovina and underline the need and possibility for the younger generations to live in a multi-ethnic and peaceful environment: her most recent work is a film about the Sarajevo women's football team titled *I Love SFK*, while her previous documentary, *The Border*, was dedicated to the friendship between renowned Bosnian rapper Adnan Hamidović-Frenkie and his Serbian friend Milan Colić. In the song "A Letter to Milan," which served as an inspiration for the documentary, Hamidović-Frenkie describes the problems of interpersonal relations in post-war Bosnia, how the world is divided into 'us' and 'them,' and that people still blame each other for wartime events. Therefore, he addresses his friend Milan, a Bosnian Serb, and wonders how he must feel when he walks around in a now Islamic Sarajevo, and that he feels similarly uneasy when he is in Republika Srpska.[2] Frenkie concludes that rec-

---

2   Republika Srpska is one of the two entities of Bosnia and Herzegovina, the other being the Federation of Bosnia and Herzegovina. Its largest city and administrative centre is Banja Luka. The entity encompasses most of the Bosnian Serb-populated portions of Bosnia and Herzegovina. Formed in 1992 at the outset of the disintegration of Yugoslavia, Republika

onciliation is not something that can be imported or forced upon, but it has to originate within the people themselves.

In the documentary *Orkestar*, which was directed by Pjer Žalica, we follow the story of the popular Yugoslav rock group from Sarajevo, Plavi Orkestar. Here, the question of nationality is deliberately put aside as the leader of the group, Saša Lošić, states that he has a problem with defining himself within given ethnic classifications. Rather, the documentary portrays how the group ceased to play during the war and how some of its members fled to Canada or Slovenia and some stayed in the besieged Sarajevo to defend it. However, a few years after the war, the band members restored contact and started playing together again. The message of this documentary kept simplistic rather than an over-dramatizing historical events: it shows that people may have gone their separate ways, but many contacts were regained after the war.

On the other hand, some of the films that were created by foreign production houses were highly contaminated with the discourse of Balkanism. According to Maria Todorova, it was only after the fall of Yugoslavia and the Yugoslav wars that a new wave of dismissive and negative connotations of the words 'Balkan' and 'Balkanization' became widespread. Todorova points out that this time around, the key role in the definition of these stereotypes was played primarily by historians and anthropologists, who tried to formulate a "scientific explanation for the violence, particularly for that perpetrated by the Serbian faction" (213).

One of the best examples of a narrative underlining the Balkan peoples' supposed tendency towards violence, quarrelsome nature, and other similar notions, is Al Jazeera's documentary *Once Upon a Time in Sarajevo*. The story is narrated by the former BBC correspondent in Belgrade Jacky Rowland. She does not hide her self-confidence, and states her mission very directly: she has come to Sarajevo to see if the three Bosnian comedians, Nele Karajlić, Zenit Đozić, and Branko Djurić-Đuro, the protagonists of the show *Top lista nadrealista*,[3] can become friends again. After losing hope to bring together three

---

Srpska, following the Dayton Accords, achieved international recognition as part of a federal Bosnia and Herzegovina.

3   Top lista nadrealista (The Surrealists' Top Chart) was a television show, which included satire, sketch, surreal and black comedy elements. It originated from short radio comedy segments, broadcasted by Radio Sarajevo in the early 1980s. The TV show Top lista was produced and aired by TV Sarajevo in three series from 1984 until 1991. The series was extremely popular in the former Yugoslavia and was considered in many respects to be prolific in depicting the situation in the former Yugoslavia and especially in Bosnia and Herzegovina before the wars of the 1990s.

individuals who clearly for whatever reason do not want to work together anymore, she concludes her failure with three sentences:

> When I set out on this journey, I wanted to find out whether the personal stories of Zenit, Nele, and Đuro reflected what had happened to their country. [...] And I think that those stories do, to a large extent, mirror recent history. [...] The question is whether Bosnians can in the future discover once again that what they share, including their sense of humour, is more important than what divides them. (47:09–47:33)

The final remarks reveal some of the documentary's contradictions and inconsistencies: if the relationships between the three men reflect what has happened, then the entire documentary is based on a rhetorical question, and consequently meaningless: the goal, then, was never to reconcile the subjects, but rather to prove that, because of their historical backgrounds, their ethnic differences and because of the quarrelsome nature of the Balkan nations, reconciliation was never possible. Moreover, the journalist's final remarks are supremely condescending and show a colonialist mentality. She emphasizes how the Bosnians (and all other Balkan nations) supposedly require the West to come and explain what is good for them and what is not. This is doubly ironic, since the motif of the know-it-all foreigner who comes to Bosnia following a misguided missionary calling was frequently used by *Top lista nadrealista*: in one of the episodes, they cause of a fight between two friends, a Muslim and a Serb, who are "as close as brothers," having known each other since childhood.

Perhaps one of the best known documentaries which examines the motif of brotherhood in the context of the disintegration of Yugoslavia is *Once Brothers* (2010), a documentary movie on the relationship between Vlade Divac and Dražen Petrović. Similarly as in the documentary *Once Upon a Time in Sarajevo*, it is hard to ignore the Balkanist perspective of American journalists and coaches, which are especially evident in the sequences describing Divac's arrival in America. Some officials could not be more patronizing; Divac is constantly criticized for not speaking English, for not being well-kept, and so on. Afterwards, their role in the film was to back up Divac's position in a dispute they had with Dražen Petrović over the war in Croatia, and to act as peacemakers in this dispute. Since Petrović died before the war in Croatia had ended, the two former friends did not have a chance to reunite. In my opinion, the biggest flaw of the film is the absence of Dražen Petrović's perspective – in the film, his stance is supported only by his mother and his brother, and Petrović cannot avoid being seen as a Croatian nationalist. This provides the impression that Divac was an innocent victim of Croatian nationalism, which was supposedly the reason why he lost contact with his Croatian teammates during the war. Thus, from the foreign perspective, inhabitants of the former of Yugoslavia are almost predestined by their nationalities which disables them to carry on with or to form multinational friendships after the disintegration of the country.

6   Conclusion

The discourse of friendship is never only a discourse about one's personal contacts or one's personal network. It is a mechanism which unravels our personal beliefs, convictions and stances which can often be misused by the prevailing power structures. Moreover, the discourse of friendship also indicates who is a part of a desired friendship (power) circle and who is excluded from the same circle, thus being left to form new, alternative connections and alternative discourses. Hence, the real promise of friendship studies lies not only in recognizing and acknowledging mainstream patterns and discourses but in balancing them with alternative narratives and perspectives of those excluded, thus providing a unique vision of historical events which we could describe as "the vision of the vanquished" (Wachtel 24–25: 2005). In order to so, scholars should balance their research on brotherhood and male friendship with subsequent experiences of female sisterhood and in the case of (post-)Yugoslavian environment, the voices of anti-war activists who refused to act upon the expectations of the newly funded nation states and understood the time of nationalism as the time when their multinational friendships demanded special attention. A concise, holistic monograph encompassing all the mentioned narratives with special emphasis on the fluid nature of the friendship discourse is – hopefully – yet to come.

Regarding that friendship also inevitably unravels our notions of how we imagine the Other, its discourse can also be very telling in the sense of exploring Orientalism, Balkanism, or other similar phenomenon which build upon (in)equality. A close reading of Kermauner's correspondence with his Serbian counterparts shows how from the 80's onward national prejudice accompanied the efforts to establish national states and were incited by politicians and public figures. Moreover, the correspondence shows that albeit having the word "friend" in the title, Kermauner's letters often sound hostile and threatening, hence revealing that the line between the friend and the enemy can be blurred very easily.

The Balkanist perspective on the (post-)Yugoslav environment is most evident in documentary movies, filmed in the last decade. While *Once Upon a Time in Sarajevo* and *Once Brothers* focus on nationalities and political disputes that supposedly arise from the different nationalities of the films' subjects, the documentary movie *Orkestar* sees the problem in nationalism as such, not in nationalities. The film is not interested in its subjects' nationalities, but whether or not someone is a "good person", as the director Pjer Žalica explains in the introduction (0:22–0:30). And while ex-Yugoslavians are making documentaries on how they find more sense in friendships that were regained or found during the times of hardship, foreign productions insist on narrating (national) disputes that are supposedly impossible to resolve.

In the case of the (post-)Yugoslav environment, friendship analysis provides the possibility to address the perils of nationalism and even suggest a way to surpass them. The given research is therefore relevant not only for scholars willing to research friendship in multi-ethnic environments but also for people living in the former Yugoslavia as a reminder and a possible suggestion of how to re-think their societies.

References

Bakić, Hayden-Milica. "Nesting Orientalisms: The Case of Former Yugoslavia." *Slavic Review*, vol. 54, no. 4, 1995, pp. 917–931.

Bartulović, Alenka. *Nismo vaši! Antinacionalizem v povojnem Sarajevu*. Znanstvena založba Filozofske fakultete v Ljubljani, 2013.

Bata Živojinović, B.M. "Nisam došao Dvorniku na sprovod jer je netko negdje bušio Srbima gume." *Index*. 28.09.2011. Acc. 30.09.2014. ⟨http://www.index.hr/sport/clanak/bata-zivojinovic-nisam-dosao-dvorniku-na-sprovod-jer-je-netko-negdje-busio-srbima-gume/574280.aspx⟩.

Bjelić, Dušan and Obrad Savić (eds.). *Balkan kao metafora*. Beogradski krug, 2003.

Black, Max. "Še o metafori." *Kaj je metafora?*, edited by Božidar Kante, Založba Krtina, 1998, pp. 91–110.

Čikeš, V. "Ponovo ćemo snimati zajedno." *TV Novosti*. Novosti, 1999–2005. Acc. 28.09.2014. ⟨http://www.tv.novosti.rs/code/navigate.php?Id=243⟩.

Derrida, Jacques. The Politics of Friendship. Trans. George Collins, London: Verso, 1997.

Dvornik, Boris. "Boris Dvornik Bati Živojinoviću." *YouTube*, 23.6.2008. Acc. 15.08.2014. ⟨https://www.youtube.com/watch?v=wIBoyoVF4d4⟩.

Granica. Film inspirisan pjesmom Pismo Milanu. Dir. Ada Sokolović. IWPR and Mebius Film.2012/2013.Film.*YouTube*, 28.4.2014. Acc. 25.04.2016. ⟨https://www.youtube.com/watch?v=b8WPZDIfHDA⟩.

Kaplan, Danny. *The Men We Loved: Male Friendship and Nationalism in Israeli Culture*. Berghahn, Oxford: Berghahn Books, 2006.

Lakoff, George and Mark Johnson. *Metaphors We Live By*. University of Chicago Press, 1980.

Maček, Ivana. "Imitation of Life." *The New Bosnian Mosaic*, edited by Xavier Bougarel, Elissa Helms, and Ger Duijzings, Ashgate, 2007, pp. 39–59.

Once Brothers. Dir. Michael Tolajian. ESPN, 2010. Film.

Once Upon a Time in Sarajevo. Dir. Jacky Rowland. *Al Jazeera Documentaries*. 12.12.2014. Film. YouTube. 13.12.2014. Acc. 15.4.2016. ⟨https://www.youtube.com/watch?v=2JCvqCqIGYA⟩.

Orkestar. Dir. Pjer Žalica. Refresh Production Sarajevo. 2011. Film.

Pavšič, Zala. "The Discourse of Friendship, Discourse of War: a Gendered Perspective of the Disintegration of Yugoslavia." Jambrešić-Kirin, Renata, Carotenuto, Silvana, Gabrielli, Maria Francesca eds., *Horror, Fear and Love*. Naples: Unior Press, 2021. Forthcoming.

Todorova, Maria. *Imaginarij Balkana*. Ljubljana, Inštitut za Civilizacijo in kulturo, 2001.

Ugrešić, Dubravka. *The Culture of Lies*. Phoenix House, 1998.

Ugrešić, Dubravka. "The Realization of a Metaphor." *The Culture of Lies*. Phoenix House, 1998, pp. 74–87.

Vrečer, Natalija. "The Lost Way of Life." *War, Exile, Everyday Life: Cultural Perspectives*, Renata Jambrešić-Kirin and Maja Povrzanović, eds., Institute of Ethnology and Folklore Reserach, 1996, pp. 133–147.

Wachtel, Nathan. *Pogled premaganih: Perujski domorodci ob španski osvojitvi: 1530–1570*. Ljubljana, Studia Humanitatis, 2005.

Index

9/11   167

Abercrombie, Nicholas   219
abyss structure, the (*mise en abyme*)
   137–138
Adriatic   193
aesthetic art   113–114
   agreeable   113–114
   fine   113–114
Ahmad, Aijaz   58n5
Al Jazeera   268, 272
Alajbegović, Božidar   227
Albahari David   193
Albania   190, 196
Alexander, Jeffrey C.   217
alien object (Marx)   45
alienation, alienated   40, 43, 45, 46, 46n1, 54
Althusser, Louis   9
Amsterdam   159, 160, 162, 164, 191, 193, 194
Anić, Vladimir   223
anti-modernism
   millennial imagining   94
   narratives of natural decline   95
   narratives of religious decline   99, 100
   pervasive sense off loss   93
anti-utopia   83–86, 88, 90–91, 93
anticipation of retrospection, the   139
Antunac, Aljoša   228
Aralica, Ivan   218, 226
arche-fossil   114
archive   108, 118, 136, 140, 141
   total   118
archive fever   140
Aristotle   110, 111, 114
Assmann, Aleida   155
Atia, Nadia   150, 153
Atwood, Margaret   93n1
aura, auratic (Benjamin)   43, 44, 53, 54
autobiographical   189, 197, 199, 200
autobiographical prose   170, 172
avant-garde   59, 73–76
   and the national   60–68
   as tradition   62–66, 71, 74
   historical   66, 73–76
   Russian   63–66, 70–71

avant-gardist   42
Aygi, Gennadiy   71

Bachelard, Gaston   200, 201
Badiou, Alain   109n2
Baker, Catherine   222
Baker, Janet   96
Bakhtin, Mikhail   43, 97, 101, 103, 104
Bakić-Hayden, Milica   264, 271
Bal, Mieke   150, 151
Balenović, Ivo   83, 101, 103, 104
Balkan/s   157, 189, 190, 192, 193, 194, 196
Balkanisation   162
Balkanism   250, 253–255, 268, 270
Barbieri, Veljko   95, 97, 98
Barker, Chris   217
Barr, Patrick   206
Barthes, Roland   117, 219
Bartulović, Alenka   262, 263, 271
Bauer, Ludwig   68, 71
Bauman, Zygmunt   205, 235
becoming (Deleuze and Guattari)   41, 46, 49, 51
becoming-woman (Braidotti)   51
Beethoven, Ludwig van   104
Beganović, Davor   153n1, 154, 165
Bekavac, Luka   108–109, 118–125, 127–141
Belobrajdić, Tanja   220, 221, 222
Benačić, Ana   222
Benjamin, Walter   39, 40, 42, 43, 44, 52, 53, 54, 75
Benjaminian   42, 52
Berger, John   53, 53n3, 54
Bergson, Henri   115, 119, 177, 179
Berlin   160, 160n11, 161
Bernardi, Bernardo   42, 45
Beronja, Vladislav   5–6, 8, 150, 154n2
Beyer, Barbara   201
Bhabha, Homi   9
Biancolelli, Pierre-François   191
Bilić, Snježana   228
binaries   151, 164
   center-periphery   151, 166
   major/minor   151
   model of nostalgia   152, 153

binary socialism 157
bioacoustics 118
Blanchot, Maurice 194
Blatnik, Andrej 82–83, 84, 85–86, 88
Bodroža, Lazar 83
body without organs (Deleuze and Guattari) 47, 48, 49, 51, 52, 171
body, bodily 41, 45, 46, 47, 48, 49, 51, 53
Bogomolets, Alexander 29
Bogue, Ronald 44
Booker, M. Keith 105
Bošković, Aleksandar 149
Bosna and Herzegovina 52, 154, 155, 156, 157, 159, 166, 190, 193
   war in 167
Bošnjak, Branimir 67
Bourdieu, Pierre 240
Bourdieusian 39 n2
Boym, Svetlana 150, 151, 152, 153, 160, 160n11, 161, 164, 200
Braidotti, Rosi 41, 51, 52, 53
Brassier, Ray 119n5, 129
Braver, Lee 109n2, 130
Brebanović, Predrag 52, 59, 61–63
Brecht, Bertolt 84
Brešan, Ivo 218
Brešan, Vinko 224
brotherhood 264, 269
brotherhood and unity 264
Brown, Dan 225
Budisavljević, Dana 235
Bukowski, Charles 224
Bulić, Vlado 227
Buonomano, Dean 28
Bürger, Peter 73–75

Callenbach, Ernest 96
Canada 193, 194, 198
capitalism 81–82, 83, 85, 86, 86n6, 88, 89, 90, 91–92
carnivalisation 101
Caruth, Cathy 234
Carver, Raymond 224
Casanova, Pascale 60n11
Cassin, Barbara 110
Catterberg, Gabriela 215
Celzijus, Nives 225
Cesarec, August 64–66, 70

Chandler, Daniel 214
Chatman, Seymour 137
Chekhov, Anton Pavlovich 103
Chicago 166, 167
Chomsky, Noam 223
Christianity 99, 101
Chronos 199
chronotopic 43, 46
Cicero 261
Cocteau, Jean 123
Coelho, Paulo 225
Cold War and literature 242
Colić, Milan 267
collectivity 151, 153, 159, 165, 168
commodities, commodification, commodifying 42, 45, 46, 217, 220, 222
communality 150, 153, 154, 161
communicability 113–114
communism 28, 31, 216, 218
conceptual (art) 40–42
conditions 112, 114, 116, 121
   of consciousness 116
   of science 112, 114, 116
consciousness 114–115, 116, 119
contemporaneity 179
contingency. See necessity
Cornis-Pope, Marsel 192
corporeal, corporeality 41, 49, 51
correlationism 130–131
cosmic horror 131–133, 140–141
counterhistory 231
Crnković Raunić, Gordana 227
Croatia 154, 191, 193
Croatian Catholic Church 100
Croatian Independence War 208, 211, 219
Croatianism 219
Čučković, Nevenka 210
Čulina, Arijana 225
cultural process 227
cultural product 222, 223, 226, 228
cultural production 216, 217, 218, 219
cultural value 222, 223, 224, 228
Culture of Lies, The 249–252, 263, 272
Curfew: Premonitions, Recollections, The (*Policijski sat: Slutnje, uspomene*) 128, 134, 139, 140
Currie, Mark 135, 139n12

INDEX

Dannenberg, Hilary   135
Davičo, Oskar   66
Davies, Jeremy   150, 153
death   261, 264, 265, 266
Dedinac, Milan   66
Deleuze, Gilles   39, 40, 41, 44, 47, 48, 49, 50, 51, 52, 109n2, 115, 154, 163, 163n12, 171n1, 174, 175, 176, 177, 180, 181, 182, 184
Denić-Grabić, Alma   197
Derrida, Jacques   130, 138n12, 140, 207, 232, 235, 261, 265, 271
description   137–138
desire, desiring machine (Deleuze and Guattari)   41, 46, 49, 50, 51, 52
Desnica, Darko   228
Desnica, Vladan   28, 32–34
de-territorialization   160, 163
diasporic   153, 165
difference   40, 41, 49, 51, 52, 53, 213, 221, 223
disavowal   149
displacement   150, 152, 154, 160, 161, 166
distrust syndrome   215
Divac, Vlade   269, 270
Djurić-Đuro, Branko   268, 269
documentary   199, 266, 267, 268, 269, 271
documentary production   230
Donat, Branimir   226
Đorđević, Bora   266
Dosse, François   40, 49, 52
Đozić, Zenit   268, 269
Dragojević, Rade   225
Drakulić, Slavenka   225, 235
Drašković, Brankica   222
Drenje   128, 134, 136, 137, 140
Drndić, Daša   235
Duda, Dean   39–40n2
Duić, Tomislav   220
duration   178
   inner (story duration), outer (discourse duration)   136, 137, 140
Dvornik, Boris   264, 265, 266, 267, 271
dystopia   83–85
   dystopian anti-modernism   94, 95
   dystopian Menippea   101, 102, 103
   dystopian trend   94
   dystopian turn   94
   gastro-dystopia   97
   simple   84

Eagleton, Mary   52
Eagleton, Terry   40, 54
East and West   263
Eastern-European exiles   242
eco-fascism   99
Eco, Umberto   120
economic recession   82
ecotopia   96
elsewhere   191, 192–193, 197
Elsie, Robert   192
Elster, Jon   45, 46, 46n1
entropic   128, 136, 140
entropy   128, 136, 140
episodic memories   199
Eposito, Elena   25
Erlebnis   196
Erll, Astrid   150, 158
eutopia   84
event (Deleuze; Guattari)   46, 53
event boundary   174
everyday   149, 155, 158, 159, 162, 163, 166
   alternative history of   156
   culture. *See also* popular culture   156
   history   156
exile   54, 159, 161, 162, 164, 166, 192–198, 241, 242, 246–247, 257
extro-science   116–118, 119
   fiction   117, 121
   world   116–118, 119
      first type   116
      second type   117–118, 119
      third type   116–117

factiality   113
facticity   113
facto-fictional   230
female (commune, continent, genealogies, pleasure, subject)   50, 51, 52
femininity   50, 51
feminist   41, 51, 52
Ferić, Zoran   225
fetish, fetishist, fetishizing (Marx)   41, 46, 52
fiction   107n1, 109, 115, 116, 117, 120, 121–122, 123, 124, 125
   documentary   176
   hyperstitional   123, 124, 125
   of memory   176, 185, 186

fiction (cont.)
    theoretical   107n1, 108, 109–110, 110n3, 111, 115, 120, 122–123, 135
    (post-)Yugoslav   109, 123
fictional confession   193, 198
fictional theory. *See* fiction
fictionalization   230, 231
ficto-factual   230
fifth risk   214
Filippini, Michele   206
film industry   227
Firestone, Shulamith   30
Fisher, Mark   107n1
Flaker, Aleksandar   61, 63–65, 68–71, 73, 224
focalization
    internal   118
    fixed   118
former Yugoslavia   189, 192
Fox, The (Ugrešić)   194–196
fragmentation   27–28, 32, 34, 36, 190, 193
    fragmentary construction of time   174
    of memory   173, 183
Frenkie-Hamidović, Adnan   267
Fukuyama, Francis   81
future   25, 28, 31–35

Gajin, Igor   83n4, 94, 127
Galijaš, Armina   149
Genette, Gerard   137, 138
Giddens, Anthony   222, 223
Goethe, Johann Wolfgang   61
Gould, Steven Jay   29
Grabar-Kitarović, Kolinda   212, 213
Gramsci, Antonio   206
grey economy   210
Grgas, Stipe   25–26
Grgić, Velimir   83, 227
Grlić, Rajko   224, 235
Gross, David   235
Grosz, Elizabeth   41
Guattari, Félix   40, 41, 48, 49, 50, 51, 52, 53, 154, 163, 163n12, 171n1, 174
Gulag   166

Hamilton Grant, Iain   129
Hamletian dilemma   195
Haraway, Donna   30
Hariri, Muhannad   116

Harman, Graham   129, 130n4, 131
Hasanbegović, Zlatko   207, 212
hegemonic discourse   206
Heidegger, Martin   109, 109n2, 139n12
Hemon, Aleksandar   149, 153, 154, 165, 166, 167
Herman, David   135
Herman, Edward S.   223
Hester, Helen   30–31
Hill, Stephen   219
historical revisionism   72, 149, 155, 213
historization, historize   40, 52
history of the future   217, 233
history   152, 154, 155, 155n5, 156
    alternative version of   154, 156
    and national identity   155
    sentimental   158, 159
    See also memory and history
Hitler, Adolf   103
Hitzke, Diana   171n1
Hofer, Johannes   151
home   151, 152, 161, 166, 191
    departure   167, 168
    homecoming   167, 168
    homesickness   161
home fear/home fire   197
home literature   191, 200
home time   191–194, 196–201
horror   131, 132
house   188, 193–194, 197–201
Hoy, David Couzens   235
Hribar, Hrvoje   224
Hume, David   116
hyperstition. *See* fiction

idem   208
identity   207, 208, 209, 210, 216, 217, 229, 230, 232, 234
    as a temporal construction   171, 175, 182
    as eternal return   180
    closeness to oneself   182
ideologization   217, 218, 227
Ilfeld, Frederic   29–30
imagined community   152
immanence   115
    immanent limit (Deleuze and Guattari)   41, 49, 52
immortality   28–29, 33–34

INDEX

impossible, the   130, 132, 133, 140, 141
individualism   247–248
innovative strategies   215
Institute for War and Peace Reporting (IWPR)   267, 272
international literary field   240–242
Invisible Committee, The   26
ipse   208
Irigaray, Luce   51
irony   153, 157, 158
Ivančić, Viktor   82, 230, 231
Iveković, Sanja   35

Jakobson, Roman   263
James, Edward   98
Jameson, Fredric   81, 81n2, 82, 83, 85, 88, 91
Jergović, Miljenko   149, 153, 154, 155, 155n5, 156, 156n, 157, 158, 159, 165, 166, 167, 222, 223, 224
Jerić, Ante   33, 134n9, 135n10
Jessup, Lynda   93
Josipović, Ivo   212
jouissance   52
Jović, Dejan   212
Joyce, James   131
Juričan, Dario   230

Kadare, Ismail   193
Kairos   199
Kant, Immanuel   107–108, 111–114, 116–118, 129, 130, 131n5, 132, 134n9
Kaplan, Danny   261, 272
Karajlić, Nele   268, 269
Kazaz, Enver   155, 156
Keightley, Emily   150, 153
Kermauner, Taras   264, 270
Khrushchev, Nikita   70
Kierkegaard, Søren   107n1
Kiev   167
Kiš, Danilo   192, 200
Kishinev   167
Komelj, Miklavž   62n12
komšiluk   262
Kopicl, Vladimir   41
Kosmos, Iva   40n1
Kosovo   191, 193, 194, 198, 199
Kovačević, Nataša   242–243
Kozarac, Josip   97

Kožul, Tonći   83
Kravar, Zoran   93, 97, 99, 104
Kreho, Dinko   40n1
Krleža, Miroslav   59, 61–66, 73, 208, 218
Kruchenykh, Aleksei   63
Kumar, Krishan   93, 94, 96, 99
Kundera, Milan   189–190

l'avenir   231, 235
LaBier, Douglas   216
Laboria Cuboniks   30–31
Lamarck, Jean-Baptiste   29
Lamont, Christopher K.   212
Lasić, Stanko   61
lateral networks   151, 167
Lears, T.J. Jackson   94
Leibniz, Gottfried Wilhelm   107, 119
Lešić-Thomas, Andrea   156n6, 158
Levanat-Peričić, Miranda   98
Levinas, Emmanuel   130
Lewis, Michael   214
Lexicon of YU Mythology   156, 156n6, 158, 164
life elsewhere   193, 197
life nowhere/everywhere   197
Lindstrom, Nicole   153n1
linearity (of time)   134, 135, 136, 140, 141
Lionnet, Francoise   151, 165
literary cosmology   192, 194
literary field   240
Little, Allan   212
Lokotar, Kruno   225, 226
longing   150, 151, 152, 159
Lošić, Saša   268
Lošonc, Mark   179
loss   150, 152, 159, 160, 161
Lovecraft, Howard Phillips   128, 129, 131–133, 140, 141
Luketić, Katarina   222
Lukić, Jasmina   41n1, 165n13
Luthar, Breda   149
Lviv   167
Lyotard, Jean-François   131
Lysenko, T.D.   29

Maccannell, Juliet Flower   52
Maček, Ivana   262, 272
machine (Deleuze)   39, 40, 46, 49, 51, 52, 53
Mandić, Igor   226, 227

Marasović, Nevio 83
Marčetić, Adrijana 40n2
Marcuse, Herbert 223
market practice 226
market-turn 226
Marković, Franjo 97
Markovina, Dragan 219
Martinis, Dalibor 35–37
Marx, Karl 45, 46, 46n1, 59, 75
Marxist 45, 46
Matanić, Dalibor 235
materialist 39n2, 40
materiality (materiality of the text) 41, 48, 54, 140, 141
Mayakovski, Vladimir 63–65, 68–71
McCarthy, Tom 122–123
mechanical reproduction/mechanically reproduced (Benjamin) 40, 42, 45, 53, 54
Meillassoux, Quentin 108–110, 112–118, 119, 124, 129–130, 134n9
melancholia 149, 152, 160
memory 149, 150, 156, 157, 159, 160, 162, 165, 166, 167, 168, 188, 191, 193, 195, 197
   affectionate/affective 149, 165
   childhood 157, 166
   collective 150, 151, 153, 154, 158, 159, 160, 163
   'confiscation of' 150, 162
   constellation 167
   counter- 162
   cultural 150, 151, 154, 168
   dynamics of 150, 151, 154
   ethno-national. *See also* national 150, 164
   fragments of 154, 158, 159, 160
   and history 155, 156, 157, 158, 159
   individual/personal 152, 153, 158, 160
   and intertextuality 161
   "knot" 161
   (rhetorical) modes of 158
   multidirectional/multidirectionality of 150, 151, 164, 165, 167, 168
   national 152, 153
   nostalgic 150, 164, 165, 168
   oppositional 168
   popular 149, 156
   post-communist 151
   post-socialist 150
   sites 157, 159, 164, 166
   social 152
   studies 8, 151
   transnational 154n2
   traumatic 166, 167
   travel/travelling 150–151, 154n2, 165
   triggers of 152, 161, 163
Menđušić, Silvana 210
messiah 123–125
   machinic 124, 125
metalepsis 124, 124n8
metanarrative 138, 141
metaphorization 262, 264
metatemporal narratives 135
Michurin, Ivan 29
migration 193
Milčec, Zvonimir 66
Milošević, Slobodan 265, 266
mimetic 127, 128, 133
minor literature (Deleuze and Guattari) 40–41, 154
minor transnationalism 151, 154, 165, 165n13
Mirković, Željko 155n5
Mishler, William 215
missing 191, 193, 194
Mitchell, William 27
Mlakić, Josip 82–83, 84, 86, 87n6, 88, 91, 95, 96, 99, 101, 104
Montaigne 261
Montažstroj collective 83
Moreno, Alejandro 215
Morris, Pam 105
Morson, Gary Soul 93
mourning 149, 261
Munday, Rod 216
museum 160
   as a memory trope 160
   Berlin as 160
   virtual museum of Yugoslavia 163
   Yugonostalgic 164
Mussolini, Benito 99
mystery 135
myth-making 152
myth/mythologization 156, 158

Nabokov, Vladimir 107n1
narrated time 136, 137

INDEX

narrative time   136
national discourse   207
national/nationalism   149, 152, 164, 165, 217, 218, 265, 270, 271, 272
   ethno-   149, 151, 155, 162, 163
   identity   152, 155, 156
   symbols and myths   152
necessary things   196
necessity   112, 113, 114, 116, 117, 118
Negarestani, Reza   107n1, 123
Nemec, Krešimir   223
neo-avant-garde, neo-avant-gardist   41, 51, 52, 62–63, 70, 74
neoliberalism   1, 2–3, 8, 12, 15
nesting of Orientalisms   264
Neumann, Birgit   174, 175, 181, 183
news publishing   227
Newton, Isaac   107
Nikolaidis, Andrej   83
Noack, Ruth   35
nomad/nomadic   161, 162, 164
nonhuman object   128, 133, 140, 141
nonhuman otherness   141
nonhuman world   127, 132, 133, 141
nostalgia, nostalgic, nostalgically   43, 44, 46, 149, 150, 151, 152, 153, 154, 157, 158, 159, 160, 160n11, 161, 164, 165, 166, 167, 168, 200–201
   reflective   150, 152, 153, 154, 160, 160n11, 164, 165
   restorative   150, 152, 164
   subversion of   166
   temporal   154, 166
   topographic   154

oblivion   175, 185, 186
Opfernarrative   191, 196
Oraić Tolić, Dubravka   61, 63–65, 67, 72–73
Orešković, Tihomir   212
Orientalism   264, 270, 271
Osborne, Peter   39

Paljetak, Luko   102n4
parliamentary democracy   209
parody   153
Pashku, Anton   192
Pavičić, Jurica   224
Pavlović, Boro   63

people's liberation movement   219
Perišić, Robert   82
Perković, Ante   222
Perrotta, Tom   116–117
Petrović, Dražen   269
Petrović, Svetozar   57n2, 59–60, 63, 68, 73, 75
Petrović, Tanja   149
Pickering, Michael   150, 153
Piketty, Thomas   8
Plavi Orkestar   268
pleasure   111, 113–114, 120, 125
pop-folk   222
Popović, Edo   82–83, 84, 87, 88, 89–90, 91, 95, 96, 99, 100, 101, 104
Popović, Koča   66
Popović, Milica   154n2
Popper, Karl   119, 119n5
popular culture   156, 158, 163, 167
post-1989   192, 194
post-avant-garde   64, 67, 74
post-colonial   165
post-communism/communist   160, 162
   'children of'   162, 165
   countries   161
   discourses   167
   subjects   165
post-memory   150
post-modern   196, 199
post-socialist   127, 149, 154, 160n11, 161
   countries   165
   mnemonic landscape   149
post-transition   214, 233
(post-)Yugoslav   3, 4, 5, 6, 7, 8–9, 10, 14, 17, 149, 150, 151, 153, 159, 161, 162, 168, 261, 262, 270, 271
   authors   149
   cultural memory   154n2
   exiles   162
   language policy   155n5, 161
   literature/literary work/literary discourse/literary production   39–41, 52, 58, 76, 82, 83, 85, 88, 151, 153, 168
   memory (discourse)/mnemonic landscape   149, 150, 153, 168
   memory-regime   155
   novel   159, 161
   studies   3, 5–6, 7, 10, 14

(post-)Yugoslav (cont.)
    subjects/subjectivity   161, 162, 163
    time   3, 6, 8–9, 14
post-Yugoslavian   193
postnational identity   229
Postnikov, Boris   40n1, 58n6, 95, 228
presencing, presenced (Osborne)   39–40, 50, 52
production (literary; of the text)   39–41, 47, 52
Propp, Vladimir   117
Protevi, John   48
Proust, Marcel   131
pseudoautobiographical discourse   139
Pušnik, Maruša   149

Rabelais, François   97, 101
Radaković, Borivoj   101, 103, 225, 226
Radstone, Susannah   168
Ramazani, Jahan   60n11
Rancière, Jacques   176, 185, 186
reconciliation   266, 267, 269
remembering
    as fiction   176
    fragmentary nature of remembering   173
    spatial perspective of remembering   174
repetition
    of difference   175, 180, 181, 183
    of time   180
    paradox of repetition   184
Republika Srpska   267, 268
resistance   216, 217, 222, 223, 226
ethmann, Petra   9–10
eatist adaptations   213
ur, Paul   134, 207, 208, 230
, Ann   150
arko   66
ć, Nenad   225
lisk   124–125
    215
3, 228
el   151, 161, 167
, 34
8, 272
191, 194, 195, 197–200

Sajko, Ivana   82
Šalgo, Judita   51–52
sameness   223
Sanader, Ivo   212, 213
Sarajevo   154, 156, 157, 158, 159, 166, 167, 262, 267, 268, 269, 271, 272
Sartre, Jean Paul   102
science   109, 111–112, 113, 114, 116–118, 121
science fiction   134, 135. *See also* fiction & extro-science fiction
Scribner, Charity   149
Searle, John   119
Second World War   207, 219
Second Yugoslavia   1, 2, 4
Sedlar, Jakov   220, 221, 222
Sekulić, Duško   215
Selimović, Meša   159
Serbia   190
Sever, Josip   57, 62–73, 76
sex, sexuality, sexual, sexually   41, 47, 48, 49, 50, 51, 53
Shanghai   167
Shaviro, Steven   110n3
Shih, Shuh-mei   141, 165
Silber, Laura   212
Simeunović, Tatjana   155n5
simulation   125
singularity   113, 114
Šnajder, Slobodan   235
Snow, Marcus   137
social malformations   218
social reproduction   215
Sokolović, Ada   267, 272
Sontag, Susan   95
Sørberg, Marius   211, 212
South-eastern Europe   192–192, 193, 200, 201
space and time   192, 193–194. *See also* time *and* spacetime
    liminal spaces of memory   178
    space of the past   174, 175
    spatial nature of time   177
    spatial structure of the lived experiences   174
    spatiality of memory   175, 177
    temporal space   176
spacetime   135
speculative fiction   135
speculative realism   108, 128–132, 135

INDEX

speculative turn 128
Spengler, Oswald Arnold Gottfried 98
Spinoza, Baruch 115
Šporer, Željka 215
Srnicek, Nick 26–27
Stalin, Joseph 71
standpoint of the present, standpoint of the past 59–61, 64, 73, 75–76
Starobinski, Jean 151
state of in-betweenness 230
state of the debt 207
statehood myth 219
Stefanović Karadžić, Vuk 67n17
Štivičić, Tena 228, 229
Strukić, Kristian 72
Stublić, Jura 266
sublime, the 130–131
Šufflay, Milan 98, 99
Suvin, Darko 83–84
system of reproduction 223
system-blame 216
Sztompka, Piotr 205, 206, 210, 214, 215

technomaterialism 30–31
temporal simultaneity 171, 177
temporal turn 5
temporal, temporality, temporally, temporalization 1, 4, 6, 10, 12, 14, 16, 17, 40, 41, 43, 52, 53, 53n3, 109, 114, 127, 128, 134–140, 232, 241, 243, 248
   nostalgic 1, 3, 4, 14
   sequential 1, 3, 9
   teleological 1, 3, 4
theoretical fiction 134n9, 135. *See also* fiction
Thiele, Kathrin 41
thing in itself 112–113, 130
thriller 134, 135
time 27–29, 39–47, 49, 52, 53, 54, 107–108, 107n1, 114, 118, 119, 121, 124, 188–198. *See also* necessity
   actual entity 107
   determinations or relations of things 107, 122
   form of intuition 107–108
timelines – disrupted, anomalous, impossible 128, 135, 136, 140
Tišma, Slobodan 39, 41–53

Tito, Josip Broz 70–71, 264
Todorova, Maria 268, 272
Todorović, Jelena 178
Tolstaya, Tatyana 97
Tomić, Ante 224, 225
Top lista nadrealista 268, 269
traditionalization 44, 52
transcendental 112, 114, 115
transcommunication. *See* communicability
transition 151, 205, 206, 207, 210, 211, 212, 213, 214, 217, 227, 231, 232, 233, 234
translated authors 241, 243–244, 257
transnational 152, 161, 163, 165, 167
   identity 160, 166
   literature 166
   memory 154n2
trauma 206, 208, 209, 210, 211, 214, 216, 217, 230, 232, 233, 234
travelling concept 151
Trump, Donald 214
Tuđman, Franjo 211, 213, 218, 219
turbo-folk 222
Turner, Bryan S. 219

Ugrešić, Dubravka 28–32, 149, 150, 153, 154, 159, 160, 160n11, 161, 162, 164, 165, 166, 167, 188, 191, 194–197, 199–201, 207, 229, 230, 263, 272
Ugričić, Sreten 83
Ujević, Tin 64–67, 73
Ukraine 166
universe
   diegetic 109, 118, 119, 121, 123, 124
USA 166, 167
utopia 93, 98, 99

value 208, 213, 216, 217, 218, 219, 220, 222, 223, 224, 225, 226, 227, 228, 233, 234, 235
Velikić, Dragan 170, 173, 174, 176, 178, 179, 185, 186
Velikonja, Mitja 149
Venturin, Radomir 63
Verde, Nora 82
Versluis, Arthur 97
Vervaet, Stijn 5–6, 8, 150, 154n2, 161
Vidojković, Marko 155n5
Vidulić, Svjetlan Lacko 40n2
Viljevo 128, 134, 138

Visković, Velimir   226
Volčič, Zala   149
Vrečer, Natalija   263, 272
Vukšić, Matija   234

Wachtel, Nathaniel   270, 272
Weber, Norbert   69
weird – fiction, tales   128, 131–133
Whitehead, Anne   175
Williams, Alex   26–27
Williams, David   159, 243
woman's woman [*žena žene*] (Tišma)   50–52
work of art   39, 40, 42, 43, 44, 45, 52, 53
Wray, Randall   27

xenofeminism   30–31

Yeats, William Butler   96
Yugo-nostalgia   149, 153, 154, 154n2, 161, 162, 163, 164, 167, 168
Yugoslav   149
    generation   149, 159
    legacy   159
    (socialist) past   149, 150, 155, 159
    socialist regime/system   149, 164
    socialism   150, 157
    socialist state   156, 157
Yugoslav literature   58–60, 62n12, 66, 73, 76
Yugoslavia   57–59, 61–64, 66–70, 72, 75, 149, 153, 157, 159, 160, 161, 162, 163, 167
    dissolution/fragmentation of   150, 160, 161, 162, 164
Yurchak, Alexei   157

Žalica, Pjer   268, 271, 272
Zeitroman   134
Zen Buddhist   199
Zima, Zdravko   226
Zink, Andrea   155n5, 166
Živanović, Miloš   83
Živković, Andreja   208
Živojinović, Bata   264, 265, 266, 272
Žmegač, Viktor   61
Zogović, Radovan   70–71

Printed in the United States
by Baker & Taylor Publisher Services